Published Volumes

Revelation of the Unknowable God, Karen L. King

Revelation
of the
Unknowable God

Revelation

of the

Unknowable God

with Text, Translation,
and Notes to NHC XI,*3* Allogenes

Karen L. King

Design and composition: Polebridge Press, Santa Rosa, California

Cover design: Illumination Graphics, Petaluma, California

Printing and binding: McNaughton & Gunn, Saline, Michigan

Text type: Galliard

Library of Congress Cataloging-in-Publication Data
King, Karen L.
    A revelation of the unknowable God / by Karen L. King.
      p. cm.
    Includes bibliographical references.
    Includes Coptic and English translations of Allogenes.
    ISBN 0-944344-44-5 (hardcover)
    1. Allogenes (Gnostic book)—Criticism, interpretation, etc. I. Allogenes (Gnostic book) English & Coptic.   II. Title.
    BT1391.K56 1995
    299′.932–dc20   95-36043

Contents

Preface

In 1945 a discovery in the Egyptian desert near the village of Nag Hammadi changed the face of Gnostic studies forever. There in a clay jar were papyrus codices containing the teachings of the ancient Gnostics themselves. One of those texts was *Allogenes* from Codex XI,3. It contains a series of divine revelations given to a character named Allogenes. The revelations describe the true nature of the divine realm, including the path to experience of the completely transcendent Unknowable God.

Through his first person narrative, the figure of Allogenes provides a model for spiritual progress and salvation. He describes how he first reacted to the revelation with fear, but then was able to turn within to seek and discover the divinity within himself. After a hundred years of preparation and further instruction from his divine helpers, he was able to ascend out of the bodily garment and attain a direct vision of the Unknowable God.

This remarkable spiritual adventure is a product of Sethian Gnosticism. Written as an apocalypse possibly in the form of an epistle, it elaborates the basic patterns of Sethian mythology in terms of current philosophical concepts and in so doing presents one of the earliest examples of apophatic (negative) theology. Indeed, the absence of explicit Jewish or Christian references may indicate that the author was attempting to appeal specifically to philosophers, like Celsus and Porphyry, who opposed Christianity.

Although the author and provenance of the work remain obscure, a Greek version of the work was probably known to the Neoplatonist philosopher Plotinus. This information, along with an analysis of the philosophical conceptuality of the text, allows the original composition of *Allogenes* in Greek to be dated to the first quarter of the third century C.E. We may speculate that the most probable provenance of the text is Alexandria in Egypt. This volume provides the Coptic text, English translation, an introduction, and extensive notes to the only surviving copy of *Allogenes*, which was translated into Coptic from a lost Greek version.

The groundwork for this edition was established during eighteen months residence in Berlin, 1982–1983, working with members of the Berlin Arbeitsgruppe für koptisch-gnostische Handscriften, under the leadership of Hans-Martin Schenke. I would like to express my thanks to the Deutsche Akademische Austauschdienst for the direct research stipend that made my residence in Berlin possible.

In the summer of 1985, support from Occidental College, through the Louis and Hermione Brown Humanities Support Fund, made it possible to travel to Cairo and make the final collation of my transcription from the original manuscript in the Coptic Museum. I want to acknowledge here my sincere thanks for this support. The experience of working directly with the manuscript was deeply rewarding, and many changes were made to the transcription.

I wish to extend a special notice of appreciation to Dr. Gawdat Gabra, Director of the Coptic Museum, and Mrs. Sumiha Abd el-Shaheed, First Curator of Manuscripts, for their generous hospitality and professional courtesy during my work at the Coptic Museum, and to James M. Robinson for allowing me to use the equipment of the Institute for Antiquity and Christianity stored in Cairo, and for his general support.

I also wish to express my appreciation to John Turner and Charles W. Hedrick, text and volume editors respectively of the Coptic Gnostic Library Project's edition of *Allogenes*, for providing me with a copy of Turner's initial transcriptions and restorations of the text for use in Berlin. My sincerest thanks for your collegial cooperation. In this same spirit, all suggested changes in this edition were made available to them and any others who requested a copy of these materials. It has been the policy of this edition, however, not to introduce restorations different from Turner's text merely for the sake of novelty. The departures from his text (described in the notes to the Coptic text below) reflect: 1) variance of his edition with my collation of the manuscript in Cairo; 2) differences of interpretation; or 3) differences in grammatical or orthographic understanding.

For the beauty and clarity of this volume, especial thanks are due to Charlene Matejovsky and Geneviève Duboscq of Polebridge Press for their professionalism in design and typesetting.

Finally, the profound debt of gratitude which I owe especially to Hans-Martin Schenke and also to other members of the Berlin working group, especially Carsten Colpe, my teacher and supporter at the Freie Universität, Hans-Gebhard Bethge, and Wolf-Peter Funk, is beyond repayment. It is no overstatement to say that without their instruction and criticism, this edition would not have been possible. In addition, they taught me the valuable meaning of scholarly community by unstinting, generous gifts of their expertise, their time, their hospitality, and of great enduring importance to me, their friendship. My sincerest thanks.

As a token of my deep respect and gratitude,
this work is dedicated to

Hans-Martin Schenke, ⲡⲣⲉϥϯⲥⲁⲃⲉ ⲛⲥⲁⲃⲉ.

"ⲡⲟⲩⲟⲉⲓⲛ ⲇⲉ ⲧⲉ ⲧⲅⲛⲱⲥⲓⲥ
ⲉⲃⲟⲗ ϩⲓⲧⲟⲟⲧⲥ̄ ⲧⲛ̄ⲡⲱϩ"

ϯϣⲡ̄ϩⲙⲟⲧ ⲛ̄ⲧⲟⲟⲧⲕ̄

Sigla

A dot placed under a letter in the transcription indicates that the letter is visually uncertain.

[ ]   Square brackets indicate a lacuna in the manuscript where writing once existed.

⟨ ⟩   Pointed brackets indicate an editorial emendation of a scribal omission or error.

[[ ]]   Double square brackets indicate a scribal deletion.

{ }   Braces indicate letters considered by the editor to have been added erroneously by the scribe.

( )   Parentheses in the translation indicate materials supplied by the translator for the sake of clarity and fluidity of the English style.

*   Text is corrupt; see note.

Abbreviations

AdvHaer	Irenaeus, *Adversus Haereses*	*NovTest*	*Novum Testamentum*
ApJohn	*Apocryphon of John*	*NTS*	*New Testament Studies*
BASP	*Bulletin of the American Society of Papyrologists*	*Post.*	Philo, *De Posteritate Caini*
		RSR	*Religious Studies Review*
BG	Papyrus Berolinensis 8502	*SBLSP*	*Society of Biblical Literature Seminar Papers*
Cat.	Aristotle, *Categories*		
Cher.	Philo, *De Cherubim*	*SJC*	*Sophia of Jesus Christ*
CH	*Corpus Hermeticum*	*StSeth*	*Three Steles of Seth*
De Prin.	Origen, *De Principiis*	*TLZ*	*Theologische Literaturzeitung*
Didask.	Numenius, *Didaskalikos*	*TriProt*	*Trimorphic Protennoia*
GosEgypt	*Gospel of the Egyptians*	*TU*	Texte und Untersuchungen
HTR	*Harvard Theological Review*		zur Geschichte
JEA	*Journal of Egyptian Archaeology*		der altchristlichen Literatur
		UnText	*The Untitled Text* in
JTS	*Journal of Theological Studies*		the Bruce Codex
Marc.	Porphyry, *Letter to Marcella*	*VC*	*Vigiliae Christianae*
NHC	Nag Hammadi Codex or Codices	*Vit.Plot.*	Porphyry, *Vita Plotini*
		ZÄS	*Zeitschrift für Ägyptische Sprache und Altertumskunde*
NHLE	*The Nag Hammadi Library in English* (3rd ed.)		
		ZNW	*Zeitschrift für die neutestamentliche Wissenschaft*
NHS	Nag Hammadi Studies		
Nich. Eth.	Aristotle, *Nichomachean Ethics*		
		Zost	*Zostrianos*

Introduction

Plot Summary

The plot of *Allogenes* does not follow the usual cosmological drama of salvation common to many Gnostic texts: the story of humankind's pitiful plight, their enslavement in the cosmos, and escape back to the world of light. Rather the narrative depicts a spiritual journey from ignorance and fear to true knowledge of self and God.

There are two significant types of structural units in *Allogenes*: the direct address of Allogenes to Messos and the revelation discourses. The first contains the narrative account by Allogenes of his experiences and his reactions to the revelations he receives. The narrative direction of the text is found here as it depicts the steady progression of Allogenes toward salvation. As Allogenes moves from fear to joy, from ignorance and disturbance of soul to knowledge, stability, praise and silence, the text provides the reader with a clear illustration of the purposeful, directed progression of the Gnostic toward salvation.

At first, Allogenes reacts to the revealer's words with fear, turning back to the distractions of the world. He is afraid that these teachings were more than he could endure in the flesh (49.38–50.17). But Iouel appears to him with a new revelation. She assures him that he has been clothed with a great power that will allow him to attain exalted knowledge.

After this second revelation, Allogenes is again greatly disturbed, but this time he turns inward to himself. In so doing he discovers within himself the light and the good, and his own divinity is manifested (52.6–13). Iouel now further empowers him and assures him that his instruction so far is perfect. He is ready now for higher, esoteric teaching; she proceeds with a third revelation.

At the end of this revelation, Allogenes does not react with fear or disturbance. Instead, he receives a vision of the glories of the perfect existents (52.13–17). This exalted vision and the words of the revealer Iouel (55.19–30) bring him to realize the deficiency of his knowledge, and he prays for a new revelation (55.31–32).

Iouel speaks one last time, promising him that after one hundred years, he will receive a truly great revelation (56.14–27). After she departs, Allogenes does not despair, but spends the hundred years preparing himself; he rejoices in himself, now confident that he is following a blessed path (57.27–39).

At the end of the appointed time, he receives a second vision. The beings of the divine hierarchy appear to him in ascending order, culminating in a vision of the Entirety. He sees Autogenes, Protophanes, Kalyptos, the aeon of Barbelo, the Triply-powered, and finally, the Entirety (58.12–26).

1

Then comes the decisive turning point in the narrative: the account of the ascent. Allogenes is seized from out of his fleshly garment and is taken up to a holy place (58.26–37). His reaction now is to give praise (58.37–38). Relying upon his own self-knowledge for stability, he turns toward the knowledge of the Entirety (58.38–59.4). The holy Powers speak to him and tell him what will come to pass (59.4–60.12). He reacts to their words with silence and self-knowledge (60.13–18).

Finally, all occurs as the Powers foretold. He first ascends past the moving Vitality up to the subsistence that is "standing and at rest according to the image of that which is truly at rest" (59.21–23). The culmination of the ascent results in a primary revelation of the Unknowable God, and through it, Allogenes achieves perfect self-knowledge (61.5–6). This knowledge of the Unknowable is defined as a kind of ignorance: "it is such that if one knows it at all, one is ignorant of it" (61.17–19).

The ascent concludes with an extensive depiction of the Unknowable in terms of negative theology (61.25–66.38). After this final revelation, Allogenes is told to go and cease seeking, for more is not possible (67.22–38).

The text ends with instructions for Allogenes to write a secret book for those who come after him who will be worthy to receive knowledge of these things (68.16–23). The final reaction of Allogenes is joy (68.25–26).

Although the reactions of Allogenes form the narrative direction of the text, the bulk of *Allogenes* is taken up with the revelation discourses, addressed to Allogenes by Iouel, the Powers, and another revealer whose identity is lost in one of the text's many lacuna. These revelations provide the knowledge of the divine hierarchy necessary for spiritual progression toward salvation.

The design of the text as a whole is drawn to convey an understanding of the nature and process of salvation to the readers. In *Allogenes*, salvation is not expressed primarily as escape from imprisonment in this world, but rather as the experience of self-recognition and knowledge of God. Similarly, the emphasis in the content of the revelations in *Allogenes* is not on cosmology and anthropology, but on epistemology and ontology, that is to say, on knowledge and direct apprehension of self and Being.

The text itself makes a distinction between "revelation" and "primary revelation" (60.38–39; 61.7–11). The first type, "revelation," is auditory and functions as preparatory instruction for the initiate. The second type, "primary revelation," is visionary and describes the direct apprehension of self and God in the mystery of ascent. This latter type is intimately connected with the Sethian rite of ascension.[1] Both types of revelation are, however, necessary for salvation and together constitute the text's message about the nature and process of salvation. The role of teaching is to prepare the soul for the road it must travel; the vision, on the other hand, is the goal itself.[2]

---

1. See Introduction, pp. 9–12.
2. See exegetical note to 59.26b–60.12a; 60.37b–61.28a.

This process is most pointedly demonstrated by the figure of Allogenes. He functions as a savior figure in two respects: 1) insofar as he wrote and hid the book, he is the mediator of divine, revelatory teaching to "those who will be worthy"; and 2) through his ascent, he provides a model for receiving the divine vision.

Both the narrative account of Allogenes' experiences and the revelation discourses belong to the text's primary concern: a description of the content and process of salvation.

The narrative structure of the text may be outlined as follows:

1. The first revelation to Allogenes (45.6–49.38a)
2. Allogenes' reaction to the first revelation (49.38b–50.17a)
3. The second revelation to Allogenes (50.17b–51.38)
4. Allogenes' reaction to the second revelation (52.6–13a)
5. The third revelation to Allogenes (52.13b–55.11a)
6. Allogenes' reaction to the third revelation (55.11b–17a)
7. The fourth revelation to Allogenes (55.17b–30)
8. Allogenes' reaction to the fourth revelation (55.31–32)
9. The fifth revelation to Allogenes (55.33–57.24a)
10. Allogenes' reaction to the fifth revelation; the first vision (57.24b–58.26a)
11. The ascent begins (58.26b–59.7a)
12. The revelation to Allogenes by the Powers concerning the ascent (59.7b–60.12a)
13. The ascent occurs as the Powers have foretold (60.12b–61.22a)
14. The revelation to Allogenes by the Powers concerning the Unknowable (61.22b–67.38)
15. The final command to Allogenes (68.16–23a)
16. Allogenes' final response (68.23b–69.1)
17. The command to Messos (69.14–19)
18. Title of the tractate (69.20)

Myth and Ritual[3]

Generation and Multiplicity

Later Platonic thought was concerned with how to preserve the transcendence of the First Principle while affirming it as the source of multiplicity. As

---

3. I choose to use the term "mythology" here to describe the narrative accounts which describe (Sethian) theology, cosmology, anthropology, soteriology, history and eschatology. My meaning is essentially the same as that of H.-M. Schenke's term "system" but avoids the difficulty of that term which may seem to imply something logically systematic. See Schenke's own elucidation of his use of "system" in "The Phenomenon," 684–685.

"Myth" is here used with emphasis upon its basic meaning of "a narrative account."

interest turned more and more toward philosophical mysticism and ascetic practice, what was at stake in this issue concerned less and less the strictly philosophical problem of description—tied to how to lead the moral life or how to structure the ideal society—than a spiritual problem concerned directly with turning the soul away from multiplicity towards union with the One. We see these tendencies at work in such diverse varieties of later Platonism as Alexandrian Christianity, Plotinus, and the Chaldaean Oracles.

Origen, for example, describes the soul's return to God through educational advancement. Students first master the moral life (the "holy virtues") and progess onward toward the attainment of wisdom. They begin with a human teacher, but progress slowly in successive lives toward that place where Christ himself is their teacher and ruler, until finally the souls are capable of receiving God who becomes "all in all" to them.[4]

Plotinus, too, sees the rise of the soul in progressive stages. The soul who wishes to attain to the Supreme begins with learning by analogies, abstractions, and by understanding the things which have derived from It. Purification and the practice of virtue are essential to this process. But then the philosopher comes to the point where all learning needs to be abandoned until "suddenly, swept beyond it all by the very crest of the wave of Intellect surging beneath, he is lifted and sees, never knowing how; the vision floods the eyes with light, but it is not a light showing some other object, the light is itself the vision."[5] At this point the seeker attains unity with the One.[6]

The Chaldean Oracles place more emphasis than do Plotinus and Origen on the purification of the soul and its vehicles from impurities, relying especially on theurgic practices and ritual at the lower stages of the ascent, followed by more purely contemplative experience.[7]

For both Origen and Plotinus, the return of the soul to unity with God or the One is the ultimate goal. The path to that goal, however, includes an intellectual study of generation, that is, of how the multitude of existents came forth from the First Principle. To be able to return to God, one must first understand the process whereby one came forth. The way of ascent is the way of descent. To these studies, the Chaldean Oracles add the use of theurgic and ritual practices.

Allogenes shares with these other Platonists the presupposition that spiritual progress requires comprehending the divine hierarchy. Like these other Platonists, *Allogenes* is interested in the problem of the generation of multiplicity from the First Principle not for its own sake, but only insofar as salvation

---

4. See *De Prin.* III,6.9.
5. *Ennead* VI.7.36; trans. by MacKenna, *Plotinus*, 590. All following translations of the *Enneads* are by MacKenna unless otherwise noted.
6. See *Ennead* VI.7.36.
7. See Majercik, *Chaldaean Oracles*, 56–85, esp. 68–75. See also Lewy, *Chaldaean Oracles and Theurgy*, 177–226.

replicates ontogeny. The pattern of spiritual progress illustrated by Allogenes can be understood only by explicating the structure of the divine hierarchy in relation to generation and multiplicity. In explicating the structure and generation of the divine hierarchy, *Allogenes* relies almost completely upon philosophical conceptuality. In describing salvation, however, the text relies most heavily upon specifically Gnostic, Sethian mythology.

Saviors and Salvation

The text's primary aim of salvation is communicated on several levels:

1. The level of the text: the writing and reading of *Allogenes* itself is part of the instruction aimed at salvation.
2. The level of the recipients: here Allogenes provides a model for human spiritual progress.
3. The level of the divine revealers: specific revealers (guardian powers) appear to human recipients providing power and knowledge.
4. The level of ontology: the structure of reality is aimed at mediation between the human and the divine; experience of true reality is salvation itself.

Salvation in *Allogenes* is the process of attaining knowledge of oneself and the divine hierarchy. The supreme goal is the vision of the Unknowable in the ascent. The process of salvation is modeled by the figure of Allogenes.[8] He begins by receiving knowledge of the higher realities through revelation. Upon learning of the existence of these blessed realities, Allogenes turns away from the multitude and looks within himself. This withdrawal brings self-knowledge and the capacity to receive further revelations. After extensive preparation (it is said to last one hundred years), Allogenes withdraws from his body and experiences an ascent to the divine world in which he receives further visions and revelations. After his return, he writes his experiences down for "those who will be worthy." Clearly the text itself is part of the salvific process since it is meant to provide at least discursive, preparatory instruction for potential Gnostics.

This presentation of salvation has much more in common with Gnostic thought than philosophy. For example, the text never indicates that philosophical investigation or moral practices play any role here,[9] although the obvious acquaintance of the text's author with current philosophical speculation seems to stand in tension with this omission. Instead the Gnostic is dependent upon the reception of revelation from divine revealers, a common motif in Sethian Gnosticism.

The Sethian text, *Zostrianos*, tells us that souls are bound by the cruel and cutting bounds of the body. They need help to escape.

8. For further discussion of Allogenes as a savior, see Introduction, pp. 44–45.
9. Compare Origen, *De Prin.* II,9 and Plotinus, *Ennead* I,2.

Therefore, powers are appointed for their salvation, and each one of them is in the world. Within the self-begotten ones corresponding to each of the [aeons] stand glories so that one who is in the [world] might be safe beside them. The glories are perfect thoughts appearing in powers. They do not perish because they [are] models for salvation [by] which each one is saved. He receives a model (and) strength from each of them, and with the glory as a helper he will thus pass out from the world . . .[10]

The view that each person in the world needs a "glory as helper" applies well to *Allogenes*. Allogenes is aided in his progress by at least three revealers: the all-glorious Iouel,[11] the Powers of the Illuminators of the aeon of Barbelo, and an unidentified male figure. The first two are clearly associated in the text with glories and powers. Iouel seems in particular to be the glory-helper assigned to Allogenes. She is his helper[12] and gives him power. In addition, the speaker at the opening of the text tells Allogenes that he has already received a guardian to instruct him (45.9–10). Whether this guardian is to be identified with Iouel or not is, however, unclear due to the preceding lacuna.

The Glories and Powers, as well as the Luminaries, seem to belong to the aeon of Barbelo. Although the text is not clear on this point, it does clearly say that they are below the Triply-powered and that they do not exist with those who exist (that is, they do not belong to the Entirety which is higher than perfect; 55.22–24). This would seem to place them in the next lower sphere, the Barbelo aeon. Since Barbelo personifies the Knowledge of the Entirety, it makes sense that the various revealer figures who appear in the text, Iouel and the Powers of the Illuminators, would be associated with her.

Another savior in the text is the Thrice-male Youth,[13] a figure well-known from other Sethian texts.[14] As H.-M. Schenke has noted, Sethian mythology closely relates Autogenes and the Thrice-male Youth to the heavenly Adam.[15] In *Allogenes*, he is sometimes associated with Autogenes,[16] but more often appears as an independent figure.[17] Turner suggests that the Christianization of Sethian texts may have led to an increasing distinction among Adamas, the Thrice-male (Youth), and Autogenes, although other forces are probably at work in *Allogenes*.[18] *In Allogenes*, the function of the Thrice-male Youth is

10. *Zost* 46.15–30; trans. Sieber, *NHLE*, 416.
11. For more information concerning Iouel, see Introduction, pp. 46–47.
12. The need for a "helper" or spiritual guide was common in this period, though such guides were usually human beings. See I. Hadot, "The Spiritual Guide."
13. See 46.10–20; 51.26–37;55.35–38; 56.12–14; 58.12–15.
14. See for example, *GosEgypt* III, 42.6; 43.16; 44.22; passim; *Zost* 44.29–31; see also H.-M. Schenke, "Das sethianische System," 170.
15. See "Das sethianische System," 170.
16. See especially *Allogenes* 55.35–38.
17. See especially *Allogenes* 46.10–20 and 58.12–15.
18. See *NHC XI*, 246–247.

clarified by describing him as "a salvation for them all" (51.34–35) and the "word deriving from a design" (51.36–37). This design or purpose is the salvation of the Gnostics, who are described at 56.12–13 as "self-begotten ones" (ΝΙΑΥΤΟΓΕΝΗϹ). *Allogenes* most often mentions him in conjunction with the triad Kalyptos-Protophanes-Autogenes, thereby disrupting the triadic order of the exposition. This disorder indicates an uneasy absorption of other traditional materials. The savior role of the Thrice-male Youth may point to a more mythological and less ontological conception of spiritual progression.

As stated above, this presentation of saviors is closely connected with Sethian mythological thinking rather than philosophy. On the other hand, the ascent in *Allogenes* does not represent the retrieval of the divine spark once and for all from its material bonds at the moment of physical death, even though the ascent is described as an extra-bodily experience. Rather, the goal of the ascent is knowledge. Neither is it clear in *Allogenes* that this knowledge provides for the ultimate release of the spiritual element from the fetters of the body, but rather the experience seems to be salvific in and of itself. Knowledge, not release, is the goal. In this sense, the ascent appears to have more in common with contemplative philosophy than Sethian myth. John Turner has argued that one can see a clear line of division among the Sethian texts[19] between those which portray the path to spiritual fulfillment "as a three-stage ascent of the soul to deity" and those which portray it "as a three-fold descent of the deity (or some aspect thereof) to the soul in the lower world."[20] In the first pattern, he says, we are dealing with Platonic traditions;[21] in the second, with primarily Jewish traditions.[22]

The saving knowledge that Allogenes achieves in the ascent is the direct vision of the divine hierarchy. Again, unlike philosophical contemplation, this ascent is made possible by the salvific structure of the divine hierarchy itself, and the ascent mirrors that structure. As was stated above, *Allogenes* is concerned with presenting the structure of the divine hierarchy, not only with regard to generation, but also with regard to salvation. The central figures here are Barbelo and her triad Kalyptos-Protophanes-Autogenes.

In Gnostic terms, Barbelo is presented as the hypostasized Gnosis (45.15–20; 51.8–14; 59.1–4). Her function in the text is extremely important because she is the figure (as Knowledge and Intellect) who gives what knowledge can be had of the Entirety and the Unknowable to the perfect individuals (Gnostics). All revealers and revelations are ultimately associated with her: powers, glories, and illuminators. In the ascent, Allogenes calls the aeon of Barbelo

---

19. For a listing of these texts, see Introduction, p. 35.
20. "The Gnostic Threefold Path," 324.
21. A similar point is made by Scopello in her consideration of Gnostic apocalypses ("Contes apocalyptiques," see esp. 340–347).
22. "The Gnostic Threefold Path," 324.

"the knowledge of the entireties" (59.2–3).[23] Through the revelation of the Luminaries belonging to her, he receives the highest revelation (59.4–7; 61.24).

Enlightenment comes through acquaintance with the three levels of the Barbelo aeon (46.11–37). First one comes to know one's own subsistence and takes a stand upon Autogenes. One then sees all those who exist individually as Autogenes exists. When one becomes like him, then one's vision is raised to the Triply-male, the thought of all those in their unity. The next step is to see Protophanes and thereby come to see the first procession of the individuals from the true existents (the Entirety). At the highest level of Kalyptos, one sees the individuals in their unity, that is, the aeon of Barbelo. Thus the text is able to describe the successive progression of the soul toward knowledge either in terms of the increasing self-knowledge of the perfect individuals or in terms of the ontological levels hypostasized by figures of the Barbelo aeon.

This possibility of ascent to knowledge is summarized at 48.6–12: "It is not impossible for them to receive a revelation of those ones (the true existents) if they come to one place (that is, ascend to the aeon of Barbelo), although it is impossible for individuals to attain to the Entirety which is located in the place that is exalted beyond perfection." Again the text reiterates the limits of the ascent: perfect knowledge of the truly transcendent Entirety is not possible.

Although, as was indicated above, the text does not clearly discuss moral practice as a preparation for the attainment of knowledge, there are several passages which may in fact hint in that direction. At 50.24–32, Iouel tells Allogenes that he will "divide those things which are difficult to be divided" in order to come to know "those things which are unknowable to the multitude." It may be that this division implies separating himself from the lower things of the world in preparation to see higher realities which "the multitude" cannot know due to their absorption in worldly and bodily concerns.[24] Again at 51.30–32, the text states that Autogenes is "continually involved with correcting the sins deriving from nature," implying that the first level of self-knowledge may be tied to purification from the dross (sins) of materiality and passion. Finally, at 52.9–13, Allogenes recalls that it was not until he turned inward that he was able to see the good inside and become divine. This "inwardness" probably indicates withdrawal from the world, a withdrawal which may well have included ascetic and contemplative practices. Thus, although not explicitly stated, the author of the text may presuppose that moral/ascetic practice or purification is necessary for the attainment of saving *gnosis.*

23. Compare *Zost* 118.9–12: "when she gave power to the one who knew her, the Barbelo Aeon, the knowledge of the Invisible, Triply-powered perfect Spirit . . ." (ⲉⲁⲥϯ ϭⲟⲙ ⲙⲡⲏ ⲉⲧⲥⲟ[ⲩⲱⲛⲥ] ⲛ6ⲓ ϯⲃⲁⲣⲃⲏⲗⲱ ⲡⲓⲁⲓⲱⲛ ϯ[ⲅⲛⲱ]ⲥⲓⲥ ⲛⲧⲉ ⲡⲓⲁ2ⲟⲣⲁⲧⲟⲛ ⲛ(ⲩⲙ[ⲧ]6ⲟⲙ ⲛⲧⲉⲗⲓⲟⲥ ⲛⲡ̄ⲛ̄ⲁ̄).

24. See exegetical note to 50.11b–15a.

The Ascent

The ascent is the central event of *Allogenes*. The first portion of the text may be read as preparation for the ascent; the second half is occupied by the account of the journey itself, the visions, and the revelation Allogenes receives.

In the first part of the text, Allogenes receives a series of revelatory discourses about the nature of the divine hierarchy. These revelations lead Allogenes from fear to rejoicing. He has come to know himself and the good which is in him; he has become divine (52.9–18; 56.14–21). Even in his embodied state, he has already had a vision of the perfect individuals (55.12–17). Iouel has told him what shall come to pass: after one hundred years, the Powers of the Illuminator of Barbelo will give him a revelation (56.21–27). Allogenes then prepares himself through the words which he has heard; he takes counsel with himself for the one hundred years (57.27–31). At the end of the hundred years, still embodied, he receives a revelation of the divine hierarchy (Autogenes, Protophanes, Kalyptos, Barbelo, the Triply-powered Invisible Spirit, and the Entirety; 58.12–26).

At this point, Allogenes is seized out of the "garment" (that is, the body) and is caught up to a holy place so transcendent that not even a shadowy image of it can appear in the world. Here he sees all those things that before he had only heard about. He begins by taking a stand upon the knowledge he has already attained of himself and turns toward a knowledge of the Entirety (which he had previously seen while embodied). There he comes upon the holy Powers. They instruct him about what he must do and what will happen. Then everything takes place as the Powers have foretold.

The ascent itself has three stages: Vitality, Subsistence, and (unknowable) Knowledge. These stages correspond to the triadic nature of the Triply-powered—Vitality-Existence-Intellection.[25]

At the peak of the experience, Allogenes comes to know himself and receives a primary revelation of the Unknowable. He is seeking the Unknowable God itself when the holy Powers intervene to tell him to stop; such seeking is impossible and will only upset the stability he has already achieved. Instead, they give him an auditory revelation of the Unknowable in terms of negative theology. After this revelation, the ascent concludes; Allogenes is told to go and seek no more.

As noted below in the discussion of genre,[26] an account of a heavenly journey is a common element of apocalypses. Allogenes shows little in common, however, with the accounts of heavenly journeys described in Jewish apocalypses. The pattern for the ascent of Allogenes is more closely tied to elaboration upon the ascent of the soul described by Plato. Three passages in

---

25. See Introduction, pp. 22–28.
26. See Introduction, p. 59.

particular are relevant: *Phaedrus* 246–250a, *Symposium* 210–212a, and *Republic* VI.507–VII.517.

From these and other texts, later Platonists drew a conviction that the soul is immortal; that it had "fallen" from a higher state, where it had contemplated true Being, to a lower state of ignorance and embodiment; and that leading a life of philosophy would help the soul to regain its "wings" and soar again to the heights, becoming perfect and god-like. The goal of the soul's ascent was to attain "the veritable knowledge of being that veritably is" (*Phaedrus* 247e). These views were widely held in the second and third centuries and clearly form the framework for understanding the ascent of Allogenes in our text.[27]

A comparison with Plotinus may prove illuminating[28] since there is some similarity in terminology which may be because both are drawing upon a common fund of intellectual resources. For example, the language of stability, which has been explored by Michael Williams, allows one to see a common usage drawn from Plato and common in Platonizing circles.[29] The context for the use of terms like "standing," "taking one's stand," "being at rest," and so forth, derive from Plato's contrast between the disturbance, confusion, and instability of corporeal existence and the quiet calm and stability of the noetic sphere. Both *Allogenes* and Plotinus use the same term "standing" to describe the soul's condition at the apex of the ascent experience.[30] The point in both cases is the same: the soul has achieved the condition appropriate for assimilation to incorporeal Being, which itself lacks any disturbance or disorder.

But while both Plotinus and *Allogenes* consider the rise of the soul to be the ultimate spiritual experience, their understandings of the goal of the ascent differ. In *Allogenes*, the culmination of the ascent is a primary vision of the Unknowable; for Plotinus, the culminating goal is not vision, but union with the One.

More importantly, the metaphysics of Plotinus are based on a radical monism. For him, all things which exist (from the second Hypostasis, Intellect, to the material world) derive from the One by a process of emanation. The return of the soul to the One, then, is a kind of reverse emanation. There is no suggestion of discontinuity; indeed Plotinus claims that a part of the soul is always turned toward the Supreme whether one is aware of it or not.

Allogenes is characterized by a milder monism.[31] The text's ontology/ontogeny are clearly monistic; everything is said to derive ultimately from the

---

27. See Dillon, *Middle Platonists*, 43–49.

28. The most relevant passages in Plotinus are *Enneads* I.6.9; IV.8.1; V.1.4; V.3.17; V.4.8–10; V.5.12; VI.7.34–36; VI.8.15; VI.9.3; VI.9.11.

29. See especially the discussion in Williams, *The Immovable Race*, 74–82 and "Stability," 819–829.

30. Compare *Allogenes* 59.9–61.22 and Plotinus *Ennead* V.5.8 and VI.9.11. See also Williams, "Stability," 822–824.

31. In the related text, *Marsanes*, the cosmic dualism of Gnosticism has effectively disappeared: ". . . in every respect the sense-perceptible world is worthy of being saved"

Invisible Spirit. But this monism is mitigated by the limit placed on the possibility of fully comprehending the Unknowable.

Gnosticism is usually described as classically dualistic, providing a sharp contrast between good and evil, God and Matter. The return of the soul to the Pleroma (the divine sphere) is conceived as an escape from imprisonment in matter, a (re)discovery of one's true self and repudiation of bodily existence. In *Allogenes*, though, we find this dualism to be relatively mild. The task of the savior, Autogenes, is to "correct the sins deriving from nature" (51.30–32), that is, the impurities of the soul deriving from contact with materiality. The only clearly operative dualism is expressed in the view that a savior (or a series of saviors and revelers) is needed at all. Neither is the ascent of Allogenes portrayed as a final escape from the body and the cosmos; although extra-corporeal, it is ultimately a ritual and contemplative process aimed at knowledge of self and God, not permanent release from the body.

As Ruth Majercik has pointed out in a comparison of Plotinus with the Chaldaean Oracles, the differences in approach between contemplation (especially based on dialectical reasoning) and ritual to achieve the rise of the soul is due to "a fundamental difference in attitude toward the soul."[32] She summarizes:

> Since Plotinus, for example, maintained that the higher (or rational) part of the soul remained unfallen, and therefore impassible, the individual need only recognize this fact, turn away (via his own moral efforts) from the material distractions of the lower soul, and return (via mental and philosophical disciplines) to his true nature—that of unfettered contemplation of the intelligible world. . . . In contrast, the Oracles place a much greater emphasis on the fall of the soul in toto; since the soul is in constant danger of becoming totally enslaved to matter, . . . there is a much greater need for aid, both divine and human, in restoring the soul to its elemental state.[33]

Allogenes does not discuss the state of the fallen soul in any detail, but one may reason, based on the account of the soul's salvation exemplified by Allogenes, that, in regard to the relative "fallenness" of the soul, *Allogenes* presumes a view somewhere between that of the Chaldaean Oracles and that of Plotinus.[34]

(5.24–26). Pearson concludes: "What we find in these tractates (*Allogenes* and *Marsanes*), in fact, is a Gnostic system in which the radical dualism of the more primitive forms of Gnosticism has been virtually abandoned in favor of a more 'monistic' understanding of reality" ("The Tractate Marsanes," 383). See also, Hans-Martin Schenke, "The Phenomenon," 614–615.

32. Majercik, *Chaldaean Oracles*, 57.
33. Majercik, *Chaldaean Oracles*, 57.
34. I do not mean to imply that *Allogenes* shares the Oracles' views concerning the nature and composition of the soul, but only the view that the soul is fallen and in need of salvation through purification, revelation, and ritual.

Without some view of the soul's fallenness, there would be no need of saviors, special revelations, ritual, and theurgic practice.

Thus while Plotinus and *Allogenes* show a good deal of similarity in language and terminology, one must exercise supreme caution, for if their underlying presuppositions about metaphysics and the nature of the soul differ, similar terminology may not carry similar meaning. It cannot be assumed, for example, that when *Allogenes* and Plotinus talk about the preparation necessary for the ascent, they mean the same thing at all. The point of greatest difference between *Allogenes* and Plotinus regards the role of cult. For Plotinus, the ascent is reached in large part by a long and rigorous preparation in philosophical study and moral practice. Even though in the end, the individual cannot attain union with the One through one's own power (union requires that the One reach out to draw the soul toward it), there can be no union without the proper preparation on the part of the individual. For *Allogenes*, the preparation of the soul includes revelation, the study of revealed texts, cultic practice, and theurgy. There is no place in Plotinus' philosophy for revelation and cult,[35] although they were employed by later Platonists such as Iamblichus and Proclus.[36]

Ritual Practice and Theurgy

Sethian cultic practice included two sacraments or mysteries: baptism and the rite of ascension.[37]

The practice of baptism has received careful attention by Jean-Marie Sevrin in his masterful study *Le dossier baptismal séthien: Études sur la sacramentaire gnostique*. The purpose of the book is to determine whether a liturgical tradition of baptism exists which is peculiar to Sethian Gnostics. The result of Sevrin's study is a convincing argument for the existence of a distinctively Sethian baptismal tradition and a description (properly conditional) of baptismal doctrine and of ritual formula used in the actual practice of baptism.[38] What he is able to show, through detailed consideration of Sethian texts and cautious, judicious argument, is that there seems to be a consistent view throughout all the texts of the significance of baptism and an assumption of its practice. The result is all the more significant because of the sensitivity he shows to the issue of metaphor, that is, the proclivity of Gnostics to "spiritualize" just about everything—including sacramental practice. He concludes:

> If one considers the rite and the formulas, it is probable that the baptism reflected by our texts is the heir of a lustral rite practiced by a sect of Jewish extraction which invoked angels and celestial powers as protec-

35. See the discussion of Armstrong, "Plotinus," (*Cambridge History*), 258–263.
36. See for example, Iamblichus, *De mysteriis* x.4–8; Proclus, *Theologia Platonica* 63.
37. See H.-M. Schenke, "The Phenomenon," 602–607.
38. For a summary, see *Le dossier baptismal séthien*, 247–290.

tors or mysterious agents of baptism, and which was marked by an especial penchant for magic. Of the Judeo-baptismal baptism—which never was a initiatory rite, but was a rite of purification that was probably repeated—of it only meager vestiges survive which can be discovered by their poor integration into the new system.

The actual baptism, indeed, no longer has anything in common with the Judeo-baptismal practice. More closely resembling Jewish proselyte baptism and above all Christian baptism, it has been altered from purification to initiation. Has it submitted to the influence of one or the other (and probably the second) of these baptisms? One is not able to exclude[39] that possibility with certainty. But the whole weight of the change appears instead to adhere to Gnostic logic: if the moment of separation or of liberation is to remain important, it has to be seen as the negative side of a salvation which is entirely achieved from on high, a return to original unity, illumination. It is this salvation which is understood to be necessary to express and to which baptism is seen to be traced. Soteriology is primary; it is this which indicates the understanding of baptism.[40]

Allogenes gives scant evidence of the practice of baptism and was not included in Sevrin's study. The only direct allusion to a baptismal connection is the restored phrase: "[these five] seals" (69.16–17).[41] A reference to anointing is also made at 52.13 and may indicate a ritual practice associated either with baptism or with the ritual of ascent. Moreover, in the ascent, *Allogenes* does invoke the angels and powers as protectors, using magical invocation. It may be that repeated baptisms ("sealings") are practiced as a part of the ritual of ascent. Other Sethian texts connect the two explicitly. *Zostrianos* (4.21–7.22), for example, connects the ascent with multiple baptisms.[42] One set of baptisms is explicitly identified with the three images of the aeon of Barbelo: Autogenes, Protophanes, and Kalyptos (*Zostrianos* 15.4–12). These images appear in *Allogenes* as stages in the ascent of Allogenes. Elsewhere in *Zostrianos*, the five sealings are explicitly associated with Autogenes:

[When I was] baptized the fifth [time] in the name of the Autogenes by each of these powers, I became divine. [I] stood upon the fifth aeon, a preparation of all [these], (and) saw all those belonging to the Autogenes who really exist. I was baptized five times . . .[43]

39. "On ne peut certes l'exlure" [sic].
40. *Le dossier baptismal séthien*, 291.
41. For more on the connection between "the five seals" and the Sethian practice of baptism, see H.-M. Schenke, "The Phenomenon of Gnostic Sethianism," 603–604; Sevrin, *Le dossier baptismal séthien*, 71–75; Pearson, "Theurgic Tendencies," 259.
42. See also Sevrin, *Le dossier baptismal séthien*, 182–203.
43. *Zost* 53.15–54.1; trans. Sieber, *NHLE*, 417. See also 6.7–7.21; 25.10–20.

Here the initiate describes the experience of baptism in the same terms in which *Allogenes* describes the experience of the ascent: the affirmation of the divine identity of the initiate and the theme of stability. Furthermore, as Sevrin notes, *Zostrianos* does not treat baptism as a rite of purification, but provides "evidence of a baptismal practice or of baptism repeated a number of times, marking the steps of a progressive initiation."[44] This progressive initiation corresponds alluringly to the progressive stages of the ascent described in *Allogenes*. John Turner suggests that baptism may itself have been understood as ascent:

> In particular, the Sethian baptismal water was understood to be of a celestial nature, a Living Water identical with light or enlightenment, and the rite itself must have been understood as a ritual of cultic ascent involving enlightenment and therefore salvation.[45]

It may therefore be the case that although *Allogenes* only alludes once to "seals," the practice of the ascent modelled by Allogenes may have been associated ritually with the practice of multiple baptisms among Sethians. *Allogenes* itself is not a liturgical text, and we should therefore not expect it to reflect much more than this slight indication of the ritual it may presuppose.

Nonetheless, that the ascent itself in *Allogenes* is not understood to be due to a purely contemplative or spiritual method, but to involve theurgic practice, is shown by the invocation in 54.11–37.[46] This invocation addresses the three aspects of the Triply-powered—Vitality (54.8), Intellection (54.15), and Existence (54.25)—culminating in a hymn praising the One (54.26–37). This sequence parallels that of Allogenes' ascent (60.19–61.14) and leads to speculation that the two may be connected.

Several points are now of importance for our discussion: the purpose of such invocation, the use of *nomina barbara* and *voces mysticae*,[47] and the connection between the invocation and a Sethian rite of ascent.[48]

The function of the invocation in the ascent is associated with the practice of theurgy in antiquity.[49] E. R. Dodds defines theurgy as follows:

> Proclus grandiloquently defines theurgy as 'a power higher than all human wisdom, embracing the blessings of divination, the purifying

---

44. *Le dossier baptismal séthien*, 203.
45. Turner, "Sethian Gnosticism," 58. See also 66–69.
46. If it is the case that the ascent in *Allogenes* is connected with a ritual context, the description of the ascent by Turner as a self-performable technique ("The Gnostic Threefold Path," 332; see also "Sethian Gnosticism," 86) is called into question.
47. See Pearson, "Theurgic Tendencies."
48. The clearest case of the existence of a ritual of ascension in our period is found in the Chaldaean Oracles (see Lewy, *Chaldaean Oracles and Theurgy*, 177–226). A more precise comparison of Sethian texts with the Chaldaean oracles is needed to clarify whether there is any connection, historical or ideological, between the two. The best discussion to date is by Majercik, *The Chaldaean Oracles*, 82–85.
49. For an excellent recent consideration of the relationship between philosophical speculation and magic, see Berchman, "Arcana Mundi."

powers of initiation, and in a word all the operations of divine possession' (*Theol. Plat.* p. 63). It may be described more simply as magic applied to a religious purpose and resting on a supposed revelation of a religious character.[50]

Both characteristics, religious purpose and supposed revelation, apply to the use of theurgy in *Allogenes*.

Birger Pearson writes that, "The ritual chanting of the divine names by the Gnostics, in any case, can easily be understood, along the lines suggested by Iamblichus, as vehicles by which man is 'called' up to the gods."[51] Pearson illustrates this suggestion with excerpts from Iamblichus' *De mysteriis*.

> . . . the soul, "leaving behind her own life, has exchanged it for the most blessed energy of the gods. If, therefore, the ascent through invocations bestows on the priests purification from passions, deliverance from generation, and unity with the divine principle, how then could anyone connect it with passions? For such (an invocation) does not draw the impassible and pure (gods) down to passibility and impurity, but, on the contrary, it makes us, who had become passible through generation, pure and immovable" (*DM* I.12; 41,16–42,5).[52]

One function of invocation, then, is to help purify the soul and draw it away from the lower, generated world upward toward unification with the divine principle.[53]

The use of *nomina barbara* is connected with this practice because these names call the gods by their proper designations.[54] Iamblichus writes:

> We think it is necessary to address the gods in a language related to them. . . . These who first learned the names of the gods, connecting them with their own proper tongue, handed them down to us, that we might always preserve inviolate, (in a language) peculiar and proper to these (names), the sacred law of tradition.[55]

The use of *voces mysticae* has a similar function. Certain sounds evoke a particular "sympathy" with the divine being who is being invoked.

---

50. *The Greeks and the Irrational*, 291.
51. "Theurgic Tendencies," 259.
52. Pearson, "Theurgic Tendencies," 260.
53. A debate raged in antiquity about whether theurgy was only of limited use in purifying the soul from the contaminations accrued in the descent of the soul, thus preparing it for ascent, or whether theurgy was efficacious in attaining the final union itself (see Majercik, *The Chaldaean Oracles*, 56–82). In the case of *Allogenes*, it is difficult to determine the role of theurgy more precisely since we lack information about the author's view of the nature of the soul or about the specific practice of the rite in a communal setting.
54. For further discussion of *nomina barbara*, see E. R. Dodds, *The Greeks and the Irrational*, 292–293.
55. *De mysteriis* VIII.4; 256, 8–15; quoted from Pearson, "Theurgic Tendencies," 258.

Allogenes provides an account of the reception of such names in a revelation, although in reality they were probably derived from Sethian teaching or practice.[56] Attributing a divine origin to the names functions to give the invocation authority and confirm its efficacy.

Is this invocation associated as well with the ascent, and more specifically, with a Sethian ritual of ascension? The clearest connection between the invocation and ascent comes from the close parallel[57] to *Allogenes* 54 in *Three Steles of Seth* 125.23–126.17.[58] The triad Existence-Vitality-Intellection appears in both texts. In addition, similar names are invoked and similar formula are used.[59] In *Three Steles of Seth*, the context is liturgical and the invocation is clearly connected with a mystery of ascent. The use of invocation in this rite is mentioned explicitly as a communal activity:

> For they bless all these individually and at one place and afterwards these shall be silent. And as they are destined, they ascend; and after silence, they descend. From the third they bless the second, after these (they bless) the first. The way of ascent is the way of descent.[60]

The passage seems to describe a ritual in which appropriate invocations to the gods are sung at each level of the ascent. The similarities with *Allogenes* point toward a common communal context and a shared knowledge of a ritual of ascent. Unlike *Marsanes*, there is no indication here of the use of magical objects or instruments in theurgic practice.[61]

The Divine Hierarchy

The Unknowable

The Unknowable is first mentioned when Allogenes receives a revelation concerning the ascent from the Powers of the Luminaries of the aeon of Barbelo. They tell Allogenes that he will achieve a first (primary) revelation of the Unknowable at the height of his ascent. They describe knowledge of the Unknowable as a kind of ignorance, a knowledge that defines the limit of what it is possible for Allogenes (or anyone) to achieve in the ascent (59.26–35). Allogenes himself tells the reader that, at the peak of the ascent experience

---

56. Similar names are found in *StSeth* and *Zost*, for example. See exegetical note to 53b–54.37.
57. For a more detailed treatment of the relationship between the two texts, see exegetical note to 53.32b–54.37.
58. There is also a similar passage in *Zost*. See exegetical note to 53.32b–54.37.
59. See exegetical note to 53b–54.37.
60. *StSeth* 127.11–21
61. Compare *Marsanes* 35*.1–5. Such instruments and objects were used in the rite of ascent described by the Chaldean Oracles. See Lewy, *Chaldaean Oracles and Theurgy*, 227–257; Majercik, *Chaldean Oracles*, 68–70, 83–85.

when he was seeking the ineffable and unknowable God (61.14–19), the Powers intervened and told him that what he was seeking is incomprehensible (61.25–28). They then gave him a description of the Unknowable primarily in negative terms (61.32–66.30). The Powers assert unequivocally that the Unknowable is unknowable in every respect (64.6–8, 10–21). Anyone who claims otherwise is impious and will receive his or her own punishment (64.21–33).

E. R. Dodds listed six ways in which "agnostos" (unknown) and cognate terms are used of God or the gods in Graeco-Roman antiquity:

A god may be (i) unknown because foreign or nameless . . . ; or (ii) unknown to (hu)mankind in general owing to the necessary limitations of human knowledge; or (iii) unknown to all who have not enjoyed a special revelation or initiation; or (iv) unknown and unknowable in his essence, but partially knowable by inference from his works or analogy with other causes; or (v) unknown and unknowable in his positive character, but definable by negations; or (vi) unknown and unknowable, but accessible in the *unio mystica* which is not properly speaking knowledge, being supralogical.[62]

Allogenes describes the Unknowable as (iii) unknown to all who have not enjoyed a special revelation or initiation (56.15–27; 64.29–33; 68.17–20); (v) unknown and unknowable in its positive character, but definable by negations (61.25–66.30); and (vi) unknown and unknowable, but accessible in the vision attained in mystical ascent which is not properly speaking knowledge, but a kind of ignorance (59.26–32; 60.8–12; 61.1–3; 61.14–19). The text explicitly denies that the Unknowable can be known by inference from its works (62.32–36; 63.9–12).[63]

Although the belief in a special revelation is a characteristic of Sethian Gnosticism,[64] the three ways used by *Allogenes* of describing God (by analogy, negation,[65] and ascent) are well established in the philosophical school tradition.[66] A particularly good example is found in the *Didaskalikos* of Albinus. He

---

62. *The Elements of Theology*, 311–312.

63. In distinction for example from Philo who argues that, despite the fact that God is ineffable (ἄρρητος), unnameable (ἀκατονόμαστος), and incomprehensible (ἀκατάληπτος), something can be known about God from his works. See Wolfson, "Albinus and Plotinus," 116–117; see also "The Knowability," 233–249; Dillon, *The Middle Platonists*, 156.

64. E. R. Dodds considers this belief to be specifically Gnostic. He writes: "Of these (six ways of describing God as unknowable), the escape by special revelation is characteristically eastern; it gave Gnosticism its name, and is exemplified in such passages as Evang. Matth. xi.27. The complete absence of this doctrine from the *Enneads* marks Platonism as being a philosophy and not a religion" (*The Elements of Theology*, 312). Concerning Plotinian thought and religion, see Armstrong, *Cambridge History*, 258–263.

65. A strong influence, if not the entire source, of the tendency to refuse to assign any positive quality to the first principle may be traced to Pythagoreanism. See John Whittaker, "Neopythagoreanism and the Transcendent Absolute," 77–86.

66. See Dillon, *The Middle Platonists*, 284–285.

illustrates the use of analogy from the sun simile in Plato's *Republic* VI, the use of negation from the *Parmenides* 137C–142A, and the ascent from Diotima's speech in the *Symposium* 210–211.[67] The author of *Allogenes* seems acquainted not only with these passages from Plato, but with the school traditions as well.

The use of negation is especially well-developed in *Allogenes*.[68] The premise of the unknowability and indescribability of the first principle seems to derive from scholastic exercises and school traditions[69] discussing Plato's *Parmenides* 137C–142A.[70] The speaker, Parmenides, concludes:

> Therefore the one in no sense *is*. It cannot, then 'be' even to the extent of 'being' one, for then it would be a thing that is and has being. Rather, if we can trust such an argument as this, it appears that the one neither is one nor is at all. And if a thing is not, you cannot say that it '*has*' anything or that there is anything '*of*' it. Consequently, it cannot *have* a name or be spoken of, nor can there be any knowledge or perception or opinion *of* it. It is not named or spoken of, not an object of opinion or of knowledge, not perceived by any creature.[71]

The presentation of the Unknowable in 61.32–67.38 is based on a denial that any of the Platonic and Aristotelian attributes or categories given for anything which exists or is intelligible can be applied to the Unknowable. In the Sophist 254D–255E, there are five attributes applied by Plato to things which really exist: being ($\tau\acute{a}$ $\check{o}\nu$ $\alpha\mathring{v}\tau\acute{o}$), movement ($\kappa\acute{\iota}\nu\eta\sigma\iota s$), rest ($\sigma\tau\acute{a}\sigma\iota s$), identity ($\tau\grave{o}$ $\tau\alpha\mathring{v}\tau o\nu$) and diversity ($\tau\grave{o}$ $\theta\acute{a}\tau\epsilon\rho o\nu$).[72] Aristotle listed ten[73] (or eight[74]) categories for the intelligible *sensu latiori*: substance ($o\mathring{v}\sigma\acute{\iota}a$), quantity ($\pi\acute{o}\sigma o\nu$), quality ($\pi o\iota\acute{o}\nu$), relation ($\pi\rho\acute{o}s$ $\tau\iota$), place ($\pi o\mathring{v}$), time ($\pi\acute{o}\tau\epsilon$), position ($\kappa\epsilon\acute{\iota}\sigma\theta a\iota$), state ($\check{\epsilon}\chi\epsilon\iota\nu$), action ($\pi o\iota\epsilon\hat{\iota}\nu$), and affection ($\pi\acute{a}\sigma\chi\epsilon\iota\nu$).[75]

---

67. See Dillon, *The Middle Platonists*, 284–285; also Wolfson, "Albinus and Plotinus," 119–124.

68. See exegetical notes to 61.22b–67.38.

69. See E. R. Dodds, "The *Parmenides* of Plato," 129–142; *The Elements of Theology*, Appendix I "The Unknown God in Neoplatonism," 310–313. He finds the doctrine of the unknowability of the One in Plotinus to be based not only on a direct knowledge of the passage quoted above from the Parmenides but also upon a knowledge of prior philosophical speculation, including Numenius (Eusebius, *Preparation for the Gospel* XI.22) and Philo (*On the Change of Names* III.58).

70. For a short summary of this passage and its application to *Allogenes*, see the exegetical notes on 62.27b–63.28a.

71. *Parmenides* 141e–142a. Translation by Francis Macdonald Cornford in *Plato* (ed. Hamilton and Cairns), 935.

72. Plotinus applied these not to the first principle, but to his second hypostasis, Being/ Intellect (*Ennead* VI.2.7–8).

73. See *Cat.* 4 and *Topics*.

74. See for example the *Posterior Analytics* A22, 83 a 21 ff., b 15 ff.

75. Plotinus gives a sharp critique of the Aristotelian categories and denies that any of Aristotle's categories except substance belongs to the primary genera (see *Ennead* VI.1; 2.13–16). He finds fault with Aristotle on precisely Platonic lines: "These thinkers (such as Aristotle) are, however, not considering the Intellectual realm in their division, which was not intended to cover all the Existents; the Supreme they overlooked" (*Ennead* VI.1.1; trans.

The revelation of the Powers denies that these categories may be applied to the Unknowable. They deny that the Unknowable exists or can come into being; that it is living, Life, or the source of life; that it knows (itself or anything else) or is known or is Intellect; that it is at rest (silent, still, at rest); that it is moved or mover or Motion; that it is essence, corporeal or incorporeal; that it is great or small; that it is defined by, contains, is, or possesses the Good or goodness, God or divinity, blessedness, or Beauty; that it gives or receives, is active or affected, is Act or Potentiality (Power); that the Unknowable has place, time or position; that it is number or creature. Rather, the Powers stress that the Unknowable transcends anything that can be said or predicated of it in its privation and incomprehensible unknowability. Thus one can claim that it exists or is substance or intellect or anything else only if one acknowledges that it is these things only in a way that is completely unknowable and incomprehensible.

This insistence on the complete incomprehensibility of the Unknowable is the most radical feature of the text's presentation of the first principle of the divine hierarchy. Yet at the same time, *Allogenes* insists that the Unknowable can be known incomprehensibly through "revelation and primary revelation." Its unknowability is therefore limited in the sense that such "unknowing knowledge" requires special initiation, revelation, and direct apprehension (in the rite of ascent)[76] and may in part be described through negation.[77]

The Invisible Spirit

The highest figure of the divine hierarchy in *Allogenes* is the Unknowable. As described above, this figure is completely transcendent, unknowable, and ineffable. In Sethian mythology, however, the highest being is often designated the Invisible Spirit,[78] a name which also appears prominently in *Allogenes*. The relationship between the Unknowable and the Invisible Spirit in *Allogenes* is never made completely clear, but at 66.16 and 66.30–38, "Invis-

MacKenna, p. 443–444). *Allogenes* presumes a similar appropriation and critique of the Aristotelian categories by later thinkers.

76. See below, p. 9.

77. Wolfson argued (in "Albinus and Plotinus," 115–130) that Albinus used Aristotle's distinction between "negation" and "privation" in his discussion of how one can form a conception of God. In "Neopythagoreanism and Negative Theology," Whittaker has shown, however, that "It is not true as Wolfson claims that in Aristotle, 'negation' in its strictly technical sense of a logical negation is contrasted with the term 'privation'" (120). It is nonetheless clear, according to Whittaker, that "Aristotle's use of the relevant terms has exercised influence upon the formulations of the via negationis which we have been considering. It is equally evident that in Aristotle these terms refer to mental acts rather than to negative statements" (122). The precise logical status of negation in Allogenes remains undetermined. (For an example of negation as abstraction, see Plotinus *Ennead* VI.8.21.) Such a process of abstraction is never explicitly discussed in *Allogenes*, though it is not possible in a text like ours, which claims to be based on revelation, to be entirely sure how the author arrived at the statements made concerning the Unknowable.

78. See *ApJohn* II.2.33 passim; *GosEgypt* III.40.13 passim; *Zost* XIII.1.20.18, passim; *Marsanes* X.1.10.19, passim; *TriProt* XIII.1.38.11, passim.

ible Spirit" appears to be used to designate the Unknowable. The designation "Unknowable" is used when the transcendence of the First Principle is expressed. The designation "Invisible Spirit" is used when the topic concerns generation, that is, when the relationship of the First Principle to the existents is discussed. It may be that the author of *Allogenes* is almost at the point of positing a being (the Unknowable) beyond the Invisible Spirit, but does not quite take so radical a step.[79]

The fullest discussion of the Invisible Spirit is at 47.9–48.32. He is a Unity or Monad encompassing everything which truly exists. He is the source and cause of all that exists; they do not have any existence apart from him, nor in some sense does he exist as such apart from those whom he has caused to exist. In quality, he surpasses anything that might be predicated of him (such as perfection, blessedness, or divinity) insofar as he is the source of all qualities and prior to all qualities in sequence. In and of himself as he is, he is incomprehensible, ineffable, and nameless. As the One, he can be described in terms of categories that apply to generated existents only as their source, not as he is in himself. Hence he is called: nonsubstantial substance, immaterial matter, numberless number, formless form, shapeless shape, powerless power, inactive activity.

Triplicity and the Triply-Powered

The number three has a long and well recognized history in religious and philosophical thought. The use of three is documented as a sacred number in ancient Near Eastern cultures, including Hebrew religion, where it suggests the idea of completeness.[80] Hermann Usener, in his study of triads in Graeco-Roman tradition, gives a long list of examples of divinities in groups of three from literature, cult, and art.[81] He shows that it was quite common to view a grouping of three gods as a unity. The triads, he argues, arise from a more original presentation of one or two unified deities to which a third is added to form a triad.[82] The impetus for this lies, he suggests, in the development of the capacity to count past two. The number two, he argues, is present in nature, while three is more abstract (past, present, future; earth, air and water). Three is important in Pythagorean arithmology[83] where it is the number for multiplicity. Aristotle presents the Pythagorean position as follows:

> For, as the Pythagoreans say, the world and all that is in it is determined by the number three, since beginning and middle and end give the

---

79. It may also be the case that the author of *Allogenes* may be having some difficulty reconciling his (philosophically expressed) views about the extreme transcendence of the Unknowable with the mythological presentation of the Invisible Spirit current in Sethian thought.
80. See the summary by Pope, "Number," III.564–565.
81. "Dreiheit," 1–47, 161–208, 321–362.
82. "Dreiheit," 321.
83. See also Burkert, *Lore and Science*, 56, 466 ff.

number of 'all,' and the number they give is the triad. And so, having taken these three from nature as (so to speak) laws of it, we make further use of the number three in the worship of the Gods. Further, we use the terms in practice in this way. Of two things, or men, we say 'both,' but not 'all': three is the first number to which the term 'all' has been appropriated. And in this, as we have said, we do but follow the lead which nature gives.[84]

The number three, then, denotes at once completeness and multiplicity. It is the symbol therefore of existence in its completeness and in the generation of multiplicity.[85]

Triads become central in later philosophical speculation in Gnosticism, Neo-Platonism, and Christian trinitarian speculation. Manchester carefully distinquishes among three triads: the Plotinian hierarchical scheme, the "schema of participation," and the noetic triad. In the first type, "the directionality of this 'one, two, three' is strongly vertical, each succeeding level dependent on its prior for a perfection and unity, which taken by itself, it lacks or has devolved into powerlessness."[86] The second type, the "schema of participation," shares the hierarchical structure of the first type, but is concerned with the relations among the hypostases. Manchester describes three states in the series of relations among the hypostases:

i. that factor unparticipated (*amethektos*), "in itself," absolute;

ii. that factor participated (*metechomenos*), which involves a self-disposition and action by the factor, not a reaction to what participates in it; and

iii. that factor as *participant* (*kata methexin, en tois metachousi, in schesei*), that is, as enacted in the derived hypostasis and now its action, no longer that of the higher hypostasis.[87]

The third type is the noetic triad, which concerns the horizontal constitution of an hypostasis. "What (this triad) articulates is not external reference but self-constitution and completion."[88] The "canonical example" he gives is the Being-Life-Mind triad of the Second Hypostasis.[89] These distinctions are important for the following description of triads in *Allogenes*.

In *Allogenes* triplicity occurs often, especially in the phrase "triply-powered"

84. Aristotle, *de Caelo* 268a, trans. McKeon, *The Basic Works*, 398.

85. Compare Philo on the number three and triads: *Quaestiones in Genesin* II,5; II,3; IV,8. The last instance is most interesting in that he connects the number three with the nature of God and being, the foundation of all knowledge (as employed by the Pythagoreans), and the ascent of the soul, ending with a statement about the inappropriateness of revealing the mysteries to the uninitiated and unworthy.

86. "The Noetic Triad," 209.

87. "The Noetic Triad," 210.

88. "The Noetic Triad," 211.

89. "The Noetic Triad," 210.

or "thrice-male." Quite often these designations have been hypostasized, for example, as the Triply-powered or the Thrice-male Youth. The ontological organization of principles is arranged hierarchically, often in triads that correspond to distinct levels, analogous to the first type of triad descibed by Manchester. Although this hierarchical triad is not articulated with anything close to the precision of Plotinus' exposition, the principle seems to be operative in *Allogenes*, especially concerning the relationship of the three hypostases, the Invisible Spirit, the Triply-powered, and Barbelo.

More prominent and more carefully worked out is a second use of triplicity which represents an attempt to create bridges between the various levels of the divine hierarchy, and which best fits Manchester's second type of triad, the schema of participation.[90] For example, the Triply-powered mediates between the levels of the Invisible Spirit and Barbelo, both of whom are also called triply-powered.[91] It is called the "ferryman" (49.8) or "steersman" (53.11–12), the mediator of the Unmeasured and Boundless.[92] A second triad, Kalyptos-Protophanes-Autogenes, particularly exemplifies the schema of participation. Here Kalyptos contains the intelligibles in their essential unity, "in themselves"; Protophanes actualizes the individual intelligibles; and Autogenes further actualizes the individuated particulars "part by part and one by one," correcting "the sins derived from nature."[93] The emphasis is upon the interrelatedness among the hierarchically ordered hypostases in the process of generation.

Triads also appear often to provide a fuller description of the triplicity of specific hypostases, and most closely parallel Manchester's third schema of the noetic triad. The Triply-powered, for example, contains the triads Vitality-Intellection-Existence and goodness-blessedness-divinity; Barbelo contains the triad Kalyptos-Protophanes-Autogenes. Each triad clearly articulates the "self-constitution and completion" of its respective hypostasis, the Triply-powered or Barbelo.

The triadic schema in *Allogenes* that has received the greatest interest because of its possible connection to later Platonism is the triad Vitality-Intellection-Existence. This triad occurs three times in *Allogenes* (49.26–38, where it is related to the Triply-powered; 61.32–38 and 62.17–22, where it is denied that the triad can be predicated of the Unknowable). The triad also appears in the account of Allogenes' ascent (59.13–32; 60.19–61.8).

---

90.   The distinction between these two triadic schemes is never entirely clear in *Allogenes*. Rather they overlap and tend to presuppose each other.

91.   See triply-powered Invisible Spirit (47.8–9; 51.8–9; 58.24–25; 66.34–36); the triply-powered aeon of Barbelo (45.20).

92.   The function of the Thrice-male Youth is as a savior (51.33–36). Though the text does not specify, it may be that this salvific role is also conceived primarily as one of mediation between the souls of the Gnostics below and the place of salvation above.

93.   See *Allogenes* 51.13–32.

The triad of Being-Life-Mind appears clearly in later Platonism with Plotinus and those who followed him.[94] E. R. Dodds traces the triad to speculation on the following section of Plato's *Sophist* 249A:[95]

> But tell me, in heaven's name, are we really to be so easily convinced that change, life, soul, understanding have no place in that which is perfectly real—that it has neither life nor thought, but stands immutable in solemn aloofness, devoid of intelligence?[96]

Hadot has argued that the triad seems to have made its way to Plotinus through the handbooks of the second and third centuries,[97] and he finds traces of the triad in a wide variety of authors, though with different implications.[98] If this is the case, the author of *Allogenes* may have picked its triad up from such a handbook. John Turner, on the other hand, has argued quite plausibly that the triad may have been introduced to Plotinus and his circle by *Allogenes*. He speculates that the triad may have arisen in Sethian mythology "as a speculative *Analogiebildung* of the 'noological' triad Prognosis-Aphtharsia-Aionia Zoe" which one finds in the *Apocryphon of John*.[99] Whatever its source, the use of the triad in *Allogenes* is tantalizingly close to that of later Platonists, though the temptation to discern hasty parallels must be avoided. The issue deserves a closer look.

Hadot summarizes the presentation of the triad in later Platonism as follows:

> For Neoplatonism after Plotinus, the triad of being, life, and thought represented at the same time an interpretation of the structure of being-in-itself and an explication of the constitution of particular beings. Being is conceived as an act of self-condition in three moments: the simple condition of itself, power going out from itself, and finally returning to itself. But this condition of itself is the act of being not yet deployed; that going out of itself, the act of living; the return to itself, the act of thinking. Nonetheless, the act of being is triple and one; each act most particularly includes the other. As for beings derived from the first being,

---

94. See E. R. Dodds, *The Elements of Theology*, 252–254; Hadot, "Être, vie, pensée," 107–141; Rist, "Mysticism," 218; P. Merlan, "Greek Philosophy," 20–21; Armstrong, "Plotinus," (*Cambridge History*), 246; Robinson, "The Three Steles of Seth," 140–141; Turner, "The Gnostic Three-fold Path," 334–339; Williams, *The Immovable Race*, 50–53; Pearson, "Marsanes: Introduction," in *Nag Hammadi Codices IX and X*, 245–246.

95. See E. R. Dodds, *The Elements of Theology*, 253; see also Hadot, "Être, vie, pensée," 107.

96. Trans. Cornford, in *Plato* (ed. Hamilton and Cairns), 993.

97. See Hadot, "Être, vie, pensée," 122, 128.

98. Plotinus seems to have developed speculation about the triad along a unique route by reading the *Sophist* 249A with Aristotle's *Metaphysics* 12 and the *Timaeus* 39E. See Hadot,"Être, vie, pensé," 113, 119.

99. Turner, "The Gnostic Threefold Path," 336–339.

the first life, the first thought, they participate more or less in these three characteristics, depending upon their proper nature.[100]

The resemblance of this presentation to that of *Allogenes* needs to be examined.

Allogenes specifically denies that life, intellect, and existence can be predicated of the Unknowable (61.32–62.23). Plotinus similarly argued that the One is beyond being, and that life and intellect cannot be predicated of it.[101] For Plotinus, the triad belonged to his second hypostasis, Intellect. In *Allogenes*, the triad is associated with the Triply-powered,[102] an hypostasis which, like Plotinus' Intellect, is beneath the first principle.

> It (the Triply-powered) is Vitality and Intellection and That-which-exists. For, then, that very one continually possesses its Vitality and Intellect and Life inasmuch as the Vitality possesses Nonsubstance and Intellection whereas Intellect possesses Life and That-which-exists. And these three are one, although they are three (considered) individually (49.26–38).

Compare this statement with Proclus:

> All things are in all things, but in each according to its proper nature: for in Being there is life and intelligence; in Life, being and intelligence; in Intelligence, being and life; but each of these exists upon one level intellectually, upon another vitally, and on the third existentially.[103]

The similarity between the two passages is immediately apparent. James Robinson and John Turner have suggested emending the *Allogenes* passage so as to make the parallel closer.[104] It then reads:

> It is Vitality and Intellection and That-which-exists. For, then, that very one continually possesses its Vitality and Intellect and the Vitality possesses Substance and Intellection whereas Intellect possesses Life and That-which-exists. And these three are one, though they are three (considered) individually.

100. Hadot, "Être, vie, pensée," 107.
101. See for example, *Ennead* V.1.7; V.2.1 and VI.7.41.
102. Compare *Zost* 15.2–12, where the triad Being-Mind-Life is associated with Kalyptos-Protophanes-Autogenes, not the Triply-powered.
103. Πάντα ἐν πᾶσιν, οἰκείως δὲ ἐν ἑκάστῳ· καὶ γὰρ ἐν τῷ ὄντι καὶ ἡ ζωὴ καὶ ὁ νοῦς καὶ ἐν τῇ ζωῇ τὸ εἶναι καὶ τὸ νοεῖν, καὶ ἐν τῷ νῷ τὸ εἶναι καὶ τὸ ζῆν, ἀλλ' ὅπου μὲν νοερῶς, ὅπου δὲ ζωτικῶς ὅπου δὲ ὄντως ὄντα πάντα. Proposition 103, text and trans. in E. R. Dodds, *The Elements of Theology*, 92–93.
104. See Robinson, "Three Steles of Seth," p. 141, n. 9. The changes Turner suggests (see note to Coptic text 49.31–33) rid us of the problematic lack of parallelism and the difficulty of "essencelessness" appearing just where we would want an expression of being. I would agree that the text as it stands is clearly corrupt and Turner's suggestions go a long way to clearing up the difficulty, though without explaining the corruption, especially the presence of the term "essencelessness."

There are three clear points of agreement between Proclus and *Allogenes*: 1) the complementarity of the terms Vitality/Intellection/Existence and Being/Life/Intellection; 2) the insistence that they are mutual; and 3) the essential unity of the three. Proclus says that the triad participates in "all things" whereas *Allogenes* ascribes the triad to one particular hypostasis, the Triply-powered. This difference is somewhat mitigated, however, in the explication Proclus gives following the above proposition. There he explains how it is that each exists in all things.

> For since each character may exist either in its cause or as substantial predicate or by participation, and since in the first term of any triad the other two are embraced as in their cause, while in the mean term the first is present by participation and the third in its cause, and finally the third contains its priors by participation, it follows that in Being there are pre-embraced Life and Intelligence, but because each term is characterized not by what it causes (since this is other than itself) nor by what it participates (since this is extrinsic in origin) but by its substantial predicate, Life and Intelligence are present there after the mode of Being, as existential life and existential intelligence; and in Life are present Being by participation and Intelligence in its cause, but each of these vitally, Life being the substantial character of the term; and in Intelligence both Life and Being by participation, and each of them intellectually, for the being of Intelligence is cognitive and its life is cognition.[105]

Insofar as the Triply-powered exists as a cause for all things that exist, they can be said to exist in relation to it as cause. Nothing can be predicated of them of which the Triply-powered is not the source; therefore they exist as a substantial predicate of it. Similarly they exist in it by participation (it is "in them" and they are "in it"). Therefore one could argue that the explication of Proclus would at least not be in contradiction to the views expressed in *Allogenes*. Proclus uses the triad concerning "all things" and *Allogenes* has hypostasized the unity of all existents in the Triply-powered. This position is most clearly expressed at 58.24–26, where the Triply-powered is identified with the transcendent Entirety.

The second part of the statement in *Allogenes* ("And these three are one, although they are three (considered) individually" [49.36–38]) finds other

---

105. ἐπεὶ γὰρ ἕκαστον ἢ κατ' αἰτίαν ἔστιν ἢ καθ' ὕπαρξιν ἢ κατὰ μέθεξιν, ἔν τε τῷ πρώτῳ τὰ λοιπὰ κατ' αἰτίαν ἔστι, καὶ ἐν τῷ μέσῳ τὸ μὲν πρῶτον κατὰ μέθεξιν τὸ δὲ τρίτον κατ' αἰτίαν, καὶ ἐν τῷ τρίτῳ τὰ πρὸ αὐτοῦ κατὰ μέθεξιν, καὶ ἐν τῷ ὄντι ἄρα ζωὴ προείληπται καὶ νοῦς, ἑκάστου δὲ κατὰ τὴν ὕπαρξιν χαρακτηριζομένου καὶ οὔτε κατὰ τὴν αἰτίαν ἄλλων γάρ ἐστιν αἴτιον οὔτε κατὰ τὴν μέθεξιν ἀλλαχόθεν γὰρ ἔχει τοῦτο, οὗ μετείληφεν, ὄντως ἐστὶν ἐκεῖ καὶ τὸ ζῆν καὶ τὸ νοεῖν, ζωὴ οὐσιώδης καὶ νοῦς οὐσιώδης· καὶ ἐν τῇ ζωῇ κατὰ μέθεξιν μὲν τὸ εἶναι, κατ' αἰτίαν δὲ τὸ νοεῖν, ἀλλὰ ζωτικῶς ἑκάτερον κατὰ τοῦτο γὰρ ἡ ὕπαρξις· καὶ ἐν τῷ νῷ καὶ ἡ ζωὴ καὶ ἡ οὐσία κατὰ μέθεξιν, καὶ νοερῶς ἑκάτερον καὶ γὰρ τὸ εἶναι τοῦ νοῦ γνωστικὸν καὶ ἡ ζωὴ γνῶσις. Proposition 103, text and trans. in E. R. Dodds, *The Elements of Theology*, 92–93.

close parallels in later literature. The anonymous *Commentary on the Parmenides of Plato* (ascribed by Hadot to Porphyry) states:

> And thus, being One and Single, that 'He-in-himself' differs, however, from itself, according to the opposition between act and existence. According to one point of view, he is now One and Single, according to another point of view, he differs from himself. For that which differs from the One is no longer One and that which is other than the Single is no longer Single. It is now the One and Single, according to the first form, that is to say, the form, power or any other name (all of which fail to indicate what is a question of something ineffable and inconceivable) of 'He-in-himself' taken in himself. But it is not One or Single, according to the contrast among existence, life, and thought. According to existence, the thinker is also the thought. But, when Intelligence goes out from existence in order to become the thinker, in order to return afterwards towards the intelligible and see itself, the thinker is then life. That is why considered according to life, Intelligence is infinite. And also existence, life, and thought are all acts insofar as one is able to say that, considered according to existence, the act is immobile, considered according to intellection, the act is turned towards itself, and finally considered according to life, the act is the going forth from existence.[106]

As Hadot has stated, the concern here is the nature of being-in-itself and of particular beings. The particular concern is the "opposition of act and existence." The expression in both Proclus and the *Parmenides Commentary* shows a knowledge of Plotinus as well as other sources, among which we may well number *Allogenes*. One must be careful here, however, not to read the clear and systematic accounts of these later sources back into *Allogenes*, as tempting as that is in the absence of a systematic presentation within *Allogenes* itself.

---

106. καὶ οὕτως ἓν ὄν καὶ ἁπλοῦν ʽτὸ αὐτὸ τοῦτοʼ (ὅμως) ἐνεργείᾳ ἑαυτοῦ διαφέρει καὶ ὑπάρξει, καὶ κατὰ ἄλλο ἄρα ἕν ἐστιν ἁπλοῦν, κατʼ ἄλλο δὲ αὐτὸ ἑαυτοῦ διαφέρει· τὸ γὰρ τοῦ ἑνὸς διαφέρον οὐχ ἓν καὶ τὸ τοῦ ἁπλοῦ ἕτερον οὐχ ἁπλοῦν. Ἓν μὲν οὖν ἐστιν καὶ ἁπλοῦν κατὰ τὴν πρώτην καὶ ʽαὐτὸ τοῦτοʼ αὐτοῦ τούτου ἰδέαν, δύναμις ἢ ὅτι καὶ χρὴ ὀνομάζειν ἐνδείξεως ⟨χ⟩άριν ἄρρητον οὖσαν καὶ ἀνεννόητον, οὐχ ἓν δὲ οὐδὲ ἁπλοῦν κατὰ τὴν ὕπαρξιν καὶ ζωὴν ⟨καὶ⟩ τὴν νόησιν. Καὶ τὸ νοοῦν καὶ τὸ νοούμενον ὑπάρξει, τὸ δὲ νοοῦν, ἥν ὁ νοῦ[ς μετε]ξ[ελθῃ] ἀπὸ τῆς ὑπάρξεως εἰς τὸ νοοῦν, ἵνα ἐπανέλθῃ εἰς τὸ νοητὸν καὶ ἑαυτὸν ἴδῃ, ἐστὶν ζωή· διὸ ἀόριστος (ὁ) κατὰ τὴν ζωήν. Καὶ πασῶν οὐσῶν ἐνεργειῶν καὶ ὡς κατὰ μὲν τὴν ὕπαρξιν ἑστῶσα ἂν εἴη ἡ ἐνέργεια, κατὰ δὲ τὴν νόησιν εἰς αὐτὴν στραφεῖσα ἐνέργεια, κατὰ δὲ τὴν ζωὴν ἐκ τῆς ὑπάρξεως ἐκνεύσασα ἐνέργεια. Fragment 14; text from Hadot, *Porphyry et Victorinus*, II.108–112.

See also Marius Victorinus, *adv. Arium* III 4, 33 (*Quod si ita est, ut unum sit vivere et intellegere, et cum unum sit esse quod est vivere atque intellegere, [substantia unum subsistentia tria sunt ista.] Cum enim vim ac sinificantiam suam habeant atque ut dicuntur et sint, necessario et sunt tria et tamen unum, cum omne, quod singulum est unum, tria sint. [Idque a Graecis ita dicitur:* ἐκ μιᾶς οὐσίας τρεῖς εἶναι τὰς ὑποστάσεις.]), op. cit. 25; and *adv. Arium* IV 5; P L 10, 116d (*Haec tria accipienda ut singula, sed ita ut qua suo plurimo sunt, hoc nominentur ut esse dicantur. Nam nihil horum quod non tria sit; esse enim, hoc est esse, si vivat, hoc est in vita sit. Ipsum vero vivere, non est vivere quod vivat intellegentiam non habere.*) quoted from Hadot, "Être, vie, pensée," 127.

Allogenes is interested in the triad (and indeed in the nature of being itself) only with reference to the ascent, as an analysis of 59.13–32 and 60.19–61.8 shows.

In the account of the ascent, Allogenes moves from Vitality to Existence ($\H{v}\pi\alpha\rho\xi\iota\varsigma$) to Knowledge. The first level of Vitality is described as an eternal, noetic motion of the Powers, formless and unbounded. From this level, Allogenes ascends to Existence, described as silent and standing at rest,[107] embracing all things in silence and inactivity. That stationary rest is the image and likeness with which Allogenes himself is clothed (a possible conflation of Platonic language about the noetic ideas with Genesis 1:22?). The final level he attains is one of "ignorant Knowledge," a revelation of what is limitless concerning the Unknowable. When Allogenes then tries to seek the Unknowable Itself, he is stopped, for that is impossible.

What we have here is a mythological expression of the triad Vitality-Intellect-Existence as levels achieved in the visionary ascent. The goal is at once self-knowledge and knowledge given through revelation and primary revelation. Here the proposition, summarized by Hadot, that knowledge is a return to Being-in-itself is expressed in a narrative of the rise of the soul to knowledge of the first principle. At the pinnacle of the ascent, Allogenes relates that:

> I came to understand what exists in me, and the Triply-powered, and the revelation of what is illimitable of it. And through a primary revelation of the First which is unknown to all, I saw the God that is beyond perfection and the Triply-powered that exists in them all (61.5–14).

The ascent of Allogenes is based upon his own self-comprehension. For Plotinus, too, the ascent is possible because of one's identity with the Supreme, since it is the wellspring of Life, Intellect, and Being. In the ascent, the soul grasps the unity of all things. In *Allogenes*, that unity is expressed hypostatically as the "Triply-powered that exists in them all"; in Plotinus, it is described as the intact identity of the emanents holding firm.

A difference between the views of *Allogenes* and Plotinus is also clear at this point. Plotinus does not see Life, Intellect, and Being as levels in the ascent,[108] but as emanations from the Supreme. Also for Plotinus, the goal is a unity of self with the Supreme,[109] whereas for *Allogenes*, the goal is self-illumination

---

107. For a discussion of the image of "standing" and "being at rest" in *Allogenes* and the *Parmenides Commentary*, see Williams, *The Immovable Race*, 50–53.

108. Although one might read *Ennead* V.1.4 in this direction?

109. Hadot has made some very important observations in this regard in relation to Plotinus. He argues plausibly that the views of later Neoplatonism are a development from an earlier Platonic triadic schema of paideia as nature, instruction, and practice, especially moral and ascetic practice ("Être, vie, pensée," 127). These were conceived as mutual aspects of each other. He concludes: "I believe that one is now able to issue the following hypothesis: the manuals which summarized the doctrine of Plato had, before Plotinus, given a special

and a kind of unknowable knowledge. In short, for Plotinus the height of the "ascent" is a mystical union with the One. The account in *Allogenes* is much more mythologized: the ascent is an extracorporeal event where the self encounters semi-hypostasized beings, and the end is not unity, but knowledge. Furthermore, as was discussed above, the ascent in *Allogenes* has a distinctly cultic context. This context is illustrated even more clearly in other Sethian texts, especially the *Three Steles of Seth* and *Zostrianos*.[110]

It should be noted at least in passing that the triad Vitality-Intellection-Existence appears elsewhere in Sethian texts (*StSeth* 122.18–23; 125.27–32; *Zostrianos* 15.4–12; 66.11–67.4; 73.6–11; perhaps 74.8–75.11). Both *Three Steles of Seth* and *Zostrianos* link the triad to the Aeon of Barbelo, and, in addition, *Three Steles of Seth* links it as well with the One (this figure is not, however, equivalent to the Unknowable in *Allogenes*). This variety illustrates the fluidity of the triad in Sethian speculation. Precisely where *Allogenes* fits into this speculation awaits a more detailed study of the history of Sethianism.

The position of the Triply-powered within *Allogenes* can be determined with some precision. A figure which appears only in a few of the Sethian texts,[111] it is identified in *Allogenes* both with the Invisible Spirit (in seven of the nine cases where the Invisible Spirit occurs)[112] and with Barbelo (once[113]).

place to the triad being-life-thought, in bringing together the division of the three divisions of philosophy with the distinction among the three steps of paideia [that is, being-mind-thought; physics, logic, and ethics; nature, doctrine and practice] . . . This parallelism in effect means that the movement of the human being toward his/her perfection coincides with the universal movement of being that is only achieved by thought and life. Human nature is only achieved by the knowledge and practice of that which conforms to nature. But this nature is only achieved in knowledge and in living as an action of God. We note, moreover, that spiritual progress is able to be conceived as a conversion; theory and practice, intelligence and life have as their sole role to be restored to the purity of being . . . The study of the triad being-life-thought in Plotinus seems to lead us to conclude that the central intuition of Plotinus is that of a life which utilizes intellectual determination in order to be joined with its source" ("Être, vie, pensée," 128–129, 137).

110. *StSeth* contains hymns which might be associated with the ascent (and descent) of the soul. In *Zost*, the triad is associated with baptisms attained in ascent: "It is the water of Life which belongs to Vitality in which you now have been baptized in the Autogenes. It is the [water] of Blessedness which belongs to Knowledge that you will be baptized in the Protophanes. It is the water of Existence [which] belongs to Divinity, and the Kalyptos" (15.4–12; trans. Sieber, *NHLE*, 408). For the replacement of Intellection with Blessedness, cf. Marius Victorinus, *Adversus Arium* 1.50; see Hadot, *Porphyre et Victorinus*, I. 62; see the discussion in Williams, *The Immovable Race*, 69–70, especially note 3.

111. *Marsanes*, *Zost*, *StSeth*, *TriProt*, *ApJohn* (BG and NHC II,*1*), and *UnText*. See exegetical note to 45.13a.

112. The designation "Invisible Spirit" appears in *Allogenes* nine times (see index for specific listings; the term occurs in two forms: ⲁⲟⲣⲁⲧⲟⲛ ⲡⲛⲁ and ⲁⲧⲛⲁⲩ ⲉⲣⲟϥ ⲙ̄ⲡⲛⲁ), four times in direct conjunction with the expression "triply-powered" (*Allogenes* 47.8–9; 51.8–9; 58.24–25; and 66.33–35), and five times singly (*Allogenes* 45.27; 49.9–10; 51.35; 64.36; and 66.16). Three of the five cases where the designation is found without the expression "triply-powered," however, concern the relation of the Invisible Spirit and the Triply-powered. At 45.27, it is said that the Triply-powered's knowledge of existents derives from

There are 15 places where the designation ΠΙϢⲘⲚⲦϬⲞⲘ ("triply-powered")
appears, either as the Triply-powered Invisible Spirit,[114] the Triply-powered
aeon of Barbelo,[115] or simply the Triply-powered.[116] These differing designations are not the product of frivolous ineptitude or nonsensical inconsistency,
but rather they function to define the Invisible Spirit, the Triply-powered, and
Barbelo as distinct hypostases, while at the same time indicating continuity
between hierarchical, ontological levels. This multiplication of hypostases
functions to protect the utter transcendence of the First Principle, while at the
same time deriving all existents from it.

The Triply-powered is, in this regard, truly the mediator between the
highest hypostasis and everything which exists.[117] It is an hypostasization of
those aspects of the Invisible Spirit which have continuity with the existents
deriving from him. Hence the Triply-powered possesses Vitality, Intellection,
and Existence—those qualities of living, thinking, and being that belong to
everything which truly exists. The mediation of the Triply-powered protects
the transcendence of the Invisible Spirit.[118]

Barbelo

The next level of the divine hierarchy is Barbelo.[119] She is again a well-
known figure in Gnostic mythology and figures prominently in Sethianism as
the consort of the Invisible Spirit; she is the second hypostasis of the divine
triad, Father-Mother-Son.[120] In *Allogenes*, her role is interpreted in terms of
current philosophical speculation as Intellect ($\nu o\hat{v}s$); and in terms of Gnostic
thought as saving Knowledge ($\gamma\nu\hat{\omega}\sigma\iota s$; see 51.8–12; 59.1–4). She is an extension of the Triply-powered and is hypostasized by turning toward him in an act
of intellection, thereby becoming bounded, eternal, and noetic (49.7–19;
53.9–17).

the Invisible Spirit. 49.9–10 describes the Triply-powered as the mediator (ferryman) of the
boundlessness of the Invisible Spirit. And finally, 64.36 describes the "Triply-powered of the
first thought of the Invisible Spirit."

113. *Allogenes* 45.20.
114. *Allogenes* 47.8; 51.8; 58.24; 66.34–35.
115. *Allogenes* 45.20.
116. *Allogenes* 45.13, 21–22; 52.19; 52.30; 53.30–31; 55.21; 61.6, 13, 20; 64.34–35.
117. See Turner, "The Gnostic Threefold Path," 334; contra Sieber, "The Barbelo
Aeon," 790.
118. *Allogenes* 48.32–38, for example, says that the triply-powered Invisible Spirit
neither gives nor receives. So whenever the individuals do receive, it is through the first
Vitality and undivided activity, that is, the Triply-powered.
119. For speculation concerning the meaning of the name Barbelo as "in four is God,"
see Leisegang, *Die Gnosis*, 186.
120. See *ApJohn* 4.36; 5.13,19, 25, 26, 31; 6.1, 5, 10, 22; 7.3, 14, 17; *StSeth* 121.21;
Zost 14.6; 36.14, 20; 37.20; 53.10; 62.21; 63.7; 83.9; 87.10; 91.19; 118.10; 119.23; 122.1;
124.11; 129.11; *Marsanes* 4.11; 8.28; 4.21; and the *TriProt* 38.9. (The name is also found
among the Nag Hammadi Codices in the non-Sethian tractate *Melchizedek* 5. 27; 16.26.)

Kalyptos, Protophanes, Autogenes

Barbelo is also described as triply-powered, male,[121] and virginal.[122] Her triplicity is manifested in the male triad: Kalyptos, Protophanes, Autogenes. This triad, also known from other Sethian texts,[123] appears in *Allogenes* three times.[124]

The three figures hypostasize the process of deriving multiplicity from intelligible unity; they are the "types and forms of the ones who truly exist."[125] Kalyptos represents the unity of all noetic (intelligible) existents; Autogenes represents their particularized individual existence; and Protophanes is the mediator between the two, their procession from unified to particularized existence.

Kalyptos ("the Hidden One) represents multiplicity in its intelligible unity. He is called the "intelligible word of these" (51.18–19). He takes on hypostatic existence when Barbelo "acts in those whom she knew," that is, the "hidden ones,"[126] the true existents[127] which exist in Kalyptos. He is called the "primal origin of blessedness."[128] Turner suggests that the name, "hidden," "may derive from the conception of the veil (κάλυμμα) as a limit (ὅρος) separating the high deity from the aeonic world."[129]

Protophanes is the "first procession of those ones."[130] That is to say, he is a hypostasization of the procession from multiplicity-in-intelligible-unity (Kalyptos) to particularized individuality (Autogenes). He actualizes individual existents through "craft, sure knowledge, or particularized nature."[131] He is described as great, male, noetic and invisible;[132] his name is Armedon (or Harmedon).[133]

Autogenes is the lowest level of the Barbelo aeon, the level of fully individuated existents. He sees all things existing individually, as he himself exists.[134] The existents are individuated "part by part and one by one" through his knowledge of them as particularized individual existents.[135] He is called good

---

121. *Allogenes* 45.18, 38; 59.6. Compare *Marsanes* 9.1–3.
122. *Allogenes* 45.18; 59.7.
123. Compare *StSeth* 119.16; 122.14–15; 123.1–6 and *Zost* 15.2–12; 20.5–9; 22.5–14; 44.23–31; 58.14–16. See also *UnText* 234.12–13.
124. *Allogenes* 45.28–46.37; 51.13–38; and 58.12–24.
125. *Allogenes* 51.14–16.
126. *Allogenes* 46.33.
127. *Allogenes* 51.15–16.
128. *Allogenes* 58.20–21.
129. "Allogenes," 247.
130. *Allogenes* 46.27.
131. *Allogenes* 51.19–25.
132. *Allogenes* 45.34–35; 46.24–25; 51.20.
133. *Allogenes* 45.36; 58.17.
134. *Allogenes* 46.14–16.
135. *Allogenes* 51.26–32.

and divine.[136] He is also described as "the savior who corrects the sins deriving from nature."[137]

Individual Beings

The existents are of two main kinds in *Allogenes*, "the true existents" ("those who truly exist") and "perfect individuals." They correspond respectively to the intelligibles in their universal and in their particular (individuated) aspects.[138]

The true existents constitute the Entirety that is higher than perfect. They are located in the Triply-powered who is their cause.[139] They are eternal potentiality,[140] the forms and images of the perfect individuals actualized in the Barbelo aeon.[141] The true existents exist in deity and blessedness and subsistence and essencelessness and non-existent subsistence.[142] They are defined as Monads.[143] The One also encompasses them in its unity.[144] They are thus the intelligibles in their unity in the One.

The perfect individuals are the intelligibles individuated as particulars and actualized in the Barbelo aeon. In philosophical terms, Barbelo can be described as Intellect actualized in particular existents. It is in her that the perfect individuals exist; they are unified insofar as they exist "in one place, being joined with Intellect,"[145] that is, insofar as they are in Barbelo. The aeon of Barbelo is thus the place all perfect individuals.

The Kalyptos-Protophanes-Autogenes triad of Barbelo expresses the nature of the intelligible existents in their multiplicity. As was said above, Kalyptos represents the unity of all individual noetic existents in Intellect;[146] Autogenes represents their particularized individual existence; and Protophanes is the mediator between the two, their procession from unified to particularized individual existence.

It is also interesting to note that *Three Steles of Seth* identifies the perfect individuals with saved Gnostics:

> We bless thee (Thrice-male), once we have been saved, as the perfect individuals, perfect on account of thee, those who [became] perfect with

---

136. *Allogenes* 58.12–13.
137. *Allogenes* 51.30–32.
138. See note to 45.6–9a.
139. *Allogenes* 49.16–18.
140. *Allogenes* 49.21–26.
141. *Allogenes* 51.14–16.
142. *Allogenes* 55.26–30.
143. See *Allogenes* 66.35–36: "The One is in all those who exist."
144. *Allogenes* 66.36–38.
145. *Allogenes* 45.6–9.
146. Though they are actualized, the perfect individuals remain in some sense a unity or unities. Philosophically expressed, the individuals are unified insofar as they are joined with "Intellect" or "Thought" (45.6–9; 46.20–22). The phrase "to be in one place" is used to describe this unity. The "place" is mythologically the Kalyptos aspect of the aeon of Barbelo.

thee who is complete, who completes, the one perfect through all these, who is similar everywhere.[147]

Since *Allogenes* stands in the same mythological tradition as *Three Steles of Seth*, we may well be able to see the perfect individuals, not only in philosophical terms as actualized existents, but also in mythological terms as Gnostic initiates.

Schematic Summary

The divine hierarchy can be summarized schematically as follows:

> *The Unknowable God*
>
> *The Invisible Spirit*
>> *Triply-powered*
>> (realm of the Entirety)
>
> *Barbelo*
> (glories; powers)
>> *Kalyptos*   (unified existents)
>> *Protophanes* (those that exist together)
>> *Autogenes*   (the perfect individuals, Gnostics)
>
> *Thrice-male Youth*
> (the self-begotten ones)

The vertical positions on the chart represent hierarchical levels, as well as ontic derivation. The three figures on the left hand side of the chart belong to the primary triad of Sethian mythology: the Invisible Spirit, Barbelo, and the Thrice-male Youth (or Autogenes).

Comparison with Plotinus

Were we now to compare this schema with Plotinus' noetic hierarchy, it becomes immediately obvious that *Allogenes* and Plotinus differ on the number of principles in the intelligible world. This was a sore point for Plotinus who charged the Gnostics with a ridiculous and unnecessary multiplication of principles.[148] It is not necessary, he says, to multiply principles in order to distinguish potentiality from actuality (τὴν μὲν δυνάμει τὴν δὲ ἐνεργείᾳ) or repose from motion (ἐν ἡσυχίᾳ τινί τον δὲ οἶον κινούμενον), or thinking from consciousness of thought (ὁ μὲν νοεῖ ὁ δὲ νοεῖ ὅτι νοεῖ). In defense of *Allogenes'* philosophical sophistication, it may be noted, however, as A. H. Armstrong points out, that these distinctions are to be found not only in Gnostic thought, but in the doctrines of other Platonists as well, including Plotinus himself![149]

---

147. *StSeth* 121.2–8; trans. Robinson, *NHLE*, 398.
148. *Ennead* II.9.1–2.
149. See *Plotinus*, vol. III, 226–227, note 1.

Allogenes displays a definite tendency to hypostasize all of the various stages of production deriving from the Supreme Principle. So where Plotinus has only two principles (the One and Intellect) and generates the latter directly from the former, *Allogenes* places a middle term (the Triply-powered) between the Invisible Spirit and Barbelo and moreover comes close to positing a further hypostasis, the Unknowable, beyond them. A comparison between *Ennead* V.4.2 and *Allogenes* shows how the characteristics of Plotinus' two principles, the Intelligible and Intellect, are divided up among three terms in *Allogenes*:

Intelligible	*Unknowable*
beyond Intellect	not Intellect[150]
remains by itself	
not deficient	not limitable[151]
discerns itself	self-comprehension[152]
beyond being	non-existing subsistence[153]
beyond Intellect	not Intellect, but more exquisite[154]
everlasting rest	at rest; stands at every time; silence; stillness[155]
	Invisible Spirit
all things in and with it	all things in it[156]
all things belong to it	provides for self[157]
it has Life in itself	
productive power of all things	cause and source[158]
Intellect (Being)	*Triply-powered*
Being	Existence[159]
Life	Vitality[160]

150. See *Allogenes* 61.36; 62.17–22.
151. See *Allogenes* 62.6–17.
152. See *Allogenes* 63.14–16, 28–32; 64.12–14.
153. The existence of the Unknowable, like Plotinus' One, is not subsistence (except incomprehensibly; 61.38–39); that is to say, it is not subsistence that can come into being (62.23–24). The Unknowable is neither corporeal nor incorporeal, but is non-existing subsistence (65.28–33).
154. See *Allogenes* 62.17–24.
155. See *Allogenes* 62.24–27; 63.33–35; 64.1; 65.26–28; 66.22, 25–30; 67.28. At 65.38 the text states that it is "more exalted than its own stillness . . ."
156. See *Allogenes* 47.11–12.
157. See *Allogenes* 48.17–19.
158. See *Allogenes* 47.13–14; 48.19–32.
159. See *Allogenes* 49.26–38.
160. See *Allogenes* 49.26–38 and 48.32–38.

Thinking	Intellection[161]
comes from great power	received power[162]

Moreover, Plotinus states that Intellect comes into being when the Intelligible abides in itself: Thinking, which is indefinite, turns toward the Intelligible and is perfected and defined by the Intelligible as Intellect. *Allogenes* describes the process of the generation of Barbelo from the Invisible Spirit in a similar fashion at 49.7–14 and 53.9–17, except that the Triply-powered appears as a mediator between the two.

Or again where Plotinus has only one principle, a tripartite Soul, *Allogenes* presents three figures (Kalyptos-Protophanes-Autogenes) who serve similar functions.[163]

These examples illustrate some relatively close similarities, as well as the differences, between *Allogenes* and the system of Plotinus.

Sethian Gnosticism

As has already been shown, *Allogenes* shows affinities with Sethian Gnosticism and with current philosophical thought. The following sections will attempt to clarify more precisely the relationship of *Allogenes* to each of these phenomena.

Sethianism

In order to understand the place of *Allogenes* with regard to Sethianism, it is necessary to know first what Sethianism is.

The name "Sethian" derives from the early Christian heresiologists. In recent times, it has been applied to a group of related texts discovered within the last century, most of which come from among the Nag Hammadi codices. According to Schenke, these include:

> *The Apocryphon of John* (NHC II,*1*: III,*1*: IV,*1*; plus the Berlin Codex version and the parallel in Irenaeus *AdvHaer* 1.29)
> *The Hypostasis of the Archons* (NHC II,*4*)
> *The Gospel of the Egyptians* (NHC III,*2*; IV,*2*)
> *The Apocalypse of Adam* (NHC V,*5*)

---

161. See *Allogenes* 49.26–38.
162. See *Allogenes* 45.25–27.
163. According to Plotinus, the soul has three parts, the first directed to the intelligibles, the third to the sensibles, and the second is in the middle between them (*Ennead* II.9.2 [5–10]). In *Allogenes*, Kalyptos represents the unity of all noetic (intelligible) existents; Autogenes represents their particularized individual existence; and Protophanes is the mediator between the two, their procession from unified to particularized existence.

The Three Steles of Seth (NHC VII,*5*)
Zostrianos (NHC VIII,*1*)
Melchizedek (NHC XI,*1*)
The Thought of Norea (NHC IX,*2*)
Marsanes (NHC X)
Allogenes (NHC XI,*3*)
Untitled Treatise (Codex Brucianus)

Included as well are the doctrines of the so-called Gnostics, Sethians, and Archontics of Epiphanius (*Panarion* 26.39–40).[164]

The Nag Hammadi texts themselves show an astonishing range of diversity.[165] Within the Nag Hammadi collection, however, some grouping is possible. The set of texts listed above has been grouped together under the designation "Sethianism"[166] based on similarities in mythology.

Although there is general agreement that these texts are mythologically related, there has been considerable debate about whether or not "Sethians" constituted a distinct, discernible sect in antiquity.[167] The primary issues under discussion are: (1) the usefulness of Christian heresiological sources; (2) the coherence and distinctiveness of Sethian teaching; (3) the use of mythology in defining group identity; (4) the self-designation of the group as "Seed of Seth" or "the Immovable Race"; and (5) the existence and role of cultic practice, especially baptism and the rite of ascension.

The original Sethian texts from Nag Hammadi, the Berlin Codex, and the Bruce Codex are not of much help in solving the dilemma of social description since their content is almost solely mythological, not historiographical. The Patristic materials are of even more dubious usefulness. Though the designation "Sethians" derives from the early Christian heresiologists, the discovery of

164. See "The Phenomenon," 588–589.
165. This fact of course has made for a considerable amount of interesting speculation about who collected these texts and why, and who hid them and why. See Hedrick, "Gnostics Proclivities," 78–94; Säve-Söderbergh, "Holy Scriptures or Apologetic Documentations?" 3–14; and Wisse, "Gnosticism and Early Monasticism," 431–440.
166. Puech first applied the term "Sethian" to the entire Nag Hammadi collection ("Les nouveaux écrits," 91–154). See also Doresse, *The Secret Books*, chapter 4. For a critique of this broad use of the appellation, see Wisse, "The Sethians and the Nag Hammadi Library," 601–607.
The use of the designation "Sethian" to describe this group of texts, although taken from the heresiologists, is nevertheless somewhat arbitrary and its use here in no way indicates acceptance of the Patristic classifications. Furthermore this usage is in accord with current judgement of most modern scholars that these texts show a significant set of internal relationships so that in some sense they belong together. The treatment of Sethianism at one of the two seminars of the International Conference on Gnosticism at Yale, 1978, is a reflection of this consensus.
167. See especially Wisse, "The Nag Hammadi Library," 601–607 and "Stalking"; H.-M. Schenke, "Das Sethianische System" and "The Phenomenon"; Tardieu, "Les livres"; Rudolph, "Die 'Sethianische' Gnosis" and the following discussion in the same volume; and Williams, *The Immovable Race*, chapter VIII.

the Nag Hammadi texts has brought into serious question the heresiologists' descriptions and classifications of various *groups*.[168] It was in their best (polemical) interests to present Gnosticism as an "absurdly fragmented movement,"[169] divided into numerous sects, each doctrinally distinct from the other, and to present, over against all this confusion and division, the *regula fidei* of the united, universal Church. Such a polemical motivation does not require us, of course, to take the opposite position and hold that there were no distinct Gnostic groups, but it does mean that we cannot unquestioningly or uncritically use the Patristic materials as sources of historically accurate evidence about them.

This fact means that we have little historical evidence at all about the persons who wrote and used these texts, and indeed considerable difficulty lies in establishing the existence of a distinct Sethian group or sect.

Hans-Martin Schenke has led the discussion in favor of the existence of a distinct and coherent Sethian teaching. He has identified the following as basic elements of Sethian mythology[170]:

Self-understanding as "the seed of Seth."

Seth is the Gnostic savior, or alternatively, Adam is the savior of his son, Seth. Both may have a heavenly and/or an earthly aspect.[171]

The heavenly place of rest for Adam, Seth, and the seed of Seth is the four aeons and illuminators of Autogenes: Harmozel, Oroiael, Daveithe, and Eleleth.

Autogenes is a member of the divine triad as the Son of the Father (often named the Invisible Spirit) and the Mother, Barbelo. This triad is itself specifically Sethian.

"Man" (Adam) in his primal form is connected with this heavenly triad.

Beneath the four lights is the realm of the Demiurge, Yaldabaoth.

The appearance of the divine Man is a result of the arrogance of Yaldabaoth and the punishment for his hybris.

Finally, Sethian mythology contains a distinctive periodization of history: the age of Adam, the age of Seth, the age of the original Sethians, and the present time.

Schenke concludes that these elements are sufficient to posit a distinct and identifiable social group:

168. The best discussion is by Wisse, "The Nag Hammadi Library." See also Wisse, "Stalking," 562–576; Rudolph, "Die 'Sethianische' Gnosis," 577–578 and the discussion following.
169. Wisse, "The Nag Hammadi Library," 221.
170. See "Das Sethianische System," 166–167.
171. For a detailed treatment of the figure of Seth in early Christian and Jewish literature, see Klijn, *Seth*.

The phenomenon and structure of our text group, its extent, the unity behind its variety, the varying density of what is essential, all this gives the impression that we have before us the genuine product of one and the same human community of no small dimensions, but one that is in the process of natural development and movement. That is, I cannot think of our documents as having no basis in a group of human beings, nor do I think of this basis as being artificial and short-lived.[172]

Recent work by John Turner takes another, but complementary approach in attempting to account for the similarities and differences among these related texts. Turner has sketched an outline of a history of Sethian Gnosticism. Based on his study of the literary relationships among the texts, he concludes:

> The result of the study suggests that Sethianism interacted with Christianity in five phases: (1) Sethianism as a non-Christian baptismal sect of the first centuries B.C.E. and C.E. which considered itself primordially enlightened by the divine wisdom revealed to Adam and Seth, yet expected a final visitation of Seth marked by his conferral of a saving baptism; (2) Sethianism as gradually Christianized in the later first century onward through an identification of the pre-existent Christ with Seth, or Adam, that emerged through contact with Christian baptismal groups; (3) Sethianism as increasingly estranged from a Christianity becoming more orthodox toward the end of the second century and beyond; (4) Sethianism as rejected by the Great Church but meanwhile increasingly attracted to the individualistic contemplative practices of third-century Platonism; and (5) Sethianism as estranged from the orthodox Platonists of the late third century and increasingly fragmented into various derivative and other sectarian gnostic groups, some surviving into the Middle Ages.[173]

This sketch offers a different approach to the problem, but leaves open the question of shifts in the sociological profile of Sethianism at various stages of its history.

An opposing view has been given by Frederik Wisse. He has argued that the evidence adduced to describe a group of "Sethians" does not satisfy the criteria of internal cohesion and external distinctiveness necessary to distinguish "a definite group of people who shared certain practices and beliefs, and who were distinguishable from other similar groups."[174] In his view, the elements listed by Schenke are not sufficient to posit the existence of a definable group:

172. "The Phenomenon," 592.
173. "Sethian Gnosticism," 56.
174. "Stalking," 564. In his 1972 article, "The Sethians," Wisse argued that scholars cannot assume "that a sect can be defined and characterized by a unique set of doctrines" (605). His position has apparently shifted, for he wrote in 1981 that: "It is therefore justified to look for a distinctive Sethian teaching to prove the existence of the sect" ("Stalking," 564).

"Either the themes in question were so common that they could not be the distinctive teaching of a sect, or they were too incidental to be given much weight."[175] He insists that the Gnostic texts we possess must be considered as "the inspired creations of individuals who did not feel bound by the opinions of a religious community,"[176] not as products of a sect or sects. The themes listed above that Schenke considers descriptive of a particularly Sethian mythology are in Wisse's view merely "free-floating theologumena"[177] which authors used "much like the amateur collector picking up pottery sherds for his shelves."[178] Due to the "unsystematic" (by which he means not logically consistent) character of these treatises, Wisse claims they are not worthy of "penetrating analysis," which would be "improper, disappointing, or the occasion of unwarranted speculation."[179] This point raises rather poignantly the question of the sociological context of "unsystematic" writings. He responds:

> The original purpose of these writings must be sought in private meditation. The intended readers would have been the esoteric group of 'like-minded' Gnostics, not in the sense of members of a sect, but as individuals with a similar attitude towards this world, other-worldly vision, and ascetic lifestyle. These books helped them to understand themselves in their estrangement from this world and oneness with their heavenly home to which they longed to return.[180]

Wisse's perspective can be criticized from several perspectives. As Hans Jonas has demonstrated,[181] what is important is not that various independent motifs can be derived from other sources and put to new uses, but how they are used by any specific text or group of texts. Wisse's thesis is of no help in this regard. Secondly, in disparaging the intellectual value of these texts, he seems to have fallen into the all-too-common judgement concerning Gnostic texts that derives from (or at least is strikingly similar to) the judgements and charges of the Christian heresiologists, views which are often used rhetorically to dismiss Gnostic texts from scholarly consideration. Wisse describes the variations in the presentation of Sethian mythology as "muddled, deformed and corrupted,"[182] and, most amazingly, he uses the fact that none of these texts present a "system" in his sense (an "expected pattern of systematic thinking and argumentation")[183] to argue that therefore it is neither proper nor possible

175. "Stalking," 573.
176. "Stalking," 575.
177. "Stalking," 575.
178. "Discussion," in *The Rediscovery of Gnosticism* (ed. Layton), vol. II, 579.
179. "Stalking," 576.
180. "Stalking," 576.
181. "Delimitation," 90–108.
182. "Stalking," 575.
183. "Stalking," 575.

to analyze the structure of these texts.[184] While I agree certainly that the Gnostics are not "system builders" comparable to systematic theologians or philosophers like Plotinus, that is not to say that they do not contain a related mythology, or as Schenke puts it, a "complex of interconnected basic beliefs and basic concepts."[185]

The establishment of a related mythology, however, does not finally resolve the question of the existence of a Sethian sect. As Michael Williams has pointed out, there are severe and important limitations in using theological and philosophical connections among texts to indicate social relationships.[186] Even use of identical materials does not necessarily indicate continuity in social profile.[187] *Allogenes* provides an excellent example of such a case. Assuming that the text mentioned by Porphyry[188] and *Allogenes* are the same, it seems that *Allogenes* was read in at least three distinct settings: the "original setting" of the Greek composition; the use of the text in the circles around Plotinus in Rome; and the Coptic translation within Codex XI and the Nag Hammadi collection in general (used by Christian monks associated with the nearby Pachomian monastery?).

In his study of the some of the Sethian texts, Williams finds, on the one hand, evidence for some kind of definable community[189]; on the other hand, he argues that the differences among the texts are best accounted for by positing a number of sects, rather than one.[190] All this needs to make us quite cautious about seeing the texts listed above as the products of a single sectarian group whose identity and social profile remained constant (or even continuous) over a period of several centuries.

Schenke has proposed that one indicator of the existence of a distinct group would be the use of a distinct, sectarian self-designation, the "seed of Seth,"[191] or the designation, "the immovable race." G. Stroumsa has made a detailed study of the terminology, "seed of Seth," in his work, *Another Seed: Studies in Gnostic Mythology*, but did not address the question of sectarian usage in any detail.[192] The more recent monograph by Michael Williams examines the

184. "Stalking," 576.
185. "Discussion," in *The Rediscovery of Gnosticism* (ed. Layton), vol. II, 685.
186. See *The Immovable Race*, 188.
187. See *The Immovable Race*, 188–189.
188. See below, Introduction, pp. 48–49.
189. See *The Immovable Race*, 186–209. He concludes: ". . . given what evidence we do have in the writings themselves I would suggest that here and there one finds elements which are most easily explained if one envisions some kind of definable community—evidence of recruitment initiative, identity-altering experiences and bridge-burning acts which could have provided clear boundaries marking passage into a special community, possible allusions to sacramental initiations, developing theory with respect to the place of the half-committed or apostates, hymnic material suggestive of a communal liturgical setting" (197).
190. See *The Immovable Race*, 197–203.
191. "Das sethianische System," 166; "The Phenomenon," 591.
192. Stroumsa does conclude: "The first Gnostics knew the 'angelological' exegesis of

origins and meaning of the phrase, "the immovable race," and asks whether it was used as a sectarian self-designation by the Sethians. He concludes that it is not "characteristically Sethian" and may not have first originated among those who wrote and used the texts grouped by Schenke as "Sethian."[193]

The strongest argument for the existence of a distinct Sethian group, however, lies in the presence of references to sacramental practice. The existence of baptismal practices, as shown by Sevrin, and evidence of a ritual of ascent, including hymnic liturgical materials, points strongly toward a distinguishable group, however much they may have had in common with those around them.[194]

Although a great deal of work still needs to be done to give us a clearer and more definite understanding of the social context of the texts under discussion, I believe that the evidence points at this stage to the existence of a distinct group or groups that we can (somewhat arbitrarily) label "Sethian" for our purposes.

Allogenes *as a Sethian Text*

Allogenes can be classified among the Sethian texts and needs to be studied in relation to them for several reasons. First of all, it shares a great deal of similar terminology and several themes with other Sethian texts. Secondly, it is often only by comparison with other Sethian texts that certain elusive names and terms in *Allogenes* become comprehensible (such as Iouel, the [five] seals, and the "quiescent eye of the revelation"). Thirdly, sections of *Allogenes* show literary relationships with sections of other Sethian texts known from Nag Hammadi (*Apocryphon of John*, *Three Steles of Seth*, *Marsanes*, and *Zostrianos*).

Certain similarities are apparent already in the flaming denunciations of the "Sethians" and "Archontics" by the Christian heresiologist Epiphanius. He writes the following about a sect he calls the Sethians:

> But from Seth, from his seed, and descending from his race there came the Christ himself, Jesus, not by birth but miraculously appearing in the world; and he is Seth himself, who both then and now visits the human race, being sent from the Mother on high. . . .They write certain books under the names of great men; they say there are seven books named after Seth, and some other different books they call Allogeneis . . .[195]

---

the Sons of God in Genesis 6 and considered the sin of the wicked angels (in its different versions) to be the source of evil. Yet these Gnostics, who considered themselves to be the pure offspring of Seth, also knew the legends built around the wicked Sethites of early times. Apparently in reaction to these trends in Jewish exegesis, they developed a theology and a *Heilsgeschichte* that was the systematic inverse of the salvation-history of Israel" (*Another Seed*, 134).

193. See *The Immovable Race*, 206–208.
194. See above Introduction, pp. 12–14.
195. *Panarion* 39.3,5; 5,1; trans. Foerster, *Gnosis*, 295.

Concerning the "heresy of the Archontics," Epiphanius writes:

> These men likewise have fabricated some apocryphal books for themselves, whose names are as follows: one book they call the Little Symphony, forsooth, another the Great Symphony. And they pile up other books for themselves, being accustomed to add to the pile whatever they read, so as to suggest that all these help to confirm their own error. They also use books called Allogeneis—for there are books bearing that name.[196]

> Again, the same persons say that Adam had intercourse with his own wife Eve and begot Seth, his own natural son. And they say that the power from on high came down together with the angels who serve the good God and caught up Seth, whom they also call Allogenes, and carried him up to some higher sphere and cared for him for some time, so that he should not be killed; and after a long time they carried him back again to this world and made him spiritual and invisible (?), so that the Demiurge had no power over him nor yet the powers and authorities of the (same) god who made the world. And they say that he no longer served the maker, the Demiurge, but had knowledge of the unnameable power, the good God who is above, and served him and gave many revelations discrediting the maker of the world and the authorities and powers. Hence they have composed books written in the name of Seth, saying that these were given them by him, and others bearing the name of Seth and of his seven sons. For they say that he begot seven sons called Allogeneis, as we have described in the case of other sects, namely the Gnostics and Sethians.[197]

This testimony attributes usage of books under the name of Allogenes to two groups, "Sethians" (or "Gnostics") and "Archontics." As was stressed above, Epiphanius' sectarian ascriptions cannot necessarily be trusted. Nonetheless, the final clause of our text, "all the books of Allogenes," seems to be a clear reference to the tradition of books written under the name of Allogenes, described by Epiphanius. And the clause indicates certainly that the author of *Allogenes* wished our text to be understood as belonging to this tradition. There is no evidence in the passages cited above, however, that Epiphanius was personally acquainted with the contents of our particular text.

Though it is not possible to accept the sectarian designations of Epiphanius uncritically, it is, on the other hand, easy to place *Allogenes* within the mythological tradition Epiphanius is treating. He identifies "Allogenes" as an alternate designation for Seth.[198] Seth is said to be a savior sent from the Mother on

196. *Panarion* 40.2,1–2; trans. Foerster, *Gnosis*, 296.
197. *Panarion* 40.7,1–5; trans. Foerster, *Gnosis*, 298.
198. Pearson notes that this tradition shows some Sethian influence on Manichaean traditions. See "The Figure of Seth in Manichaean Literature," 155.

high—in Allogenes' case, he is sent by the Father of the Entirety[199]; he was "caught up" to some higher sphere by powers who serve the good God[200]; he did not serve the maker but had knowledge of the ineffable power,[201] and gave many revelations.[202] This description of Seth accords well with that of Allogenes in our text.

On the other hand, *Allogenes* makes no mention of Adam, Eve, or Seth, nor is the text concerned with occurrences in this world or figures like the Demiurge who belong to it. Indeed there is no evidence of any explicitly Jewish or Christian figures or influence. The text, in fact, by excluding even the name of Seth, presents itself as a completely pagan text of a mythical-philosophical character.[203] This is interesting for two reasons: comparison with other Sethian texts leads one to conclude that the Sethian tradition behind the text has been "paganized"; and 2) this "paganization" appears among a group of texts, some of which show a tendency towards *Christianization*.[204] The reason for excluding Jewish (and Christian?) names and themes can only be to appeal to a group of persons to whom Judaism and Christianity did not appeal. Given the extensive use of philosophical materials, that group appears to have been Graeco-Roman philosophers (like Celsus and Porphyry?).

When we turn to comparison with the primary Sethian texts listed above, it becomes clear that *Allogenes* shares enough characteristics and other specific terminology with them to be clearly included among the Sethian texts identified by Schenke. Of the distinctive elements of Sethian mythology identified by Schenke, only the second, third, and fourth of these elements apply directly to *Allogenes*. The last four themes deal with the lower world, topics not addressed in the text at all. The following discussion will treat each of the first four elements separately, as well as discuss the figure of Iouel and the literary relationships of *Allogenes* to other Sethian texts.

The Seed of Seth   According to Schenke, the self-definition of the Sethian community lies in their understanding of themselves as "the seed of Seth."[205] They are the spiritual race descended from Seth,[206] the children descended

---

199. *Allogenes* 50.24–32.

200. Compare *Allogenes* 58.26–37.

201. Compare *Allogenes* 50.1–36.

202. Compare *Allogenes* 68.16–20.

203. Turner has come to a similar conclusion. See "Sethian Gnosticism," 56, 58, 86. He argues that this movement toward philosophy with "an increasing emphasis on self-performable techniques of spiritual ascent with its attendant possibilities for individualism possibly entailed a further weakening of communal awareness traditionally grounded in ritual and primordial history" (86).

204. *GosEgypt*, *ApJohn*, *TriProt*, and *Melchizedek*. For discussion of the "Christianisierung" of Sethian Gnosticism, see H.-M. Schenke, The Phenomenon," 607–612; Turner, "Sethian Gnosticism," 58.

205. See "Das Sethianische System," 166, and "The Phenomenon," 592.

206. H.-M. Schenke sees these as the genos of those who are by nature to be saved. L. Schottroff, in "Animae naturaliter salvandae," has given a lucid and convincing argument

from the seven sons of Seth, called Allogeneis.[207] In *Allogenes*, the phrase "seed of Seth" never occurs, but there are three possible references to a group identity.

The first at 56.28–30 indicates that Allogenes needs to receive a revelation lest he suffer the loss of his "genos." Since Allogenes is to communicate his revelation to "those who will be worthy," the revelation is given to him in his capacity as savior/teacher. Those he is to save can be seen in the designation "genos" and also in the reference to "those who will be worthy" (68.19). The latter are the recipients of the secret book he is to write and may possibly refer to initiated members of the group.

The third reference at 56.[13] refers more obliquely to the heavenly "Autogeneis" ("self-begotten ones") who exist for the Triply-male. *Zostrianos* (46.15–22) also mentions "Autogeneis" that contain glories that act as helpers for souls locked in the fetters of the world. It may be that the Autogeneis of *Allogenes* have an identity and function similar to those of *Zostrianos*: they may be the heavenly powers that provide patterns of salvation for the "genos" of Allogenes.[208]

None of these instances offers conclusive evidence of the existence of a group sharing a common self-designation. In each case, the references do not clearly show any sectarian identity, but could simply refer loosely to spiritually advanced persons. *Allogenes* alone would not support the theory of the existence of a Sethian group. But, taken in consideration with other Sethian texts that offer greater evidence of sectarian identity, the references in *Allogenes* would be compatible with the existence of such a group.

The Savior   The model of salvation in our text is Allogenes. He is not an historical person, but a pseudonymous[209] figure of mythic and salvific importance.

---

that what the heresiologists characterized as an elitist determinism on the part of Gnostic sectarians was not really seen that way by the Gnostics themselves. Chapter seven of M. Williams' book, *The Immovable Race*, discusses the meaning of the designation, "seed of Seth," in terms of group membership. Williams writes: "I am convinced that what to us might sound initially like a self-designation brandished among cocky sectarians as an affirmation of their innate privileged status vis-a-vis the rest of humanity, may in fact have been intended in quite the opposite spirit. Although they go about it in more than one way, all five of the texts which contain the designation seem to be saying that to belong to the immovable race is nothing more nor less than to be truly and perfectly Human, to realize full Human potential—a potential which is in theory open to anyone who 'seeks and finds,' but which in practice is achieved only by certain persons" (172). If this is the case—and I believe Schottroff and Williams are correct—, the meaning of Gnostic esotericism and determinist elitism needs to be seriously rethought.

207. See Epiphanius, *Panarion* 40.7.5. A second designation for the Sethian community, "the immovable race," has been the subject of a detailed study by Williams (*The Immovable Race*). The phrase appears some dozen times in five Sethian texts from Nag Hammadi, but does not appear in *Allogenes*.

208. Compare also the *SJC* III,4.99.31–100.16 and parallels.

209. Pseudonymity is a characteristic common to revelation discourses.

The name "Allogenes" in Greek means literally "he of another race," that is, the "stranger" or "foreigner." As was noted above, Epiphanius understands "Allogenes" to be an alternate designation for Seth. According to Birger Pearson, the identification of Seth with Allogenes stems from a speculative interpretation of Genesis 4.25 (LXX), where Seth is referred to as "another seed" (σπέρμα ἕτερον). Seth is said to be the son of Adam "according to his form and image" (κατὰ τὴν ἰδίαν αὐτοῦ καὶ κατὰ τὴν εἰκόνα αὐτοῦ).[210] The term ⲀⲖⲖⲟⲅⲉⲚⲎⲤ or the variations, "alien" (ⲀⲖⲖⲟⲅⲉⲚⲒⲟⲤ) and "other race," (ⲔⲉⲅⲉⲚⲟⲤ) appear in two other Sethian texts in relation to Allogenes:

> . . . the aeon of the aeons, he who begets himself, and he who comes forth from himself, and the alien one (ⲀⲖⲖⲟⲅⲉⲚⲎⲤ), the uninterpretable power of the ineffable Father.[211]

> . . . the aeon of the aeons, Autogenes, self-begotten, self-producing, alien (ⲀⲖⲖⲟⲅⲉⲚⲒⲟⲤ), the really true aeon.[212]

In praising the son, Autogenes:

> You are from another race (ⲔⲉⲅⲉⲚⲟⲤ) and it is situated above another race. For now you are from another race, and it is situated above another race. You are from another race, for you are not similar.[213]

In these texts the tendency to project the earthly figures of Adam and Seth into the heavenly plane can be seen.[214] Here the designation of Allogenes is applied to a figure who represents at once the savior and the saved. Allogenes is the savior insofar as it is he who was sent from above[215] and it is he who is to pass on the revelations he has received to those who are worthy by writing this secret book[216]; but insofar as Allogenes himself is in need of, and receives revealed knowledge in order to return to his proper place above,[217] he represents *par excellence* the whole race of those who are to be saved. The purpose of the text is to convey salvation. Allogenes provides both the message of and the pattern for salvation. The content of the revelations and the pattern of individual salvation exemplified in the visions, auditions, and experiences of Allogenes are salvific. By hearing the revelations, preparing himself, ascending out of the body to heights where he sees and ponders things that are truly existent and unknowable, Allogenes achieves perfection and divinity. He comes to

---

210. Genesis 5.3 LXX. See Pearson, "The Figure of Seth in Gnostic Literature," 486 ff. Pearson also shows clearly that the sources for Seth traditions in Gnosticism are Jewish not Egyptian (500–503; see also "Egyptian Seth," 25–43).
211. *GosEgypt* IV.50.17–23; trans. Wisse, *Nag Hammadi Codices III,2 and IV,2*, 52–55.
212. *GosEgypt* III.41.5–7; op. cit.
213. *StSeth* 120.1–6.
214. See Pearson, "The Figure of Seth in Gnostic Literature," 503.
215. *Allogenes* 50.24–33.
216. *Allogenes* 68.16–35.
217. *Allogenes* 50.33–36.

know himself, to be still, to take a firm stand: these are the images of salvation. In Carsten Colpe's terminology, Allogenes is a true "redeemed Redeemer" as well as *"salvator salvandus."*[218]

As noted above, the Sethian depiction of periodization of history, each with its own savior figure, does not appear in *Allogenes*, whose sole concern is with a description of the higher realms of being and the ascent. Allogenes does not appear as an eschatological savior such as is found in other Sethian texts.

The Luminaries   The names of the four illuminators do not appear in Allogenes. But we may be justified in seeing these figures behind the "Powers of the Luminary/ies of the aeon of Barbelo."[219]

The Divine Triad   The divine triad, Father-Mother-Son, appears in the text in an elaborated form. Two interwoven presentations can be traced:

		Unknowable
(Father)	Invisible Spirit	Invisible Spirit
		Triply-powered
(Mother)	Barbelo	Barbelo
		Kalyptos
		Protophanes
		Autogenes
(Son)	Autogenes	Thrice-male Youth

The term "Father" appears only once in the text[220]; "Mother" and "Son" do not appear at all. The specifically Sethian triad of the Invisible Spirit, Barbelo, and Autogenes does, however, appear. The final column represents an elaboration of that pattern, especially by giving each member of the triad a triple aspect (Invisible Spirit—Triply-powered; Barbelo—Kalyptos/Protophanes/Autogenes; Autogenes—Thrice-male Youth[221]). In certain respects, the presentation of the divine hierarchy in *Allogenes* may be seen as an attempt to explicate the Sethian triad in terms of current philosophical discussion.

Iouel   Iouel appears in *Allogenes* as a revealer figure. Nothing is said about her except that she appears and gives revelations to Allogenes. Once he begins his ascent, she is replaced as the revealer by "the Powers of the Luminaries of the aeon of Barbelo." The only clue inside the text to her identity and status is her title: "the all glorious" (literally "She-to-whom-all-the-glories-pertain").[222]

---

218. See *Die religionsgeschichtliche Schule*, 189 ff, and "Vorschläge."
219. See *Allogenes* 56.25–27; 59.5–6; 61.24.
220. *Allogenes* 50.26.
221. On the association of Autogenes with the Thrice-male Youth, see above, pp. 6–7.
222. Scopello argues that Iouel and Barbelo have the same attributes and functions and suggests that they may be interchangeable entities ("Youel et Barbélo," 375).

Comparison with other Sethian texts in this case is quite helpful. The name appears in two Sethian texts: *Gospel of the Egyptians* and *Zostrianos*.[223] In the former text, Iouel appears as the male-virginal consort of the Thrice-male Youth, the fourth member of the pentad: Invisible Spirit, Barbelo, Thrice-male Youth, Iouel, and Esephech. *Zostrianos* states that "Kalyptos really exists and with him is located the all glorious Iouel, the male-virgin glory, through whom the all-perfect ones are seen" (125.11–17). In both texts, she is associated with salvation.

G. Scholem has connected the name Iouel with the angel Yahoel, or Yoel, whose name is a clear abbreviation of the Tetragrammaton YHWH.[224] In Jewish texts, Yahoel figures as the angel who appeared to Abraham (*Apocalypse of Abraham*) and, in a twelfth century manuscript, Yahoel is presented as Abraham's teacher and the angel who invites Moses to ascend to heaven.[225] The figure of Iouel thus provides a definite, though obscure connection of *Allogenes* to Jewish thought.

Literary Relationships to Other Sethian Texts   There are two sections of *Allogenes* which have close similarities with other texts: *Allogenes* 54.11–37 with *Three Steles of Seth* 125.23–126.16 and *Zostrianos* 51.24–52.24; 86.13–88; and *Allogenes* 62.27–63.28 with *Apocryphon of John* BG 24.6–25.10; II.3.17–36; III.5.2–6.3; IV.4.28–5.32.[226] The first set of passages contains theurgic hymns, and the relationship among the texts is best accounted for, not by literary dependence of one text upon others, but by access to the same community traditions. The second case is more difficult. John Turner assumes the closeness of the two passages means that "*Allogenes* is documentarily dependent on some version of the *Apocryphon of John*."[227] Michel Tardieu has argued, on the other hand, that both texts are exercises in scholastic logic applied to the first hypothesis of Plato's *Parmenides*; one does not need to presume borrowing in either direction to account for the close similarities.[228] In both cases, closer study is needed to determine more precisely the nature of the relationship among or between these passages. They show, at any rate, a further tie of *Allogenes* to other Sethian texts.

In addition, there are close similarities in conceptuality and specific terminology between *Allogenes* and three other Sethian texts: *Three Steles of Seth*,

223. *GosEgypt* III.50.2; 53.25; 55.22; 62.6; IV.56.[20]; 59.23; and *Zost* 52.14; 54.17; 63.11; 125.14.
224. See "Merkabah Mysticism," 68 n. 105.
225. See Scholem, "Merkabah Mysticism," 68–69. See also *Jewish Gnosticism*, 41–42. See also the comments of Scopello, "Youel et Barbélo," 376–378.
226. For more detailed treatment, see exegetical notes to 53.32b–54.37 and 62.27b–63.28a.
227. Turner, "The Gnostic Threefold Path," 329.
228. See Tardieu, *Écrits Gnostiques*, 250; see also exegetical note to 62.27b–63.28a.

Marsanes, and *Zostrianos*. All of them use similar current philosophical terminology and present salvation in terms of an ascent (rather than a descent of a
savior or set of saviors); all contain references to the Triply-powered and to the
Kalyptos-Protophanes-Autogenes triad. The resemblances in many other
respects suggest a similar provenance. Again, a detailed study is needed in
order to clarify their relationships.[229]

In conclusion, *Allogenes* clearly belongs to a tradition, reported by Epiphanius, which designates Seth as "Allogenes" and attributes various books to
him. In addition, *Allogenes* may be classified among the group of writings
which Schenke designates as "Sethian." It shows the closest affinity with a
subset of these texts (*Three Steles of Seth*, *Marsanes*, and *Zostrianos*). It is likely
that the earliest *Sitz im Leben* of the Greek text is to be found with a definable
group which used these texts and practiced baptism and the rite of ascent, and
which, for the sake of convention, may also be called "Sethian."

The Gnostics of Plotinus

Porphyry, in his *Life of Plotinus*, attests to one or more revelations under the
name of "Allogenes"[230] known to Plotinian circles in Rome:

> There were in (Plotinus') time many Christians and others, and sectar-
> ians who had abandoned the old philosophy, men of the school of
> Adelphius and Aculinus, who possessed a great many treatises of Alex-
> ander the Libyan and Philocomus and Demonstratus and Lydus, and
> produced revelations by Zoroaster and Zostrianus and Nicotheus and
> Allogenes and Messus and other people of the kind, deceived themselves
> and deceiving many, alleging that Plato had not penetrated to the depths
> of intelligible reality. Plotinus hence often attacked their position in his
> lectures, and wrote the treatise to which we have given the title "Against
> the Gnostics."[231]

This allusion by Porphyry leads to the supposition that in *Allogenes* we possess
a Coptic version of the Greek text known to and refuted by Plotinus.

Plotinus wrote against the Gnostics and engaged Porphyry to write against
the Christians and Zoroastrians. His arguments against Gnostic views indicate

---

229. See the sketch by Turner, "Sethian Gnosticism," 79–85. For a brief comparison of
Marsanes with *Allogenes*, see Pearson, "Introduction to Codex X," *Nag Hammadi Codices IX
and X*, 242–246.
230. Interestingly, the passage also mentions books attributed to Messos, the addressee
of *Allogenes*. The name "Messos" is otherwise not mentioned in the Nag Hammadi collection.
231. *Vit. Plot.* 16; trans. Armstrong, *Plotinus*, I.45.

a knowledge of and interest in positions he opposed. Similarly, the inferiority of *Allogenes'* translation into Coptic should not lead modern scholars to suppose that Plotinus and his circle would not have taken the text seriously. We know from the translation of Plato's *Republic* 588A–589B into Coptic, also found in the Nag Hammadi collection (VI,5), that the literary artistry and logical clarity of the original should not be judged from a translation alone. The slavishness and the ignorance of the translator of *Allogenes* make themselves apparent at many places. One interesting example is found at 65.32. The passage says of the Unknowable that: "On the one hand, it is corporeal, being in a place; on the other hand, it is incorporeal, being in a house . . ."[232] Here the translation of ἐν τῷ οἰκείῳ ("belonging to, conformable to the nature of")[233] as ϨΝ ΟΥΗΕΙ (literally, "in a house") has rendered the sense impossible. Instead of "the Unknowable is incorporeal, being in a house," the original meaning is closer to "the Unknowable is incorporeal as is fitting for it." Such occurrences not only make it clear that the underlying text was Greek, but also ought to make us cautious about denying the seriousness with which the Greek original may have been met in Platonist circles.

On the other hand, there is no irrefutable evidence from Plotinus' writings against the Gnostics in *Enneads* III.3; V.8; V.5; and II.9 (=30–33) that Plotinus knew a Greek version of *Allogenes*. Charges which he could have made against *Allogenes* could also have been directed against a number of other Gnostic writings: multiplication of hypostases in the noetic realm, plagiarism and perversion of Plato, magical practices, and false other-worldliness. What *Allogenes* does *not* contain is materials against which Plotinus could charge a misunderstanding of the demiurge, the creation and nature of the cosmos, or the devaluation of the body and the material universe. These arguments do not, however, provide any evidence that Plotinus did not know *Allogenes* among other Gnostic texts. Indeed the author left out the areas of Sethian thought that potentially would be the most problematic for philosophers, that is, the Sethian portrayal of the soul's fall, the negative devaluation of the cosmos, and the periodization of history into four epochs. The absence of these topics in *Allogenes* may have made it more persuasive to philosophers and a rather difficult target against which to direct an attack.

Hans-Martin Schenke has argued indeed that the Gnostics known to and refuted by Plotinus were Sethians.[234] If further study should confirm this thesis, it would be a further argument in favor of identifying our *Allogenes* with the text mentioned by Porphyry.

The evidence, then, does not allow us to conclude decisively whether or not

---

232. *Allogenes* 65.30–32.
233. Liddel and Scott, *A Greek-English Lexicon*, 1029. Armstrong translates the phrase "in its own proper way of life" (*Plotinus* V, 147).
234. See "The Phenomenon," 613–614; and H.-M. Schenke's review of Elsas in *TLZ* 102 (1977), 644–46.

Plotinus and those in his circle knew a Greek version of *Allogenes*, but it does seem highly probable that they did.

The supposition that *Allogenes* was indeed one of the texts known to Plotinian circles in Rome finds a further foundation in the use of technical philosophical language and conceptuality by *Allogenes*. What is certain is that there was communication between philosophers and Sethians in antiquity. The author of *Allogenes* has clearly had some training in philosophy, though like so many others, his Platonism has turned in a specifically religious direction.

The particulars of *Allogenes*' connections with current philosophical speculation have been treated above and in the notes.[235] It remains here to summarize the most important features.

The closest connection between *Allogenes* and contemporary philosophical speculation lies in the use of shared terms and concepts concerning the description of the nature of the highest Being (especially with reference to the unknowability of the One), the composition of the divine hierarchy (especially in the employment of triads), the generation of multiplicity from unity (or from the One who is not number), and the rise of the soul to vision and knowledge of the truly divine. The most definite way in which the Gnostic views of *Allogenes* belong to the sphere of philosophical Platonism appears in the text's decided tendency toward monism. On the other hand, *Allogenes* shows a distinct difference from Plotinian speculation in the employment of Sethian mythology, especially in the multiplication of divine hypostases, the hypostasization (personification) of philosophical concepts, and the emphasis placed upon a need for revelation and communal cultic practice. (It shares the use of prayer and theurgy with later Platonism, however.)

We have seen not only a borrowing of philosophical terms and concepts, but also their transformation. This transformation has taken place primarily by setting them in the context of Sethian Gnostic mythology and cult. What appears as "borrowing" is in fact a kind of rethinking, a product of translation or interpretation across ideologies or world views. This process is employed to elaborate the text's primary concern: a description of the process of spiritual progress and salvation. The work combines in a unique and surprisingly coherent manner traditional Sethian materials (its basic mythological pattern, theurgic prayers, and the ritual of ascension) with contemporary philosophical speculation on the nature of being and the return of the soul to the divine. The intent seems to be to "reveal" the more subtle implications of Sethian mythology. The work does not reduce Sethian mythology to a philosophical system nor allow either mythology or philosophical conceptuality to control the generative flow of the text.

Allogenes is to be classed generally among the Platonizing religious litera-

235. See also Turner, "The Gnostic Threefold Path" and "Gnosticism and Platonism."

ture of antiquity such as Hermeticism, Platonizing Christianity, Valentinian-ism, and the Chaldaean Oracles—and Neoplatonism itself.[236]

Since *Allogenes* is specifically Sethian, the fact that it contains no specifically Jewish or Christian elements of Sethian mythology is quite odd. It seems indeed that the author has consciously excluded such elements and instead formed the presentation of Sethianism in terms of contemporary (early third century) Platonic speculation. This may have been done, not only because that was how this author actually understood Sethian tradition, but perhaps also in order to appeal to educated readers with philosophical interests who were hostile to Christianity. Thus Plotinus may have been roused to the refutation of Gnosticism by an active Sethian attempt to reach a pagan philosophical audience.[237] This attempt must have had some success or a refutation would not have been necessary.

Traces of this success are perhaps still visible in later post-Plotinian Plato-nism, for example in the use of theurgy and the presence of specific termi-nology such as the triad Being-Life-Mind.[238] Though I have not yet found it possible to show any clear instance where *Allogenes* has influenced later Pla-tonic thought—in every instance similarities could be due to reliance on sources shared by both (for example, the extremely close similarity in language and conceptuality between *Allogenes* and the *Commentary of the Parmenides* attributed by Hadot to Porphyry could show a direct influence by *Allogenes* on the *Parmenides Commentary* or the relationship could stem from knowledge of a common school tradition)—, three points make such influence at least possible if not demonstrable:

1. *Allogenes* can be dated chronologically prior to Plotinus and was probably known to him and his circle.
2. Portions of the preserved text show striking similarities in language and conceptuality to later Platonists.
3. Certain topics were of burning interest both to some later Platonists and to Sethian Gnostics. Chief among these was the religious interest in the rise of the soul to God. That Gnostics would turn to the writings of Platonists concerning the nature of the soul is just as natural as that Platonists might turn to Gnostics concerning revela-tion, theurgy, and the ritual of the ascent.

---

236. Armstrong admits that "the philosophy of Plotinus is also a religion" (*The Cam-bridge History*, 259). The argument could be made even less ambiguously concerning the later Neoplatonists, especially those among whom theurgy figures prominently.

237. In contrast, Perkins has argued that *Allogenes*, along with *Zostrianos*, can be under-stood as an attack on Platonic mysticism (*Gnostic Dialogue*, 40).

238. See Introduction, pp. 22–28.

Genre

So far we have discussed various aspects of *Allogenes'* narrative structure, its historical settings, and intellectual connections. This section will focus upon a literary analysis of the text, drawing heavily upon the work of David Hellholm.[239] The categories are organized roughly according to the six dimensions he lists "from which genre designations ought to derive their characteristics."[240] These dimensions provide categories which illuminate much about the ways in which *Allogenes* communicates its message of spiritual progress and salvation. Rather than simply list isolated elements, Hellholm's categories allow the interrelatedness of each of the dimensions to become more apparent in order to show how this web of interrelationships constitutes the meaning(s) of the text.

In the end, the analysis does not result in a clear taxonomic genre classification of *Allogenes*. But the crucial ways in which the text operates at the generic level, mixing generic characteristics and manipulating readers' expectations, do lead to the possibility of a less static way of regarding genre and taxonomy.

Literary Dimensions

The text's literary dimensions are concerned with function (pragmatics), content (including settings), and various aspects of form.

Four functions can be identified for *Allogenes*:

Authorization of message
Connection with cultic practice
Encounter with Greek philosophy
Representation of a model for spiritual progress and salvation

The communication situations both inside and external to the text need to be discussed in order to understand the interrelationship of these functions to the macro-structure and contents of *Allogenes*.

There are minimally two external communication situations apparent: that of the Greek text and that of the Coptic translation. These two aspects indicate at least two different sets of readers. Based on the considerations of content and background discussed above, it can be assumed that the text had a Sethian readership in Greek that was interested in the authoritative message of the text,

---

239. Not only the categories, but much of the terminology and conceptuality of what follows is taken from Hellholm's "The Problem of Apocalyptic Genre." I have modified many aspects to suit *Allogenes*, and Hellholm is obviously not responsible for these many modifications and inventions. Nonetheless, his article is the primary inspiration for the analysis which follows and that needs to be duly noted with respect.

240. Hellholm, 34; see 34–35.

its model of spiritual progression, and its connection with the rite of ascent. External information further allows us to speculate that one set of Greek-speaking readers belonged to the circles of Plotinus in Rome, and that *Allogenes* had a corresponding polemical function in this encounter with Greek philosophy. The relative lack of a speculative philosophical tradition in the Coptic language allows us to suggest that the polemical confrontation with Greek philosophy was not a particular function for the readership(s) of the Coptic translation.

The Coptic readership is even more difficult to determine. The number and type of orthographic errors indicates that our text was one of a number of copies of *Allogenes* in Coptic.[241] For whom the translation was made and to what uses the copies were put remain matters of pure speculation. The inscription of our one surviving copy of *Allogenes* within a codex containing Valentinian texts indicates that the audience for this copy was not exclusively Sethian. Furthermore, the discovery of Codex XI among a collection of codices exhibiting a wide variety of contents[242] and showing paleographic resemblances with other codices in the collection,[243] raises problems for determining the more precise milieu of the collection as a whole. Scholars have suggested that the collection might have been a Gnostic library, that it might have been intended for use by the Christian monks of upper Egypt, or that the collection may have been slated for use as the basis for an anti-heretical work. However one addresses the problem, it is highly likely that *Allogenes* had a variety of readerships in Coptic even as it did in Greek, both among those who valued its teachings and those who wished to combat them. Determination of anything more definite is ruled out by lack of evidence, either within or outside of the text.

Each of these communication situations may have emphasized different functions of the text: Sethians may have read the text for its authorization of teaching, its relation to cultic practice, or its model of spiritual progression. The encounter with Greek philosophy may have relied upon the authorization of its message in revelation for claims to a superior teaching, as well as the content of the revelations themselves. Later Coptic readers may have found little interest in the encounter with Greek philosophy, and turned more toward understanding the text's model of spiritual progression. A Christian heresiologist may have found the text valuable to demonstrate the pagan character of heretical thought, here turning the encounter with philosophy to a new purpose. And so on. We can only speculate. But the analysis of communication settings implied within the text's functions and contents allows us to dismiss the notion of a single setting, function, or meaning for *Allogenes*, while affirming the interrelatedness of these aspects with each other.

241. See below, Introduction, p. 61.
242. See *NHLE*.
243. See Introduction, pp. 63–64.

The communication situations within the text are also related to the text's functions. These situations can be ordered hierarchically by how they are embedded within each other:

Written text of *Allogenes* to readers
Allogenes/Messos to "those who will be worthy"
Allogenes to Messos
Revealers to Allogenes
Utterance of Gnosis(?) within revelation from Iouel and the description
   of the ascent within the revelation from the Powers

The main line of communication is from the divine revealers to "those who will be worthy" through the mediation of Allogenes (and secondarily of Messos) through the medium of the written (and hidden) book. The communication levels assure the primary function of *Allogenes*: to authorize the message of the text. Embedding the speech of Gnosis (53.32–55.11) and the account of the ascent within the speeches of the revealers (Iouel and the Powers) serves further to authorize the rite of ascent, and quite possibly the invocation by Gnosis as part of that rite. Together, the authorized message and elements of ritual form the text's model of spiritual progression and salvation.

Considerations of content (text-semantics) include:

Subject matter:
   Descriptions of the other-world (divine hierarchy)
   Progressive reactions of the recipient (Allogenes)
   Ascent through other-world (divine hierarchy)
   Paraenesis (preparatory teaching, command to be still, and so on)
   Command to write the book by other-worldy mediator
Persons/characters:
   Other-worldly mediators or revealers (Iouel, Powers, ?)
   This-worldly recipients (Allogenes)
   Addressees of recipient's revelation (Messos and "those who will be
      worthy")
Time and Place:
   Time: Anytime (unspecified, general, universal)
   Places: this place (50.28 presumably this-world);
      a holy place (58.31–34, the transcendent other-world)

All of these elements are intimately interrelated to the other dimensions of the text, for function and form cannot be considered apart from content.

The settings of the text define reality by distinguishing between this-world and the transcendent other-world of the divine hierarchy. *Allogenes* makes it clear that the true reality is that of the divine sphere; the existence of this-world is derivative and unstable. Meaning is gained in this-world only through access to the other-world by revelatory teaching and preparation for the ascent.

The pseudonymous character of *Allogenes* might also be discussed here. As a kind of everyhuman, on the one hand, and as a circumlocution for Seth, on the other hand, Allogenes represents every person who is not at home in the world, who seeks the higher realities, and who may be one of "those who will be worthy," the Sethians. His name is at once an invitation and a mystery to be uncovered: the fictive character of the name invites the reader to discover what mystery it hides, what the identity of the Foreigner might be, and in so doing, discover one's own true identity. The name is a pointer toward a foreign, higher reality.

The narrative structure of *Allogenes* is composed of alternating sets of revelation discourses and narrative responses set within an epistolary framework of address from Allogenes to Messos. Each new episode is marked by a change in speaker or level of communication. The beginning of the ascent is additionally marked by changes in time (after a hundred years)[244] and place (from this-world to the holy, transcendent other-world),[245] indicating a major division of the text.[246]

Five major divisions may be postulated:

1. The epistolary prescript (not preserved; 45.1–5[247])
2. Revelations from Iouel to Allogenes and his responses (45.6–58.26a) containing the first five revelations to Allogenes and his responses
3. The ascent (58.26b–67.38) containing the revelation from the Powers concerning the ascent, the ascent itself, and the revelation from the Powers concerning the Unknowable
4. The final command to Allogenes (68.16–23a)
5. The final address to Messos (68.23b–69.19) containing the final response of Allogenes and his command to Messos

The first and last divisions provide the epistolary frame for the text and the most general level of communication within the written text. The second and fourth divisions take place on the level of this-world, but involve communication between this-world and the other-world. This level illustrates the linear progression of the spiritual aspirant from fear to joy, from ignorance to enlightenment. The placement of the third division at the center of the text emphasizes the central importance of the Powers' message and the central importance of the ascent itself. Here the division between this-world and the other-world is overcome.

Some have argued that the division of the text into two distinct parts is due

244. *Allogenes* 58.7–8.
245. *Allogenes* 58.26–34.
246. The division of the text into two episodes has been often noted (see for example, Wire "Introduction," 176).
247. See exegetical note to 45.1–5.

to the reproduction or harmonization of different sources.[248] However true that may be, the final arrangement shows a congruence between form and content. The difference in the place of revelation (this-world or the other-world) corresponds to the difference in the content of the revelations (the lower levels of the divine hierarchy or the Unknowable). Moreover, the teachings given by Iouel function as preparatory instructions, while the elevation to an other-worldly location signals the transcendent character of both the content of the revelation and Allogenes' experience. While drawing upon different source materials may account for some differences in tone and content between the two sections and for certain inconsistencies, the text's form capitalizes upon those differences. They have been placed in generically strategic locations that underscore the differences and that use them to exemplify different conditions of spiritual knowledge and advancement. Thus the "disjunction" felt in the difference in content and style between the two sets of revelations is strategic for the text and marked clearly by changes in speaker (from Iouel to the Powers) and place (from this-world to the other-world).

There are two additional structural features of the text that are of interest. The first is the embedding of a magical utterance by some divine figure at 53.36–37 and the following theurgic prayer within the third revelation discourse from Iouel. The theurgic prayer has similarities with sections of *Three Steles of Seth*, where the material appears in the context of the liturgy for the ascent.[249] As was noted above, this embedding seems to function to authorize the use of this prayer by claiming divine, revelatory origins for its contents.

The second structural feature is the repetition of the account of the ascent. At 58.26b–59.7a, it looks as though the ascent has begun. It is interrupted by the discourse of the Powers instructing Allogenes about what will occur in the ascent. The narrative account of the ascent which follows closely parallels the discourse of the Powers. Placing the first account in the mouths of the divine revealers suggests several possible functions. It might indicate to the reader that one only gains the ascent upon invitation and initiative by the divine world, not through one's own efforts, however strenuous. It might serve to

---

248. Wire notes the following: the content of the revelations in the two sections differs, the first is more mythical, the second more philosophical; the names of the mythological figures from Iouel's revelations are missing in the revelations from the Powers; and, in her opinion, the ascent and revelations of the Powers form "a unified and fluid piece of writing" ("Introduction," 177). She concludes that the ascent and final revelation are compositions of the author, while: "If Part II is seen to have evolved through increasing abstraction in a cultic tradition, the Youel revelations in Part I may be the older myths and prayers now revised and relegated to the task of cosmological introduction before the 'primary revelation of the Unknowable One' (59,28–30). The author may be seeking to harmonize old and new by this ordering of materials, perhaps also by philosophical additions to Part I on the privative divine in its tripartite being (47,7–49,38; 53,10–32) and by mythological motifs in the opening of Part II, such as the vision of Barbelo, the translation to a holy place and the Luminaries giving instructions for a journey (58,7–60,12)" ("Introduction," 178).

249. See below Introduction, pp. 14–16, and the exegetical notes to 53.32b–54.37.

authorize the ascent further by making it, too, the product of divine revelation, not simply one person's account of his own spiritual adventures. Certainly repetition emphasizes the significance of the event. Or it might serve to preserve the structural balance of the text, which always sandwiches a revelation discourse between Allogenes' accounts of his spiritual progress. The possibilities are not mutually exclusive.

The text itself, as a revealed, secret writing, functions first and foremost as the medium of its own communication. Containing within itself the command for its own generation, the written text becomes not only product, but reproduces the production of its own discourse.

Within *Allogenes* are also other media that transfer direct speech into indirect speech: the epistle, which carries the revelation discourses as indirect speech; and the (third) revelation discourse, which transforms the utterance of Gnosis (?) and the theurgic prayer into indirect speech. The effect is to remove the speech to a distance (the transcendent sphere), while providing access through divine mediation. The media bridge the distance between this-world and the other-world.

In addition to the act of writing itself, formal media include: direct speech (discourse), indirect speech, vision, divine epiphany, and theurgic invocation. Each medium conveys a distinguishable communication act.

Representation in *Allogenes* is conveyed through narrative, descriptive, instructive, and imperative modes of presentation. This dimension also includes the shorter generic types within *Allogenes*: the epistle, revelation discourses, philosophical-mythical treatise, the ascent narrative (as a kind of brief travel narrative), and theurgic prayer.

The discernment of smaller forms may provide clues to the use of prior materials[250] or to the compositional history of the text. The combination of those forms, however, is an essential characteristic element of the genre. This perspective is important for understanding generic literary expectations in antiquity. For example, the use of the smaller form of the speech (discourse) is an essential contribution to the text's function to authorize the message of *Allogenes*. To stop by noting that the content of those speeches closely parallels materials conveyed elsewhere in other media (such as prayer or philosophical treatises) would miss the importance of the incorporation of materials into a new genre for new purposes. The ancients were less interested than we are in the question of originality, and more interested in the question of origins as authorization. Here the combination of smaller forms is done in a fashion that shapes the meanings of the text as a whole, while authorizing the text's specific teachings about the nature of reality and the path toward spiritual attainment.

These examples begin to demonstrate how the various dimensions of the

---

250. Specific cases of possible literary dependence or relation to other literatures are taken up in the exegetical notes.

text are interrelated. Function, content, and form all contribute the threads which constitute the pattern of possible meanings conveyed by *Allogenes* to its various readerships. The short generic types, the various media and modes of respresentation, each allow readers to comprehend sections of the text as coherent wholes and allow readers with various interests access to different pieces of the pie, so to speak. The fabric as a whole provides a model of purposeful direction toward spiritual attainment, making room for a wide variety of human emotions, actions, and experiences, such as teaching and learning, prediction and preparation, giving and receiving, hearing and seeing, fear and joy.

Taxonomy

The discussion so far has attempted to analyze the generic characteristics of *Allogenes*. This analysis provides the basis for determining the taxonomic classification of the text. This task is limited, however, by the absence of comparable analyses for other possibly related texts, such as the Sethian treatises from Nag Hammadi. For example, *Allogenes* has been classified with Sethian texts, but the taxonomic connections to Sethianism discussed above are based almost solely upon similarities in content, especially in descriptions of the divine hierarchy and the connection to the Sethian ritual of ascent. Among these texts, *Allogenes* shows the greatest similarities with *Three Steles of Seth*, *Zostrianos*, and *Marsanes*. The last two correspond very closely to *Allogenes* in form as well as content. Like *Allogenes*, they are narrated in the first person, with the speaker identified in the title. They contain revelation discourses given by various divine speakers and an ascent narrative. *Three Steles of Seth* is generically different, being made up of hymnic materials, but its mythological content clearly belongs to the same set of texts as *Allogenes*, *Zostrianos*, and *Marsanes*, and apparently it was used in conjunction with an ascent similar to that described in *Allogenes*. The results of this attempt at classification are, however, quite tentative, and based upon only the most general considerations of content and form.

Similarly, several suggestions have been made in the past regarding the generic taxonomy of *Allogenes*, but with only tentative results. Ann Wire[251] has described *Allogenes* as a revelation discourse, but that category is too broad

---

251. See Wire, "Introduction," 175–176. She describes this genre as follows: "Characteristic of this genre are the speaker's self-introduction, reference to the person addressed, narrative of events including the appearance of a divine being, a record of the divine pronouncements, an account of the speaker's reaction, and closing instructions on the preservation of the document" (175). The remainder of her discussion of form and composition is taken up with considerations about the literary unity of the text and its borrowings. The brevity of her discussion and the focus upon compositional history, however, leaves the question of genre and taxonomy largely open. Moreover, the characteristics are so general that a wide variety of texts could be included in this category, from the Gospel of John to the Book of Revelations.

and general for a precise generic classification. In his discussion of the Sethian treatises, Hans-Martin Schenke[252] does try to account for all three elements of genre (form, content, and function) and even their interrelationship, but, despite its importance, his discussion is very cursory and he does not attempt a taxonomic classification for *Allogenes*.

The most adequate classification of *Allogenes* is among ancient apocalypses. The most thorough analysis to date is that of Francis Fallon,[253] using the paradigm developed by John Collins. Unfortunately the paradigm does not include a consideration of function. This deficiency is a serious one since *Allogenes* diverges most sharply from apocalypses with regard to function.

Comparison with the paradigm of Hellholm,[254] shows that the closest similarities of *Allogenes* with apocalypses are in form. Both are characterized by the following elements:

Narrative framework
Epistolary prescript and/or postscript[255] . . .
Heavenly journey to an other-worldy place of revelation
Account of vision(s)
Interpretation of vision(s)
Discourse of mediators
Dialogues between mediator(s) and receiver . . .
Communications embedment . . .
Pseudonymity[256]

Missing from *Allogenes* are only: "Removal to a this-worldly place of revelation . . . Quotations of the Supreme Divinity . . . (and) Pictorial language."[257] One prominent characteristic of *Allogenes* not listed is the emphasis upon the recipient's reaction to revelation. The ascent might also be considered a characteristic of form, as well as of content.

252. "The Phenomenon," 597–607, 612–616.
253. Collins defines the genre of apocalypse as follows: "'Apocalypse' is a genre of revelatory literature with a narrative framework, in which a revelation is mediated by an otherworldly being to a human recipient, disclosing a transcendent reality which is both temporal, insofar as it envisages eschatological salvation, and spatial insofar as it involves another, supernatural world" ("Introduction," 9). Collins also gives a "master paradigm" of the genre, listing those elements of both the framework of the revelation and its content which define apocalypse as a specific literary genre of antiquity ("Introduction," 5–8). Fallon then applied this definition and paradigm specifically to Gnostic apocalypses, *Allogenes* among them. (For a list and discussion of these texts, see Fallon, "The Gnostic Apocalypses," 123–158.) The result of his analysis was to show that *Allogenes* shares most of the elements of the apocalypse genre. Excluded are only those elements which involve history and its accompanying eschatology. Although the work of Collins and Fallon is extremely important, the analysis is limited by the absence of considerations of function.
254. "The Problem of Apocalyptic," 22–23.
255. See exegetical note to 45.1–5.
256. Hellholm, "The Problem of Apocalyptic," 23.
257. Hellholm, "The Problem of Apocalyptic," 23.

Again comparison with Hellholm's paradigm shows that *Allogenes* lacks many of the most distinctive characteristic contents of apocalypses, including eschatology, the periodic division of cosmic history, and combat between dualistic powers. But it does contain many of the other contents characteristic of apocalypses:

Description of the other-world . . .
This-worldy recipients
Addressees of recipient's revelation
Paraenesis
Command to the recipient to reveal and/or write by other-worldly
    mediator
Sytematization of numbers, etc.[258]

Where *Allogenes* differs most decisively from apocalypses, however, concerns function. Comparison with Hellholm's paradigm[259] shows that it has only one function in common with apocalyptic: the authorization of the text's message, a function common to all revelation discourses. Its other functions (to provide a model of spiritual progress, its connection with the Sethian ritual of ascent, and its encounter with Greek philosophy) are not characteristic of apocalypses. Nor is the text intended for a group in crisis, exhorting its believers to steadfastness or repentence, promising a final vindication of redemption, as is characteristic of apocalypses.

Many of the similarities between apocalypses and *Allogenes* stem no doubt from characteristics belonging to the broad generic category of revelatory writing.[260] Part of the confusion about whether *Allogenes*, and indeed many Gnostic texts, should be classified as apocalypses may be due to the fact that there are striking similarities to apocalypses in form and content, while at the same time significant differences in content and especially in function are displayed. Despite the tentative nature of the comparison, it seems that the best taxonomic classification of *Allogenes* is as a subgenre of apocalypses.

Hellholm makes three observations that are pertinent to our discussion here. First of all, he notes that none of the individual characterists he lists in his paradigm are unique to apocalypses.[261] Secondly, no single text contains all the characteristics listed in the paradigm.[262] Finally, it is not only the number of characteristics that a text possseses, but also the "type, the sequential order and the interrelationship of these characteristics to each other" that must be considered.[263] These observations stress the fluidity of generic construction

258. Hellholm, "The Problem of Apocalyptic," 22–23.
259. Hellholm, "The Problem of Apocalyptic," 23.
260. See Hellholm, "The Problem of Apocalyptic," 30. Wire's classification of *Allogenes* as a revelation discourse applies here.
261. Hellholm, "The Problem of Apocalyptic," 23–24.
262. Hellholm, "The Problem of Apocalyptic," 23–24.
263. Hellholm, "The Problem of Apocalyptic," 25; see also p. 16.

and the possibilities for creative manipulation within the parameters of generic constraints. The uneasy placement of *Allogenes* within any taxonomic category affirms the fluidity with which generic conventions are employed in the text.

Date and Provenance

Only a single fragmentary copy of *Allogenes* survives from antiquity. That copy came to light in an important manuscript discovery in 1945. Although precise details of the find remain obscure, reports of the find agree that a large clay jar containing twelve codices and one tractate was discovered at the base of Jebel el-Tarif near the village of Hamra Dam, ten kilometers northwest of Nag Hammadi in Egypt.[264]

The original composition of *Allogenes* in Greek[265] can be dated to the first quarter of the third century, because it is highly probable that a Greek version may have been known to Plotinus.[266] The number and type of scribal errors in our one extant Coptic manuscript indicate that it is one of a number of copies from a Coptic original.[267] It may reasonably be supposed that translation into Coptic took place sometime in the third century C.E. since the extant manuscript can be dated to the early fourth century C.E..

The geographical provenance of *Allogenes* is uncertain. Translation into Coptic does not necessarily mean that the original was composed in Egypt, although it certainly establishes the fact that it was known and read there. Other points, however, also point toward Egypt, especially Alexandria, as a possible provenance. Epiphanius located the Sethians in Egypt,[268] and *Allogenes* contains many elements of Sethian mythology. Furthermore, the text explicates its mythology in terms of philosophical speculation consonant with that taught in Alexandria. And, on the other hand, the fact that the text was known to the circles of Plotinus in Rome[269] is not necessarily an argument for a Roman origin. Finally, scholars have suggested that the origin of related texts, especially *The Three Steles of Seth*,[270] is to be sought in Egypt. These

---

264. See Robinson, "Introduction" to *The Facsimile Edition of the Nag Hammadi Codices* (brochure); "Preface" to *The Facsimile Edition of the Nag Hammadi Codices (Codices XI, XII, and XIII*, vii; "On the Codicology," 16–17; "The Discovery," 206–224; and "The Discovering and Marketing of Coptic Manuscripts," 97–114.

265. See below, Introduction, p. 66.

266. See below, Introduction, pp. 48–49.

267. See below, Introduction, p. 65.

268. See *Panarion* 39.1.2.

269. See Porphyry, *Vit. Plot.* 16, and Introduction, pp. 48–49.

270. Tardieu places *The Three Steles of Seth* in the area of Assuit, near the supposed birthplace of Plotinus, at about the same time ("Les Trois Stéles de Seth," 599). E. R. Dodds, however, questions the reliability of the tradition that Plotinus was born in Egypt ("The *Parmenides* of Plato," 129–130, note 2).

points in conjunction make a case for the origins of *Allogenes* in Egypt, though such a suggestion remains necessarily speculative.

Nothing can be said with certainty about the author of *Allogenes* except that this person was intimately acquainted with Sethian mythology and sacramental practice, as well as with contemporary philosophical speculation.

Manuscript

As stated above, *Allogenes* is preserved in only one fragmentary manuscript discovered in December, 1945. In 1952, the codex was deposited in the Coptic Museum in Old Cairo and, in 1959, was given the inventory number 10547. Its official numbering (Nag Hammadi Codex XI; tractate 3) is that of the Coptic Museum, UNESCO, *The Facsimile Edition of the Nag Hammadi Codices*, and of this edition.[271]

Codex XI is a papyrus codex of a single quire originally bound in a leather cover.[272] According to James M. Robinson, the cover of the Codex may be grouped with Codices I, III, and VII in terms of construction.[273] The quire consists most probably of two rolls from which nine or ten sheets respectively were cut.[274] In addition, Robinson notes:

. . . (among others) Codex XI seem(s) on first glance to belong with the majority that were cut from right to left. But since in each case the *kollemata* on the right side overlap those on the left, one may assume (though other alternatives may not be excluded) that, before or after cutting, the roll or stack of sheets had been rotated 180 degrees. If one may assume it was standard to cut from right to left, then one should assume the roll was first rotated 180 degrees and then cut from right to left.[275]

The codex contains three complete texts, albeit in fragmentary form, and the beginning of a fourth:

1. *The Interpretation of Knowledge*
2. *A Valentinian Exposition*
   a. On the Anointing
   b. On Baptism A and B
   c. On the Eucharist A and B

271. See Robinson, "Preface" *The Facsimile Edition Codices XI, XII, and XIII*, vii, for a listing of previous numberings.
272. For a description of the condition of the codex, see Robinson, "Preface," *Facsimile Edition. Codices XI, XII, and XIII*, ix-xiii. The leather cover is now preserved separately.
273. See Robinson, "Construction," 170–190.
274. See Robinson, "Codicology," 28–29.
275. Robinson, "Codicology," 26.

3. *Allogenes*
4. *Hypsiphrone*

The present pagination of the *Facsimile Edition* was determined with some difficulty due to the rather serious damage to the codex.[276] Only in one case does the pagination numbering survive (19/20), and then only on a detached fragment. Our text extends according to the present pagination of the *Facsimile Edition*, from page 45 to approximately the middle of the remainder of page 71. It is, however, agreed that the pagination of 59–74 should be shifted to 57–72. Robinson writes:

> Between [56] and [57] there was a now missing stub that connected to [15/16] and was the end of the papyrus roll from which sheets were cut (compare Codices VII and VIII). A dark blot at the same position on both [56] and [57] confirms that these pages were separated, not by a complete folio, but only by a stub that protruded little further than the inner margin. Therefore, the pagination of plates 4 and 63–78 is to be reduced two numbers.[277]

With this correction, the text of *Allogenes* extends from 45–69, twenty-four folio pages in total.

In general, the length of the pages extends from 36–39 lines; the text of *Allogenes* ends at approximately line 20 on page 69. The construction accords with that of the Nag Hammadi Codices in general: all recto pages have horizontal fiber patterns; all verso pages have vertical fiber patterns, as is expected since the tractate is located in the second half of a one quire codex.

The condition of the pages varies considerably. A number of fragments have been placed and are noted in the introductory volume to the *Facsimile Edition*.[278] Pages 45/46 and 47/48 are completely missing approximately the first four or five lines and are marred by several lacuna of considerable size. The entire inner margin of 45/46 is missing. Pages 49/50, 51/52, and 53/54 are also missing the first four to five lines, with the exception of a fragment, replaced from page 57/58 so as partially to restore lines one to three of folio 45/46. Otherwise these three folios are in relatively good condition, containing only a few small to medium-sized lacuna located mostly toward the upper parts of the folios. Pages 55/56 are the worst preserved of the entire text. Approximately lines one to nine or ten are missing completely. In addition somewhat more than half of the inner side of the folio is missing. Pages 57/58 are missing lines one to four, as well as sections on lines five to fourteen, but are otherwise in excellent condition. Similarly 59–64 are in relatively excellent

---

276. See Robinson, "Preface," *Facsimile Edition. Codices XI, XII, and XIII*, xi-xiii.

277. See Robinson, "Preface," *Facsimile Edition. Codices XI, XII, and XIII*, xiii; see also "Codicology," 24.

278. See 126–128, plates 19–22.

condition. Pages 59/60 and 61/62 show minimal lacunae in lines one to eleven; pages 63/64 in lines one to fourteen with an additional small lacuna at lines 16–18. Pages 65/66 and 67/68 are missing approximately the first 14–15 lines. And pages 65/66 show more or less serious areas of deterioration at lines 15–22; pages 67/68, in lines 16–18. In addition, deterioration of lines 32–34 on page 68 makes an occasional letter uncertain. The final page, 69, is extremely fragmentary. Approximately lines one to 14 are missing completely. The remaining six lines of text belonging to *Allogenes* are marred by lacunae.

In summary, a sufficient portion of the manuscript is preserved to allow the content and themes to be determined, but the considerable damage to the manuscript requires caution in many matters of exact description.

Orthography

The texts of Codex XI were inscribed by two scribes; texts one and two, and texts three and four, respectively. The handwriting style of *Allogenes* (and the following pages of *Hypsiphrone*) is related to, or identical with, that of Codex VII.[279] The style shows a more distant relationship with that of the scribe who copied Codices IV, V, VI, VIII, and IX. The style of these codices is also characterized by rounded forms and hooked elements. The hand of our scribe is uniform and legible, producing a text that (where preserved) is a pleasure to read. The left margin in particular is straight and clear. The right margin shows some variation of one to two letters. The only dramatic deviation is at 65.25 where the scribe extends into the margin at such length that one might speculate that the letters M̄N̄T̄ were originally forgotten and had to be corrected with a marginal addition.

The supralinear stroke (functioning as a syllable marker) appears regularly above single consonantal sonants (ρ, м, ν, and λ) which form syllables of their own, or above two or more consonants of any sort[280] forming syllables of their own. The supralinear stroke over single or double consonants is generally in the rounded form of the circumflex; whereas over three or more consonants, the stroke is straight. The circumflex, like the stroke above two consonants, generally extends from the middle of the first to the middle of the second. Occasionally it shifts slightly to the right or left, as may be expected in a hand-inscribed text. The stroke above two consonants is therefore in principle no longer than that above one. The length of the stroke above three or more

---

279. Robinson follows Krause's analysis of the classification of scribal hands. He concludes: ". . . The scribe who wrote I.3 wrote the first two tractates of Codex XI. The scribe who wrote the late two tractates of Codex XI also wrote Codex VII" ("Codicology," 17). In H.-M. Schenke's opinion, with which I concur, this position cannot be maintained with certainty.

consonants extends in principle from the end of the first consonant to the beginning of the last consonant.

A characteristic feature of the orthography of *Allogenes* (and one which provides clear evidence of a relation to the orthography of Codices IV, V, VI, VII, VIII, and IX) is the normal appearance of the stroke above the complex ϩⲓ in every form (ϩ̄ⲓ, ϩ̄ⲓⲛⲁ, ϩ̄ⲓⲧ̄ⲛ̄, and so forth). The stroke is sometimes round, sometimes straighter. Its function remains obscure since it is not a syllable marker and has no other apparent, necessary function. In addition, strokes appear consistently above standard contractions (for example, ⲡ̄ⲛ̄ⲁ̄ and ⲭ̄ⲥ̄) and more irregularly as emphasizing strokes above proper names. Never does a stroke appear at the end of a line to indicate a final ⲛ, though the scribe had ample opportunity to use this commonplace feature of Coptic orthography.

The hook[281] appears only with the letter ⲧ and functions as a syllable divider, the normal function of a hook in Codices IV–X. The hook looks like, and probably is, a ligature with the apostrophe.

The raised dot is used frequently, though not entirely consistently, to divide syntactical units. In this function it is usually, though not always, reliable.

In a few cases, difficulties of orthography may be ascribed to errors of copying. These are all indicated in the critical apparatus of the text. The following is a summary of the most significant errors:

ⲥⲉⲙⲉⲛ (as nomen) for ⲥⲉⲗⲙⲉⲛ	1
haplography of ⲟⲩ-	
ⲟⲩⲱⲛϩ for ⲟⲩⲟⲩⲱⲛϩ	5
ⲉⲩⲁⲁⲃ for ⲉⲩⲟⲩⲁⲁⲃ	1
dittography of ⲟⲛⲧⲱⲥ	1
omission of ⟨ⲉⲩϣⲟⲟⲡ⟩	1
omission of emphasizing stroke above proper names	18[282]

Other types of difficulties with grammar, syntax, and/or sense may not be so easily ascribed simply to scribal error, but indicate a more serious corruption of our one surviving copy of *Allogenes*. At 67.36, grammar requires the restoration of an object for ⲉⲓⲙⲉ. The incorrect suffix pronoun is given five times.[283] At 50.18, an impossible use of ⲡⲉⲝⲁⲥ ⲝⲉ with the vocative occurs. The omission of critical syntactical elements (ⲡⲉ, ⲧⲉ, circumstantial ⲉ-)

---

280. This practice differs from the supralinear stroke system of Nag Hammadi Codex II and XIII where supralinear strokes appear only above sonora. The system of our text is more standard.

281. Also termed "flag" or "serif."

282. The most explicit examples include ⲛⲟⲏⲑⲉⲩ (54.20) and ⲁⲫ̄ⲣⲏⲁⲱⲛ (54.23–24). The emphasizing stroke never appears above Allogenes, only once above Messos (68.28), and twice above Barbelo (46.34 and 58.21).

283. 45.23; 49.11; 54.16; 58.26; 60.18.

occurs in four cases.[284] Eight additional cases of corruption in the text, mostly likely through omission, are marked with the sigla ⟨ ⟩.[285] On two other occasions[286] corruption has made the text so obscure that it is hard to speculate about what would be required to give them either a grammatical or narrative sense; these instances are marked by the sigla *. In one case (59.8–9), it appears that several words, in themselves yielding no clear grammatical or narrative sense, have been misplaced. All these occurences are clearly marked in the text and critical apparatus. These difficulties indicate quite clearly that the text is not everywhere in order and, along with the serious damage to the physical materials themselves, they present the greatest difficulty to the student of *Allogenes*.

It is of course impossible at our present state of research into the language of the Nag Hammadi texts, and indeed of Coptic dialects in general, to be equally certain about the kind and degree of corruption in all these cases. The omission of εροϥ after ειμε (67.36) or the appearance of the suffix pronoun -c for -ϊ (60.18), can be more easily explained perhaps as scribal errors or misunderstanding. Grammar and sense at any rate require their correction. Other cases are less easily understood, let alone explained, and one is often left with an unsatisfying suspicion that perhaps the text is in order, the scholar in confusion. One may question, for example, whether the adverbial usage of πϣορπ̄ at 68.31 is a scribal error for ⲛ̄ϣⲟⲣⲡ̄ or whether unbeknownst to us πϣορπ̄ as an adverb falls within the comprehensible purview of normal usage, perhaps as a rendering of πρῶτος.

Language

As noted briefly above, the surviving manuscript of *Allogenes* is a Coptic translation from Greek. This fact is illustrated in particular by two Coptic readings which make sense only as misunderstandings and mistranslations of an underlying Greek text: ϩ̄ⲛ ⲟⲩⲏⲉⲓ for ἐν τῷ οἰκείῳ (65.32) and ⲧⲁⲙⲓⲟ for ποιόν by misreading ποιητόν (63.[8]).[287]

Notwithstanding some minor alternations in normative usage given below, *Allogenes* is written in a standard Sahidic[288] which is, for the Nag Hammadi collection, astonishingly pure. In contrast to Codices II and XIII, for example, final clauses are always formed using the III Future. The crucial preposition ε-

---

284. 45.9; 47.34; 48.36; 61.34.
285. 46.9; 52.29; 57.9; 61.38; 63.35; 65.23–24; 67.31, 37.
286. 59.8–9; 65.34.
287. For further comment, see the respective exegetical notes to 65.22b–66.30a and 62.27b–63.28a.
288. See Shisha-Halevy, "Sahidic"; Satzinger, "On the Origin"; Kasser, "Prolégomènes."

("to, towards") is always used consistently in all its forms (ⲉϥⲥⲱⲧⲙ ⲉ-, ⲉⲃⲟⲗ, ⲉϩⲟⲩⲛ, etc.). The text, nonetheless, does show both internal variation and occasional deviance from the standard of classical (Biblical) Sahidic. These cases are partly due to limited influence coming from upper Egyptian dialects,[289] influence one would naturally expect in a manuscript coming from the area of Nag Hammadi. Other deviations, however, are more unexpected and are thus more significant, including elements which are peculiar to our text.

Before attempting to discuss the significance of these phenomena, it is necessary to determine specifically which elements come into consideration. Then one may determine the degree and kind of influence, and finally the problem of significance can be addressed.

I have listed below all elements showing internal (normative) variation or deviation from standard, classical Sahidic. These elements are divided into three larger divisions: 1) internal variants comprehensible within the scope of standard Sahidic; 2) features giving evidence of a specific dialectical influence; and 3) non-Sahidic traits peculiar, if not unique, to *Allogenes*. Under each of these divisions are headings supplying general categories under which the various alternatives are more or less naturally grouped. Following each item is given the number of occurrences in *Allogenes*. Items themselves in parentheses indicate standard Sahidic terms which do not occur at all in *Allogenes* but which are supplied for purposes of comparison.[290]

1. Internal variants of *Allogenes* comprehensible within the scope of standard Sahidic

These occurrences can usually be interpreted as orthographic variants, though Spross ⲛ and the absence of ϩ may be consequent upon pronunciation.

-ⲉⲓ for -ⲓ̈

ⲗⲉⲓ	22	ⲗⲓ̈	10
ⲉⲗⲉⲓ	2	(ⲉⲗⲓ̈)	
ⲉⲧⲁⲉⲓ	5	ⲉⲧⲁⲓ̈	2
ⲙⲙⲟⲉⲓ	2	ⲙ̄ⲙⲟⲓ̈	4
	31		16

Other forms (ⲉⲓ̈, ⲉⲓ̈ⲉ, ⲛⲉⲓ̈, etc.) show no variation.

---

289. See Kasser, "Dialects," "Prolégomènes," and "Les Dialectes coptes"; Satzinger "On the Origin."

290. This systematic presentation of the notable linguistic features of *Allogenes* is aimed not only at clarity of description, but also at providing information in a manner that will allow for ready comparison with the features of other texts. The presentation here is based on the model of H.-M. Schenke, though its faults are my own.

ı for ∈ı

ıмє	2	єıмє	30
ıнє	2	єıнє	2
ıⲱⲧ	1	(єıⲱⲧ)	
	5		32

These forms are somewhat rare in Sahidic outside the Nag Hammadi Codices, especially ıмє and ıнє.[291] In Middle Egyptian[292] they appear with some regularity.[293] Their usage in *Allogenes* is thoroughly inconsistent. For example, both єкıмє and єкєıмє appear.[294]

ı for ∈ı with stems derived from Greek

єнєргı	7	єнєргєı	1
ємєλı	2	(мєλєı)	
хрıλ	3	(хрєıλ)	
	12		1

-ү (following є) for oү

after є		all other cases	
ү-	18	(oү-)	
үнⲧλ⸗	8	oүнⲧλ⸗	3
үн	1	oүн/oүнⲧє-	4
	27		7

-ү appears regularly for oү in construction with є-.

-нoү for -нү

ⲧλхрнoү	1	ⲧλхрнү	1
ⲑⲃⲃıнoүⲧ	1	(ⲧⲃⲃıнү)	
	2		1

λ for н (?)

ⲃλрⲃλλⲱ	1	ⲃλрⲃнλⲱ	1

The difference here is perhaps due merely to scribal error and is no real orthographic variant. It is at any rate not a Coptic word. The phenom-

291. See Kasser, *Compléments au dictionnaire du Crum*.
292. See H.-M. Schenke, "On the Middle Egyptian Dialect."
293. See H.-M. Schenke, "Introduction" to *Das Matthäus-Evangelium*. For further discussion of the principle on which this irregularity is based, see Polotsky, *Collected Papers*, 437.
294. See *Allogenes* 60.11 and 55.20 or 59.12 respectively.

enon of writing ⲁ for ⲏ does, however, occur in Coptic,[295] as well as elsewhere with foreign names.[296]

Absence of doubled vowels

ⲙⲟϣⲉ	1	(ⲙⲟⲟϣⲉ)
ⲧⲱⲛ	1[297]	(ⲧⲱⲱⲛ or ⲧⲱⲟⲩⲛ)

These cases form an exception to the otherwise normalized usage of standard Sahidic double vowels (for example, ⲉⲧⲃⲏⲏⲧ⸗, ϫⲱⲱⲙⲉ, etc.). Both forms occur occasionally in Sahidic.

Presence of Sprossvokal

ⲡⲱϣⲉ	1[298]	ⲡⲱϣ	2
ⲟⲩⲱϣⲉ	3[299]	ⲟⲩⲱϣ	1
ⲙⲛ̄ⲧⲥⲁⲉⲓⲉ	2	ⲙⲛ̄ⲧⲥⲁⲉⲓ	1
	6		4

ⲙⲛ̄ⲧⲥⲁⲉⲓ apppears only once and may be a scribal error.[300]

Absence of ⲛ of Spross ⲛ

ϣⲟⲙ̄ⲧ	7	(ϣⲟⲙ̄ⲛ̄ⲧ)	
ϣⲙ̄ⲧ-	2	ϣⲙ̄ⲛ̄ⲧ-	13
ⲛ̄ⲥⲁⲃⲟⲗ	1	ⲛ̄ⲥⲁⲛⲃⲟⲗ	2
	10		15

Absence of ϩ[301]

ⲁⲣⲉϩ (with prefix)	2[302]	ϩⲁⲣⲉϩ (as verb)	1
ⲁⲣⲙⲏⲗⲱⲛ	2[303]	ϩⲁⲣⲙⲏⲗⲟⲛ	1

Metathesis of ϩ (with ϫ)

ϣⲁϫϩ⸗	2	ϣⲁϩϫ⸗	3

295. See P. Kahle, *Bala'izah*, 59–60.
296. See G. Horner, *The Coptic Version of the New Testament in the Southern Dialect*, Acts 5.36; and Codex Glazier (G67), Pierpont Morgan Library.
297. Occurs also at NHC VII. 36.18–19.
298. Occurs also in NHC VII; see index in Krause, *Christentum am Roten Meer*.
299. Occurs also at NHC VII. 10.26–27; 50.21; see also index in Krause, *Christentum am Roten Meer*.
300. The text is emended by Turner.
301. Layton notes that this is a common feature of Sahidic as well as Lycopolitan. See *Nag Hammadi Codex II*, I, 14.
302. Occurs also in NHC II.
303. One case is restored. See index.

Because the word itself is completely unattested outside *Allogenes*, we can infer on the basis of the vowel quality alone that ϣⲁϩⲝ- is standard. There are similar occurrences of metathesis with ϩ also in NHC II.[304]

Qualitative of ⲙⲟⲩϩ

ⲙⲉϩ   2   (ⲙⲏϩ)

The use of ⲙⲉϩ is unusual, though a possible Sahidic spelling of the qualitative of ⲙⲟⲩϩ; nonetheless, one would expect (ⲙⲏϩ).

2. Features specifically giving evidence of dialectical influence

In *Allogenes*, these influences come from Achmimic[305] or Lycopolitan,[306] particularly the former.

ⲁ for ⲟ

ⲉⲁⲩ	1	ⲉⲟⲟⲩ	7
ⲗⲁⲉⲓⲟ̄ⲉ	2	ⲗⲟⲉⲓⲟ̄ⲉ	1
ⲛ̄ⲧⲁϥ	3	ⲛ̄ⲧⲟϥ	4[307]

Forms of the Qualitative

ⲉ	12	ⲟ	3
ⲧⲟⲉ	2	ⲧⲟ	1
	14		4

The use of ⲉ rather than ⲟ as the qualitative of ⲉⲓⲣⲉ in particular emphasizes a sharper influence from Achmimic than Lycopolitan. The spelling of the qualitative of ϯ as ⲟⲧⲉ occurs also in NHC V.58.22 and VI.9.16. In all cases, it appears only within the expression ⲧⲟⲉ ϩⲓⲱⲱ- ("to clothe"). If it points to any specific influence, it is Upper Egyptian.

Supralinear Stroke for ⲉ

ϩⲛ̄   1   ϩⲉⲛ   5

ϩⲛ̄ is the standard spelling in P, and in Lycopolitan it is frequently the preferred variant.

304. See Layton, *Nag Hammadi Codex II*, I, 14.
305. See Nagel, "Akhmimic."
306. See Nagel, "Lycopolitan"; Funk, "How Closely Related"; Kasser, "Relations" and "Orthographe."
307. Both ⲛ̄ⲧⲁϥ and ⲛ̄ⲧⲟϥ appear as a particle with ⲁⲗⲗⲁ. Only the cases of ⲛ̄ⲧⲟϥ used as a particle with ⲁⲗⲗⲁ are counted here, not when used as a personal pronoun.

ε for ⲁ

(in stressed or unstressed position)

ⲚⲦⲈ⸗	1	ⲚⲦⲀ⸗	14
ⲞⲨⲚⲦⲈ⸗	1	ⲞⲨⲚⲦⲀ⸗	18
ⲦⲈⳘⲞ	3	ⲦⲀⳘⲞ	8
	5		40

(in pretonic syllable)

ⲚⲈⲀ⸗	4	(ⲚⲀⲀ⸗)	

(imperative prefix)

ⲈⲘⲞⲨ	1	(ⲀⲘⲞⲨ)	
ⲈⲚⲀⲨ	1	(ⲀⲚⲀⲨ)	

ⲞⲨⲀⲈⲦ⸗ (with Ⲧ)[308]	1	ⲞⲨⲀⲀ⸗	12

The form ⲚⲈⲀ⸗ is extremely rare, appearing only in the Nag Hammadi Codices.[309]

The imperative prefix Ⲉ- is typical of Achmimic and one variety of Lycopolitan.[310] Westendorf lists ⲈⲘⲞⲨ as Old Coptic or Late Egyptian.[311] ⲈⲚⲀⲨ is also rare, appearing as the standard form in the Bodmer Papyrus Lamentations and Nag Hammadi Codices V and VI.[312]

Ⲁ for ε

Ⲉ⸗Ⲁ	1	Ⲉ⸗Ⲉ	13
ⲘⲀ⸗	1	ⲘⲈ⸗	1
ⲘⲀⳘ-	1	ⲘⲈⳘ-	3
ⲚⲦⲀⲢⲈ⸗	3	ⲚⲦⲈⲢⲈ⸗	2
	6		19

Conditional

ⲈϢⲀ-	1	ⲈⲢϢⲀⲚ-	3

Although ⲈϢⲀ- occurs as a conditional form in non-literary Sahidic in at least one case,[313] its alternating occurrence with the normal Sahidic ⲈⲢϢⲀⲚ- is notable.

---

308. Occurs also at NHC VII.70.4–5.
309. Occurs at NHC II.64.15–16; V.46.10; VI.69.7; VI.71.30; VII.64.20; VII.72.24.
310. See especially the *Apocryphon of James* (NHC I,2).
311. Westendorf, *Koptisches Handwörterbuch*, 5.
312. Lamentations I.9; NHC V.19.11, 28; 24.12; 59.17; VI.13.5; 37.24.
313. Crum lists an occurrence from the monastery of Epiphanius; *Coptic Dictionary*, 59.

p̄- as a prefix deriving verb stems borrowed from Greek

with p̄- 24 without p̄- 3

Standard Sahidic does not employ any prefix (p̄-, ep-, or eλ-) to derive stems from Greek, in contrast with all other dialects except Middle Egyptian. The use of a prefix in all but three cases in *Allogenes* indicates a strong non-Sahidic influence.

Negative III Future

ne⸗ 6 n̄ne⸗ 1

The usage of ne⸗ is almost normative, showing a significantly strong agreement with Achmimic and Lycopolitan.

3. Peculiar or characteristic traits of *Allogenes*

Reduplication of n̄ before vowels

	Reduplicated	*Not reduplicated*
n̄- (genitive particle)	0	1 [314]
n̄- (with complementary infinitive)	0	2 [315]
n̄- (preposition "in," "through," etc.)	0	6 [316]
n̄- (dative preposition)	0	2 [317]
n̄- (negative particle with λn)	16 [318]	0
n̄- (particle of equivalence)	7 [319]	11/12? [320]
n̄- (attributive particle before oγ)	0	7 [321]
n̄- (attributive particle before λ/e)	23 [322]	24 [323]
n̄- (introducing object before oγ) [324]	7 [325]	18 [326]
	53	71

314. Appears once before article oγ- (64.20).
315. Appears twice before λ/ei (60.4; 50.6).
316. Appears four times before oγ (47.16; 50.25; 54.25; 66.31) and twice before λ (49.14; 63.15).
317. Appears twice before oγ (49.15; 52.22).
318. For occurrences, see index.
319. Appears before oγ twice (61.32; 62.1), before other vowels five times (see index for occurrences).
320. Appears before oγ ten (eleven?) times (46.7 [?]; 48.13, 20, 30; 49.15, 16; 55.27, 29; 59.28; 60.11; 64.20) and before e (proper name) once (48.13).
321. Appears at 45.20; 57.34; 59.28; 60.38; 61.9; 63.14; 64.20.
322. See index for occurrences.
323. Appears at 47.8; 48.23, 23, 24, 26, 29, 35; 49.1; 51.10, 11; 53.25, 26, 27; 54.9; 55.20, 30; 58.12, 20, 23, 24; 60.25; 61.10; 64.35; 65.33.
324. There are no occurrences of n- (introducing object) before any vowels other than oγ.
325. Appears at 47.25; 58.9; 61.36; 62.15, 18; 63.33; 65.33.
326. Appears at 48.7; 49.5; 50.16; 51.6; 53.36; 56.32; 57.7; 59.26; 61.4 62.4, 11, 24; 64.22, 24, 27; 65.22, 35; 67.29.

This characteristic reduplication of ⲛ occurs in other Nag Hammadi Codices, for example in NHC II,[327] but is not to be associated peculiarly with any dialect.[328]

Reduplication of ⲙ before a nasal

ⲙⲙⲛ̄	4	ⲙⲛ̄	2
ⲙⲙⲛ̄ⲧⲉ-/ⲙⲙⲛ̄ⲧⲁ⸗	2	ⲙⲛ̄ⲧⲁ⸗	2
ⲙⲙⲛ̄ⲛ̄ⲥⲱ⸗	1	ⲙⲛ̄ⲛ̄ⲥⲁ-/	
		(ⲙⲛ̄ⲛ̄ⲥⲱ⸗)	1
	7		5

As with the reduplication of ⲛ̄, reduplication of ⲙ occurs in other Nag Hammadi Codices.[329] It is tempting to see the reduplication of ⲙ in ⲙⲙⲛ̄ⲛ̄ⲥⲱ⸗ as a scribal error, but this form also occurs in Nag Hammadi Codex II.[330]

Relative Forms

ⲉⲧⲉ⸗	5	ⲉⲧ⸗	5
ⲉⲧⲁ⸗	22	ⲛ̄ⲧⲁ⸗	6
	27		11

These forms show a variation in two distinct paradigms of the relative. In the perfect, usage varies apart from any consideration of whether the form is employed as strict relative or in temporal function. Similarly, the use of ⲛ̄ⲧⲁⲣⲉ⸗/ⲛ̄ⲧⲉⲣⲉ⸗ interchangeably with the temporal functioning of the relatives ⲛ̄ⲧⲁ⸗/ⲉⲧⲁ⸗ presents a mixing of paradigms. This occurrence is not a specific feature of any particular dialect but rather suggests that the text is not absolutely of a purely consistent character. In Bohairic, the normal temporal is ⲉⲧⲁ⸗; in Middle Egyptian, ⲉⲑⲁ⸗ and ⲉⲧⲉ ϩⲁ⸗; in all other dialects, ⲛ̄ⲧⲉⲣⲉ⸗ (on rare occasion with ⲛ̄ⲧⲁ⸗).

Negative of circumstantial present

ⲉϥ-....ⲁⲛ	4
ⲉⲛⲅ-...ⲁⲛ	1
ⲉⲛⲥⲉ-...ⲁⲛ	3
	8

---

327. See Nagel, "Grammatische Untersuchungen," 404 ff.
328. See Layton, *Nag Hammadi Codex II*, I, 12.
329. For example NHC II and V; see Nagel, "Grammatische Untersuchungen," 406, and Funk, *Die zweite Apokalypse des Jakobus*, index.
330. See Nagel, "Grammatische Untersuchungen," 406.

Negation of the relative without ⲛ

ⲉⲧⲉⲥ-...ⲁⲛ   1

Negation of II Present

ⲛ̄ⲛⲉϥ-...ⲁⲛ   2

Only the reduplication of ⲛ here is not standard Sahidic.

III Future with relative converter

ⲉⲧⲉϥⲉ   1

The appearance of the III future with a relative converter is very unusual, especially in Sahidic.

Extraposition (duplication) of conjugation base/ⲟⲩⲛ̄ⲧⲉ-[331]

ⲁ- (pre-nominal perfect) ...ⲁ⸗   2
ⲟⲩⲛ̄ⲧⲉ-...ⲟⲩⲛ̄ⲧⲁ⸗   2

II Perfect

ⲉⲁ-   1
ⲉⲁϥ   1

This phenomenon is one of the most striking peculiarities of *Allogenes*. The forms are identical in all respects with the circumstantial perfect, so that only the strongest pressure of the syntactical evidence requires that these forms be understood to be functioning in II perfect tense. The possibility that the text is not in order does not seem likely in these cases (50.12 and 66.32) since such considerations in general affect only difficulties occurring in the process of transmission or are due to difficulties the translator had with technical Greek philosophical terminology. Neither appears to be the case here. A further consideration is the fact that there is no other converter of the II perfect, so that it seems possible that the II perfect is converted only with ⲉ-—and this not once, but twice.[332] Furthermore, Wolf-Peter Funk has pointed out in conversation that there is reason for suspicion that the circumstantial perfect is functioning as a II perfect at several instances in Nag Hammadi Codex VII.[333] In that text, however, standard II perfect forms are present.

---

331. For further discussion of this unusual phenomenon, see Schenke, "Bemerkungen," 418.
332. For further discussion of this phenomenon, see Schenke, "Bemerkungen," 419.
333. See VII.49.20ff; 59.19ff; 67.31ff.

Apodotic
εϥϲωⲧⲙ̄   4

New Lexical Items
ⲡⲓⲟⲩⲁⲧⲟ   1/2?[334]
ϣⲱⲝ̄ϩ   3
ϣⲁⲝϩ꞊/ϣⲁϩⲝ꞊   4
ⲁⲧϣⲁⲝ̄ϩϥ   1

Schenke notes that comparison with the Fayumic translation of the *Epistle of Jeremiah* V.12 provides evidence that ⲟⲩⲁⲧⲉ was a common expression for "a multitude," making it possible to provide the addition of the demonstrative article ⲡⲓ-.[335]

The word ϣⲱⲝ̄ϩ appears eight times in *Allogenes*, one of which is partially reconstructed. Schenke traces this term philologically to an Egyptian term meaning "limit, restrict."[336]

In summary, the language of *Allogenes* is, despite the features noted above, a highly standardized Sahidic with only minor normative variations. The minor variations of vocalization would have caused no problems for those who wrote, copied, read, or heard this text. On the other hand, certain difficulties may ultimately be accountable to scribal errors. This possibility is naturally higher in the case of forms appearing only once (for example, ⲃⲁⲣⲃⲁⲗⲱ, ⲙ̄ⲙⲛ̄ⲧ꞊, ⲧⲁⲭⲣⲏⲟⲩ, ⲟⲩⲁⲉⲧ꞊). Most forms which occur only once, however, seem to conform to typical patterns of exceptions (for example, ⲛ̄ⲧⲉ꞊ and ⲟⲩⲛⲧⲉ-; ⲉ꞊ⲁ, ⲙⲁ꞊, and ⲙⲁϩ-; ⲛⲥⲁⲃⲏⲗ; ⲛⲥⲁⲃⲟⲗ; ⲓⲱⲧ; ⲉⲁⲩ; ϩⲛ̄; ⲙ̄ⲙⲛ̄ⲛ̄ⲥⲱ꞊; ⲉⲙⲟⲩ and ⲛⲁⲩ) and represent a variant type within Sahidic.

Only minimal influence from Upper Egyptian dialects appears; that of Lycopolitan in relation to Achmimic is particularly weak. Evidence of dialectical influence in *Allogenes* may not be interpreted as an indication of any specific geographical location for the translation or copying of the text.

334. One of the two occurrences is restored.
335. See "Bemerkungen," 420.
336. See "Bemerkungen," 419–420.

Facing page: NHC XI,69. Concluding page of *Allogenes* with the title and decoration. In contrast to modern practice, in antiquity it was common to put the title of a work at the end of the text. Here the last lines of the work and the title are set apart by a few strokes of decoration, marking a clear break between this work and the beginning of the next text in this codex, *Hypsiphrone*. *Photograph courtesy of the Institute for Antiquity and Christianity, Claremont, California. Used by permission.*

Revelation
of the
Unknowable God

45

45 ¹⁻⁵ [   ]
⁶ [   ]ⲉⲩⲉ ⲛ̄ⲕ[ⲁ]
⁷ [ⲧⲁ ⲟ]ⲩⲁ ⲛ̄ⲧⲉⲗ[ⲓⲟⲥ ⲁ]ⲩⲱ ⲉⲩⲕⲏ
⁸ [ϩⲓ ⲟ]ⲩⲙⲁ ⲧⲏⲣⲟⲩ [ⲉⲩϩ]ⲟⲧⲡ̄ [ⲉ]ⲡⲓ
⁹ [ⲛⲟⲩ]ⲥ

ⲡⲓⲣⲉϥⲁⲣⲉϩ ⲛ̄[ⲧⲁ]ⲉⲓⲧⲁ[ⲁ]ϥ ⟨ⲡⲉ⟩
¹⁰ [ⲛ̄ⲧ]ⲁϥⲧⲁⲙⲟⲕ· ⲁⲩ[ⲱ] ⲧ̄ϭⲟ[ⲙ] ⲉⲧ
¹¹ [ϣⲟ]ⲟⲡ ⲛ̄ϩⲏⲧⲕ̄ ⲧⲉ ⲛ̄ⲧⲁⲥⲡⲟ[ⲣⲱ̄ⲥ]

45.9 Turner reads: ⲛ̄[ⲧⲁ]ⲉⲓⲧⲁⲁϥ, without ⟨ⲡⲉ⟩. The addition of ⲡⲉ is necessary grammatically if ⲡⲓⲣⲉϥⲁⲣⲉϩ ⲛ̄ⲧⲁⲉⲓⲧⲁⲁϥ ⟨ⲡⲉ⟩ ⲛ̄ⲧⲁϥⲧⲁⲙⲟⲕ is understood to be a nominal (cleft) sentence. The construction is parallel to that in 45.11.

The first revelation to Allogenes

45.1–5 The text begins in a lacuna. We may suppose that the first lines contained a short epistolary address from Allogenes to Messos since *Allogenes* is narrated directly to a specific figure, Messos. The practice of writing pseudonymous letters of exhortation, often in the name of a renowned teacher, was common in antiquity, especially for purposes of paraenesis (see Stowers, *Letter Writing*, 36–40, 91–152; Perkins, *Gnostic Dialogue*, 46–47).

Comparison with the *Apocryphon of James* is useful here. There is no literary dependence between or similiarity in the contents of the two texts. Interestingly enough though, the literary conventions of the pseudonymous epistle/apocalypse seem to be used in a parallel fashion. If one analyzed the Nag Hammadi texts (and those of the Berlin Codex) according to the grammatical use of personal address, *Allogenes* and the *Apocalypse of James* stand out. In all the other texts, either the narrative is impersonal (that is, the text is narrated by an impersonal author) and the addressees are not in the text at all, or the scribe or an unidentified impersonal narrator ascribes the text to some author and identifies the addressees in the texts. For example, in the *Gospel of Thomas*, an impersonal narrator ascribes the sayings to Jesus and identifies Didymos Judas Thomas as the scribe. The title confirms the ascription. The entire narrative, however, is impersonal. When Thomas is mentioned in the text, it is in the third person. While this of course says nothing about authorship, it says a good deal about generic conventions. In the non-epistolary texts from Nag Hammadi, the author and addressees are either absent or are identified only secondarily in the title or in a short note at the beginning or end.

The *Apocalypse of James* is an apocalypse written in the form of an epistle (see the analysis of Perkins, *The Gnostic Dialogue*, 46–47), addressed from James to a figure whose name is partially obscured by a lacuna. Like *Allogenes*, the *Apocryphon of James* concludes with a commission to the addressee to proclaim the teachings given in the epistle, but only to those who are worthy.

45 ¹⁻⁵ [   ]

⁶ ". . .] for they are

⁷ per[fect indi]viduals [a]nd are all located

⁸ [toge]ther [in that they] are [jo]ined [with]

⁹ [intell]ect.

⟨It is⟩ the Guardian w[ho]m I gave (to you)

¹⁰ [who] instructed you; an[d] it is the Power which

¹¹ [exi]sts in you that procl[aimed itself]

45.7–8 Or: "they are all located in one place."
45.11–12 Or: "that spread itself often in speech."

These similarities lead me to speculate that the missing lines at the beginning of our text may have included an epistolary introduction from Allogenes to his son, Messos. This would be sufficient to satisfy the minimal form required of an epistle. If the introductory lacuna contained such an address, then the generic macro-structure of *Allogenes* would be that of the (pseudo)-epistle, that is, the whole apocalypse is an epistolary narration to Messos.

The extant text opens during the first revelation to Allogenes. Whether the revealer is Iouel or some other figure is in doubt (see notes to 50.17b–21a and 68.16–23a).

The lacuna contains the main clause to which the following three circumstantial clauses belong.

45.6–9a The first three circumstantial clauses, as restored, are ordered in a parallelism that is a common stylistic trait of *Allogenes*.

The topic of these clauses is "the individuals" (see pp. 31–32), which we may understand in Platonic terminology to be the particulars, the individuated intelligibles. They exist individually (ⲕⲁⲧⲁ ⲟⲩⲁ) and are perfect (ⲧⲉⲗⲓⲟⲥ). But though individuals, they are all situated in or at one place; they are unified insofar as they are joined with Intellect (ⲛⲟⲩⲥ). This statement expresses the essential unity of intelligible substance, which is at once universal and particular (individuated). (Compare *StSeth* 124.7–25; Plato, *Timaeus* 51D–52B; Plotinus, *Ennead* V.7.1; Porphyry, *Sententiae* 22; *Corpus Hermeticum* XXI; Turner, "Allogenes," 243; Williams, *The Immovable Race*, 62–63.)

45.9b–12 A grammatical parallelism appears here between two cleft sentences. The stressed elements are ⲡⲓⲣⲉϥⲁⲣⲉⲍ ⲛ̄ⲧⲁⲉⲓⲧⲁⲁϥ ("the Guardian whom I gave to you") and ⲧ̄ϭⲟⲙ ⲉⲧϣⲟⲟⲡ ⲛ̄ϩⲏⲧⲕ̄ ("the Power which exists in you"). The other two relative clauses (ⲛ̄ⲧⲁϥⲧⲁⲙⲟⲕ and ⲛ̄ⲧⲁⲥⲡⲟⲣⲱ̄ⲥ) are glosses expanding upon their antecedents: the Guardian instructed Allogenes; the Power extended itself as speech. That parallelism of construction seems to imply an identification between "the Guardian" and "the Power." The Guardian is also described as a "Power." The term ⲡϭⲟⲙ is here hypostasized;

¹² [ⲛ̄ϣⲁ]ϫⲉ ⲟⲩⲙⲏⲛϣⲉ ⲛ̄ⲥⲟⲡ
¹³[ⲡⲓⲉⲃ]ⲟⲗ ϩ̄ⲙ ⲡⲓϣⲙ̄ⲛ̄ⲧ̄ϭⲟⲙ· ⲡ[ⲏ]
¹⁴ [ⲛ̄ⲧⲉ ⲛⲏ] ⲧⲏⲣⲟⲩ ⲉⲧ[ϣ]ⲟⲟⲡ ⲟ[ⲛ]
¹⁵ [ⲧⲱⲥ] ⲙ̄ⲛ ⲡⲓⲁⲧϯ [ϣ]ⲓ ⲉⲣⲟϥ ⲡⲓ
¹⁶ [ⲟⲩⲟ]ⲉⲓⲛ ϣⲁ ⲉⲛ[ⲉϩ ⲛ̄]ϯⲅⲛⲱ

compare 67.17 where it is not. (For further discussion of the "Powers," see p. 45.) It is also possible that the Guardian is to be identified with Iouel.

The Guardian is clearly a teacher of a special sort. The concept of the Guardian may be related to the belief in the personal daimon that was common in antiquity. The daimon was believed to be the inner possession of an individual from birth, determining one's destiny wholly or in part. (See, for example, Plato, *Timaeus* 90A, C; *Phaedo* 107D; *Republic* 617D–E, 620D–E; see also the discussion and notes of Dodds, *The Greeks*, 42–43, 289–91.) Plotinus found the topic of sufficient interest to devote an entire treatise to it (*Ennead* III.4 "On our Allotted Guardian Spirit"). Porphyry describes an incident in his *vita Plotini* where the guardian spirit of Plotinus was revealed by theurgic practice to be a god (*vit. Plot.* 10)! In *Allogenes*, the Guardian is specifically given to Allogenes in order to provide preparatory instruction for his ascent. (Compare 50.11–17; 52.16–17.) Turner identifies the Guardian with Iouel ("Allogenes," 244).

It is difficult to understand what is implied by Turner's restoration of the phrase ⲛ̄ⲧⲁⲥⲡⲟⲣϣ̄ⲥ ⲛ̄ϣⲁϫⲉ ("who/which extended herself/itself as speech"). The phrase "extension by speech" could indicate the power of prophecy possessed by Allogenes or, alternatively, it could be the inner voice of the Guardian speaking to Allogenes as part of his preparatory instruction. The parallelism of construction with ⲛ̄ⲧⲁϥⲧⲁⲙⲟⲕ suggests an identification between "instruction" and "extension by speech," in which case ⲛ̄ⲧⲁⲥⲡⲟⲣϣ̄ⲥ ⲛ̄ϣⲁϫⲉ is perhaps best understood as a metaphor for the process of instruction.

This instruction had already taken place "often" before the present revelation, indicating extensive preparation for the teaching that follows.

45.13–22a This grammatical unit lacks a clear subject and verb. It is either a continuation of the lost beginning of the text, or more likely is simply a list.

The primary problem of interpretation regards the referent for the nominal phrases. It could be knowledge, the Guardian, or a referent lost in the lacuna. Since, however, the Guardian is a kind of mythologization or hypostasis of the noetic connection of Allogenes with mind, the distinction between knowledge and Guardian is probably not significant.

45.13a (Concerning the Triply-powered, see pp. 20–29). Compare *Ap-John* BG 28.1; 39.13; II,*1* 5.8; *Marsanes* 7.17–18; 7.23–24; 8.19–20; 9.8–9; 9.20–21; 9.25; *StSeth* 121.32; 123.23; *TriProt* 37.26–27; *UnText*

¹² often [in spe]ech.
¹³(He is) [the one deri]ved from the Triply- powered.
¹⁴ [Among] all [these] that tr[uly] exist,
¹⁵ it (alone is) with the Unmea[sured]. (It is) the
¹⁶ etern[al lig]ht of that know[ledge

> **45.13–22a** The pronominal references here are ambiguous. I interpret the text as
> paraphrased: The Guardian derives from the Triply-powered. Of all those that
> exist, the Triply-powered alone is with the Unmeasured. The Triply-powered is
> the eternal light of the knowledge which appeared. The knowledge is Barbelo: the
> male-virginal glory, the first of the aeons; she derives from the single triply-
> powered aeon. The single triply-powered aeon is the Triply-powered who truly
> exists.

(ⲧⲣⲓⲁⲩⲛⲁⲙⲓⲥ) 231.20; 233.6; 234.16; 235.21; 236.6; 239.12; 240.5–6;
243.13, 23; 244.25–245.1; 246.1; 246.12–13, 26; 248.24–25; 249.7, 10, 15;
252.16–17; 272.[6]–7, 8; (ϣⲟⲙⲧⲉ ⲛⲁⲩⲛⲁⲙⲓⲥ) 252.3; *Zost* 97.2–3.

The Guardian is described as ⲡⲓⲉⲃⲟⲗ ϩⲙ ⲡⲓϣⲙⲛ̄ⲧϭⲟⲙ ("he from the Triply-
powered"). ⲡⲓⲉⲃⲟⲗ ϩⲙ clearly indicates a derivative ontic and epistemic status, though it does not specify how he was derived, whether from emanation,
production, or in some other way. It is stated elsewhere that Intellect (mythologically personified in Barbelo) is derived from the Triply-powered in an act
of self-reflection (see p. 29).

45.13b–15a There are two grammatical options for the referent of the
phrase ⲡⲏ ⲛ̄ⲧⲉ ⲛⲏ ⲧⲏⲣⲟⲩ ⲉⲧϣⲟⲟⲡ ⲟⲛⲧⲱⲥ ⲙⲛ̄ ⲡⲓⲁⲧϯϣⲓ ⲉⲣⲟϥ: the phrase
describes either 1) the knowledge (or Guardian) who derives from the Triply-
powered or 2) the Triply-powered itself. The second option is the only one
that is congruent with the presentation of the metaphysical hierarchy in the
rest of the text. In that case, two interpretations of the phrase are possible: the
Triply-powered is 1) among all those beings who truly exist with the Unmeasured or 2) it is that one who, of all those who truly exist, is with the Unmeasured. The first interpretation understands the Triply-powered to be one of the
true existents; the second sees it as an exception, that is, of all those true
existents, the Triply-powered alone is with the Unmeasured. The second reading more clearly expresses the role of the Triply-powered as a mediator of the
Invisible Spirit (see 45.25–27; 49.9–10; 64.36; Introduction pp. 28–29).

(Concerning ⲛⲏ ⲧⲏⲣⲟⲩ ⲉⲧϣⲟⲟⲡ ⲟⲛⲧⲱⲥ ["all those who truly exist"], see
pp. 31–32.)

45.15b–17a The term "*gnosis*" sometimes appears, as here, as a semi-
hypostasized figure (compare 49.19; 51.10), but more often it is not hypostasized (compare 53.8–9, 19–20; 59.1, 2; 63.15; 64.10–11, 21). Elsewhere
Barbelo is associated with *gnosis* (see 51.8–12; 59.1–4).

The genitive ⲛ implies that "that knowledge (*gnosis*) which appeared" either
comes from or belongs to "the eternal light." The Triply-powered is the light

17 [ⲥⲓⲥ ⲛ̄]ⲧⲁⲥⲟⲩⲱ̣[ⲛ̄ϩ] ⲉⲃⲟⲗ· ⲡⲓ
18 [ⲉⲟⲟ]ⲩ ⲛ̄ϩⲟⲟⲩⲧ [ⲙ̄]ⲡ̣ⲁⲣⲑⲉⲛⲟⲥ
19 [ⲡϣⲟⲣ̄ⲡ̄] ⲛ̄ⲛⲉⲱⲛ ⲡⲓⲉⲃⲟⲗ ϩⲛ̄
20 [ⲟⲩⲉⲱ]ⲛ ⲛ̄ⲟⲩⲱⲧ ⲛ̄ϣⲙ̄ⲛ̄ⲧ̄
21 [ϭⲟⲙ ⲡⲓ]ϣ̣ⲙ̄ⲛ̄ⲧ̄ϭⲟⲙ ⲉⲧϣ̣[ⲟ]
22 [ⲟⲡ ⲟⲛⲧⲱ]ⲥ·
ϫ̣ⲉ ⲉⲧⲁⲩϩⲟ[ⲣ]
23 [ⲕ̄ϥ ⲁⲩⲡⲟⲣ]ϣ̣̄ ⟨ϥ̄⟩ ⲉⲃⲟⲗ· ⲁⲩⲱ̣

45.17 Turner restores: ⲉ]ⲧⲁⲥⲟⲩⲱ[ⲛ̄ϩ].
45.18 Turner restores: [ⲁⲗⲟ]ⲩ ("youth").
45.22–23 Or: ⲉⲧⲁⲩϩⲟ[ⲧⲡ̄ϥ ⲁϥⲙⲟⲟ]ϣⲉ ⲉⲃⲟⲗ ("When it was joined, it went forth."). The advantage of this second possible restoration is that it does not require emending the text.
45.23 The manuscript reads:]ϣⲉ ⲉⲃⲟⲗ· ⲁⲩⲱ.
45.23 Supralinear stroke over ϣ is restored; letter is clear.

of Barbelo, who is described here as "that knowledge (*gnosis*) which appeared." In *Allogenes*, light is often a metaphor for the capacity to illuminate, to make understanding possible (see 52.10–11; 57.34; 58.27; and especially 60.11). The metaphor refers here to the saving capacity of Barbelo to give knowledge about the Triply-powered Invisible Spirit.

45.17b–22a The description of Barbelo continues here. She is male and virginal (compare 59.5–7). "Male" is found in many other ancient texts as a metaphor for the transcendent, spiritual, noetic, non-material sphere in contrast to that of the "female" sphere of sexuality, materiality, lust, and death. For example, the Sethian treatise *Zostrianos* reads:

> Do not baptize yourselves with death nor entrust yourselves to those who are inferior to you instead of to those who are better. Flee from the madness and the bondage of femaleness and choose for yourselves the salvation of maleness. You have not come to suffer; rather, you have come to escape your bondage. (131.2–10; trans. Sieber, *NHLE*, 430)

Similarly, "virginity" implies a metaphorical purity and transcendence over the pollutions of the material realm of passion and appetite. Wisse argues ("Flee Femininity," 297–307) that the social milieu for the theme of anti-femininity found in a variety of Gnostic texts belongs to an encratic setting. The coupling of the themes of masculinity and virginity here fits well with his thesis, and may add evidence that *Allogenes* was written in such a milieu.

In the *Apocryphon of John*, Barbelo is described as a "glory" (II,1.4.36–5.2; see also p. 6). Turner's restoration of the term ⲁⲗⲟⲩ ("youth") at 45.18 is not consistent with usage elsewhere in the text, where the term is used only of the Thrice-male Youth.

Barbelo is the first of the aeons (compare *StSeth* 121.20); she derives from a triply-powered aeon, that is, she derives from the Triply-powered.

¹⁷ w]hich appe[ar]ed, the
¹⁸ male virginal [glor]y,
¹⁹ [the first] of the aeons, the one who derives from
²⁰ [a] single triply-[powered aeo]n.
²¹ (It is) [the] Triply-powered which [trul]y e[x]ists.
  ²²For when it was still[ed]
²³ ⟨it⟩ [was exten]ded and

45.22b–30 Again the pronominal references are ambiguous. I interpret the text as paraphrased: When the Triply-powered was stilled, it was extended, and when it was extended, it became perfect. And the Triply-powered received power from all those who truly exist insofar as it knows them in the perfect Invisible Spirit. And the Triply-powered came into being in an aeon (Barbelo) that knew the existents because she knew the Invisible Spirit (or the Triply-powered?).

Feminine pronouns are used with Barbelo here, but it should be noted that the text uses both masculine and feminine pronouns for Barbelo. "Her" gender is not metaphorically significant in this text, unlike other Sethian texts where her role as "mother" or "consort" is stressed (see, for example, *ApJohn* II.*1*,6.10–13). It is her "masculinity" that carries meaning.

The description of the Triply-powered as a being that "truly exists" (45.21–22) indicates its exalted ontic status (see p. 31).

Being "single" (ογωτ; 45.20) implies a lack of division, indicating a unity or monad.

45.22b–30 εταγ is equivalent to the Sahidic εντεπε, I. perfect affirmative with relative conversion in supplementary function (*Nebenfunktion*) as a temporal (see Schenke, *Das Matthäus-Evangelium*, 191). The form appears to be a temporal since the sentence begins with an antecedentless relative perfect.

The Triply-powered takes on form as the aeon of Barbelo through an act of self-extension. Plotinus also uses the metaphor of extension to describe the process whereby Mind, a vestige of the formless Supreme principle, takes on form through its extension into plurality (*Ennead* VI.7.17; compare also *Allogenes* 48.18–25; 49.7–14.) Like Plotinus, lines 45.25–30 understand ontological generation as an act of intellection. (Compare also Albinus *Didask.* 10 and Plotinus *Ennead* V.2.1.10 ff; V.2.1.3–13.) P. Merlin summarizes Albinus' position as follows:

Having introduced the difference between 'the father,' 'celestial intelligence,' and the cosmic soul, Albinus says that the father implants intelligence in the soul, and then (the 'then' taken in a non-temporal sense) turns the soul towards himself, so that the soul now can contemplate the intelligibles and fill itself with ideas and forms.(ch. 10)

("Greek Philosophy," 69)

Our text expresses a similar, though not identical, conception. Unlike Albinus and Plotinus who discuss the problem of how multiplicity could arise

[ⲉⲧⲁⲩⲡⲟⲣ]ϣ̣̄ϥ̄ ⲁϥⲣ̄ⲧⲉ[ⲗⲓ]ⲟ̣ⲥ·
[ⲁⲩ]ⲱ̣ ⲁ̣ϥ̣ϫ̣ⲓ̣ [ϭ]ⲟⲙ ⲉⲃⲟⲗ [ⲛ̄ϩⲏ]
[ⲧⲟⲩ ⲧ]ⲏⲣⲟⲩ· ⲉϥⲉⲓⲙ̣[ⲉ ⲉⲣⲟⲟⲩ]
[ϩ̄ⲙ̄ ⲡⲓⲁ]ϩⲟⲣⲁ̣[ⲧⲟⲛ] ⲙ̄ⲡ̣̄[ⲛ̄ⲁ̄]
[ⲛ̄ⲧⲉⲗⲓⲟⲥ·] ⲁⲩⲱ̣ ⲁ̣ϥ̣ϣ̣[ⲱⲡⲉ]
[ϩ̄ⲛ̄ ⲟⲩ]ⲉ̣ⲱⲛ· ⲉⲥⲉⲓⲙ[ⲉ ⲉⲣⲟⲟⲩ]
[ϫⲉ ⲁ]ⲥⲉⲓⲙⲉ ⲉⲡⲏ ⲉ[ⲧ̄ⲙ̄]ⲙ̣ⲁⲩ
[ⲁⲩ]ⲱ̣ ⲁⲥϣⲱⲡⲉ ⲛ̄ⲕⲁⲗⲩ̣[ⲡ]ⲧ̣ⲟⲥ
[ⲉⲧⲁ]ⲥ̣ⲣ̣̄ⲉ̣ⲛⲉⲣⲅⲓ ϩⲛ̄ ⲛⲏ ⲉⲧ̄ⲥ̄
[ⲥⲟ]ⲟ̣ⲩⲛ ⲙ̄ⲙⲟⲟⲩ· ⲟⲩⲡⲣⲱ
[ⲧⲟ]ⲫⲁⲛⲏⲥ ⲡⲉ ⲛ̄ⲧⲉⲗⲓⲟⲥ ⲛ̄
[ⲛⲁ]ⲧⲛⲁⲩ ⲉⲣⲟϥ ⲛ̄ⲛⲟⲩⲥ
[ϫⲉ]ⲁ̣̄ⲣ̄ⲙ̄ⲏ̄ⲇ̄ⲱ̄ⲛ̄· ⲉⲥϯ ϭⲟⲙ
[ⲇⲉ] ⲛ̄ⲛⲓⲕⲁⲧⲁ ⲟⲩⲁ· ⲟⲩ̄ⲅ̄ ϩⲟ
[ⲟⲩ]ⲧ ⲧⲉ̣ ⲉⲥⲟ ⲇⲉ ⲕⲁⲧⲁ ⲟⲩⲁ

45.26–27 Turner restores: ⲧ]ⲏⲣⲟⲩ· ⲉϥⲉⲓⲙ[ⲉ ⲉⲣⲟϥ ⲙ̄ⲛ̄ ⲡⲓⲁ]ϩⲟⲣⲁ̣[ⲧⲟⲛ] ("he knows himself and the Invisible").
45.29 Turner restores: ⲉⲥⲉⲓⲙ[ⲉ ⲉⲣⲟⲥ] ("knows herself"). The restoration of ⲉⲣⲟⲟⲩ, rather than ⲉⲣⲟϥ or ⲉⲣⲟⲥ, is based on a comparison with 45.32–33 (ⲛⲏ ⲉⲧ̄ⲥ̄ⲥⲟⲟⲩⲛ ⲙ̄ⲙⲟⲟⲩ).
45.30 Turner restores: [ϫⲉ ⲉ]ⲥⲉⲓⲙⲉ ⲉⲡⲏ ⲉ[ⲧ̄ⲙ̄]ⲙ̣ⲁⲩ.
45.32 Supralinear stroke over ⲣ is restored.
45.36 Turner restores: [ⲛ̄ϩ]ⲁ̄ⲣ̄ⲙ̄ⲏ̄ⲇ̄ⲱ̄ⲛ̄·. Compare 54.12; 58.17.

out of the One, our text is not interested in cosmic production *per se*, but in how one achieves knowledge. The text presumes that it is not possible by nature for a lower being to know a higher one. The lower being must "receive power" from a higher being in order to gain higher knowledge. Here, the Triply-powered receives power from those which exist in the perfect Invisible Spirit. (Compare 47.11–12 and 66.34–38 which state explicitly that the existents are encompassed by the Invisible Spirit.) That knowledge (*gnosis*) is hypostasized by the aeon of Barbelo. Her capacity for self-understanding is based upon knowledge of the Invisible Spirit, since every being turns to the being above it for knowledge and power. (Compare Plotinus, *Ennead* VI.7.35 ff.; *ApJohn* 4.22–6.11 where the first Ennoia of the father, Barbelo, alone calls forth knowledge from him.)

45.31–46.7a This section gives a capsule summary of the triply-powered nature of Barbelo as Kalyptos, Protophanes, and Autogenes (see pp. 30–31). This male triad hypostasizes the progression of existents from substantial unity to individuated differentiation. The meaning of the three names shows the progressive process of explicit generation: hidden (Kalyptos), (first)-ap-

²⁴ [when] it [was exten]ded, it became pe[rf]ect.
²⁵ [An]d it was em[po]wered b[y]
²⁶ [them a]ll insofar as it kno[ws them]
²⁷ [in the perfect In]visi[ble] Sp[irit].
²⁸ And it ca[me into being]
²⁹ [in an] aeon that kno[ws them]
³⁰ [because] she knows T[h]at one.
   ³¹[An]d she became Kalyptos
³² [as] she began to act in those whom she
³³ [kn]ows. He is a
³⁴ perfect,
³⁵ [i]nvisible, noetic Pro[to]phanes
³⁶ [named] Armedon. [For] insofar as she empowers
³⁷ the individuals, she is a triply-
³⁸ m[a]le being. But insofar as she exists individually . . .

45.31 "Kalyptos" means "a hidden one."
45.33–34 "Protophanes" means "a first-appearing one."
45.38 Or: "existing one-by-one, one after another." See exegetical note.

pearing (Protophanes), (self)-generated (Autogenes). Such production is not yet material; all belong to the intelligible realm.

For the distinction between the individuals and the true existents, see pp. 31–32.

The particulars are at once differentiated ("exist as individuals"; 46.6) and unified ("are at one place"; 46.6–7), repeating the assertion of 45.6–9. The "place" where they are located is the Intellect, that is, the intelligible sphere of the aeon of Barbelo.

In our text, the name Armedon/Harmedon is always an epithet of Protophanes, the second image in the triad of the aeon of Barbelo. (Concerning the name ⲁⲣⲙⲏⲇⲱⲛ, see also 54.12; compare 58.17 ⲑⲁⲣⲙⲏⲇⲱⲛ.) The name (with both spellings) also appears relatively frequently in Sethian literature:

in relation to Protophanes (compare *Zost* 127.7–11: ⲁⲩⲱ ⲛⲁⲓ̈ ⲙⲉⲛ
ⲉⲩⲛ2ⲣⲁⲓ̈ 2ⲙ ⲡⲓⲡⲣⲱⲧⲟⲫⲁⲛⲏⲥ ⲛ ⲧⲉⲗⲓⲟⲥ ⲛ ⲁⲣⲙⲏⲇⲱⲛ ⲛ 2ⲟⲟⲩⲧ·
†ⲉⲛⲉⲣⲅⲓⲁ ⲛⲧⲉ ⲛⲁ[ⲓ̈] ⲧⲏⲣⲟⲩ ⲉⲧ ϣⲟⲟⲡ 2ⲓ ⲟⲩⲙⲁ·);
as the first Aeon (*TriProt* 38.34; *Zost* 120.3);
as one of the Lights (*Zost* 119.5);
or in a theurgic invocation (*StSeth* 126.12; *Zost* 86.19).

The phrase ⲟⲩ̄ 2ⲟⲟⲩⲧ ⲧⲉ (45.37–38) describes Barbelo as a triply-male being; this triplicity is hypostasized as Kalyptos, Protophanes, and Autogenes.

46 ¹⁻⁵ [   ]

⁶ ⲉⲩⲕⲁ[ⲧⲁ ⲟⲩⲁ ⲙⲉⲛ ⲉⲩⲍ̄ⲓ ⲟⲩ]

⁷ ⲙⲁ

ⲗⲉ [ⲭⲉ ⲉⲥ]ⲟ ⲛ̄ⲟⲩϩ[ⲩⲡⲁⲣ]

⁸ ϫⲓⲥ ⲛ̄ⲧ[ⲉ ⲛⲁⲓ̈] ⲁⲩⲱ ⲉⲥⲛ[ⲁⲩ]

⁹ ⲉ[ⲛ]ⲏ ⲧⲏ[ⲣ]ⲟⲩ ⟨ⲉⲧϣⲟⲟⲡ⟩ ⲟⲛⲧⲱⲥ {ⲟ[ⲛⲧⲱⲥ]}

¹⁰ ⲟⲩⲛ̄ⲧⲁ[ⲥ] ⲙ̄ⲙⲁⲩ ⲙ̄ⲡⲓⲁⲩ[ⲧⲟⲅⲉ]

¹¹ [ⲛ]ⲏⲥ ⲛ̄ⲛⲟⲩⲧⲉ· ⲉⲧⲁⲥⲉ[ⲓⲙⲉ]

46.7 Supralinear stroke over ⲛ is restored; letter is clear.
46.9 Turner emends: ⲉⲛⲏ ⲧⲏ[ⲣ]ⲟⲩ ⟨ⲉⲩϣⲟⲟⲡ⟩ ⲟⲛⲧⲱⲥ ⲟ[ⲛ]. The position of ⲟⲛ
here is extremely unusual and leaves the line in the manuscript quite short. More
probable is a scribal error repeating ⲟⲛⲧⲱⲥ, as restored above. The emendation of
ⲉⲧϣⲟⲟⲡ instead of ⲉⲩϣⲟⲟⲡ is in accordance with the standard usage of the text
(compare 45.14; 56.11–12).
46.10 Supralinear stroke over first ⲙ is restored.

These three represent the active aspects of the second being in the divine
hierarchy ("insofar as she empowers the individuals, she is a triply-male being"
45.36–38).

The term 'male' here clearly does not refer to biological sexuality or gender,
but connotes a kind of transcendental perfection (see above, note to 45.17b–
22a). In ancient Pythagorean thought, as described by Aristotle, 'male' and
'female' belong to a set of ten opposites, identifying the male with positive
principles (limit, odd, one, right, resting, straight, light, good, square) and the
female with negative principles (unlimited, even, plurality, left, moving,
crooked, darkness, bad, oblong). (See Aristotle, *Metaphysics* 986a 22; Burkert,
Lore and Science, 51–52.) Williams states that "within *Zostrianos* the contrast
between 'femaleness' (†ⲙ̄ⲛ̄ⲧϣⲓⲙⲉ) and 'maleness' (†ⲙ̄ⲛ̄ⲧϩⲟⲟⲩⲧ) apparently
expresses this ascetic disassociation from the body" (*The Immovable Race*, 99).
In our text, however, there is no evidence for ascetic practice (though it would
not be inconsistent with the teaching of the text).

The expressions "to empower" (ⲭⲓ ϭⲟⲙ; 45.24) and "to receive power"
(†ϭⲟⲙ; 45.36) appear frequently in the text. They denote the direction in
which "capacity" or "potentiality" is directed, always from a higher to a lower
being. In *Allogenes*, the capacity to give or receive is either 1) the capacity to
come into being or 2) the capacity for knowledge of higher things (for example, 50.6; 52.15). The two meanings are, however, closely linked; indeed
'being' and 'knowing' in this text are nearly synonymous. Both are conceived
hierarchically; there are pyramidal gradations of being and of knowing.
Knowledge of higher things can only come to a lower being from beings that
have a higher ontological status. The power or capacity to be, to know, and to
act is dependent upon one's place in that hierarchy.

At 45.38, the phrase ⲕⲁⲧⲁ ⲟⲩⲁ (*καθ' ἕνα*; "one at a time") is used distribu-
tively to indicate a whole divided into parts. Above at 45.20, the Barbelo aeon

46 ¹⁻⁵ [   ] . . .

⁶ [on the one hand,] they exist in[dividually], (but) on the
other hand, they [exist to]gether.

⁷[For, inasmuch as she exi]sts as a s[ubsis]tence
⁸ o[f those] (individuals) and s[ees]
⁹ a[l]l tho[s]e ⟨who⟩ truly ⟨exist⟩,
¹⁰ [she] possesses the divine Au[togen]es.
¹¹ When she came to k[now]

46.6–7 Or: "at one place."
46.10–11 "Autogenes" means "self-generated one."

is described in her wholeness as ογωτ ("single"); now the text expresses her
multiplicity, εϲο κατα ογα ("existing individually").

46.7b–37 This section describes for the first time the process of salvation
(see pp. 5–8). The previous section, 45.31–46.7, described the successive
devolution of beings from the Invisible Spirit. First the Triply-powered, then
Barbelo and her triply-male aspects, Kalyptos, Protophanes, and Autogenes.
Now the same figures are described in reverse order, beginning with Autogenes.

The point of the previous section was the origins of the multiplicity of
being. The point of this section is to describe the return of the (particular) soul
(the referent of feminine pronouns in 46.7–17 and of masculine pronouns in
46.22–36) to knowledge of its true nature and origins and of the true nature
and origins of Being itself. The passage presents a description of the ascending
levels of the aeon of Barbelo: Autogenes, Protophanes, Kalyptos, Barbelo.
This sequence presupposes a movement from plurality ("existing as individuals") toward unity ("existence at one place"). This movement defines the
process of salvation: moving from knowledge of lower things to that of higher
things through a direct vision based upon self-knowledge.

An alternative understanding of the passage is based on reading the feminine pronominal references in 46.7–17 as references to Barbelo. One could
argue that this reading is preferable for two reasons: 1) The direct antecedent,
and hence the proper grammatical referent, is Barbelo not the soul. 2) This
reading rids us of the difficulty of accounting for the pronominal shift from the
feminine in 46.7–17 to the masculine in 46.22–36, since the text uses both
gender pronouns to refer to Barbelo. The counter-argument is that this reading poses three new problems: 1) What is the antecedent or referent of the
masculine pronoun in 46.22–37? 2) How is 46.7–22 related to 46.22–37?
3) It is impossible to comprehend why Barbelo, who is Intellect, should need
to come to know her hypostasis and take her stand (46.11–14); in the rest of
the text, only lower beings, exemplified by Allogenes, need to come to self-
knowledge and stability (compare 58.38–59.1). To presume that Autogenes,

¹² ετετε τωc ν̄ζυπα[ρξιc]

¹³ αγω ν̄ταρεcαζεραт̄[c̄ ζιx̄ν̄]

¹⁴ παï εαϥναγ ενη т[нρογ εγ]

¹⁵ ϣοοπ [κ]ατα ογα ν̄θ[ε ετ̄ϥ]

¹⁶ ϣοο[π м̄]мοc· αγω ε[cϣαν]

¹⁷ ϣωπ[ε εν]тοϥ πε· ε[cε]

¹⁸ ναγ επι[ϣ]м̄ν̄т̄ζοογ[т ν̄]

¹⁹ νογτε· †6ομ ετx[οcε ε]

²⁰ πνογτε· тεν[νοια τε]

²¹ ν̄τε ναï тнρογ ετϣ[οοπ]

²² [ζ]ῑ ογμα εϥϣα[νмοϣτογ]

²³ [εϥ]мογ ϣ̄т̄ м̄[πιπρωτοφα]

²⁴ νнc ν̄νο6 ν̄ζοο[γт . . . .]

²⁵ [.].[. . .ν̄ν]ογc· †ϣ[ο]p̄[π̄ ν̄]

46.13 Turner restores: ν̄ταρεcαζεραт[c̄ αcν̄] ("when she stood, she brought").
46.16–17 Turner restores: αγω ε[таγ] ϣωπ[ε εν]тοϥ πε· ε[γνα] ("And [when they] become as he is, [they shall]").
46.22 Supralinear stroke over ι is restored.
46.23 Supralinear stroke over м is restored.
46.25 Turner restores: [.].[. . .ν]ογc.
46.25 Supralinear stroke over p is restored.

Protophanes, and Kalyptos do not belong to Barbelo by nature, since they derive from her, is inconceivable. One might suggest that the mythology has clouded the philosophical clarity of the presentation, but that only leaves open the question of the passage's purpose and presumes the text is incoherent. On the other hand, understanding the soul to be the pronominal referent connects the passage to the most important theme of the text: that the hierarchical structure of ontology reflects the path to saving knowledge. 45.31–46.11 describes the structure of Being, beginning at the highest level and moving downward; 46.11–37 describes the process and stages of knowledge, beginning with the lowest level and moving upward.

46.11b–22a The soul must first know its own true self, its ζυπαρξιc ("subsistence"). This term refers here to the essential existence of the individual (soul) rooted in the Autogenes aspect of Barbelo (see 46.8–11). Based on a knowledge of self, the soul is able to "take a stand" upon Autogenes. This stability allows the soul to understand the nature of individual or particular existence. Again 'knowing' and 'being' are linked: when one becomes as Autogenes is, one knows (sees) what he knows (sees). The soul then can see the divine Triply-male, described in lines 46.18–22a. The Triply-male is Barbelo. She is described here as divine, a power beyond divinity, the thought of all those who exist in unity.

¹² her own subsi[stence]

¹³ and when she took her sta[nd upon]

¹⁴ This one, a being that saw a[ll] those [that]

¹⁵ exist [in]dividually a[s it] (itself)

¹⁶ exis[ts], and w[hen she]

¹⁷ becom[es what] it is, [she will]

¹⁸ see the divine [Tr]iply-mal[e],

¹⁹ the power that su[rpasses]

²⁰ god. [She is] the th[ought]

²¹ of all those that ex[ist]

²² [to]gether. If one [were to consider them]

²³ [one would] consider [the]

²⁴ great, ma[le . . .]

²⁵ [. . .] no[etic Protopha]nes.

46.21–22 Or: "that exist at one place."
46.25 "Protophanes" means "first-appearing one."

For further discussion of the phrase "to take a stand," see below, note to 58.38b–59.4.

Note the balanced presentation of lines 46.7–11a with 11b–22. In 46.7–11a, the Autogenes aspect of Barbelo is described as the subsistence of the particulars and the vision of those who truly exist. This aspect, Autogenes, is divine (46.11). In 46.11b–22, the soul discovers first its subsistence as an individual (and thus participates in Autogenes who is the subsistence of the individuals), and then is able to receive a vision of the divine Triply-male, the thought of those who exist in unity (that is, "those who truly exist").

To state that Barbelo is a power that "is higher than god" (46.19b–20a) is only to emphasize her exalted nature and the inadequacy of words and concepts such as "god" and "divinity" to describe her. The phrase is more poetry than philosophical proposition.

46.20b–22a states that Barbelo is the thought of all the unified existents. They are in fact unified insofar as she thinks them and they are joined with her. (Compare 45.6–9.)

In other Sethian texts (for example, *ApJohn* II,*1*,5.4), Barbelo is called the "first thought" of the Father or Invisible Spirit. (Compare also *Allogenes* 48.13 and 53.27–28.)

46.22b–30a Following Autogenes, the next stage of the soul's enlightenment is Protophanes. Based on a vision of those who truly exist (in unity in the mind of Barbelo), the soul is able to focus on Protophanes, the hypostasization of the procession of particularized multiplicity from unity.

²⁶ [⳨ⲓⲏ ⲛ̄]ⲧⲉ ⲛⲁⲓ̈ ⲉϣⲱⲡ[ⲉ ⲉϥ]
²⁷ [ϣⲁ]ⲛⲛⲁⲩ ⲉⲣⲟⲥ [ⲉϥⲛⲁⲩ]
²⁸ [ⲟⲛ ⲉⲛⲓⲟ]ⲛ̄ⲧ[ⲱ]ⲥ [ⲉⲧϣⲟⲟⲡ]
²⁹ [ⲉϯ]ϣⲟⲣⲡ̄ ⲛ̄⳨ⲓⲏ ⲁ[ⲉ ⲛ̄ⲛⲏ ⲉⲧ]
³⁰ ⳨ⲓ [ⲟⲩ]ⲙⲁ· ⲡⲏ ⲁⲉ ⲉⲧⲁ[ϥⲛⲁⲩ]
³¹ ⲉⲛ[ⲁ]ⲓ̈ ⲁϥⲛⲁⲩ ⲉⲡⲓⲕⲁⲗ[ⲩⲡⲧⲟⲥ]
³² ⲉϣⲱⲡⲉ ⲁⲉ ⲉϥϣⲁⲛⲛ[ⲁⲩ ⲉ]
³³ ⲡⲟⲩⲁ ⲛ̄ⲧⲉ ⲛⲓⲕⲁⲗⲩⲡⲧ[ⲟⲥ ⲉϥ]
³⁴ ⲛⲁⲩ ⲉⲡⲓⲉⲱⲛ ⲛ̄ⲃⲁⲣⲃⲁⲗⲱ [ⲡⲓ]
³⁵ ⲭⲡⲟ ⲁⲉ ⲛ̄ⲛⲁⲧⲙⲓⲥⲉ ⲛ̄ⲧ[ⲉ ⲡⲏ]
³⁶ ⲉϣⲱⲡⲉ ⲉⲣϣⲁⲛⲟⲩⲁ ⲛ̄[ⲁⲩ]
³⁷ ⲉⲣⲟϥ ⲭⲉ ⲡⲱⲥ ⲉϣⲁϥⲱ[ⲛ̄⳨]

47 ¹⁻⁴ [   ]
⁵ [. . . . . . . ⲁⲕⲥⲱⲧ̄]ⲙ̄ [ⲉⲧⲃⲉ ϯ]
⁶ ⲡⲉⲣ[ⲓ]ⲟⲩⲥⲓⲁ ⲙ̄ⲡ]ⲟⲩⲁ ⲡⲟⲩⲁ
⁷ ⲙ̄ⲙⲟⲟⲩ ⳨ⲛ̄ ⲟ[ⲩⲧⲁ]ⲭⲣⲟ· ⲉⲧⲃⲉ
⁸ ⲡⲓϣⲙ̄ⲛ̄ⲧ⳽ⲟⲙ [ⲁⲉ] ⲛ̄ⲁ⳨ⲟⲣ[ⲁ]ⲧⲟ[ⲛ]·
⁹ ⲙ̄ⲡⲛ̄ⲁ ⲥⲱⲧⲙ̄·
[ϥϣ]ⲟⲟ[ⲡ] ⲉⲟⲩ[ⲁ]
¹⁰ ⲡⲉ ⲛ̄ⲛⲁⲧⲛⲁⲩ ⲉⲣ[ⲟϥ ⲉϥ]ⲟ ⲛ̄ⲛⲁ[ⲧ]

47.5 Turner restores: [ⲉⲧⲃⲉ ⲧ]. Supralinear stroke over ⲙ is restored.
47.10 Supralinear stroke over second ⲛ is restored.

46.30b–34a The highest being of the Barbelo triad is Kalyptos, the hypostasization of the unity of the particulars. That Kalyptos, like his fellows, is both singular and multiple is shown by the phrase ⲡⲟⲩⲁ ⲛ̄ⲧⲉ ⲛⲓⲕⲁⲗⲩⲡⲧⲟⲥ ("the one of the hidden ones"). When the soul reaches the level of Kalyptos, it understands the unity (the "Hidden one") behind multiplicity ("the hidden ones"). This comprehension allows it to receive a vision (or understanding) of Barbelo since the individuals are unified in her (compare 45.6–9).

46.34–37 [ⲡⲓ]ⲭⲡⲟ ⲁⲉ ⲛ̄ⲛⲁⲧⲙⲓⲥⲉ ⲛ̄ⲧ[ⲉ ⲡⲏ] (lines 34–35) is in extraposition with ⲉⲣⲟϥ in line 37.

The "unborn offspring" are the individual, noetic existents belonging to Barbelo.

47.5–48.38 This section provides a description of the Triply-powered Invisible Spirit (see also pp. 19–29).

47.5–9a These lines provide a transition from a description of the process of salvation to a revelation about the Invisible Spirit. At this point, Allogenes

26 Wh[eneve]r [one]

27 sees the first procession of those ones, [one will also see]

28 [those who t]ru[l]y [exist]

29 [since] (it is) the first procession [of those who are]

30 to[ge]ther. This one, however, when he saw

31 those ones, he saw Kal[yptos].

32 For whenever one s[ees]

33 the One of the hidd[en] ones, [one will]

34 see the aeon of Barbelo.

35 But as regards [the] unborn offspring belonging [to That one],

36 if one s[ees]

37 how it li[ves] . . .

47 1–4 [   ] . . .

5 [you have hear]d [about this]

6 superabu[n]dan[ce of e]ach one

7 of them with [cer]tainty.

8 [But] hear (now) about the Triply- powered Invis[i]bl[e]

9 Spirit!

[He ex]is[ts] as an

10 invisib[le] On[e], [bei]ng

46.30 Or: "at one place."
46.31 "Kalyptos" means the "hidden one."
46.33 Here the term for "hidden ones" is "kalyptos" with the plural definite article. Hence there is a connection between seeing Kalyptos ("the hidden one"; 46.31) and seeing the "hidden ones" (46.33).
46.37 Or: "how he lives . . ."
47.8–9 Or: "the invisible, spiritual Triply-powered."

has come to a firm understanding about the lower hypostases; now he will receive revelation about the Triply-powered Invisible Spirit.

The name of the figure discussed is ⲡⲓϣⲙⲛ̄ⲧ̄ϭⲟⲙ ⲛ̄ⲁϩⲟⲣⲁⲧⲟⲛ ⲙ̄ⲡ̄ⲛ̄ⲁ̄ (47.8–9). Coptic grammar understands ⲡⲓϣⲙⲛ̄ⲧ̄ϭⲟⲙ to be the kernel of the sentence, and ⲛ̄ⲁϩⲟⲣⲁⲧⲟⲛ and ⲙ̄ⲡ̄ⲛ̄ⲁ̄ to be modifiers (that is, "the Invisible, Spiritual Triply-powered"). It is possible, however, to understand ϣⲙⲛ̄ⲧ̄ϭⲟⲙ and ⲁϩⲟⲣⲁⲧⲟⲛ as modifiers of ⲡ̄ⲛ̄ⲁ̄, since ⲡ̄ⲛ̄ⲁ̄ is a noun (in Greek) and the name of the highest figure. The "Invisible Spirit" is a commonplace in Sethian texts.

47.9b–38 This passage provides a description of the Invisible Spirit couched in primarily philosophical terminology. Its primary point is to emphasize his surpassing transcendence and his relation to the existents.

¹¹ ⲧⲁϩⲟϥ ⲛⲁⲩ ⲧⲏⲣⲟⲩ ⲉⲟⲩⲛ̄

¹² ⲧⲁϥ ⲛ̄ⲛⲏ ⲧⲏⲣⲟⲩ ϩⲣⲁⲓ̈ ⲛ̄ϩⲏⲧ̄[ϥ]

¹³ [ⲉⲩ]ϣⲟⲟⲡ ⲅⲁⲣ ⲧⲏⲣⲟⲩ ⲉⲧⲃ[ⲏ]

¹⁴ [ⲏⲧ̄ϥ· ⲉ]ⲩⲧⲉⲗⲓⲟⲛ ⲡⲉ ⲁⲩⲱ ⲉ

¹⁵ [ⲛⲉ]ⲁϥ ⲉⲧⲉⲗⲓⲟⲥ· ⲁ[ⲩ]ⲱ ⲉⲩⲙⲁ

¹⁶ ⲕⲁⲣⲓⲟⲥ ⲡⲉ· ⲉⲟ[ⲩⲁ ⲡ]ⲉ ⲛ̄ⲟⲩⲟ

¹⁷ ⲉⲓϣ ⲛⲓⲙ· ⲁⲩⲱ [ⲉϥ]ϣⲟⲟⲡ ⲛ̄

¹⁸ [ϩⲏⲧⲟ]ⲩ ⲧⲏⲣⲟⲩ· ⲉⲩⲁⲧϣⲁϫⲉ

¹⁹ [ⲙ̄ⲙ]ⲟϥ [ⲡ]ⲉ ⲛ̄ⲛⲁⲧϯ ⲣⲁⲛ ⲉⲣⲟϥ

²⁰ [ⲉⲟⲩⲁ] ⲡⲉ ⲉϥϣⲟⲟⲡ ⲉⲃⲟⲗ ϩⲓ

²¹ [ⲧⲟⲟⲧⲟ]ⲩ ⲧⲏⲣⲟⲩ· ⲡⲏ ⲉⲧⲉ [ⲉ]

²² [ϣⲱⲡⲉ ⲉⲣϣⲁ]ⲛⲟⲩⲁ ⲣ̄ⲛⲟⲉ[ⲓ ⲙ̄]

²³ [ⲙⲟϥ ⲙⲉϥⲟⲩ]ⲉϣ ⲗⲁⲁⲩ ⲉϥ

²⁴ [ϣⲟⲟⲡ ϩⲁⲧ]ⲉϥⲉϩⲏ ⲛ̄ⲧ[ⲉ] ⲛⲏ

²⁵ [ⲉⲧⲉ ⲟⲩⲛ̄ⲧⲁ]ⲩ ⲛ̄ⲛⲟⲩϩ̣[ⲩ]ⲡⲁⲣ

²⁶ [ϫⲓⲥ· ⲛ̄ⲧⲟϥ] ⲅⲁⲣ ⲡⲉ ⲧⲡ[ⲏⲅ]ⲏ

47.12 Supralinear stroke over ⲧ is restored; letter is clear.
47.14 Restoration of [ⲏⲧ̄ϥ· by Turner; restoration of ⲉ] by King.
47.26 Turner restores: ⲛ̄ⲧⲁϥ.

He exists (47.9b). Behind the Coptic ϣⲟⲟⲡ and ϣⲱⲡⲉ, we can perhaps read the Greek distinction between Being and becoming. If so, this verb defines his ontological status as Being.

The implications of the Invisible Spirit's ontological status as Being are spelled out in detail in what follows (47.9b–21a). He is One or single, that is, he is a monad. He is invisible, an attribute which follows from his incorporeality; he is not sensible. He is incomprehensible to the individuated particulars, even though he contains them. The adjective ⲁⲧⲧⲁϩⲟϥ should probably be understood in both of its implications: 1) spatially he cannot be reached or touched, and 2) intellectually he cannot be known. Hence he is ineffable and unnameable.

He is the cause of all existents (47.13–14); he is the source or fount from which they were all sent forth (47.26–28). He is also the place of the existents. They exist in him (47.11–12) and at the same time, insofar as it can be said that he has subsistence (ϩⲩⲡⲁⲣϫⲓⲥ), he exists in and through them (47.17–18). Thus they cannot "comprehend" him, because they are in him. And they cannot surpass him in excellence (47.22–26) because he is in them and is their source. Yet his existence in and through them does not imply a loss of his essential oneness (47.16–17, 20–21).

This discussion concerning the relation of the Triply-powered Invisible

11 i[n]comprehensible to them all, containing
12 all those inside [himself]–
13 for it is be[cause of him that they] all exist–
14 [(for) he is] perfect and is
15 [gre]ater than perfect, a[n]d is blessed;
16 he is On[e] at
17 all times and exists
18 in them all; he is ineffable,
19 unnameable;
20 [he is a single] One who exists thr[ough]
21 them all–that one who is such that
22 [if] one should concei[ve]
23 [him, one would not de]sire anything which
24 [exists pri]or to him amon[g] those
25 [who have] s[u]bsis[tence].
26 For he is the so[urc]e

47.14 Or: "He is a perfect one."
47.15 Or: "He is a blessed one."
47.23–26 This sentence may reflect a misunderstanding by the Coptic translator of the underlying Greek text which probably meant to state that nothing which has substance could exist prior to the Invisible Spirit.

Spirit to the existents is expressed in philosophical terms. Although there was considerable discussion among the philosophical schools concerning what qualities could be properly attributed to primary substances, all the schools accept certain definitions and propositions laid out in Aristotle's *Categories*. Thus the language used to describe the Invisible Spirit implies:

that those things which are in him have no existence apart from him (see *Cat.* II, 1a);
that he is a primary substance insofar as everything is present in him (see *Cat.* V, 2b);
and that the existents are correlative to the Invisible Spirit insofar as he is their source (hence one can say he exists through them; see *Cat.* VII, 7b).

The entire phrase following ⲡⲏ (in line 21) is an elaboration of ⲡⲏ in free apposition. Lines 47.21b–26a express the Invisible Spirit's superiority in quality. There is, however, some confusion in the Coptic or in Turner's restoration at line 24, since the phrase seems to imply that the existents are in some sense "prior" to the Invisible Spirit. This flatly contradicts lines 13–14 and 26–28. The sense of the passage must be that nothing that possesses subsistence exists

²⁷ [ⲛ̄ⲧⲁⲩⲧⲁⲩⲟⲟⲩ ⲧⲏⲣ]ⲟ̣[ⲩ ⲉ]ⲃⲟⲗ
²⁸ [ⲛ̄ϩⲏⲧⲥ̄· ⲉⲩϣⲟⲣⲡ̄ ⲡⲉ ϩⲁⲑⲏ ⲛ̄]
²⁹ [ⲧⲙ̄ⲛ̄ⲧⲧⲉ]ⲗⲓⲟⲥ ⲛⲉ[ⲩϣⲟⲣⲡ̄ ⲡⲉ]
³⁰ [ϩⲁⲑⲏ ⲙ̄]ⲙ̄ⲛ̄ⲧⲛⲟⲩⲧ[ⲉ ⲛⲓⲙ·]
³¹ ⲁ[ⲩⲱ] ⲉⲩϣⲟⲣⲡ̄ ⲡⲉ ϩⲁ[ⲑⲏ ⲙ̄]
³² ⲙ̄ⲛ̄[ⲧ̄]ⲙⲁⲕⲁⲣⲓⲟⲥ ⲛⲓⲙ[·] ⲉϥ
³³ ⲥⲁϩⲛⲉ ⲛ̄ⲥⲁ ϭⲟⲙ ⲛⲓⲙ· ⲁⲩⲱ
³⁴ ⲟⲩⲟⲩⲥⲓⲁ ⟨ⲡⲉ⟩ ⲉⲩⲙ̄ⲛ̄ⲧⲁⲧⲟⲩⲥⲓⲁ
³⁵ ⲡⲉ ⲉⲩⲛⲟⲩⲧⲉ ⲡⲉ ⲉⲙ̄ⲛ̄ ⲙ̄ⲛ̄
³⁶ ⲧⲛⲟⲩⲧⲉ ϩ̄ⲓ̈ⲭⲱϥ· ⲡⲏ ⲉⲧⲉ
³⁷ ⲡⲓϩⲟⲩⲉ ⲟⲩⲱⲧ̄ⲃ ⲛ̄ⲧⲉ ⲧⲉϥ
³⁸ ⲙ̄ⲛ̄ⲧⲛⲟϭ ⲙ̄ⲛ̄ ✝ⲙ̄ⲛ̄ⲧⲥⲁⲉⲓ ⲛ·

48 ¹⁻⁵ [   ]
   ⁶ [ϭ]ⲁⲙ·
        ⲟⲩⲁ[ⲧϭⲁⲙ ⲁⲛ] ⲧ[ⲉ ⲛ̄ⲧⲁⲩ]
   ⁷ ⲉⲭⲓ ⲛ̄ⲟⲩⲱⲛ̄[ϩ̄ ⲉ]ⲃⲟⲗ ⲛ̄ⲧ[ⲉ] ⲛⲁⲓ̈
   ⁸ ⲉϣⲱⲡⲉ [ⲉⲩϣ]ⲁⲛⲉⲓ ⲉⲩⲙⲁ·

47.30 Supralinear stroke over ⲙⲛⲧ is restored; ⲛⲧ letters are clear.
47.32 Supralinear stroke over ⲙⲛⲧ is restored; ⲙ is clear.
47.33 Supralinear stroke over ⲛ is restored.
47.38 Turner emends: ✝ⲙ̄ⲛ̄ⲧⲥⲁⲉⲓ⟨ⲉ⟩·.
48.7 Supralinear stroke over second and third ⲛ's and dots over ⲓ are restored; the
letters of the third ⲛ and ⲓ are clear.

prior to the Invisible Spirit. Hence if one can conceive him, nothing else is
desirable.

The category of quality applies to the Invisible Spirit as well, insofar as one
can say the he is blessed (47.15–16). Yet the text states outright that he is
beyond perfection (47.14–15), that he is prior to everything that has subsistence (47.23–26); he is prior to perfection, divinity and blessedness (47.28–
33). According to Aristotle's *Categories* 12, one can use the word 'prior' in five
senses. Three could possibly be meant here:

1. he is prior in terms of sequence (he is their source, 47.26);
2. he is prior in the sense that what is better and more honorable has a
   natural priority (he is beyond perfect, 47.14–15);
3. he is prior as cause to effect (he sent them all forth, 47.27–28; he
   provides for every power, 47.32–33).

His priority thus is not temporal or simply a matter of order, but in substance,
quality, and power. The text states that the Invisible Spirit is their cause *out of*
which (substance), *from* which (relation), *in* which (place), and *prior to* which

27 [from which they were al]l [sent] forth;
28 [he is prior to]
29 [per]fect[ion], being [prior]
30 [to every] divinit[y]
31 a[nd] prior t[o]
32 every blessedness since he
33 provides for every power. And
34 ⟨he is⟩ a nonsubstantial substance;
35 he is a god above whom there is no
36 god—the one who is such that
37 the great surpassing of his
38 greatness and the beauty . . .

48 1-5 [   ] . . .
     6 [p]ower.
        I[t] is [not] im[possible for them]
     7 to receive a revela[ti]on o[f] those ones
     8 if [they] come to one place,

(quality), they exist. These four categories are, in Aristotle's view, those which are applicable to the non-material sphere: substance, relation, place, and quality. This position places *Allogenes* in opposition to Plotinus who argues that the category of quality (as well as quantity, time, position, state, action and affection) is not applicable to the intelligible world (see *Ennead* II.6).

Yet, while Aristotle can hold that: "The most distinctive mark of substance appears to be that, while remaining numerically one and the same, it is capable of admitting contrary qualities" and that substances do so by "themselves changing" (*Cat.* V, 4a), *Allogenes* will insist that the Invisible Spirit is both ογϲιа ("substance") and м̄ñ̄тагоγϲιа ("substancelessness"). The point is that while the Invisible Spirit can be said to be primary substance in terms of substance, relation, place, and quality as was outlined above, on the other hand, he is not subject to change even when seeming to admit of contrary qualities. In this latter sense he is not substance in Aristotelian terms.

The Invisible Spirit does possess qualities—deity, greatness, and beauty are predicated of him—but only to the most superior degree (47.35b–38; compare *Cat.* V, 4a. lines 2–4). Here, as elsewhere in the text, the statements of quality seem more poetic praise, such as is found in the *Three Steles of Seth*, than precise philosophical statement.

48.6–12a Concerning the individuals and those who truly exist, see pp. 31–32 and note to 45.6–9a.

This passage provides an example of the principle that differentiation and

⁹ επιΔΗ [ογⲘⲚ]ⲧⲁⲧ6ⲁⲙ ⲧⲉ ⲛ̄
¹⁰ ⲧⲉ ⲛⲓⲕ[ⲁⲧⲁ ο]ⲅⲁ ⲉⲧⲁ2ⲉ ⲡⲧⲏⲣ̄ϥ
¹¹ ⲉⲧⲕ[ⲏ 2̄]ⲙ̄ [ⲡ]ⲙⲁ ⲉⲧⲭⲟⲥⲉ ⲉⲧⲉ
¹² ⲗⲓⲟⲥ· ⲉϣⲁⲅⲭⲓ ⲇⲉ ⲉⲃⲟⲗ 2̄ⲓⲧⲟ
¹³ οⲧⲥ̄ ⲛ̄ⲟⲅϣⲟⲡ̄ⲡ ⲛ̄ⲉⲛⲛ[ο]ⲓⲁ·
¹⁴ [ⲛ̄]ⲑⲉ ⲙ̄ⲡϣⲱⲡⲉ ⲁⲛ·
                            ⲁⲗ[ⲗⲁ ⲣⲱ]
¹⁵ ⲉϥ† ⲙ̄[ⲡ]ϣⲱⲡⲉ ⲙ̄ⲛ [ⲡ]ⲏ [ⲉⲧ]
¹⁶ 2ⲏⲡ ⲛ̄ⲧ[ⲉ] ⲑⲩⲡⲁⲣ3ⲓⲥ· ⲉϥ[ⲁ2]

48.9 Turner does not restore the supralinear stroke above ⲙⲛ̄.
48.11 The supralinear stroke above ⲙ is restored.
48.14 The supralinear stroke above the ⲛ is partially preserved.

individuation are considered to be processes of degeneration. This view is common in Platonism (see, for example, Origen, *De Prin.* II,1.1, and II,9.2 and 6, where the explanation of evil is tied to the fall of created rational minds away from oneness with the Father into diversity and variety). Zandee summarizes:

> Gnosticism and Neoplatonism have in common the consideration of unity as a higher level of being. Plurality is a transition to a lower level. It is progress to turn oneself from differentiation into oneness.
>
> (Zandee, *Terminology*, p. 24)

Presupposing this principle, *Allogenes* is concerned with the question of what lower, differentiated individuals can know of the Entirety (that is, of those who truly exist). It states that, on the one hand, individuals *per se* cannot themselves attain the Entirety, but they can receive a revelation of it if they are able to "come to one place," that is, if they achieve a state of unity.

This interpretation of the passage supposes that the plural pronoun (ⲛⲧⲁⲩ and ⲉⲩϣⲁⲛ, lines 6 and 8 respectively) refers to ⲛⲓⲕⲁⲧⲁ ⲟⲩⲁ ("the individuals," line 10). The strongest argument for taking ⲛⲧⲁⲩ and ⲉⲩϣⲁⲛ together is the use of the verb ⲉⲓ ("come"). If the plural referred to the ideas, one would expect ⲕⲏ ("situated"), as in line 11 below. ⲛⲁⲓ ⲉϣⲱⲡⲉ ⲉⲩϣⲁⲛⲉⲓ ⲉⲩⲙⲁ ("those who exist having come to one place," lines 7–8) refers to ⲡⲧⲏⲣϥ ("the Entirety," line 10). The second sentence (lines 9–12a) thus provides the key to understanding the first (lines 6–8): it is impossible for individuals to understand something of those who truly exist, unless the individuals themselves attain to unity.

That unity could possibly be attained in cultic practice (compare *StSeth* 120.26–121.14). In the context of *Allogenes*, unity may refer to the visionary ritual of ascent whereby the (Gnostic) soul rises above its inferior state of multiplicity, division, and instability toward a vision of the transcendent Entirety.

⁹ although it is impossi[bl]e
¹⁰ for in[dividu]als to attain to the Entirety
¹¹ which is loc[ated i]n [the] place that is exalted beyond
¹² perfection. For it is through
¹³ a first thou[g]ht that they receive,
¹⁴ not [in] the manner that pertains to (the realm) of becoming.
　　Bu[t indeed]
¹⁵ it is to (the realm) of becoming and (to) [t]h[at]
¹⁶ hidden one belong[ing] to subsistence that he gives, pro[vi]ding

48.11–12 Or: "the place that is higher than perfect."
48.13 "First thought" is probably a Coptic rendering of the Greek Protennoia.

The phrase ετκη ϩⲙ ⲡⲙⲁ ετχοϲε ετⲉⲗⲓοϲ ("which is loc[ated i]n [the] place that is exalted beyond perfection"; 48.11–12a) expresses the utter transcendence of the Entirety.

A second possibility for interpreting this passage is to restore ⲛⲧⲁⲕ ("for you") instead of ⲛⲧⲁⲩ ("for them") in line 6. The sentence would then be understood: "it is not impossible for you (Allogenes) to receive a revelation of the Entirety in its unity." This restoration, however, is less congruent with what follows where the subject is in the plural.

48.12b–14a The object of χⲓ in line 12 is understood to be the same as in line 7: ⲛⲟⲩⲱⲛϩ ⲉⲃⲟⲗ ("revelation"). The revelation is mediated by the first thought (Ennoia), that is, Barbelo (compare with *ApJohn* II.*1*, 4.21–5.11 and *Allogenes* 53.27–28). Turner suggests that "first thought" may "refer intentionally both to (human) pre-noetic intuition . . . and to divine revelation in quasi-hypostatic form" ("Allogenes," 250).

The phrase ⲛ̄ⲑⲉ ⲙ̄ⲡϣⲱⲡⲉ ⲁⲛ ("not in the manner of becoming") is an adverbial qualifier of χⲓ ("receive"). ⲡϣⲱⲡⲉ is here the equivalent to the Greek γίνεσθαι. The import of the phrase is that revelation cannot be received by those who are bound to the lower ontological level of becoming, but only by those who belong to the higher noetic sphere of Being. Like the phrase "higher than perfect," this phrase is meant to stress the transcendent nature of the revelation. The phrase further implies that true knowledge is mediated solely through divine revelation, not through the kind of knowledge obtained from lower beings or through the study or contemplation of generated things.

48.14b–17a The text here makes a parenthetical remark, explaining the relation of the Invisible Spirit to the sphere of becoming. The phrase "the hidden one belonging to subsistence" clearly refers to the Kalyptos aeon of Barbelo (compare 45.31–33; 46.7–9). The import of the sentence here is thus to explain that even though revelation does not pertain to the realm of

¹⁷ ne n̄cⲱ[q n̄]ϩⲱⲃ nim· ϫe ⲡⲏ

¹⁸ n̄toq e[te]qeϣⲱⲡe eqϣⲁn

¹⁹ ⲣ̄noei m̄moq· ⲡⲁï ⲇe ⲡe [oⲩⲁ]

²⁰ eqⲕⲏ eϩⲣⲁï n̄oⲩⲗⲁ[eiⲇe n̄ϣⲱ]

²¹ [ⲡ]e m̄n oⲩⲡⲏⲅⲏ· ⲁⲩⲱ [oⲩϩⲩ]

²² [ⲗ]ⲏ n̄nⲁtϩⲩⲗⲏ [m̄n oⲩⲏⲡe]

²³ n̄ⲁtⲏⲡe [m̄n oⲩeiⲇoc n̄ⲁt]

²⁴ eiⲇoc[·] m̄n oⲩm[oⲣⲫⲏ n̄ⲁt]

²⁵ mo[ⲣ]ⲫⲏ· m̄n o[ⲩⲁtϭⲁm m̄n]

²⁶ oⲩ[ϭ]ⲁm[· m̄]n̄ o[ⲩoⲩciⲁ n̄ⲁt]

²⁷ oⲩ[c]ḭ[ⲁ m̄n oⲩ . . . .]

²⁸ [. . . . . . m̄n oⲩeneⲣⲅiⲁ]

²⁹ [n̄ⲁten]eⲣⲅiⲁ ⲁ[ⲩⲱ eqe]

³⁰ [n̄oⲩⲣe]qcⲁϩne n̄[te ϩn̄cⲁϩ]

³¹ n[e m̄]n̄ oⲩm̄n̄tnoⲩt[e n̄]te

³² tm̄n̄tnoⲩte

48.20–21 Restoration of n̄oⲩⲗⲁ[eiⲇe by King; restoration of n̄ϣⲱⲡ]e by Turner.
48.23 The supralinear stroke over n is restored; the letter is clear.
48.27 Turner restores: [oⲩⲕinⲏcic], a Greek term otherwise not attested in *Allogenes*.
48.28 Turner restores: [n̄ⲁtⲕim· m̄n oⲩeneⲣⲅiⲁ].
48.29 Turner restores: ⲁ[ⲗⲗⲁ eqe] ("Yet he is").
48.30 The supralinear stroke over n is restored.
48.31 Turner restores the supralinear stroke above the second m̄n even though it is clear in the *Facsimile Edition*, 54.
48.32 The supralinear stroke over mn is restored; the letter m is clear.

becoming, the unified individuals (Kalyptos) and everything that has come into being ultimately derive from the Invisible Spirit.

eqcⲁϩne n̄cⲱq n̄ϩⲱⲃ nim ("he provides everything for himself") is a statement of the self-sufficiency of the deity that guards against possible charges that the Invisible Spirit lacks unity or transcendence, charges which might be implied by the derivation of becoming from the transcendent realm (compare 66.25–28).

48.17b–19a ϫe ⲡⲏ n̄toq is to be understood as a reduced cleft sentence with the absolute pronoun under the influence of the *Verstarker* n̄toq. ⲡe has dropped out. (See Polotsky, *Collected Papers*, 400; Schenke, *Das Matthäus-Evangelium*, 193.)

This sentence affirms that the self-generation of the Invisible Spirit comes about through self-comprehension (compare 63.14–16, 28–30).

48.19b–32a This passage discusses the relation of the Invisible Spirit to everything which exists.

¹⁷ everything for [himself]. For it is that one
¹⁸ himself wh[o w]ill come into being if he
¹⁹ conceives himself. For this one is [One]
²⁰ who is situated as a ca[use of Be]ing
²¹ and a source and [an]
²² immaterial [matt]er [and a]
²³ numberless [number and a] form[less
²⁴ form] and a sha[p]e[less]
²⁵ s[hape] and a [powerless one with]
²⁶ [p]ower [a]nd a [non]sub[st]an[tial]
²⁷ [substance and a . . .]
²⁸ [. . . and an ina]ctive
²⁹ [activity], a[lso being]
³⁰ [a] provide[r] o[f provi]si[ons]
³¹ [a]nd a divinit[y o]f
³² divinity.

The Invisible Spirit is the One (compare 48.20).

The conjunctive ⲁⲅⲱ (48.21) joins the statement that the Invisible Spirit is the cause and source of everything (48.20–21a) with the explanation of how he is the cause and source in terms of predicates and their privatives (48.21b–32a). Matter (ὕλη), number, form (εἶδος), power, substance (οὐσία), and activity (ἐνέργεια) can all be predicated of everything that exists. These apply to the Invisible Spirit, however, only as source and cause, not in and of himself. They apply to him in the sense that everything which exists derives from him, but these predicates do not describe him as he is in himself. He can, however, be described metaphorically as a "provider of provisions" and a "divinity of divinity"; the first phrase stresses his role as sustainer, the second his exalted status.

Compare Plotinus, *Ennead* V.1.7. 18–27. Plotinus calls the One, the "Form of the Firsts, the Formless Form" (*Ennead* VI.7.17). Similarly, the Invisible Spirit of *Allogenes* is the source of everything, without himself being numbered among those things.

A second possible interpretation of this passage is that these "opposites" are both contained in the One. Whittaker writes that:

An ultimate One might be understood to transcend the opposites in either of two ways. Either (1) the One combines in itself in some manner the opposing characteristics of both sides of the Pythagorean table of opposites, or (2) the One transcends the opposites in the sense that though the opposites are derived from it they are not present in it.

("Neopythagoreanism and the Transcendent Absolute," 77)

ⲁⲗ[ⲗ]ⲁ [ⲉ]ϣⲱ

³³ ⲡⲉ ⲉⲩϣⲁⲛⲭⲓ ⲉϣⲁⲩⲭⲓ ⲉⲃⲟⲗ

³⁴ ϩⲛ ⲧϣⲟⲣⲡ ⲙ̅ⲙⲛ̅ⲧⲱⲛϩ̅· ⲙⲛ̅

³⁵ ⲟⲩⲉⲛⲉⲣⲅⲓⲁ ⲛ̅ⲁⲧⲡⲱⲣⲝ̅·

³⁶ ⲟⲩϩⲩⲡⲟⲥⲧⲁⲥⲓⲥ ⟨ⲧⲉ⟩ ⲛ̅ⲧⲉ ⲧϣⲟ

³⁷ ⲣⲡ̅ ⲛ̅ⲧⲉ ⲡⲟⲩⲁ ⲉⲧϣⲟⲟⲡ

³⁸ ⲟⲛⲧⲱⲥ· ⲟⲩⲙⲁϩϲⲛ̅ⲧⲉ ⲇⲉ

49

¹ ⲛ̅ⲉⲛⲉⲣⲅⲓⲁ ⲉ[   ]

² [. .]ⲇⲉ ⲡⲉ ⲡⲉ[   ]

³ [. . . . .]ⲟⲩⲧ[   ]

⁴ [   ]

⁵ [. . .]. . .[. . .ⲟ]ⲩⲛ̅ⲧ[ⲁϥ ⲛ̅]

⁶ ⲟⲩⲙ̅ⲛ̅ⲧⲙⲁⲕ[ⲁⲣⲓⲟⲥ] ⲙⲛ̅ ⲟⲩⲙ̅[ⲛ̅ⲧ]

⁷ ⲁⲅⲁⲑⲟⲥ·

48.36 Turner does not emend.
49.5 The supralinear stroke above ⲛ is restored; the letter is clear.
49.6 The supralinear stroke above the third ⲙ is restored.

The problem with option one here is that the predicates listed in 48.19b–32a are not really "opposites" in the Pythagorean sense (like male and female, right and left), but predicates of existence. They do not express opposites, but deny predication altogether.

48.32b–49.7a This statement continues the presentation of the relation of existents to the One. Though he is their source and cause, they do not receive life and activity from him directly. "Activity" here refers specifically to "existence in action" as opposed to δύναμις ("power, potentiality"). (See Aristotle, *Metaphysics* 8, 6; Plotinus, *Ennead* V,4.2.) They receive from an hypostasis of the One who truly exists. This hypostasis, Vitality, is later attributed to the Triply-powered (49.28–30) and also appears independently during Allogenes' ascent (59.13–15; 60.19–20). The point again is to indicate, on the one hand, that everything has its ultimate source in the One, but, on the other hand, that the One is itself beyond life and activity. Compare Plotinus:

> Giving need not comport possessing; in this order we are to think of a giver as a greater and of a gift as a lower; this is the meaning of origin among real Beings. First there must be an actualized thing; its laters must be potentially their own priors; a first must transcend its derivatives; the giver transcends the given, as a superior. If therefore there is a prior to actuality, that prior transcends Activity and so transcends Life.

But [w]henever
33 they receive, it is
34 from the first Vitality and
35 an undivided activity that they receive.
36 ⟨She is⟩ an hypostasis of the
37 First belonging to the One who truly exists.
38 But a second

49   1 activity [. . .   ]
    2-4 [   ]
    5 [. . . He po]sess[es]
    6 ble[ssed]ness and
    7 goodn[ess].

49.7-21 This passage is difficult to read because of the lack of clarity regarding the antecedents of the pronouns. I interpret the text as is paraphrased: For whenever the Triply-powered is recognized as the (mediating) ferryman of the boundlessness of the Invisible Spirit, for the Triply-powered is situated in the Invisible Spirit, Barbelo will turn herself toward the Invisible Spirit in order that Barbelo might understand what the Triply-powered is, that is, the Triply-powered which is in the Invisible Spirit, and in what manner the Invisible Spirit (or the Triply-powered?) exists. And the Triply-powered was becoming a salvation for everyone, insofar as the Triply-powered exists as a cause for those who truly exist. For through the Triply-powered, the Invisible Spirit's Knowledge looked out— for it is the Triply-powered who knows what the Invisible Spirit is." See exegetical notes and the Introduction pp. 28-29 for further comments.

The Intellectual-Principle contains life, and the giver of this life is therefore a principle of greater good, of greater worth than Life; in gaining life the Intellectual-Principle had no need to look for it to any given in possession of Life's variety.   (*Ennead* VI.7.17)

(See also Hadot, "Être, vie, pensée," 133-137.)

48.38b-49.7a One might speculate that the lacuna here included a description of the second and third hypostases of the triad Vitality-Intellection-Existence (compare 49.26-38; see pp. 20-28). The terms "blessedness" and "goodness" (49.6-7) might also be associated with the triad (see 58.12-21). Compare *Zostrianos* 15.4-12, where the following triads are associated:

Vitality	Autogenes	(Goodness?)
Knowledge	Protophanes	Blessedness
Existence	Kalyptos	Divinity

Allogenes 52.29-32 states clearly that the Triply-powered exists in blessedness

ϫⲉ [ⲉϣⲱ]ⲡⲉ ⲉⲩϣ[ⲁⲛ]
8 ⲡ̅ⲛⲟⲉⲓ ⲙ̅ⲙⲟϥ ⲙ̅[ⲡⲓⲣⲉ]ϥϫⲓⲟⲟⲣ
9 ⲛ̅ⲧⲙ̅ⲛ̅ⲧⲁⲧ̅ⲛ̅ⲁⲣ[ⲏⲭⲥ̅] ⲛ̅ⲧⲉ ⲡⲁ
10 ϩⲟⲣⲁⲧⲟⲛ ⲙ̅ⲡ̅ⲛ̅[ⲁ̅ ⲉⲧⲕ]ⲏ ⲛ̅ϩⲣⲁ[ⲓ̈]
11 ⲛ̅ϩⲏⲧϥ̅ ⲉⲥⲕⲱⲧⲉ ⲙ̅ⲙⲟ⟨ⲥ⟩ ⲉⲣ[ⲟϥ]
12 [ϩ̅]ⲓⲛⲁ ϫⲉ ⲉⲥⲉⲉⲓⲙⲉ ϫⲉ ⲟⲩ ⲡⲉ
13 [ⲡⲏ ⲉ]ⲧⲛ̅ϩⲣⲁⲓ̈ ⲛ̅ϩⲏⲧϥ̅· ⲁⲩⲱ ϫⲉ
14 [ⲉ]ϥ[ϣ]ⲟⲟⲡ ⲛ̅ⲁϣ ⲛ̅ϩⲉ·
ⲁⲩⲱ ⲛ[ⲉ]
15 [ⲣ]ⲉⲡⲁⲓ̈ ϣⲱⲡⲉ ⲛ̅ⲟⲩⲟⲩϫⲁⲓ̈ ⲛ̅
16 [ⲟ]ⲩⲟⲛ ⲛⲓⲙ· ⲉϥϣⲟⲟⲡ ⲛ̅ⲟⲩ
17 ⲗⲁⲉⲓⲃⲉ ⲛ̅ⲛⲓⲟⲛⲧⲱⲥ ⲉⲧϣⲟ
18 ⲟⲡ· ⲉⲃⲟⲗ ⲅⲁⲣ ϩⲓⲧⲙ̅ ⲡⲁⲓ̈ ⲁⲥⲃⲱ
19 ϣⲧ ⲉⲃⲟⲗ ⲛ̅ϭⲓ ⲧⲉϥⲅⲛⲱⲥⲓⲥ·

49.11 Turner does not emend. The manuscript reads: ⲙⲙⲟϥ. The supralinear stroke over ⲙ is restored; the letter is clear.
49.12 The supralinear stroke over ϩⲓ is restored.
49.15 The dots over the first ⲓ are restored; the letter is clear.

and goodness, so we may tentatively suggest that the Triply-powered may also be the pronominal antecedent here.

49.7b–38a This section describes the Triply-powered and its relation to the Invisible Spirit, Barbelo, and the existents.

49.7b–14a The first sentence uses poetic imagery to describe the role of the Triply-powered as the mediator between Barbelo and the Invisible Spirit. The metaphor of a ferryman crossing boundlessness expresses the relationship of the Triply-powered to the Invisible Spirit. The use of the term ⲧⲙ̅ⲛ̅ⲧⲁⲧ̅ⲛ̅ⲁⲣⲏⲭⲥ̅ ("boundlessness"; 49.9) is particularly appropriate. The term suggests "the boundless seas" at the same time that it stresses the philosophical requirement for a mediator between what is transcendent (and therefore boundless and without form) and what is generated (and therefore bounded, having taken on form).

In Plato's *Parmenides* (137D–E), the One is described as ἀπείρων ("boundless"; ⲁⲧ̅ⲛ̅ⲁⲣⲏⲭⲥ̅). Insofar as the One is one, it cannot have parts; having no parts, it can have no beginning, middle, or end and is thus boundless. Compare Plotinus on the relation between the One and Life:

The Life was a vestige of that Primal, not a life lived by it; Life, then as it looked towards That was undetermined; having looked it had determination though That had none. Life looks to unity and is determined by it, taking bound, limit, form. But this form is in the shaped, the shaper

For [wh]eneve[r] it is
8 recognized as [the] ferry[ma]n
9 of the bo[und]lessness of the
10 Invisible Spir[it, being sit]uated
11 in him, she will turn ⟨herself⟩ towar[d him]
12 [in] order that she might understand what it is,
13 [that wh]ich is in him and
14 in what manner he [ex]ists.
     And
15 it was becoming a salvation for
16 every[o]ne, insofar as it exists as a
17 cause for those who truly
18 exist. For through this one
19 its Knowledge looked out—

had none; the limit was not external as something drawn about a magnitude; the limit was that of the multiplicity of the Life there.
                    (*Ennead* VI.7.17; trans. MacKenna)

The concept here is quite similar to that of *Allogenes*, especially when we note our text's association of the One with the Invisible Spirit and the association of Vitality (Life) with the Triply-powered. (Also compare *Allogenes* 63.1–5 concerning the Unknowable.)

A nautical metaphor is also used by Numenius (Des Places, fr. 18; Leemans, fr. 27) to describe how the demiurge (as helmsman) looks to the ideas (stars) in establishing the bonds of harmony around matter (in sailing the seas). Both the helmsman and the ferryman are metaphors for mediation, though they mediate between different levels of the ontological hierarchy. Nautical metaphors, however, are common in Graeco-Roman literature so that there is no reason to posit any kind of literary dependence between *Allogenes* and Numenius.

49.14b–18a This sentence is meant as an explanatory expansion of ⲉϥϣⲟⲟⲡ ⲛ̄ⲁϣ ⲛ̄ϩⲉ ("in what manner it exists"; 49.14a). The Triply-powered exists in the Invisible Spirit as that to which causality may be properly applied. In this sense, the Triply-powered is closely identified with the One, which in 48.20 is called ⲗⲁⲉⲓⲟⲉ ("cause"). This is to say, the One or Invisible Spirit is the absolute and ultimate source of everything which exists, but the Triply-powered is the actual cause of multiplicity in the intelligible realm.

The Triply-powered is a "salvation for everyone" in two senses. First, it is their ontological root. And secondly, it is the mediator of all possible knowledge of the Invisible Spirit through Barbelo. These points are made explicit in what follows.

²⁰ ϫε ⲛ̄ⲧⲟϥ ⲉⲧⲥⲟⲟⲩⲛ ϫε ⲟⲩ
²¹ ⲡⲉ· ⲉⲙⲡⲉⲛⲁϊ ⲁⲉ ⲛ̄ⲗⲁⲁⲩ ⲉⲃ[ⲟⲗ]
²² [ⲛ̄ⲥ]ⲁⲛⲃⲟⲗ ⲛ̄ⲛⲉⲅⲉⲣⲏⲩ· ⲟⲩ[ⲧⲉ]
²³ ⲟⲩϭⲁⲙ· ⲟⲩⲧⲉ ⲟⲩⲧⲁϫⲓⲥ· ⲟⲩ
²⁴ [ⲧ]ⲉ ⲟⲩⲉⲁⲩ. ⲟⲩⲧⲉ ⲟⲩⲉⲱⲛ·
²⁵ [ⲛ̄]ⲧⲟⲟⲩ ⲅⲁⲣ ⲧⲏⲣⲟⲩ ϩⲉⲛϣⲁ
²⁶ [ⲉ]ⲛⲉϩ ⲛⲉ·

ⲧⲙ̄ⲛ̄ⲧⲱⲛ̄ϩ ⲙⲛ̄
²⁷ ⲧⲙ̄ⲛ̄ⲧⲉⲓⲙⲉ· ⲙⲛ̄ ⲡⲉⲧϣⲟ
²⁸ ⲟⲡ ⲛ̄ⲧⲟϥ ⲡⲉ· ⲧⲟⲧⲉ ⲅⲁⲣ ⲡⲏ
²⁹ ⲉⲧⲉ ⲡⲁϊ ⲡⲉ ⲟⲩⲛ̄ⲧⲁϥ ⲛ̄ⲧⲉϥ
³⁰ ⲙ̄ⲛ̄ⲧⲱⲛ̄ϩ ⲉϥⲙⲏⲛ· ⲙⲛ̄ ⲧⲛⲟ
³¹ ⲏⲧⲏⲥ ⲁⲩⲱ ⲡⲱⲛ̄ϩ· ⲉⲟⲩⲛ̄
³² ⲧⲉ ⲧⲙ̄ⲛ̄ⲧⲱⲛ̄ϩ ⲟⲩⲛ̄ⲧⲉⲥ ⲛ̄
³³ ⲧⲙ̄ⲛ̄ⲧⲁⲧⲟⲩⲥⲓⲁ ⲙⲛ̄ ⲧⲙ̄ⲛ̄ⲧ
³⁴ ⲉⲓⲙⲉ· ϯⲛⲟⲏⲧⲏⲥ ⲉⲩⲛ̄
³⁵ ⲧⲁⲥ ⲙ̄ⲡⲱⲛ̄ϩ ⲙⲛ̄ ⲡⲉⲧϣⲟ
³⁶ ⲟⲡ· ⲁⲩⲱ ⲡⲓϣⲟⲙ̄ⲧ ⲟⲩⲁ
³⁷ ⲛⲉ· ⲉⲩⲉ ⲛ̄ϣⲟⲙ̄ⲧ ⲕⲁⲧⲁ
³⁸ ⲡⲟⲩⲁ ⲡⲟⲩⲁ·

ⲁⲛⲟⲕ ⲁⲉ ⲛ̄
³⁹ ⲧⲁⲣⲓⲥⲱⲧⲙ̄ ⲉⲛⲁϊ ⲡⲁϣⲏⲣⲉ

49.31–34 Turner indicates: {ⲡⲱⲛ̄ϩ· ⲉⲟⲩⲛ̄ ⲧⲉ} ⲧⲙ̄ⲛ̄ⲧⲱⲛ̄ϩ ⲟⲩⲛ̄ⲧⲉⲥ ⲛ̄(ⲧⲙ̄ⲛ̄ⲧⲁ)ⲧⲟⲩⲥⲓⲁ ⲙⲛ̄ ⲧⲙ̄ⲛ̄ⲧⲉⲓⲙⲉ·.

49.18b–21a The sentence may be paraphrased: "For it is through the Triply-powered that knowledge of the Invisible Spirit becomes accessible to Barbelo; for it is the Triply-powered which knows what the Invisible Spirit is." Barbelo is the source of saving knowledge through the mediation of the Triply-powered.

ⲛ̄ⲧⲟϥ ⲉⲧⲥⲟⲟⲩⲛ ϫε ⲟⲩ ⲡⲉ is to be understood as a reduced cleft sentence (see above, note to 48.17b–19a).

At 49.18–19, *gnosis* ("knowledge") is hypostasized and identified with Barbelo (compare *Marsanes*: 9.2–4; see also *ApJohn* II.*1*,4.26–5.11; Irenaeus, *AdvHaer* I.29.1; *StSeth* 123,15–17; *Zost* 118.10–12).

49.21b–26a Those who truly exist are completely transcendent. It cannot be said that they produce anything, that is, anything of a lower kind, such as powers, orders, glories, or aeons.

49.26b–38a For consideration of this section, see pp. 24–27.

This statement ends the first speech of a revealer, possibly Iouel, to Allo-

²⁰ for it is that which knows what
²¹ he is—inasmuch as these ones did not produce anything
²² [ex]cept themselves, nei[ther]
²³ a power nor an order no[r]
²⁴ a glory nor an aeon.
²⁵ For they are all eter[n]al
²⁶ beings.
　　It is Vitality and
²⁷ Intellection and That-which-exists.
²⁸ For, then, that
²⁹ very one continually possesses its
³⁰ Vitality and
³¹ Intellect and Life inasmuch as
³² the Vitality possesses
³³ Substancelessness and
³⁴ Intellection, whereas Intellect
³⁵ possesses Life and That-which-exists.
³⁶ And these three are one,
³⁷ although they are three (when considered)
³⁸ individually."
　　But
³⁹ when I heard these things, my son

genes. The statement by Turner that the speech was made *by Allogenes* to Iouel is surely incorrect (see "Allogenes," 253). Even if the second singular pronominal reference in 50.11 is to Iouel, that does not explain the first section of the text as a speech from Allogenes.

In the left margin next to lines 38–39, there is an ink marking shaped like a pointed bracket, the purpose of which is obscure. Turner suggests that it may mark the transition to a new section ("Allogenes," 253).

At 49.28 ⲧⲟⲧⲉ ("then") seems to function as a logical, not merely a temporal, connective.

As noted above (pp. 24–27), this passage is problematic. The complexity of the sentence (49.26b–38a) may be due in part to an only partially successful attempt to express certain subtle distinctions in philosophical terminology. "Being" (or "That-which-exists") and "Non-being" are expressed in three strikingly different phrases: ⲡⲏ ⲉⲧⲉ ⲡⲁⲓ ⲡⲉ, ⲡⲉⲧϣⲟⲟⲡ, and ⲧⲙⲛ̄ⲧⲁⲧⲟⲩⲥⲓⲁ. One could perhaps read the difficult ⲙⲛ̄ⲧⲁⲧⲟⲩⲥⲓⲁ ("substancelessness") as an attempt at translating ὑπερούσιος ("beyond substance"). "Life" appears both with and without the abstracting prefix ⲙⲛ̄ⲧ: ⲙⲛ̄ⲧⲱⲛϩ̄ and ⲱⲛϩ̄; it is unclear,

50   ¹ [ⲙⲉⲥⲥⲟⲥ ⲁⲉⲓ ⲣ̄]ⲍ̣ⲟⲧⲉ ⲁⲩⲱ
     ² [ⲁⲉⲓⲕⲟⲧⲧ̄ ⲉⲡⲓⲟ]ⲅ̣ⲁⲧⲟ· ⲉ̣[   ]
     ³ [ⲙ]ⲉ̣ⲉ̣ⲅⲉ̣[   ]
     ⁴ [   ]
     ⁵ [. . .] . [   ]
     ⁶ [ⳁ]ϭⲟⲙ ⲉ[ⲛⲏ ⲉⲧⲟ̄]ⲙ̄ϭⲟⲙ ⲛ̄ⲉⲓⲙⲉ
     ⁷ [ⲉ]ⲛⲁⲓ̈ ⲉ[ⲃⲟⲗ ⲍ̄ⲓⲧ̄]ⲛ̄ ⲟⲩⲱⲛ̄ⲍ̣ ⲉ
     ⁸ ⲃⲟⲗ ⲉⲛ[ⲉⲁϥ ⲛ̄]ⲍ̣ⲟⲅⲟ· ⲁⲛⲟⲕ ⲁⲉ
     ⁹ ⲁⲉⲓϭⲙ̄ϭ[ⲟⲙ]ⲉ̣ⲅⲛ̄ ⲟⲩⲥⲁⲣⲝ̄ ⲧⲟ
     ¹⁰ ⲍ̄ⲓⲱⲱ[ⲧ ⲁⲉⲓ]ⲥⲱⲧⲙ̄ ⲉⲛⲁⲓ̈ ⲉⲃⲟⲗ
     ¹¹ ⲛ̄ⲧⲟⲟⲧ̄ⲕ̄ [ⲁ]ⲅ̣ⲱ ⲉⲧⲃⲉ ⳁⲥⲃⲱ

50.1–2 Or: ⲁⲩⲱ [ⲙⲡⲓⲕⲟⲧⲧ̄ ⲉⲡⲓⲟ]ⲅⲁⲧⲟ· "But I did not turn myself toward the multitude." In this case, the ⲁⲩⲱ is understood as an adversative καί.
50.6 Supralinear stroke over ⲛ is restored.
50.7 Supralinear stroke over ⲛ is restored; letter is clear.
50.11 Supralinear stroke over ⲧⲕ is restored; the letter ⲕ is clear.

however, what the significance of this differentiation is. Similarly, the text may present a subtle, but obscure distinction between ⲛⲟⲏⲧⲏⲥ ("perceptible to the mind, intellectual") and ⲙ̄ⲛ̄ⲧⲉⲓⲙⲉ ("what is associated with knowledge, what is characteristic of knowledge").

Allogenes' reaction to the first revelation

49.38b–50.17a Here we learn about Allogenes' reaction to the words of the first revelation.

49.38b–50.2 Allogenes is frightened and turns toward the multitude (concerning the construction of ⲡⲓⲟⲅⲁⲧⲟ, see p. 74). "The multitude" is a metaphor for the lower things of this world which are considered to be distractions from higher spiritual concerns. Plotinus illustrates the consequences of the soul's distraction from contemplation of the One using the metaphor of a chorus:

> We resemble a chorus which surrounds its leader, whose members, none-theless, do not always sing in time because they allow their attention to be distracted by some exterior object. If, however, they turned towards their leader, they would sing well and really be with him. In a similar way, we too always turn around the One. If not, we should dissolve and cease to exist. But our glance does not remain fixed on the One. When, however, we look to it, we attain the end of our desires and find rest. Then we dance around it, without dissonance, a truly divine dance.
>
> (*Ennead* VI.9.8; trans. Katz, 152–153.)

Since, however, Allogenes is given further revelation in what follows and becomes divine, perhaps he did not yield to the temptation to "turn toward

50   ¹ [Messos, I became] frightened and
    ² [I turned toward the m]ultitude [   ]
    ³ [th]ink [   ]
    ⁴⁻⁵ [   ] . . .
    ⁶ [em]powers [those who are a]ble to understand
    ⁷ these things t[hroug]h a much gr[eater] revelation.
    ⁸ But I
    ⁹ had the po[wer] (to understand these things)—despite (the fact) that I am clothed in flesh.
    ¹⁰ [I] heard these things from
    ¹¹ you. [A]nd it is because of the teaching

50.6–7 Or: "[gives] power t[hroug]h a much gr[eater] revelation to [those who are a]ble to understand these things."

the multitude" despite his fear. One might then restore: ⲁⲩⲱ ⲙ̄ⲡⲓⲕⲟⲧⲧ ⲉⲡⲓⲟⲩⲁⲧⲟ ("and I did not turn toward the multitude"). The problem with this restoration is the usage of ⲁⲩⲱ ("and"); it could be understood, with some difficulty, as the improper translation of an adversative καί.

50.6–8a The adverbial clause ⲉⲃⲟⲗ ϩⲓⲧⲛ̄ ⲟⲩⲱⲛϩ̄ ⲉⲃⲟⲗ ("through revelation") can grammatically be taken either with ϯϭⲟⲙ ("empower") or ϭⲙϭⲟⲙ ⲛ̄ⲉⲓⲙⲉ ⲉⲛⲁⲓ̈ ("be able to understand these things"). There are two options for translation: "empowers through a superior revelation those who are able to understand these things" or "empowers those who are able to understand these things through a superior revelation." Compare 50.24–25; 52.15; 61.3–4. The meanings are not mutually exclusive.

50.8b–10a ⲁⲉⲓϭⲙϭⲟⲙ ("I was able") presupposes ⲛ̄ⲉⲓⲙⲉ ⲉⲛⲁⲓ̈ ("to understand these things"). Allogenes is able to understand the words of revelation despite the fact that he is in a lowly incarnate state. The body is apparently not an obstacle to enlightenment. Although it is couched in reserved tones, the statement suggests a less negative attitude toward the material world and the body than one finds in modern descriptions of Gnosticism.

The qualification ("despite the fact that I am clothed in flesh") may be a defense against the accusation that Allogenes claims to have knowledge of matters that only higher, non-corporeal beings could possess. This view may be further confirmed by his statement below in 50.15–17 that his teaching was beyond what was proper for his estate.

50.10b–11a The restoration of ⲁⲉⲓ is in asyndetic construction with the previous sentence.

Grammar indicates that the second singular pronominal antecedent is Messos, but that makes no sense in this context. One would wish to see ⲛ̄ⲧⲟⲟⲧⲥ̄ or ⲛ̄ⲧⲟⲟⲧϥ̄ where the antecedent was a specified revealer figure like Iouel.

¹² ετⲛ̅ϩⲏⲧⲟⲩ· ⲉⲁⲡⲓⲙⲉⲉⲩⲉ

¹³ ετⲛ̅ϩⲏⲧ ⲁϥⲡⲱⲣⲝ̅ ⲛ̅ⲛ[ⲏ] ⲉⲧ

¹⁴ ϫⲟⲥⲉ ⲉ[ⲡ]ϣⲓ ⲙ̅ⲛ̅ ⲛⲓⲁⲧ[ⲥ]ⲟⲩ[ⲱ]

¹⁵ ⲛⲟⲩ· ⲉⲧⲃⲉ ⲡⲁⲓ †ⲣ̅ϩⲟⲧⲉ ⲙ[ⲏ]

¹⁶ ⲡⲱⲥ ⲁⲧⲁⲥⲃⲱ ⲁⲥⲉⲓⲣⲉ ⲛ̅ⲟⲩ

¹⁷ ⲗⲁⲁⲩ ⲡⲁⲣⲁ ⲡⲉⲧⲉϣϣⲉ·

ⲁⲩⲱ

¹⁸ ⲧⲟⲧⲉ ⲡⲉϫⲁⲥ ⲛⲁⲓ ⲟⲛ {ϫⲉ} ⲡⲁ

¹⁹ ϣⲏⲣⲉ ⲙⲉⲥⲥⲟⲥ ⲛ̅ϭⲓ ⲧⲁⲛⲓⲉ

50.18 The appearance of ϫⲉ here following ⲡⲉϫⲁⲥ is incorrect since ϫⲉ should introduce a direct or indirect quotation, not the speaker.

50.11b–15a The teaching, which is based upon revelation, allows the thought of Allogenes to distinguish exalted and unknowable matters or beings. The question is what is he to distinguish them *from*. (Usually ⲡⲱⲣϫ is followed by the preposition ⲉ-/ⲁ-, to separate or divide *from*.) In 50.29–30 below, Iouel tells Allogenes that his mission is precisely this: to divide things difficult to divide. What are these things that are difficult to divide? Comparison with *Zostrianos* provides a possible clue. At the beginning of the text, the savior, who was sent into the world on account of the "living elect," says:

ⲉⲧⲁⲉⲓⲡⲱⲣϫ ⲙ̅ⲡⲓⲥⲱⲙⲁⲧⲓⲕⲟⲛ ⲛ̅ⲕⲁⲕⲉ ⲉⲧⲛ̅ϩⲣⲁⲓ̈ ⲛ̅ϩⲏⲧ· ⲙⲛ ⲡⲓⲯⲩⲭⲓⲕⲟⲛ ⲛ
ⲭⲁⲟⲩⲥ ϩⲛ ⲟⲩⲛⲟⲩⲥ ⲙⲛ †ⲙⲛ̅ⲧⲥ̅ϩⲓⲙⲉ ⲛ̅ⲛⲉⲡⲓⲑⲩⲙⲓⲁ [.]ⲁⲓ̈ ⲉⲧⲛ ⲡⲓⲕⲁⲕⲉ·
ⲉⲙⲡⲓⲣ ϩⲱⲃ ϭⲉ ⲉⲣⲟⲥ· ⲉⲧⲁⲉⲓϭⲓⲛⲉ ⲙ̅ⲡⲓⲁⲧⲛ ⲁⲣⲏϫϥ ⲛ̅ⲧⲉ ⲧⲁϩⲩⲗⲏ· ⲁⲩⲱ
ⲁⲉⲓⲥⲟϩⲉ ⲛ̅†ⲕⲧⲓⲥⲓⲥ ⲉⲧⲙⲟⲟⲩⲧ ⲉⲧϩⲣⲁⲓ̈ ⲛ̅ϩⲏⲧ ⲙⲛ ⲡⲓⲕⲟⲥⲙⲟⲕⲣⲁⲧⲱⲣ
ⲛ̅ⲛⲟⲩⲧⲉ ⲛ̅ⲛⲉⲥⲑⲏⲧⲟⲛ· ⲉⲗⲉ[ⲓ]† ϩⲛ ⲟⲩϭⲟⲙ ⲛ̅ⲛⲟⲩⲟⲉⲓϣ ⲛ̅ⲧⲉ ⲡⲧⲏⲣϥ ⲛ̅ⲛⲏ
ⲉⲧⲛ̅ⲧⲁ[ⲩ] ⲙⲙⲁⲩ ⲙ̅ⲙⲉⲣⲓⲕⲟⲛ ⲛ̅ϣⲙⲙⲟ·

After I parted from the somatic darkness in me and the psychic chaos in mind and the feminine desire [. . .] in the darkness, I did not use it again. After I had found the infinite part of my matter and I reproved the dead creation within me and the divine cosmocrater of the perceptible (world), I preached powerfully about the All to those with alien parts.
(*Zost* 1.10–22; trans. Sieber, *Nag Hammadi Codex VIII*, 30–31)

In both contexts, ⲡⲱⲣϫ seems to be a metaphor for a mental activity of discernment that allows one to separate the higher self from the body and its base passions. It is unclear whether the meaning is 1) to distinguish those that are exalted from those that are unknowable (like the perfect individuals from those who truly exist) or 2) to distinguish what is exalted and unknowable from the lower things of the perceptible world. The latter is the more probable meaning.

¹² that is in them, that the thought
¹³ which is in me separated those things that
¹⁴ are exalted beyond [mea]sure and are un[k]no[w]able.
¹⁵ For this reason I am frightened l[e]st
¹⁶ my teaching had
¹⁷ exceeded what is fitting.
       And
¹⁸ then the all-glorious Iouel spoke to me also, my
¹⁹ son Messos.

50.18 Literally: "she to whom all the glories pertain, Iouel."

As Valantasis observes (*Spiritual Guides*, 120, n. 24), the process of separating or dividing (see 50.28–30) probably refers to *diairesis*, an intellectual process which uses identity, difference, and similarity to categorize the relations among substances (see Berchman, *From Philo to Origen*, 64–68).

Of great grammatical interest here is the form ⲉⲁ- (in extraposition with the tense marker ⲁ⸗). The form ⲉⲁ- looks like a circumstantial perfect, but functions as a II perfect. A similar occurrence is found in 66.30–33 (without extraposition): ⲉⲃⲟⲗ ϩⲙ ⲡⲏ ⲉⲧⲁϩⲉⲣⲁⲧϥ ⲛ̄ⲟⲩⲉⲓⲱ ⲛⲓⲙ· ⲉⲁϥⲟⲩⲱⲛϩ̄ ⲉⲃⲟⲗ ⲛ̄ϭⲓ ⲟⲩⲱⲛϩ̄ ⲛ̄ϣⲁ ⲉⲛⲉϩ·. This usage is similar to that of Middle Egyptian, a dialect also found in this vicinity, which does not distinguish between the circumstantial and II perfect forms. Both appear as ⲉϩⲁ⸗. Since the form ⲉⲁ⸗ is clearly functioning as a II perfect in 50.12 and 66.32, the only issue is whether the forms here should be labeled as II perfect (as I do below) or whether one would rather classify them as circumstantial forms with a secondary function (the II perfect).

50.15b–17a An instance of extraposition of the conjugation base appears at line 16: ⲁⲧⲁⲥⲃⲱ ⲁⲥⲉⲓⲣⲉ.

There are at least three possible interpretations of this sentence: 1) Allogenes was frightened that his teaching, concerning exalted and unknowable matters or beings, had surpassed what was appropriate for a mortal. 2) He was frightened that he would be persecuted by others because his teaching concerned matters that were not fitting in the eyes of other persons or that were more exalted than their teachings. 3) He was afraid that he had gone too far and drawn the wrong conclusions. Valantasis has also suggested that the sentence might be "an attempt to indicate that the new revelation takes precedence over the old" (*Spiritual Guides*, 136). I tend to interpret the matter according to the first option based on the connection with 50.9–10, but any of the suggestions is defensible.

²⁰ [ο]ογ τηρογ ιογηλ· αϲϭωλ[π]
²¹ [ν]αϊ εβολ· αγω πεϫαϲ ϫε μ[ε]
²² ρεϣογον νιμ ϲωτμ εναⲓ
²³ εβολ ενινοϭ νϭομ ογα[γ]
²⁴ ω παλλογενηϲ αγϯ ϩιω
²⁵ ωκ νογνοϭ νϭομ· τη ε
²⁶ ταϥτααϲ ϩιωωκ νϭι πιωτ
²⁷ ντε πτηρϥ πιϣα ενεϩ ϩα
²⁸ θη εμπατεκει επιμα· ϩι
²⁹ να νη ετμοκϩ μπορϫογ
³⁰ ϫε εκεπορϫογ· αγω νη
³¹ ετε ννατϲογωνογ μ
³² πιογατο ϫε εκεειμε ε
³³ ροογ. αγω νγνογϩμ ε
³⁴ ϩραϊ επετε πωκ· πη ε
³⁵ ταϥϣορπ ννογϩμ μν
³⁶ πη ετε μαϥρχρια ννα ϩμεϥ

The second revelation to Allogenes

50.17b–21a The adverb ον ("again" or "also") may indicate that Iouel was the speaker of the first revelation or it may simply refer to the fact that she, in addition to the first revealer, spoke now to Allogenes. The lacuna at the beginning of the text makes the solution unclear.

The title of Iouel, τανιεοογ τηρογ ιογηλ ("She-to-whom-all-the-glories-pertain Iouel") is standard in the text (also compare *Zost* 125.13–14). It is an attestation of her exalted nature and a titular invocation of praise. (For further discussion of Iouel, see pp. 45–46.)

Though the meaning of this passage is clear (Allogenes tells Messos that Iouel appeared and spoke to him), the text is clearly corrupt. Not only is ϫε in line 18 impossible since it is not followed by a direct or indirect quotation, but the repetition of πεϫαϲ (in lines 18 and 21) is also odd. The intrusion of the vocative after πεϫαϲ ϫε (that is, after direct address by Allogenes to Messos) is most disturbing. πεϫαϲ ναϊ ον ϫε ("she spoke to me also . . .") introduces no quotation, as expected by the use of ϫε. The text as it now stands is translatable but it departs widely from standard Coptic expression.

The name "Messos" appears here for the first time (without restoration). The identity of this figure is obscure. He is identified in the text as the "son" of Allogenes, a reference no doubt to a spiritual, not biological relationship. The revelations of Allogenes have been recorded for him (68.26–31). As H.-M. Schenke points out, Messos will have to retrieve this book from the clutches of the demon who protects it, hidden on a mountain. If one were to read *Allo-*

²⁰ She appea[r]ed
²¹ to me and said:
²² "N[o]t everyone is able to hear the[se] things
²³ except the great powers alo[ne],
²⁴ O Allogenes. You were clothed
²⁵ with a great power, that (power)
²⁶ with which the Father
²⁷ of the Entirety, the eternal one, clothed you
²⁸ before you came to this place in
²⁹ order that you will divide those things that are difficult to be
divided
³⁰ and (in order that) you will come to know those things
³¹ that are unknowable to
³² the multitude.
³³ And (afterwards) you will escape
³⁴ up to that which is yours, which
³⁵ is already saved and
³⁶ does not need to be saved.

50.33–36 Or: "And you will escape up to the one who is yours, who is already saved and does not need to be saved."
50.36 Or: "to save himself."

genes in terms of the Sethian schema of the ages of humanity, it might be that the book has been left for Messos to retrieve on the mountain after the flood waters had receded. Schenke suggests that it is even possible to ask "whether the Messos of our text is not simply a Sethian adaptation and detachment (*Verfremdung*) of Moses, who received the holy scriptures on Sinai from the Lᴏʀᴅ" ("Bemerkungen," 422). If this intriguing possibility is true, the reference to Messos only emphasizes how much was obscured by the platonizing removal of all the explicitly Sethian-Jewish references within *Allogenes*. The connection between Messos and Moses remains only in deeply shadowed allusions.

50.21b–36 This passage describes, in highly mythological terms, the role of Allogenes as savior (see pp. 5–8, 43–45). More than any other, this passage illustrates the distinctly Gnostic character of *Allogenes*. The savior is sent by the Father; he is "clothed" with power from on high; his mission is to bring saving discernment; he goes down to the lower places and (after fulfilling his mission) escapes back up to his proper place. In the course of his mission below, while being in the flesh, he requires power and revelations. In this sense, he is a Gnostic "saved-savior." (For fuller discussion of the term, "saved savior," see Rudolph, *Gnosis*, 121–131.)

51 ¹⁻⁵ [   ]

⁶ ϩ H.[. .].[. . . . . Ñ]ⲁⲕ [ÑⲞⲨ]
⁷ ⲈⲒⲀⲞⲤ Ñ[Ñ ⲞⲨⲰ̄Ñ]ϩ ⲈⲂⲞⲖ [·]
⁸ⲠⲒϢⲞⲘ̄Ⲧ [Ñ6ⲞⲘ Ñ]ⲚⲀⲦⲚⲀⲨ
⁹ ⲈⲢⲞϤ Ñⲡ̄Ñⲁ̄ Ⲉ[ⲤⲔ H Ñ]ⲤⲀⲂⲞⲖ Ñ
¹⁰ ⲘⲞϤ Ñ6Ⲓ ⲞⲨⲄⲚⲰ[ⲤⲒⲤ Ñ]ⲀⲦⲠ[Ⲱ]
¹¹ ϢⲈ ÑⲀⲦⲤⲰⲘⲀ [Ñ]ϢⳘ[Ⲁ Ⲉ]ⲚⲈϩ
¹² ⲔⲀⲦⲀ ⲐⲈ ⲈⲦϨ̄Ñ Ñ[Ⲓ]ⲈⲰⲚ ⲦⲎⲢ[ⲞⲨ]
¹³[Ⲉ]ϤϢⲞⲞⲠ Ñ6Ⲓ ⲠⲒⲈⲰⲚ ÑⲂⲀⲢⲂ[H]
¹⁴ [Ⲗ]Ⲱ· ⲈⲨÑⲦⲀϤ ⲞⲚ ÑⲚⲒⲦⲨⲠⲞⲤ
¹⁵ Ñ̄Ñ ⲚⲒⲈⲒⲀⲞⲤ ÑⲦⲈ ⲚⲒⲞⲚⲦⲰⲤ

51.6 Turner does not restore a supralinear stroke over the first ɴ. Second ɴ is restored by King.
51.7 Turner reads and restores: Ñ[Ñ ⲞⲨⲰ̄Ñ]ϩ ⲈⲂⲞⲖ [Ñ]. This restoration is not possible since the genitive following an indefinite article, (ⲞⲨ)ⲞⲨⲰⲚϩ ⲈⲂⲞⲖ, must be ÑⲦⲈ, but there is not enough room for this restoration.
51.9 Supralinear stroke over ⲠⲚⲀ and ⲙ are restored; letters ⲠⲚⲀ are clear.

Line 50.24 is the first place in the extant text where Allogenes is mentioned by name. (For discussion of the meaning of the name "Allogenes," see p. 44.)

The title of "the Father of the Entirety, the Eternal one" belongs more to Gnostic mythology than to philosophical conceptualization. Although he is here called "eternal," other passages in *Allogenes* make it clear that he is not subject to time. The term ⲠⲒϢⲀ ⲈⲚⲈϩ is thus an epithet of praise rather than an integral part of the text's philosophical speculation.

Concerning ϨⲒⲚⲀ ⲚH ⲈⲦⲘⲞⲔϨ̄ Ñ̄ⲠⲞⲢⳘ̄ⲞⲨ ⳘⲈ ⲈⲔⲈⲠⲞⲢⳘ̄ⲞⲨ· ("in order that you will divide those things that are difficult to be divided"; 50.29–30), see above, note to 50.11b–15a.

ⲚH ⲈⲦⲈ ÑⲚⲀⲦⲤⲞⲨⲰⲚⲞⲨ Ñ̄ⲠⲒⲞⲨⲀⲦⲞ ⳘⲈ ⲈⲔⲈⲈⲒⲘⲈ ⲈⲢⲞⲞⲨ (50.30–33) could refer either to impersonal or personal objects: "those things that are unknowable to the multitude" or "those divine beings who are unknowable to the multitude." Either is comprehensible in the context of *Allogenes*.

The phrase ⲠⲈⲦⲈ ⲠⲰⲔ ("that which is yours"; 50.34) might refer either to the heavenly abode of Allogenes or to his heavenly double (such as is described in the "Hymn of the Pearl" in the *Acts of Thomas*). It could also be understood personally ("he who is yours"), though the referent would be unclear. Turner suggests that the phrase may mean "one's blessedness of self-knowledge" ("Allogenes," 253).

Similarly, the appositional phrase ⲠⲎ ⲈⲦⲀϤⲢ̄ϢⲞⲢⲠ̄ ÑⲚⲞⲨϨ̄Ⲙ Ñ̄Ñ ⲠⲎ ⲈⲦⲈ ⲘⲀϤⲢ̄ⲬⲢⲒⲀ Ñ̄ⲚⲀϨⲘⲈϤ can be understood personally or impersonally ("that which is saved and does not need to be saved" or "he who is saved and does not

51 1-5 [   ] . . .

6 [to] you [a]
7 form a[nd a revelat]ion.
    8It is [ou]tside of the Triply-[powered] Invisible
9 Spirit that i[s situated]
10 an indi[vi]sible
11 bodiless, e[te]rnal Know[ledge]
12 as in al[l] t[he] aeons.
    14aIt is possessing (the following) that
13 the aeon of Barb[el]o exists:

> **51.12** The phrase "as in all the aeons" can also be understood to modify the following sentence: "As in all the aeons, the aeon of Barbelo exists . . ."

need to be saved"). Compare the praise given to the highest member of the divine hierarchy in *Three Steles of Seth* 125.18–21:

> You are them all for you save them all, he who was not himself saved nor does he save through them.

The subject of 50.35–36 could be the Invisible Spirit or the Triply-powered (compare *Allogenes* 49.14–18). It is just as likely, however, that the phrase refers to Allogenes himself as the saved-savior. The impersonal meaning of the phrase makes little sense. I interpret the phrase to mean: And (afterwards) you will escape up to your heavenly abode for you are already saved and do not need to be saved.

ϤϢⲟⲣⲡ̄ ⲛ̄ⲛⲟⲩϨⲙ (line 35) is best understood as a *Prae-verbal* (see Funk, "Zur Syntax des koptischen Qualitatives," 99–100. He translates: "jener der schon gerettet ist.")

51.8–37 This passage describes the aeon of Barbelo. See pp. 29–31.

51.8–12 *Gnosis* ("knowledge") is clearly a personified figure here. Since knowledge involves duality (the knower and what is known; see the discussion of this view by Rist, *Plotinus*, chapter 4) and hence multiplicity, it is said that Knowledge is an hypostasis separate from the Invisible Spirit. It is said to be situated "outside" of the Triply-powered Invisible Spirit (compare *Zost* 76.20–22). This knowledge concerns what is indivisible, incorporeal, and eternal.

The last phrase ("as in all the aeons") can be understood either with what precedes or with what follows.

The easy transition to a description of Barbelo in the next sentence establishes a connection between Barbelo and personified Knowledge.

51.13–32a This whole passage is a description of Barbelo, combining philosophical terms and concepts with elements of Sethian myth (see pp. 5–8,

¹⁶ ετϣοοπ· †ⲍⲓⲕⲱⲛ ⲛ̄τε
¹⁷ πικⲁⲗυπτοϲ· ευⲛ̄ⲧⲁϥ ⲁε
¹⁸ ⲙ̄πιϣⲁⲭε ⲛ̄ⲛοεⲣοⲛ ⲛ̄τε
¹⁹ ⲛⲁ ⲉϥⲧⲱⲛ ⲍⲁ πιⲡⲣⲱⲧοφⲁ
²⁰ ⲛⲏϲ ⲛ̄ⲍοουⲧ ⲛ̄ⲛουϲ ⲕⲁⲧⲁ
²¹ ου ⲍⲓⲕⲱⲛ· ⲉϥ̄ⲣⲉⲛⲉⲣⲅⲓ ⲁε
²² ⲍⲛ̄ ⲛⲓⲕⲁⲧⲁ ⲟⲩⲁ· ⲉⲓⲧⲉ ⲍⲛ̄ οⲩ
²³ ⲧⲉⲭⲛⲏ· ⲉⲓⲧⲉ ⲍⲛ̄ οⲩⲉπⲓϲⲧⲏ
²⁴ [ⲙ]ⲏ· ⲉⲓⲧⲉ ⲍⲛ̄ οⲩφⲩϲⲓϲ ⲙ̄

45, and notes to 45.31–46.37). The hypostases (Barbelo, Kalyptos, Protophanes, and Autogenes) belong to Sethian myth; their description as stages in the process of generation is here given in philosophical terms. The triad Kalyptos-Protophanes-Autogenes is described with the technical terms εἶδος ("form"), τύπος ("type"), and εἰκών ("image"). Our author uses these terms as though they were interchangeable. One is reminded by this language of the widespread view that the (Platonic) ideas are located in the mind of God.

The description of each hypostasis is followed by a circumstantial clause with ⲁε (17, 21, and 27) describing his status and/or cosmological or soteriological functions. The section can be summarized as follows:

Barbelo possesses:
　the types and forms of those who truly exist:
　　1. the image of Kalyptos
　　　the intelligible word
　　2. the image of male, noetic Protophanes
　　　actualized in individuals
　　3. the image of divine Autogenes
　　　knowing each one, actualizing them part by part, and one by one;
　　　the savior who corrects sins deriving from nature.

As described above (p. 30), Kalyptos represents the unity of noetic existents in Intellect; Autogenes represents their particularized individual existence; and Protophanes is the mediator between the two—he is the procession from unified to particularized existence.

Protophanes is actualized (ἐνεργεῖν) in particulars by any one of three possible methods:

　1. τέχνη. According to Aristotle's usage (*Nich.Ethic* 6.1140a), "craft" is a technical term for knowledge of individual instances from which a knowledge of general causes comes. Its goal is generation.

¹⁴ᵇ(she possesses) also the types
¹⁵ and the forms of the ones who truly
¹⁶ exist; the image of
¹⁷ Kalyptos who possesses
¹⁸ the intelligible word of
¹⁹ these ones; (Barbelo) bears the
²⁰ male, noetic Protophanes as
²¹ an image who is further actualized
²² in the individuals, either by a
²³ craft or in sure knowledge
²⁴ or in a particular nature;

> **51.17** "Kalyptos" means "hidden one."
> **51.20** "Protophanes" means "first-appearing one."

2. ἐπιστήμη. The term may imply knowledge of the Ideas and perhaps refers to a more typical type of Platonic generation where the Demiurge (Protophanes?) looks to the Forms (the "hidden ones" of Kalyptos?) for knowledge with which to bring about the generation of particular things (the sphere of Autogenes?).

3. Particularized φύσις. According to Aristotle, "nature is a source or cause of being moved and of being at rest in that to which it belongs primarily, in virtue of itself and not in virtue of a concomitant attribute" (*Physics* II.1 [192b21–23]).

Based on a comparison with *Corpus Hermeticum Exc. Stob.* IV,2–3, Turner suggests alternatively that craft and skill are applied to the intelligence within humans, particularized nature (which he translates "partial instinct") applies to the type of intelligence appropriate for animals ("Allogenes," 254).

Autogenes plays the role of savior: he is concerned with correcting the sins deriving from nature (51.30–32). The term used here, ⲧⲁϩⲟ ⲉⲣⲁⲧ⸗ ("to set upright," "establish") may be connected with the theme of stability (ⲁϩⲉⲣⲁⲧⲥ⸗) which appears elsewhere in the text (see note to 58.38b–59.4a). Both terms derive from ⲱϩⲉ and can translate the Greek ἱστάναι. According to Williams, the term appears in Gnostic (and often in specifically Sethian) contexts to refer to "that which *transcends* movement or change, that which belongs to the Platonic realm of the immutable" (*The Immovable Race*, 14). The stability of this realm contrasts with the realm of nature, which is in constant flux. Thus the phrase "to set upright the sins deriving from nature" does not necessarily imply a radical Gnostic dualism or ascetic ethic, but could merely refer to a return to the ideal of Platonic stability, involving only a mild

25 ΜΕΡΙΚΟΝ· ΕΥⲚΤⲀϥ ⲘΠΙ
26 ⲀΥΤΟΓΕΝΗⲤ ⲚΝΟΥΤΕ ΚⲀ
27 ΤⲀ ΟΥⲌ̅ΙΚⲰΝ· ΕϥΕΙΜΕ ⲆΕ
28 ΕΠΟΥⲀ ΠΟΥⲀ ⲚΤΕ ΝⲀΪ· Εϥ
29 Ⲣ̄ΕΝΕΡΓΕΙ ΚⲀΤⲀ ΜΕΡΟⳞ ⲀΥⲰ
30 ΚⲀΤⲀ ΟΥⲀ ΕϥΟΥΗⲌ ΕϥΤⲀⲌΟ
31 ⲚΝΙΝΟΒΕ ΕΡⲀΤΟΥ ΝΙΕΒΟⲖ
32 Ⲍ̅Ⲛ ϯΦΥⳞΙⳞ· ΟΥⲚΤⲀϥ Ⲙ̄
33 ΠΙϢΟΜ̅Ⲧ̅ Ⲛ̄ⲌΟΟΥΤ ⲚΝΟΥ
34 ΤΕ ΕΥΟΥΧⲀΪ ⲚΤΕΥ ΤΗ
35 ΡΟΥ Μ̅Ⲛ̅ ΠΙⲀⲌΟΡⲀΤΟΝ Μ̅ΠⲚ̅Ⲁ̅
36 ΟΥϢⲀΧΕ ΠΕ ΕΒΟⲖ Ⲍ̅Ⲛ̅ ΟΥϢΟ
37 ΧΝΕ ΠΕ ΠΙⲀⲖΟΥ ⲚΤΕⲖΙΟⳞ
38 ⲀΥⲰ ΤΕΪⲌΥΠΟⳞΤⲀⳞΙⳞ ΟΥⲀ

52 1-5 [   ]
6 [. . .].[   ] ⲀⳞ
7 [Ⲣ̄6]ⲀΒⲌΗ[Τ Ⲛ̄6Ι ΤⲀⲯⲨ]ΧΗ[·] ⲀΥⲰ
8 [Ⲁ]ΕΙⲢ̄ ΕΒ[ΟⲖ ⲀΕΙϢ]Τ]ΟⲢ̄Τ̄Ⲣ̄ ΕΜⲀ

51.37 Turner emends: ⟨ⲚΤΟϥ⟩ ΠΕ ΠΙⲀⲖΟΥ ⲚΤΕⲖΙΟⳞ. This emendation is not, however, necessary; the reiteration of the superfluous ΠΕ does not require emendation.
52.6 Turner reads: Ⲁ[Ⳟ].
52.7 Restoration is by H.-M. Schenke. The word 6ⲀΒⲌ[ΗΤ] appears in fragment 2, page 81 of the *Facsimile Edition*.

dualism. Contact with the lower realm of nature leads to instability, a condition that needs rectifying.

At 58.13, the Thrice-male Youth is called the savior, although how the term is meant there is not discussed. The two figures are explicitly connected in the section which follows.

51.32b–37 For discussion of this passage and the Thrice-male Youth, see pp. 6–7. See also, Turner, "Allogenes," 247–248, 254.

The *logos* is identified with Autogenes in *Gospel of the Egyptians* III, 49.18; 53.13.

Allogenes' reaction to the second revelation

52.6–13a The speech of Iouel has broken off in the lacuna. The text reopens with a description of Allogenes' reaction to the words of Iouel in the second revelation. He became fainthearted and fled, being greatly disturbed.

25 (Barbelo) possesses the
26 divine Autogenes as
27 an image who further knows
28 each one of these, (and) who is
29 actualized part by part and
30 one by one, being continually involved with correcting
31 the sins deriving from
32a nature. He,
35 along with the Invisible Spirit,
32b possesses
33 the divine Thrice-male
34 as a salvation for them all.
37 This perfect Youth
36 is a word deriving from a design.
　　38 And this hypostasis . . ."

52 1-5 [　　　　　　　　　　　　]
　6 [. . . my]
　7 so]ul [became w]eak and
　8 I fle[d. I was] greatly [dis]turbed.

51.26 "Autogenes" means "self-generated one."

In contrast, however, to his reaction to the first revelation, he does not turn to the lower things of this world even though he is frightened, but instead he turns inward. When he does, Allogenes perceives within himself light and good, metaphors of his own divinity. He comes to recognize that which is divine in himself. On this basis, he is ready for further empowerment and revelation.

There is a close parallel in *Zost* 44.17–23 to this conception that contemplative practice leads to understanding one's divine character:

εϣωπ εϥϣα[ΝΟΥ]ωϣ ΠΑΛΙΝ ΟΝ ε[Ι]ε ϥΠωΡ[Χ Ν]C[Α]ΒΟΛ ΝΝΑЇ
ΤΗΡΟΥ· ΑΥω Ν[ΤΟϥ] ΝϥΡ ΑΝΑΧωΡΙ[Ν ε]ΡΟϥ ΜΑΥΑ[Αϥ] ΠΑЇ ΓΑΡ
ϣΑ[ϥϣ]ωΠε [Ν]ΝΟΥ[Τ]ε ΑϥΡ ΑΝΑΧω[ΡΙ]Ν εΠΝΟΥΤε ΠΑЇ

If it [wishes], then it again parts from them all and withdraws into itself [alone], for it can become divine by having taken refuge in god.

　　　　　(Sieber, *Nag Hammadi Codex VIII*, 108–111)

Allogenes' experience of self-understanding is a preparation for his ascent (see below, exegetical note to 58.38b–59.4a). The language used, though

⁹ ⲧⲉ· ⲁⲅ[ⲱ ⲁⲉ]ⲓⲕⲟⲧⲧ̄ ⲉⲣⲟⲉⲓ
¹⁰ ⲟⲩⲁ[ⲁⲧ· ⲁ]ⲉⲓⲛⲁⲩ ⲉⲡⲓⲟⲩⲟ
¹¹ ⲉⲓⲛ ⲉ[ⲧⲕⲱ]ⲧⲉ ⲉⲣⲟⲉⲓ ⲙ̄ⲛ ⲡⲓ
¹² ⲁⲅⲁⲑⲟⲛ ⲉⲧⲛ̄ϩⲏⲧ ⲁⲉⲓⲡ̄ⲛⲟⲩ
¹³ ⲧⲉ·

      ⲁⲩⲱ ⲁⲥⲭⲱϩ ⲉⲣⲟⲓ̈ ⲟⲛ ⲛ̄[61]
¹⁴ ⲧⲁⲛⲓⲉⲟⲟⲩ ⲧⲏⲣⲟⲩ ⲓ̈ⲟⲩⲏ̄ⲗ
¹⁵ ⲁⲥϯ ϭⲟⲙ ⲛⲁⲓ̈· ⲡⲉⲭⲁⲥ ⲭⲉ ⲉ
¹⁶ ⲡⲓⲁⲏ ⲁⲧⲉⲕⲥⲃⲱ ⲁⲥⲣ̄ⲧⲉⲗⲓⲟⲥ
¹⁷ ⲙ̄ⲛ ⲡⲓⲁⲅⲁⲑⲟⲛ ⲉⲧⲛ̄ϩⲏⲧⲕ̄
¹⁸ ⲁⲕⲉⲓⲙⲉ ⲉⲣⲟϥ· ⲥⲱⲧ̄ⲙ ⲉⲧⲃⲉ
¹⁹ ⲡⲓϣⲙ̄ⲛ̄ⲧϭⲟⲙ· ⲛⲏ ⲉⲧⲉⲕⲛⲁ
²⁰ [ϩ]ⲁⲣⲉϩ ⲉⲣⲟⲟⲩ ϩ̄ⲛ ⲟⲩⲛⲟϭ ⲛ̄
²¹ ⲥⲓⲅⲏ ⲙ̄ⲛ ⲟⲩⲛⲟϭ ⲙ̄ⲙⲩⲥⲧⲏⲣ[ⲓ]

52.10 Turner does not restore raised dot.

highly mythological, reflects also the philosophical view, such as one finds exemplified in Plotinus, that the first stage in the soul's return to the One is self-apprehension (see *Ennead* V.1.12) and that the goal of the philosophical enterprise is to become divine (or at least to achieve "likeness to God.") The reason for beginning with oneself is to discover that divinity within, to become divine (see *Ennead* I.2.6; VI.9.9). Plotinus describes his own experience as follows:

> Often I have woken up out of the body to myself and have entered into myself, going out from all other things; I have seen a beauty wonderfully great and felt assurance that then most of all I belonged to the better part; I have actually lived the best life and come to identity with the divine; and set first in it I have come to that supreme actuality, setting myself above all else in the realm of Intellect.
>
> (*Ennead* IV.8.1.1–8; trans. Armstrong, *Plotinus*, IV, 397)

(See also O'Daly, *Plotinus' Philosophy*; Rist, *Plotinus*, chapters 16 and 17; Armstrong, "Plotinus" [*Cambridge History*], 258–263.)

The third revelation to Allogenes

52.13b–19a As a consequence of Allogenes' self-recognition, Iouel appears to him again. Iouel anoints (or touches) him and conveys power that enables him to receive her words. (Concerning anointing, see pp. 12–14; concerning "giving" or "receiving power," see above, note to 45.22b–30.)

⁹ An[d] I turned inward toward myself
¹⁰ alo[ne]. I perceived the light
¹¹ th[at sur]rounds me and the
¹² good that is in me; I became
¹³ᵃdivine.

    And
¹⁴ the all-glorious Iouel
¹³ᵇanointed me again,
¹⁵ empowering me. She said:
¹⁶ "Since your instruction has become perfect
¹⁷ and you have come to know the good that is in you,
¹⁸ hear (now) about
¹⁹ the Triply- powered.

    These (are words) that you will
²⁰ [gu]ard in great
²¹ silence and great mystery.

52.13b Or: "Iouel touched me again."
52.14 Literally: "she to whom all the glories pertain, Iouel."

The words also confirm that his education and self-knowledge have reached a level where he is ready for further instruction. Iouel commands him to hear now about the Triply-powered. This topic, however, is delayed and does not begin until 52.29.

52.19b–28 Instead of providing revelation about the Triply-powered as she had promised at 52.18–19, Iouel continues with a warning about the esoteric character of what she is about to tell him. The words Allogenes will hear are to be guarded fiercely in "silence" and "mystery" from those who are not worthy, those who have not attained to teaching about the exalted Entirety. At 58.24–26, the Triply-powered is identified with the Entirety.

The terms "silence" and "mystery" imply not only that the contents of the revelation are esoteric, but they also suggest a cultic setting. The recipients, "those who are worthy," may be initiates who have received preparatory instruction and/or cultic initiation. The minimum content of such preparatory instruction was apparently teaching about "the Entirety that surpasses perfection." Thus Iouel's warning indicates that the content of the revelation which follows is to be communicated only (in a cultic setting?) to persons who have received the necessary preparatory instruction or initiation. Whether or not this setting was part of an ascension or baptismal rite (see pp. 12–16) is impossible to determine with certainty. It is nonetheless a setting in which one could imagine that this text, or at least portions of it, may have been read.

²² ⲟⲛ ϫⲉ ⲛⲁⲓ̈ ⲙⲉⲩϫⲟⲟⲩ ⲛ̄ⲟⲩ
²³ ⲟⲛ ⲛⲓⲙ ⲉⲃⲟⲗ ⲉⲛⲏ ⲉⲧⲙ̄ⲡⲱϣⲁ
²⁴ ⲛⲏ ⲉⲧⲉ ⲟⲩⲛ̄ϭⲟⲙ ⲙ̄ⲙⲟⲟⲩ
²⁵ ⲉⲥⲱⲧⲙ̄· ⲟⲩⲧⲉ ⲙ̄ⲡⲉⲧⲉϣ
²⁶ ϣⲉ ⲁⲛ ⲡⲉ ⲉϫⲟⲟⲩ ⲉϩⲣⲁⲓ̈ ⲉⲩ
²⁷ ⲅⲉⲛⲉⲁ ⲛ̄ⲛⲁⲧⲥⲃⲱ ⲉⲧⲃⲉ ⲡⲓ
²⁸ ⲧⲏⲣϥ̄ ⲉⲧϫⲟⲥⲉ ⲉⲧⲉⲗⲓⲟⲥ·
²⁹ⲟⲩⲛ̄ⲧⲁⲕ ⲇⲉ ⲙ̄ⲙⲁⲩ ⟨ . . . ⟩

ⲉⲧⲃⲉ

³⁰ ⲡⲓϣⲟⲙⲧ̄ ⲛ̄ϭⲟⲙ· ⲡⲏ ⲉⲧϣⲟ
³¹ ⲟⲡ ϩⲛ̄ ⲟⲩⲙⲛ̄ⲧⲙⲁⲕⲁⲣⲓⲟⲥ
³² ⲙⲛ̄ ⲟⲩⲙⲛ̄ⲧⲁⲅⲁⲑⲟⲥ· ⲡⲏ
³³ ⲉⲧⲉ ⲛ̄ⲗⲟⲉⲓϭⲉ ⲉⲛⲁⲓ̈ ⲧⲏⲣⲟⲩ·
³⁴ ⲉⲥϣⲟⲟⲡ ϩⲣⲁⲓ̈ ⲛ̄ϩⲏⲧϥ̄ ⲛ̄ϭⲓ
³⁵ ⲟⲩⲙⲛ̄ⲧⲛⲟϭ ⲉⲛⲁϣⲱⲥ
³⁶ ⲉϥϣⲟⲟⲡ ⲉⲟⲩⲁ ⲡⲉ ϩⲛ̄ ⲟⲩ

53 ¹⁻⁴ [   ]
⁵ ϣⲟ[   ]
⁶ ⲛ̄ⲧⲉ ϯϣ[   ]
⁷ ⲑⲉ ⲁⲛ ⲉⲃ[ⲟⲗ   ]
⁸ ϩⲣⲁⲓ̈ ϩⲛ̄ ⲟⲩⲧⲁϩⲟ [ⲙⲛ̄ ⲟⲩⲅⲛⲱ]
⁹ ⲥⲓⲥ ⲙⲛ̄ ⲟⲩⲉⲡⲓ[ⲥⲧⲏ]ⲙ[ⲏ·

52.29 Turner emends: ⲟⲩⲛ̄ⲧⲁⲕ ⲇⲉ ⲙ̄ⲙⲁⲩ ⟨ⲛ̄ⲛⲁⲓ̈⟩ ⲉⲧⲃⲉ.
53.6–7 Turner restores: ⲛ̄ⲧⲉ ϯϣ[ⲟⲣⲡ̄ ⲛ̄ⲉⲛⲛⲟⲓⲁ ⲡⲏ ⲉ]ⲑⲉ ⲁⲛ ⲉⲃⲟⲗ ϩⲛ̄ ⲛⲏ ⲉⲧϣⲟⲟⲡ] ("of the F[irst Thought, which] does not fall away [from those who dwell]"). The standard negation of the sentence would be ⲉⲧⲉ ⲛ̄ϥϩⲉ ⲁⲛ. ⲉⲧϩⲉ ⲁⲛ is possible, but in this case the line division should be ⲉⲧ/ϩⲉ.
53.9 Turner does not restore raised dot.

ⲛⲏ in line 19 is a loose second object of ⲥⲱⲧⲙ in line 18.

For the use of the full form of the relative ⲉⲧⲉⲕ for ⲉⲧⲕ̄, see H.-M. Schenke, "On the Middle Egyptian Dialect."

52.29–30a The text appears corrupt here. One expects something like: "But you have the (necessary) instruction. Hear now about the Triply-powered." Furthermore, the repetition of ⲉⲧⲃⲉ ⲡⲓϣⲟⲙⲧ̄ ⲛ̄ϭⲟⲙ clearly is a literary device to provide continuity between lines 18–19 and 30 ff. The corruption, following the sudden change of topic and seeming intrusion of lines 19–28, leads one to ask if those lines of warning are a secondary insertion. One can easily imagine the occasion for such an addition, stemming

22 For these are not spoken to
23 everyone, but only to those who are worthy,
24 those who have the capacity
25 to hear. Nor is it fitting
26 to utter these things
27ᵃabout the
28 Entirety that surpasses perfection to a
27ᵇgeneration that is uninstructed.
    29But you possess ⟨. . .⟩
    Concerning
30 the Triply-powered: It
31 exists in blessedness
32 and a state of goodness,
33 as the cause for all these.
34 It is in it that
35 an immense greatness exists.
36 It is in a . . . that it exists being One . . .

53 1–5 [   ]
    6 of the [. . .]
    7 not ou[t of . . .]
    8 in comprehension [and]
    9 [know]ledge and sure under[sta]nd[ing].

> 52.24 "Capacity": or "power."

from a wide circulation that drew unwanted criticism, perhaps such as that of Plotinus.

52.30b–36 These lines describe the Triply-powered. The phrase ϨN ογμⲚⲦⲘⲀⲕⲀⲣⲓⲟⲥ ⲘⲚ ογμⲚⲦⲀⲅⲀⲑⲟⲥ ("in blessedness and a state of goodness") is an adverbial phrase modifying Ϣⲟⲟⲡ ("exists"). The use of the prefix ⲘⲚⲦ before these terms reinforces the transcendence of the Triply-powered. It is not merely good and blessed, but the qualities of goodness and blessedness themselves define the state of its existence. Furthermore, the Triply-powered is the cause for all things (see 49.16–18 and note); it is great in quantity (52.34–35; compare *Ennead* V.8.9 24–28), and, although the sentence beginning on the last line of page 52 is incomplete, it may affirm that the Triply-powered is One.

53.6–9a Although the lacuna at the top of this page makes the context unclear, the appearance of the three terms ⲦⲀϨⲟ ("attain, comprehend"),

ⲁⲩⲱ]

10 ⲁϥⲕⲓⲙ ⲍ̄ⲛ ⲟⲩⲙ̄[ⲛ̄]ⲧ̄ⲁⲧⲕⲓⲙ

11 [ⲛ̄]ϭⲓ ⲡⲏ ⲉⲧ̄ⲙⲙⲁⲩ ⳥ⲣⲁⲓ̈ ⳥ⲙ̄ ⲡⲉⲧ

12 [ⲣ̄]⳥ⲙ̄ⲙⲉ· ⳥ⲓ̄ⲛⲁ ⲭⲉ ⲛⲉϥⲱⲙⲉⲥ

13 ⲉ⳥ⲟⲩⲛ ⲉⲡⲓⲁⲧ̄ⲛⲁⲣⲏⲭ̄ϥ ⲉⲃⲟⲗ

14 ⳥ⲓⲧⲟⲟⲧ̄ⲥ̄ ⲛ̄ⲕⲉⲉⲛⲉⲣⲅⲓⲁ ⲛ̄ⲧⲉ

15 ⲧ̄ⲙⲛ̄ⲧⲉⲓⲙⲉ· ⲁⲩⲱ ⲁϥⲃⲱⲕ

16 ⲉ⳥ⲟⲩⲛ ⲉⲣⲟϥ ⲟⲩⲁⲁϥ· ⲁϥⲟⲩ

17 ⲱⲛ̄⳥ ⲉⲃⲟⲗ ⲉϥⲉ ⲛ̄ⲧ̄ ⲧⲟⲱ ⲛⲓⲙ·

53.10 Supralinear stroke over ⲙⲛⲧ is restored; the letter ⲙ is clear.

ⲅⲛⲱⲥⲓⲥ ("*gnosis*, knowledge"), and ⲉⲡⲓⲥⲧⲏⲙⲏ ("*sure understanding*, knowledge") is especially intriguing. The first term is related to the theme of stability (see above, note to 51.13–32a); the second is a technical term for salvation through knowledge; and the third is the technical philosophical term used to distinguish true knowledge (ἐπιστήμη) from opinion (δόξα).

53.9b–17 This passage again takes up the problem of the origin of Being and can be understood by comparison to 45.22–30 and 49.7–18. Several metaphors and concepts are similar:

The term here is "steersman" instead of "ferryman" as in 49.8, but both terms are metaphorical descriptions of the Triply-powered as mediator.

The nautical metaphor of 49.7–18 is present here in the phrase "lest he should *sink*." (53.12)

The act of generation was described in 45.22–30 as "extending" himself; in 49.11, as "turning herself." Here one talks about "immovably moving" as a "noetic activity" directed inward. "To move immovably" may mean simply that he moved without himself being moved. The Coptic ⲁⲧⲕⲓⲙ may be a translation of the Greek ἀκίνητος or ἀμετακίνητος (see Plato, *Timaeus* 40B).

The concept of the "unmoved mover" is of course important in Aristotelian metaphysics and was also of considerable importance in the metaphysical discussions of later Platonists, though not necessarily with the same implications.

The result of the act in 45.28–30 is the coming into being of the Triply-powered as the aeon of Barbelo; in 49.11–19, it is knowledge which comes into being. Here the pronominal referents remain obscure, but analogy with 45.22–30 and 49.7–18 would permit identifying them with Barbelo and the Triply-powered.

[And]

11 he who is there in the steersman

10 moved immovably

14 through another activity of

15a intellection—

12 lest he should sink

13 down into the Boundless one.

15b And he went

16 into himself; he

17 appeared having set all limits.

53.11–17 The antecedent of the pronoun "he" in these sentences is probably Barbelo. See exegetical note to 45.17b–22a.
53.14–15 Or: "through a different activity of intellection."

In 49.9–10, the text mentions "the boundlessness of the Invisible Spirit." Here is mentioned "the Boundless," to be understood as the Invisible Spirit.

Comparison with these two other passages, therefore, allows the following paraphrase of 53.9b–17:

Barbelo, being present (potentially) in the steersman (the Triply-powered), moved motionlessly by a noetic activity—lest he (Barbelo) should sink down into the Boundless (the Invisible Spirit). And Barbelo went into himself. He (Barbelo) appeared having set all limits.

One can compare again Plotinus, *Ennead* VI.7.17:

The Life was a vestige of that Primal, not a life lived by it; Life, then, as it looked towards That was undetermined; having looked it had determination though That had none. Life looks to unity and is determined by it, taking bound, limit, form.   (trans. MacKenna, *Plotinus*, 575)

The concept in both *Allogenes* and Plotinus seems to be quite similar: the Supreme (the One/Primal or the Invisible Spirit) is undetermined or "boundless." The potential of all things (Life, the Triply-powered) takes on determination (as Intellect, Barbelo) by "looking" or some such "noetic activity." Both Plotinus and *Allogenes* are addressing a similar problem: how multiplicity arises from transcendent Unity. And the solutions they present are also similar: everything is present potentially in the Primal Unity (the One or Invisible Spirit); it becomes actualized by some noetic movement.

The phrase ϩⲣⲁⲓ ϩⲙ ⲡⲉⲧⲣ̄ϩⲙ̄ⲙⲉ ("in the steersman"; 53.11–12) can be taken either with ⲁϥⲕⲓⲙ ("he moved") or with ⲡⲏ ⲉⲧⲙ̄ⲙⲁⲩ ("he who is

¹⁸ⲡⲓⲧⲏⲣϥ ⲉⲧϫⲟⲥⲉ ⲉⲧⲉⲗⲓⲟⲥ·
¹⁹ ⲉϥⲉ ⲛ̄ϣⲟⲣⲡ̄ ⲙⲉⲛ ⲉϯⲅⲛⲱ
²⁰ ⲥⲓⲥ ⲛ̄ϯ϶ⲉ ⲉⲃⲟⲗ ϩⲓⲧⲟⲟⲧ ⲁⲛ
²¹ ⲉⲡⲓⲁⲏ ⲙ̄ⲙⲛ̄6ⲟⲙ ⲉⲡⲓⲧⲉ϶ⲟ
²² ⲛ̄ⲧⲉⲗⲓⲟⲥ ⲉⲩⲉⲓⲙⲉ ⲉⲣⲟϥ ⲛ̄
²³ ϯ϶ⲉ ⲁⲉ ⲡⲁⲓ̈· ⲉⲧⲃⲉ ⲡⲓⲙⲉ϶
²⁴ ϣⲟⲙⲧ̄ ⲛ̄ⲕⲁⲣⲱϥ ⲛ̄ⲧⲉ ϯⲙⲛ̄ⲧ
²⁵ ⲉⲓⲙⲉ· ⲙⲛ̄ ϯⲙⲉ϶ⲥ̄ⲛⲧⲉ ⲛⲉ
²⁶ ⲛⲉⲣⲅⲓⲁ ⲛ̄ⲁⲧⲡⲱⲣⲝ̄ ⲉⲧⲁⲥⲟⲩ
²⁷ ⲱⲛ̄϶ ⲉⲃⲟⲗ ϩⲛ̄ ϯϣⲟⲣⲡ̄ ⲛⲉⲛ
²⁸ ⲛⲟⲓⲁ ⲉⲧⲉ ⲡⲓⲉⲱⲛ ⲡⲉ ⲛ̄ⲃⲁⲣ
²⁹ ⲃⲏⲗⲱ· ⲙⲛ̄ ⲡⲓⲁⲧⲡⲱϣ ⲛ̄
³⁰ ⲛⲓⲛⲉ ⲙ̄ⲡⲱϣ· ⲙⲛ̄ ⲡⲓϣⲙⲛ̄ⲧ
³¹ 6ⲟⲙ· ⲙⲛ̄ ϯϩⲩⲡⲁⲣϫⲓⲥ ⲛ̄ⲛⲁ
³² ⲧⲟⲩⲥⲓⲁ ⲙⲛ̄ ϯ6ⲟⲙ·

ⲁⲥⲟⲩ
³³ ⲱⲛ̄϶ ⲉⲃⲟⲗ’ ⲉⲃⲟⲗ ϩⲓⲧⲛ̄ ⲟⲩⲉ
³⁴ ⲛⲉⲣⲅⲓⲁ ⲉⲥϩⲟⲣⲕ̄ ⲙ̄ⲙⲟⲥ
³⁵ ⲁⲩⲱ ⲉⲥⲕⲱ ⲛ̄ⲣⲱⲥ ⲉⲁⲥϯ
³⁶ ⲛ̄ⲟⲩϩⲣⲟⲟⲩ ⲛ̄ϯ϶ⲉ ϫⲉ ⲍⲍⲁ
³⁷ ⲍⲍⲁ ⲍⲍⲁ·

ⲛ̄ⲧⲉⲣⲉⲥⲥⲱⲧⲙ̄
³⁸ ⲁⲉ ⲉϯ6ⲟⲙ· ⲁⲩⲱ ⲁⲥⲙⲟⲩϩ

53.20 According to sense, the particle ⲁⲛ negates only ⲉⲃⲟⲗ ϩⲓⲧⲟⲟⲧ.
53.32 Turner emends: ⲧⲟⲩⲥⲓⲁ⟨·⟩ ⟨ⲁⲩⲱ⟩ ϯ6ⲟⲙ{·}.

there"). First reading: "he who is there moved motionlessly in the steersman lest he should sink down into the boundless one . . ." Second reading: "he who is there in the steersman moved motionlessly" etc. The two readings are not mutually exclusive.

The term ⲕⲉ before ⲉⲛⲉⲣⲅⲓⲁ ("activity"; line 14) can be understood as a "wrong" activity that would lead him to sink, or it can be taken with the next phrase "he went into himself," in which case the activity would be positive, implying a "different" activity.

53.18–32a The transcendence of the Entirety makes perfect knowledge of it impossible.

Such knowledge of the Entirety as is possible cannot be made known by Iouel, but only through "him" (presumably Barbelo since "he" is the source of saving knowledge for those below). Even then, such knowledge is clearly limited: compare 61.25–32.

¹⁸The Entirety which surpasses perfection,

¹⁹ being, on the one hand, prior to that

²⁰ knowledge, (is) in no way (made known) through me—

²¹ since it is not possible (for me to attain) perfect comprehension—

²² but, on the other hand, as far as it is made known

²³ (such knowledge is possible) through him, because of the

²⁴ third silence of the

²⁵ Intellection and the second

²⁶ undivided activity that

²⁷ appeared from the first

²⁸ thought—which is the aeon of

²⁹ Barbelo—together with the indivisible

³⁰ likeness of the utterance and the Triply-

³¹ powered and the subsistenceless

³² subsistence and the power.

She

³³ appeared through an

³⁴ activity, being still

³⁵ and silent after she uttered

³⁶ a sound in this manner: 'ZZA

³⁷ ZZA ZZA.'

But when she heard

³⁸ this power, and she was full. . .

53.29–30 Or: "divided indivisible likeness."

ⲡⲓⲧⲏⲣ̄ϥ ⲉⲧⲭⲟⲥⲉ ⲉⲧⲉⲗⲓⲟⲥ ("the Entirety which surpasses perfection"; line 18) is the antecedent of the pronominal references in 53.19 and 22 in extraposition.

For the possible meanings of the term "prior" (line 19), see above, note to 47.9b–38; Aristotle, *Cat.* 12.

ⲁⲛ (line 20) negates only ⲉⲃⲟⲗ ϩ̄ⲓⲧⲟⲟⲧ.

The unusual placement of ⲇⲉ in line 23 indicates that the force of the ⲙⲉⲛ/ⲇⲉ opposition is between "me" (Iouel) and "him."

The aeon of Barbelo appears again as a triad in 53.23b–32a: the first thought, the second undivided activity, and the third silence of intellection. In other Sethian texts (for example *ApJohn* II,1,5.4), Barbelo is called the "first thought" (*pronoia*) of the Father or Invisible Spirit.

The phrase following ⲉⲧⲃⲉ ("because of"; line 23) could concern either

54 1-4 [   ]
  5 [   ]..e
  6 [   ]ⲗⲉ ⲛ̄ⲧⲕ
  7 [   ]ⲩⲥ· ⲥⲟⲗⲙⲓⲥ·
  8 [ⲕ]ⲁⲧⲁ ⲧ̄ⲙ̄ⲛ̄ⲧⲱⲛ̄ⲅ̄
  9 [ⲉⲧ]ⲛ̄ⲧ[ⲁⲕ ⲙ̄ⲛ̄] ⲧ̄ϣⲟⲣⲡ̄ ⲛ̄ⲉⲛⲉⲣ
  10 [ⲅ]ⲓⲁ ⲧⲏ ⲉⲧ[ⲉ] ⲉⲃⲟⲗ ⲙ̄ⲙⲟⲥ ⲧⲉ
  11 ⲧ̄ⲙ̄ⲛ̄ⲧⲛⲟⲩⲧⲉ· ⲛ̄ⲧⲕ ⲟⲩⲛⲟϭ
  12 ⲁⲣⲙⲏⲗⲱⲛ· ⲛ̄ⲧⲕ ⲟⲩⲧⲉⲗⲓⲟ[ⲥ]
  13 ⲉⲡⲓⲫⲁⲛⲉⲩ· ⲕⲁⲧⲁ ⲗⲉ ⲧ̄ⲉⲛ[ⲉ]ⲣ
  14 ⲅⲓⲁ ⲗⲉ ⲉⲧⲛ̄ⲧⲁⲕ· ⲧ̄ϭⲟⲙ ⲙ̄ⲙⲉⲅ
  15 ⲥ̄ⲛⲧⲉ ⲙ̄ⲛ̄ ⲧ̄ⲙ̄ⲛ̄ⲧⲉⲓⲙⲉ· ⲧⲏ ⲉ
  16 ⲧⲉ ⲉⲃⲟⲗ ⲙ̄ⲙⲟ⟨ⲥ⟩ ⲧⲉ ⲧ̄ⲙ̄ⲛ̄ⲧⲙⲁ
  17 ⲕⲁⲣⲓⲟⲥ· ⲁ̄ⲩⲧⲟⲏⲣ· ⲃⲏⲣⲓ̄ⲑⲉⲩ·

54.5 Turner restores:].ⲛⲉ.
54.9 Supralinear stroke above the first ⲛ is restored.
54.16 The manuscript reads: ⲙ̄ⲙⲟϥ.

what follows or what precedes, though the former construction would be highly unusual. If one takes the phrase with what precedes, it seems to indicate how knowledge of the Entirety is made known—through thought, noetic activity, and silence (the Barbelo aeon), and from indivisible utterance (the Triply-powered), and subsistenceless subsistence (the Invisible Spirit). As will be seen below, knowledge of the Entirety cannot be conveyed in discursive revelation, such as Iouel gives, but only through a vision (primary revelation) of the divine hierarchy through ascent (see 60.10–61.1).

53.32b–54.37 See pp. 14–16.

It is difficult to decide who the (feminine) speaker of the invocation is. Robinson ("Three Steles of Seth," 134) has suggested Iouel, but if so then the speaker of the sounds, "ZZA ZZA ZZA," would be different from the speaker of the invocation. The emendation of Turner (see "Allogenes," textual note to 53.32) supposes the speaker is a "power," but then the referent of the feminine pronoun in 53.37b remains unexplained. Schenke has suggested that the speaker may be hypostasized knowledge (*gnosis*). This suggestion works well since the antecedent is feminine and knowledge was the topic of the previous sentence (see 53.19–20).

The first sounds spoken, "ZZA ZZA ZZA," would seem to be an esoteric name or invocation. Compare *Marsanes* 25.12–32.5; *Zost* 118.21; 127.1–5 (especially zoe zeoe . . . zosi zosi zao ziooo zesen zesen); *GosEgypt* 66.8–22; *TriProt* 38.29; the Hermetic *Discourse on the Eighth and Ninth* 56.17–22

54 ¹⁻⁵ [   ]

⁶ ['. . .] but you are [. . .]

⁷ [. . .] us! Solmis!

⁸ [. . . ac]cording to the Vitality

⁹ [that is] you[rs and] (according to) the first activity

¹⁰ from whom

¹¹ divinity derives. You are great,

¹² O Armedon! You are perfect,

¹³ O Epiphaneus! But according to the activity

¹⁴ that is yours, the second power

¹⁵ and the Intellection,

¹⁶ from whom

¹⁷ blessedness derives, (I invoke you), O Autoer! Beritheus!

(especially the name Zozazoth), 62.4–18. See also Dornseiff, *Das Alphabet* and Pearson, *Codex IX and X*, 236–238; 292–308.

There is a clear parallel to portions of this invocation in *Three Steles of Seth:*

ⲚⲦⲔ ⲞⲨⲀ ⲚⲦⲔ ⲞⲨⲀ ⲔⲀⲦⲀ ⲠⲢⲎⲦⲈ ⲈⲦⲈ ⲞⲨⲚ̄ ⲞⲨⲀ ⲚⲀϪⲞⲞⲤ ⲈⲢⲞⲔ ϪⲈ ⲚⲦⲔ
ⲞⲨⲀ ⲚⲦⲔ ⲞⲨⲠⲚ̄Ⲁ ⲚⲞⲨⲰⲦ ⲈϥⲞⲚϨ̄· ⲈⲚⲚⲀϯ ⲢⲀⲚ ⲈⲢⲟⲔ ⲚⲀϢ Ⲛ̄ϨⲈ· Ⲛ̄ϥⲚ̄ⲦⲀⲚ
Ⲙ̄ⲘⲀⲨ ⲀⲚ· ⲚⲦⲞⲔ ⲄⲀⲢ ⲠⲈ ϯϨⲨⲠⲀⲢϪⲒⲤ ⲚⲦⲈ ⲚⲀ ̈Ⲓ ⲦⲎⲢⲞⲨ· ⲚⲦⲞⲔ ⲠⲈ ⲠⲰⲚϨ
ⲚⲦⲈ ⲚⲀ ̈Ⲓ ⲦⲎⲢⲞⲨ· ⲚⲦⲞⲔ ⲠⲈ ⲠⲚⲞⲨⲤ ⲚⲦⲈ Ⲛ[Ⲁ ̈Ⲓ] ⲦⲎⲢⲞⲨ· ⲚⲦⲞⲔ [ⲈⲦⲈ ⲚⲀ ̈Ⲓ]
ⲦⲎ[ⲢⲞ]Ⲩ ⲦⲈⲖⲎⲖ ⲚⲀⲔ ⲚⲦⲞⲔ ⲀⲔⲞⲨⲈϨⲤⲀϨ[Ⲛ]Ⲉ Ⲛ̄ⲚⲀ ̈Ⲓ ⲦⲎⲢ[Ⲟ]Ⲩ
Ⲉ[ⲦⲢ]Ⲉ[ⲨⲚ]ⲞⲨ[Ϩ]Ⲙ̄ ϨⲘ̄ ⲠⲈⲔ ϢⲀ[ϪⲈ.]...[.] [ ]Ⲙ Ⲙ̄Ⲙ[ⲞⲞⲨ]· ⲠⲒⲈ[ⲞⲞⲨ]
ⲚϢⲰⲢ̄Ⲡ ⲈⲦϨⲀϪⲰϥ [ⲠⲒⲔ]Ⲗ̄Ⲥ ⲠⲘ[Ⲁ]ⲔⲀⲢⲒⲞⲤ ⲤⲎⲚⲀⲰⲚ [ⲈⲦⲀϥ]ϪⲠⲞ ⲈⲂⲞⲖ
Ⲙ̄ⲘⲞϥ ⲞⲨⲀⲀ[ϥ ...]ⲚⲈⲨ. ⲘⲈϤⲚⲈⲨ· ⲞⲠⲦⲀⲰⲚ· ⲈⲖⲈⲘⲀⲰⲚ ⲠⲒⲚⲞϬ Ⲛ̄ϬⲞⲘ·
ⲈⲘⲞⲨⲚⲒⲀⲢ· ⲚⲒⲂⲀⲢⲈⲨ· ⲔⲀⲚⲆⲎϤⲞⲢⲈ· ⲀϤⲢⲎⲆⲰⲚ· Ⲁ̄ⲎⲒϤⲀⲚⲈⲨⲤ· ⲚⲦⲞⲔ ⲈⲦⲈ
Ⲛ̄ⲀⲢⲘⲎⲆⲰⲚ ⲚⲀ ̈Ⲓ ⲠⲒⲢⲈϥϪⲠⲈ ϬⲞⲘ· ⲐⲀⲖⲀⲚⲀⲐⲈⲨ· Ⲁ̄ⲚⲦⲒⲐⲈⲨⲤ· ⲚⲦⲞⲔ
ⲈⲦϢⲞⲞⲠ Ⲛ̄ϨⲢⲀ ̈Ⲓ Ⲛ̄ϨⲎⲦⲔ ⲘⲀⲨⲀⲀⲔ· ⲚⲦⲞⲔ ⲈⲦϨⲀϪⲰⲔ ⲘⲀⲨⲀⲀⲔ· ⲀⲨⲰ Ⲙ̄Ⲙ̄Ⲛ
Ⲛ̄ⲤⲰⲔ Ⲙ̄ⲠⲈⲖⲀⲀⲨ Ⲉ̄Ⲓ ⲈⲨⲈⲚⲈⲢⲄⲈⲒ·

You are one! You are one, as an individual can say to you "You are one! You are a single living spirit." In what manner shall we name you? We do not have it (any appropriate way to name you). For you are the Subsistence of them all. You are the Life of them all. You are the Intellect of them all. You are him in whom they all rejoice. You commanded them all, causing them to be saved by your word [. . .] the [firs]t g[lory] which is before him. The Hidden one (Kalyptos). The Blessed one. Senaon who alone begat himself [. . .]neu. Mepheu. Optaon. Elemaon. The great power. Emouniar. Nibareu. Kandephore. Aphredon. Deiphaneus. You are he who is Armedon to me. O power-begetter. Thalanatheu. Antitheus. You are he who exists within yourself alone. You are he who is

¹⁸ ⲎⲢⲓⲅⲉⲛⲁⲱⲣ· ⲱⲣⲓⲙⲉⲛⲓⲉ· ⲁⲣⲁ
¹⁹ ⲙⲉⲛ· ⲁⲗⲫⲗⲉⲅⲉⲥ· ⲏⲗⲏⲗⲓⲟⲩⲫⲉⲩ·
²⁰ [ⲗ]ⲁⲗⲁⲙⲉⲩ· ⲓⲉⲑⲉⲩ· ⲛⲟⲏⲑⲉⲩ[·]
²¹ ⲛⲧⲕ ⲟⲩⲛⲟϭ ⲡⲏ ⲉⲧⲉⲓⲙⲉ ⲉⲣⲟ[ϥ]
²² ϥⲓⲙⲉ ⲉⲡⲧⲏⲣϥ· ⲛⲧⲕ ⲟⲩⲁ ⲛ
²³ ⲧⲕ ⲟⲩⲁ ⲡⲏ ⲉⲧⲛⲁⲛⲟⲩϥ ⲁⲫⲣⲏ
²⁴ ⲁⲱⲛ· ⲛⲧⲟⲕ ⲡⲉ ⲡⲉⲱⲛ ⲛⲧⲉ
²⁵ ⲛⲉⲱⲛ ⲡⲏ ⲉⲧϣⲟⲟⲡ ⲛⲟⲩⲟ
²⁶ ⲉⲓϣ ⲛⲓⲙ·
     ⲧⲟⲧⲉ ⲁⲥⲥⲙⲟⲩ ⲉ
²⁷ ⲡⲓⲟⲩⲁ ⲧⲏⲣϥ ⲉⲥϫⲱ ⲙⲙⲟⲥ
²⁸ ϫⲉ ⲗⲁⲗⲁⲙⲉⲩ· ⲛⲟ[ⲏⲑ]ⲉⲩ· ⲥⲏ
²⁹ ⲛⲁⲱⲛ· ⲁⲥⲓⲛⲉ[ⲩ·ⲁ]ⲣⲓⲫⲁⲛⲓⲉ
³⁰ ⲙⲉⲗⲗⲉⲫⲁⲛⲉⲩ[·] ⲉⲗⲉⲙⲁⲱⲛⲓ·
³¹ ⲥⲙⲟⲩⲛ· ⲟⲡⲧⲁⲱⲛ· ⲡⲏ ⲉⲧ
³² ϣⲟⲟⲡ· ⲛⲧⲟⲕ ⲡⲉ ⲡⲉⲧϣⲟ
³³ ⲟⲡ ⲡⲓⲉⲱⲛ ⲛⲧⲉ ⲛⲉⲱⲛ· ⲡⲓ
³⁴ ⲁⲧϫⲡⲟ ⲉⲧϫⲟⲥⲉ ⲉⲛⲓⲁⲧϫⲡⲟ

54.21 Turner restores: ⲉⲣⲟ[ⲕ] in keeping with the second person address, but more properly it should be restored ⲉⲣⲟϥ to correspond to the construction with ⲡⲉ and to forms in lines 21, 23, and 24.
54.24 The scribe did not complete the supralinear stroke over ⲁⲱⲛ.
54.29 Turner restores: [ⲩ· ⲱ].

before yourself alone and after you there is not anyone to enter into activity.   (125.23–126.17)

It is especially important to note here the presence of the triad Subsistence (Existence), Life, and Intellect (125.28–32). As discussed above pp. 26–28, this triad connects the invocation with the ascent itself.

Konrad Wekel notes five perspectives that lead one to see a close relationship between these two passages: 1) Both texts give an invocation in the second person style ("You . . ."). 2) Apparently the invocation takes place in distinctive steps as is shown by 3) the appearance of magical words and names. 4) Some of the same names appear, as well as 5) the same and similar formulas (see *Drei Stelen des Seth*, 181–190). He concludes: "The comparison that has been carried out leads to the conclusion and result that the two passages within the texts known to us apparently present materials formed through liturgical use" (*Drei Stelen des Seth*, 190; see also Robinson, "The Three Steles of Seth," 133–136, and H.-M. Schenke, "The Phenomenon," 601–602.)

18 Erigenaor! Orimenios! Aramen!
19 Alphleges! Elelioupheus!
20 [L]alameus! Ietheus! Noetheus!
21 You are great! Whoever knows [him],
22 knows the Entirety. You are One!
23 You are One, that one who is good, O Aphredon!
24 You are the aeon of
25 aeons who exists at
26 every time.'
    Then she praised
27 the entire One, saying:
28 'Lalameus! Noetheus!
29 Senaon! Asineus[! A]riphanios!
30 Mellephaneus[!] Elemaoni!
31 Smoun! Optaon, that one who
32 exists! You are he who
33 exists, the aeon of aeons, that
34 unbegotten one who surpasses the unbegotten ones,

A second parallel may exist in *Zostrianos* 88, though the extremely poor condition of the manuscript makes an assessment uncertain. What remains of the text can be translated:

9 bless [. . .]
10 Be[ritheus, Erigneaor]
11 Or[imeni]os Ar[amen]
12 Alphl[ege], Elilio[upheus],
13 Lalamenus, Noetheu(s) [. . .]
14 Great is your name! [. . .]
15 He is strong! He who knows
16 brings truth to all. You are
17 one! You are one! You are one! Sious, E[. . .]
18 Aphredon, you are the [aeon]
19 of the aeons of the
20 great, perfect, first
21 Hidden one (Kalyptos) of the [. . .]
22 activity, and [. . .]
23 [. . .]
24 his image [. . .]
25 of his [. . .

35 ⲓ̈ⲁ̅ⲧ̅ⲟ̅ⲙ̅ⲉ̅ⲛ̅ⲉ̅· ⲛ̅ⲧⲟⲕ ⲟⲩⲁⲁⲕ
36 ⲉⲧⲁⲩϫⲡⲟ ⲛⲁⲕ ⲛ̅ⲛⲓⲁⲧⲙⲓ
37 ⲥⲉ ⲧⲏⲣⲟⲩ· ⲡⲓⲁⲧϯⲣⲁⲛ ⲉ

55
1 [ⲣⲟϥ]
2–9 [ ]
10 [ ].[ ]
11 [ⲙ̅ⲛ̅ⲧ̅]ⲉ̣ⲓⲙⲉ
ⲁ
12 [ⲛⲟⲕ ⲇⲉ ⲛ̅ⲧⲁⲣⲓ]ⲥ̣[ⲱ]ⲧ̅ⲙ̅ ⲉⲛⲁ̈ⲓ ⲁⲉⲓ
13 [ⲛⲁⲩ ⲉⲛⲉⲟⲟⲩ] ⲛ̅ⲛ̣ⲓ̣ⲕⲁⲧⲁ ⲟⲩⲁ
14 [ⲛ̅ⲧⲉⲗⲓⲟⲥ ⲁⲩ]ⲱ̣ ⲛⲓⲡⲁⲛⲧⲉⲗⲓⲟⲥ
15 [ⲛⲏ ⲉⲧϣⲟⲟⲡ ϩ̅ⲓ̅]ⲟ̣ⲩⲙⲁ· ⲙ̅ⲛ̅ ⲛⲓ
16 [ⲡⲧⲏⲣ̅ϥ̅ ⲉⲧϣⲟⲟⲡ ⲉ]ⲧ̣ϩⲁⲑⲏ ⲛ̅ⲛⲓⲧⲉ
17 [ⲗⲓⲟⲥ·
ⲡⲁⲗⲓⲛ] ⲟⲛ ⲡⲉϫⲁⲥ ⲛⲁ̈ⲓ
18 [ⲛ̅ϭⲓ ⲧⲛⲟϭ ⲛ̅] ⲛ̣ⲉⲟⲟⲩ ⲓ̈ⲟ̅ⲩ̅ⲏ̅ⲗ̅·
19 [ϫⲉ ⲡⲁⲗⲗⲟⲅⲉ]ⲛⲏⲥ ϩ̅ⲛ̅ ⲟⲩⲉⲓ
20 [ⲙⲉ ⲛ̅ⲁⲧⲉⲓⲙⲉ] ⲉⲕⲉⲓⲙⲉ· ϫⲉ ⲡⲓ
21 [ϣⲟⲙⲧ ⲛ̅ϭⲟ]ⲙ ϥϣⲟⲟⲡ ϩⲁ

55.11 Restoration by King.
55.16 Turner restores: [ⲡⲁⲛⲧⲉⲗⲓⲟⲥ ⲉ]ⲧ̣ϩⲁⲑⲏ ("[all-perfect ones who] are before").
55.17 Restoration by H.-M. Schenke. See fragment four of page 82, *Facsimile Edition*, where ⲡⲁ]ⲗⲓⲛ ⲟⲛ[may actually occur.
55.18 Turner restores: [ⲛ̅ϭⲓ ⲧⲁⲛ̅ⲛⲟϭ]ⲛ̣ⲉⲟⲟⲩ.

In what little remains, we see the following parallels to *Allogenes*: the form of invocation is the same; certain names (Be[ritheus], Or[imeni]os, Ar[amen], Alphl[ege]s, Elilio[upheus] or Elelioupheus, Lalameus, Noetheu(s) Aphredon, and Kalyptos) and phrases ("You are one!"; "Aphredon, you are the aeon of aeons") are found in both passages, as well as more common terms such as "activity."

Trimorphic Protennoia 38.33–39.5 describes four aeons, each associated with three names:

first aeon:	Armedon, Nousa[nios, Armozel]
second aeon:	Phaionios, Ainios, Oroiael
third aeon:	Mellephaneus, Loios, Daveithai
fourth aeon:	Mousanios, Amethes, Eleleth

³⁵ Iatomenos! It is for you alone
³⁶ that all the unbegotten ones were begotten.
³⁷ The unnameable one . . .'

55^{1–10} [   ]
¹¹ [. . .] know[ledge]."
        ¹²[For after I] had he[a]rd these things, I
¹³ [saw the glories] of the [perfect] individuals,
¹⁴ [an]d the all-perfect ones,
¹⁵ [those that exist to]gether and the
¹⁶ [entireties t]hat exist before the
^{17a}per[fect ones.]
        [Then again]
¹⁸ [the one to whom great] glories [pertain], Iouel,
^{17b}said to me:
¹⁹ "[Alloge]nes, it is with an [unknowing]
²⁰ know[ledge] that you know that the
²¹ [Triply-powe]red exists

55.15 Or: "in one place."

Each aeon gives and receives glory and all together the glories bless the Perfect Son. Again, the hymnic context of these names appears clearly (compare 38.24 ff.; 39.12 ff.). (For further discussion, see Wekel, *Die Drei Stelen des Seth*, 181–91; H.-M. Schenke, "Phenomenon," 601; Robinson, "Three Steles of Seth," 133–136; G. Schenke, *Die dreigestaltige Protennoia*, 116.)

The forms in lines 12–13, 17–22, 23–24, 28–32, and 35 are all vocatives. Even пн єтϣооп in lines 31–32 is a Coptic vocative.

Turner takes ñток оуаак єтаγхпо нак ñнιатмιсє тнроγ as a vocative; grammatically it can also be a shortened cleft sentence: "It is for you alone that all the unbegotten ones were begotten" (54.35–37).

One can also see here some sloppiness on the part of the scribe. He has left off the distinguishing stroke from ноноєγ in line 20 and аωн in line 24.

54.37–55.11 The hymn of praise breaks off in a lacuna.

The second revelation appears to end at 55.11.

Allogenes' reaction to the third revelation

55–56 This leaf, containing pages 55–56, is the most fragmentary in the codex. It contains portions of revelations from Iouel and the response of Allogenes.

²² [ⲑⲏ ⲛ̅ⲛⲁ ⲧ ⲧⲏⲣⲟ ⲩ] ⲛ̅ⲥⲉ ⲱ ⲟ ⲟⲡ ⲁⲛ
²³ [ⲛ̅ⲑⲉ ⲛⲏ ⲉⲧ ⲱ ⲟ]ⲟⲡ ⲛ̅ⲥⲉ ⲱ ⲟ ⲟⲡ
²⁴ [ⲁⲛ ⲍ ⲓⲟ ⲩ ⲙⲁ] ⲙ̅ⲛ̅ ⲛⲏ ⲉⲧ ⲱ ⲟ ⲟⲡ
²⁵ [ⲛⲁ ⲧ ⲛⲉ ⲛⲉⲧ ⲱ]ⲟⲟⲡ ⲟ ⲛⲧ ⲱ ⲥ
²⁶ [ⲁⲗⲗⲁ ⲛⲁ ⲧ ⲧⲏⲣ]ⲟ ⲩ ⲉ ⲩ ⲱ ⲟ ⲟⲡ
²⁷ [ⲛ̅ⲟⲩ ⲙ̅ⲛ̅ⲧ̅ⲛ ⲟ ⲩ]ⲧⲉ ⲙ̅ⲛ̅ ⲟ ⲩ ⲙ̅ⲛ̅ⲧ̅
²⁸ [ⲙⲁⲕⲁⲣⲓⲟⲥ ⲙ̅ⲛ̅] ⲟ ⲩ ⲍ ⲩ ⲡⲁⲣⲍⲓⲥ·
²⁹ [ⲁ ⲩ ⲱ ⲛ̅ⲟⲩ ⲙ̅ⲛ̅ⲧ̅]ⲁⲧⲟ ⲩ ⲥ ⲓⲁ ⲙ̅ⲛ̅
³⁰ [ⲟ ⲩ ⲍ ⲩ ⲡⲁⲣⲍⲓⲥ] ⲛ̅ⲁⲧ ⲱ ⲱ ⲡⲉ·
  ³¹[ⲁ ⲩ ⲱ ⲧ ⲟ ⲧⲉ ⲁ]ⲉ[ⲓ]ⲧ ⲱ ⲃ̅ⲍ̅ ⲭⲉ ⲉⲣ ⲉ
³² [ⲡⲟ ⲩ ⲱ ⲛ̅ⲍ̅ ⲉ ⲃ]ⲟ ⲗ ⲱ ⲱ ⲡⲉ ⲛⲁ ⲧ
  ³³[ⲁ ⲩ ⲱ ⲧⲟⲧⲉ ⲡⲉ]ⲭⲁⲥ ⲛⲁ ⲧ ⲛ̅ϭⲓ
³⁴ [ⲧⲁ ⲛⲓⲉ ⲟⲟ ⲩ] ⲧⲏⲣⲟ ⲩ ⲓ̅ⲟ̅ ⲩ̅ ⲏ̅ ⲗ̅
³⁵ [ⲭⲉ ⲡⲓⲁ ⲩ ⲧⲟ ⲅ]ⲉⲛⲏⲥ ⲙⲉⲛ
³⁶ [ⲡⲉ ⲡⲓ ⲱ ⲙ̅ⲛ̅]ⲧ ⲍ ⲟ ⲟ ⲩ ⲧ ⲉ ⲩ
³⁷ [ⲗⲁⲁ ⲩ ⲡⲉ ⲕⲁⲧ]ⲁ ⲟ ⲩ ⲟ ⲩ ⲥ ⲓⲁ·
³⁸ [ⲟ ⲩ ⲙ̅ⲛ̅ⲧ̅ⲁⲧⲟ ⲩ]ⲥ ⲓⲁ ⲁⲉ ⲡⲉ ⲡⲓ

56 ¹⁻⁷ [   ]
   ⁸ [ⲉ]
   ⁹ [ⲃ]ⲟ ⲗ[   ]
   ¹⁰ ⲛⲏ ⲉⲧ ⲱ ⲟ[ⲟ]ⲡ [ⲍ̅ⲛ̅ ⲟ ⲩ ⲥ ⲩ ⲥ ⲧⲁ]
   ¹¹ ⲥⲓⲥ ⲙ̅ⲛ̅ ⲧ̅[ⲅ]ⲉ[ⲛⲉⲁ ⲛ̅ⲧⲉ ⲛⲏ]
   ¹² ⲉⲧ ⲱ ⲟ ⲟⲡ ⲟ[ⲛⲧ ⲱ ⲥ· ⲉ ⲩ ⲱ ⲟ]

55.22 Turner restores: [ⲑⲏ ⲛ̅ⲛⲓⲉ ⲟ ⲟ ⲩ].
55.23 Turner restores: [ⲙ̅ⲛ̅ ⲛⲉⲧ ⲱ ⲟ]ⲟⲡ ("[among those who ex]ist").
55.24 Restoration by King.
55.25 Turner restores: [ⲟ ⲩ ⲧⲉ ⲛⲏ ⲉⲧ ⲱ]ⲟ ⲟⲡ ("[nor those who ex]ist").
55.30 Or: [ⲟ ⲩ ⲙ̅ⲛ̅ⲧ̅ⲱ ⲱ ⲡⲉ].
55.35–36 Turner restores: [ⲭⲉ ⲱ̅ ⲡⲁⲗⲗ ⲟ ⲅ]ⲉⲛⲏⲥ ⲙⲉⲛ[ⲧⲟⲓ ⲡⲓ ⲱ ⲙ̅ⲛ̅]ⲧ ⲍ ⲟ ⲟ ⲩ ⲧ ("'O Allogenes, of course, [the Triple-] Male'").
55.37 Turner restores: [ⲗⲁⲁ ⲩ ⲡⲉ ⲛ̅ⲥ]ⲁ ("[something beyon]d").
55.38 Turner restores: [ⲉⲛⲉ ⲩ ⲁⲧⲟ ⲩ]ⲥ ⲓⲁ ("[were he insubstantial]").

55.12–17a See pp. 31–32.
After hearing about the Triply-powered, Allogenes asks about the perfect individuals and the all-perfect ones.

The fourth revelation to Allogenes

55.17b–30 These lines contain Iouel's response to Allogenes' query concerning the existents.

²² be[fore them all]. They do not exist

²³ [as do those which (truly) ex]ist. They do [not] exist

²⁴ [together] with those who exist.

²⁵ [These are those who] truly [ex]ist.

²⁶ᵃBut it is in

²⁷ [deit]y and

²⁸ [blessed]ness [and] subsistence

²⁹ [and] insubstantial[ity] and

³⁰ [a] non-existent [subsistence]

²⁶ᵇthat [al]l [these] exist."

³¹[And then I] prayed that

³² [the revelatio]n would be given to me.

³³ᵃ[And then]

³⁴ the all-[glorious] Iouel

³³ᵇsaid to me:

³⁵ "[This Autog]enes is, on the one hand,

³⁶ [thric]e-male, being

³⁷ [something with res]pect to substance;

³⁸ on the other hand, he is [an insub]stantial [being], the . . .

56 ¹⁻⁸ [   ] . . .

⁹ [fr]om [. . .]

¹⁰ those which exi[s]t [in associa]tion

¹¹ together with the [gen]era[tion of those]

¹² who t[ruly] exist. [It is]

55.24 Literally: "[in one place]."
55.34 Literally: "she to whom all the glories pertain, Iouel."
55.35 "Autogenes" means "self-generated one."

Allogenes' reaction to the fourth revelation

55.31–32 The reaction of Allogenes to Iouel's speech is given; he asks for further revelation which follows.

The fifth revelation to Allogenes

55.33–38 This passage may suggest an association of Autogenes with the Thrice-male (attested elsewhere in the text, see pp. 6–7).

56.12b–14a ε2ρλϊ ε- is equivalent to the Greek preposition εἰς. See Col. 1.16 εἰς αὐτόν.

¹³ ⲟⲡ ⲛ̄ϭⲓ ⲛⲓⲁⲩⲧ[ⲟⲅⲉⲛⲏⲥ ⲉ]

¹⁴ ϩⲣⲁⲓ̈ ⲉⲡⲓϣ[ⲙ̄ⲛ̄ⲧϩⲟⲟⲩⲧ·

ⲉ]

¹⁵ ϣⲱⲡⲉ ⲉⲕϣⲁ[ⲛϣⲓⲛⲉ ϩ̄ⲛ ⲟⲩ]

¹⁶ ϣⲓⲛⲉ ⲉϥϫⲏ[ⲕ ⲉⲃⲟⲗ· ⲧⲟⲧⲉ]

¹⁷ ⲉⲕⲉⲉⲓⲙⲉ ⲉⲡ[ⲓⲁⲅⲁⲑⲟⲛ ⲉⲧⲛ̄]

¹⁸ ϩⲏⲧⲕ̄· ⲧⲟⲧⲉ ⲉ̇[ⲕⲉⲉⲓⲙⲉ ⲉⲣⲟⲕ]

¹⁹ ϩⲱⲱⲕ· ⲡⲏ ⲉⲧ[ϣⲟⲟⲡ ⲉϩⲣⲁⲓ̈ ⲉ]

²⁰ ⲡⲛⲟⲩⲧⲉ ⲉⲧⲣ̄[ϣⲟⲣⲡ̄ ⲛ̄ϣⲟⲟⲡ]

²¹ ⲟⲛⲧⲱⲥ·

ⲙ̄ⲛ̄ⲛ̄[ⲥⲁ ϣⲉ ⲅⲁⲣ ⲛ̄]

²² ⲣⲟⲙⲡⲉ ⲉϥⲉ[ϣⲱⲡⲉ ⲛⲁⲕ ⲛ̄]

²³ ϭⲓ ⲟⲩϭⲱⲗⲡ̄ ⲉⲃ[ⲟⲗ ⲛ̄ⲧⲉ ⲡⲏ ⲉ]

²⁴ ⲃⲟⲗ ϩⲓⲧⲟⲟⲧϥ̄[ⲛ̄ⲥⲁⲗⲁⲙⲉⲝ·]

²⁵ ⲙ̄ⲛ ⲥⲉ⟨ⲗ⟩ ⲙⲉⲛ· ⲙ̄[ⲛ̄ ⲛⲓϭⲟⲙ ⲛ̄ⲧⲉ]

²⁶ ⲫⲱⲥⲧⲏⲣ ⲛ̄ⲧ[ⲉ ⲡⲓⲉⲱⲛ ⲛ̄ⲃⲁⲣ]

²⁷ ⲃⲏⲗⲱ· ⲁⲩⲱ ⲡ [   ]

²⁸ ⳟϣⲉ ⲉⲣⲟⲕ ⲛ̄[ⲅⲉⲓⲙⲉ ⲉⲣⲟϥ]

²⁹ ⲛ̄ϣⲟⲣⲡ̄ ϫⲉ ⲛ[ⲉⲕϯ ⲟⲥⲉ ⲙ̄ⲡⲉⲕ]

³⁰ ⲅⲉⲛⲟⲥ ⲉϣ[ⲱⲡⲉ . . . . .]

³¹ ⲧⲟⲧⲉ ⲉϣⲱⲡ[ⲉ ⲉⲕϣⲁⲛϫⲓ]

³² ⲛ̄ⲟⲩⲉⲛⲛⲟ[ⲓⲁ ⲛ̄ⲧⲉ ⲡⲏ· ⲧⲟⲧⲉ]

³³ ⲉϣⲁⲩϫⲱⲕ [ⲙ̄ⲙⲟⲕ ⲉⲃⲟⲗ ϩⲙ̄]

³⁴ ⲡϣⲁϫⲉ ⲉϩ[ⲣⲁⲓ̈ ⲉⲡϫⲱⲕ ⲉⲃⲟⲗ·]

56.19 Turner restores: ⲉⲧ[ϣⲟⲟⲡ ⲉⲃⲟⲗ ϩⲙ̄].
56.21 Restoration by King. While Turner has adopted most of the restoration, he has changed ⲣⲁⲣ for ⲁⲉ. Note, however, that the translation still presumes γάρ. The supralinear stroke over the second ⲛ is restored.
56.24 Turner does not restore the raised dot.
56.25 Turner restores: ⲙ̄[ⲛ̄ ⲁ̄ⲣ.ⲙ̄ ⲛⲓ]. The supralinear stroke over the second ⲙⲛ is restored; the letter ⲙ is clear.
56.27–28 Turner restores: ⲡ[ⲓⲡⲁⲣⲁ ⲡⲉⲧ]ⳟϣⲉ ⲉⲣⲟⲕ ⲛ[ⲉⲕⲉⲓⲙⲉ ⲉⲣⲟϥ] ("that beyond what is fitting for you, you shall not know"). The supralinear stroke above ϣ in line 28 makes the reconstruction in line 27 difficult since it does not occur elsewhere in the text with ϣϣⲉ (see index). The supralinear stroke over ⲛⲅ is restored.
56.29 Turner does not place a dot below the second ⲛ.
56.30 Turner restores: ⲉϣ[ⲱⲡⲉ ⲁⲉ ⲛ̄ϯϩⲉ].

The sentence may connect the Thrice-male with the self-generated ones.

56.14b–37 As the text is reconstructed, the antecedent of ⲡⲏ in line 19 is ⲡⲓⲁⲅⲁⲑⲟⲛ in line 17. Compare 52.11–12.

¹⁴ for the Th[rice- male] that
¹³ the sel[f-begotten] ones [ex]ist.
       ¹⁵[W]henever you [seek with a]
¹⁶ perfe[ct] inquiry, [then]
¹⁷ you will know th[e good that is]
¹⁸ in you. Then [you will know]
¹⁹ yourself, that which [exists for]
²⁰ the truly [pre-existent] god.
       ²¹[For] af[ter one hundred]
²²ᵃyears,
²³ a revelation abo[ut That one]
²²ᵇwill [be given to you]
²⁴ through [Salamex]
²⁵ and Se⟨l⟩men an[d the Powers of]
²⁶ the Luminary o[f the aeon of
²⁷ Bar]belo. And the [. . .]
²⁸ it is fitting for you to [know him]
²⁹ first so that [you will not suffer the loss of your]
³⁰ race. I[f . . .]
³¹ then when[ever you receive]
³² a thoug[ht about that one, then]
³³ᵃit is [from]
³⁴ᵃthe word
³³ᵇthat [you] will be made comple[te]
³⁴ᵇfo[r the completion.]

56.13 The term for the "self-begotten ones" is Autogenes with the plural definite article. Hence the name associates these beings with the figure of Autogenes, here called the Thrice-male.

As the text is reconstructed, the form ετρϣορπ̄ ñϣοοπ in line 20 is a *Prae-verbal* (see Funk, "Zur syntax des koptischen Qualitativs").

Lines 56.21–27 seem to contain an allusion to what will occur later (compare 58.7–11; 59.4–7).

Concerning the "Luminary of the aeon of Barbelo" (56.24–27), see above p. 45; *Zost* 29.1–19. The names Salamex and Selmen are restored from *Zostrianos* (see, for example, 54.20; 62.18; 63.19–20; 64.8).

Concerning the term renoc ("race") in 56.30, see pp. 42–43.

57.1–3 The facsimile edition incorrectly placed a fragment at 57.1–3 (plate 63) which has now been correctly replaced at 49.1–3 (see *Facsimile*, p. XVII).

³⁵ ⲁⲩⲱ ⲧⲟⲧⲉ [ϣⲁⲕϣⲱⲡⲉ ⲛ̅ⲛⲟⲩ]
³⁶ ⲧⲉ· ⲁⲩⲱ ϣ[ⲁⲕⲣ̅ ⲧⲉⲗⲓⲟⲥ·
                                          ⲉⲕϫⲓ]
³⁷ ⲙⲉⲛ ⲙ̅ⲙⲟⲟ[ⲩ   ]

57 ¹⁻⁴ [   ]
⁵ [..].. ⲡϣⲓⲛ[ⲉ   ]
⁶ [..] ϯ̄ⲍⲩⲡⲁⲣϫ[ⲓⲥ   ]
⁷[ⲉ]ϣⲱⲡⲉ ⲉⲥϣⲁ[ⲛⲁⲙⲁϩⲧⲉ ⲛⲟⲩ]
⁸ [ⲗ]ⲁⲁⲩ ⲉϣⲁⲩⲁⲙⲁ[ϩⲧⲉ ⲙ̅ⲙⲟⲥ ⲉⲃⲟⲗ]
⁹ [ϩⲓ̅]ⲧ̅ⲙ ⲡⲏ ⲉⲧⲙ̅ⲙⲁⲩ· ⲙ̅ⲛ̅ ⟨...⟩ ⲉⲃⲟⲗ ϩ̅ⲓ̅
¹⁰ ⲧⲟⲟⲧ̅ϥ ⲙ̅ⲡⲏ ⲉⲧⲟⲩⲧⲁϩⲟ ⲙ̅ⲙⲟϥ
¹¹ [ⲉ]ⲧⲉ ⲡⲁⲓ ⲡⲉ· ⲁⲩⲱ ⲧⲟⲧⲉ ⲉϣⲁϥ
¹² ϣⲱⲡⲉ ⲉⲛⲉⲁϥ ⲛ̅ϩⲟⲩⲟ ⲛ̅ϭⲓ ⲡⲏ
¹³ [ⲉ]ⲧⲧⲉϩⲟ ⲁⲩⲱ ⲉⲧⲉⲓⲙⲉ ⲛ̅ϩⲟⲩⲟ̂·
¹⁴ ⲉ[ⲡ]ⲏ ⲉⲧⲟⲩⲧⲁϩⲟ ⲙ̅ⲙⲟϥ ⲁⲩⲱ
¹⁵ ⲉⲧⲟⲩⲉⲓⲙⲉ ⲉⲣⲟϥ· ⲉϣⲱⲡⲉ
¹⁶ ⲇⲉ ⲉϥϣⲁⲛⲉ̅ⲓ ⲉϩⲣⲁⲓ ⲉⲧⲉϥⲫⲩ
¹⁷ ⲥⲓⲥ ϣⲁϥⲑ̅ⲃⲃⲓⲟ· ⲛⲓⲫⲩⲥⲓⲥ ⲅⲁⲣ
¹⁸ ⲛ̅ⲛⲁⲧⲥⲱⲙⲁ ⲙ̅ⲡⲟⲩⲣ̅ϣⲃⲏⲣ ⲉ
¹⁹ ⲗⲁⲁⲩ ⲙ̅ⲙ̅ⲛ̅ⲧⲛⲟϭ· ⲉⲩⲛ̅ⲧⲁⲩ
²⁰ ⲛ̅ⲧⲉⲓ̈ϭⲟⲙ ⲉⲩϩ̅ⲛ̅ ⲧⲟⲡⲟⲥ ⲛⲓⲙ·
²¹ ⲁⲩⲱ ⲉⲛⲥⲉϩ̅ⲛ̅ⲗⲁⲁⲩ ⲛ̅ⲧⲟⲡⲟⲥ
²² ⲁⲛ· ⲉⲛⲉⲁⲩ ⲉⲙ̅ⲛ̅ⲧⲛⲟϭ ⲛⲓⲙ·
²³ ⲁⲩⲱ ⲥⲉⲑ̅ⲃⲃⲓⲏⲟⲩⲧ ⲉⲙ̅ⲛ̅ⲧⲕⲟⲩ
²⁴ ⲉⲓ ⲛⲓⲙ·
        ⲛⲁⲓ ⲇⲉ ⲛ̅ⲧⲁⲥϫⲟⲟⲩ ⲛ̅

57.9 Turner does not note corruption, but ⲁⲩⲱ is expected as the connective between two prepositional phrases. With ⲙ̅ⲛ̅, the repetition of ⲉⲃⲟⲗ ϩⲓⲧⲟⲟⲧ̅ϥ is not necessary. After ⲙ̅ⲛ̅ one expects a noun equivalent, not a preposition. The supralinear strokes above ⲙⲛ and ϩⲓ are restored; the letter ⲙ is clear.

57.7–15a The form of the comment is very general (note the use of ⲗⲁⲁⲩ). The point is a common one: to know, one must first be known. The one who comprehends is greater than whoever is comprehended. The divine first knows its objects and through this divine comprehension, the objects' self-knowledge becomes possible. (Compare, for example, I. Cor 13.12b; Phil 3.12b–13a; *CH* 10.15; Philo, *Cher.* 115; Porphyry, *Marc.* 13.)

35 And then [you will become
36 div]ine. And [you will become perfect].
   37On the one hand it is . . . that [you receive] the[m] . . .

57 1-4 [   ]
   5 [. . .] the inqui[ry . . .]
   6 [. . .] the subsisten[ce   ].
      7[W]henever she [apprehends]
   8 [an]yone, she will [herself] be apprehe[nded]
   9 [b]y that one and ⟨. . .⟩ through
   10 that very one who is (himself) comprehended.
   11 And accordingly, that one
   13 [w]ho comprehends and who knows
   12 becomes greater
   14 than [o]ne who is comprehended and
   15 known.
   16 For whenever one comes to one's
   17 nature, one is humbled. For incorporeal natures
   18 do not have a share
   19 of any greatness since they have
   20 the capacity such that they are in every place
   21 and are not in any place,
   22 being greater than any greatness;
   23 and they are humbler than any smallness."
      24aBut after

57.15b–24a The category of quantity does not apply to incorporeal beings. Place similarly does not apply in any sense that would indicate corporeal existence. These lines qualify the statement in 57.12 that the one who knows is "greater," lest that seem to imply quantity or place are appropriate categories for incorporeal beings.

This section concludes Iouel's final revelation to Allogenes.

Allogenes' reaction to the fifth revelation; the first vision

57.24b–39 Iouel now departs from Allogenes. He has achieved a certain stability and does not "loose his hold" of the words he has heard. He prepares himself through them for the ascent. It is possible that this instruction and preparation are necessary for the ascent ritual. At any rate, Allogenes finds his "counsel" within, not from other teachers or writings. That the process of

²⁵ ϭι ⲧⲁⲛⲓⲉⲟⲟⲩ ⲧⲏⲣⲟⲩ ⲓ̅ⲟ̅ⲩⲏⲗ·
²⁶ ⲁⲥⲡⲱⲣⲝ̅ ⲉⲃⲟⲗ ⲙ̅ⲙⲟⲓ̈ ⲁⲥⲕⲁ
²⁷ ⲁⲧ· ⲁⲛⲟⲕ ⲇⲉ ⲙ̅ⲡⲓⲕⲁ ⲧⲟⲟⲧ
²⁸ ⲉⲃⲟⲗ ϩ̅ⲛ ⲛⲓϣⲁⲭⲉ ⲉⲧⲁⲓ̈ⲥⲱⲧ̅ⲙ̅
²⁹ ⲉⲣⲟⲟⲩ. ⲁⲉⲓⲥⲟⲃⲧⲉ ⲙ̅ⲙⲟⲓ̈ ⲛ̅
³⁰ ϩⲏⲧⲟⲩ· ⲁⲩⲱ ⲛⲉⲓ̈ϣⲟⲭⲛⲉ ⲙ̅
³¹ ⲙⲟⲉⲓ ⲡⲉ ϩ̅ⲛ ϯϣⲉ ⲛ̅ⲣⲟⲙⲡⲉ·
³² ⲁⲛⲟⲕ ⲇⲉ ⲛⲉⲓ̈ⲧⲉⲗⲏⲗ ⲙ̅ⲙⲟⲓ̈ ⲉ
³³ ⲙⲁⲧⲉ ⲉⲓ̈ϣⲟⲟⲡ ϩ̅ⲛ ⲟⲩⲛⲟϭ
³⁴ ⲛ̅ⲟⲩⲟⲉⲓⲛ ⲙ̅ⲛ ⲟⲩϩ̅ⲓⲏ ⲙ̅ⲙⲁ
³⁵ ⲕⲁⲣⲓⲟⲥ· ⲭⲉ ⲛⲏ ⲙⲉⲛ ⲉⲧⲁⲉⲓ
³⁶ ⲙ̅ⲡϣⲁ ⲛ̅ⲛⲁⲩ ⲉⲣⲟⲟⲩ. ⲁⲩⲱ
³⁷ ⲟⲛ ⲛⲏ ⲉⲧⲁⲉⲓⲙ̅ⲡϣⲁ ⲛ̅ⲥⲱ
³⁸ ⲧ̅ⲙ̅ ⲉⲣⲟⲟⲩ· ⲛⲏ ⲉⲧⲉϣϣⲉ
³⁹ ⲛ̅ⲧⲉ ⲛⲓⲛⲟϭ ⲛ̅ϭⲟⲙ ⲟⲩⲁⲁⲩ

58 ¹⁻⁴ [   ]
⁵ [   ]. ⲉⲛ .[   ]
⁶ [   ]ⲃ ⲛ̅ⲧⲉ ⲡⲛⲟ[ⲩ]
⁷ [ⲧⲉ
    ⲉⲧⲁ̣ϥⲛⲁ]ⲛ ⲉϩⲟⲩⲛ ⲛ̅ϭⲓ [ⲡⲓ]
⁸ [ⲭⲱⲕ ⲉⲃⲟⲗ ⲛ̅ⲧ]ⲉ ϯϣⲉ ⲛ̅ⲣⲟⲙⲡ[ⲉ]
⁹ [ⲁ]ϥ[ⲉⲓ]ⲛ[ⲉ] ⲛⲁⲓ̈ ⲛ̅ⲛⲟⲩⲙ̅ⲛ̅ⲧⲙⲁⲕ̣[ⲁ]

58.7 Turner restores: ⲉⲧⲁϥϩⲛⲁ]ⲛ.
58.9 The supralinear dots above ι are restored; letter is clear.

preparation is difficult is indicated by the fact that this stage of preparation is said to have taken "one hundred years." Noting that according to Biblical tradition (Gen 5:6–8) Seth lived for 912 years, Hans-Martin Schenke has suggested that the Sethian identification of Allogenes with Seth (see above p. 44) might afford an explanation for this unusually long period of time while providing further evidence that the text presupposes an identification of Allogenes with Seth (see "Bemerkungen," 422).

Allogenes has now moved far from his initial reaction of fear and has reached a stage of rejoicing: he exists in a "great light" and upon a "blessed path." Both metaphors are to be understood in the context of the spiritual path of illumination he is following.

57.35–39 states that the things he has heard and seen are elevated. (Compare 50.22–24.)

25 the all-glorious Iouel
24bspoke these things,
26 she parted from me; she left
27 me. But I did not loose my hold upon
28 the words that I heard.
29 I prepared myself through
30 them. And I took counsel
31 with myself for those hundred years.
32 For I rejoiced greatly in myself,
33 existing in a great
34 light and upon a blessed path
35 for, on the one hand, I became
36 worthy to see and
37 also to
38 hear those things which are fitting
39 for the great powers alone. . .

58 1–5 [   ]
6 [   ] of g[od].
7a[When the]
8 [completion o]f those hundred years
7b[dre]w nigh,
9 it [bro]ug[ht] me a ble[s]sedness

57.25 Literally: "she to whom all the glories pertain, Iouel."

58.1–3 The facsimile edition incorrectly placed a fragment at 58.1–3 (plate 64) which has now been correctly replaced at 50.1–3 (see *Facsimile,* p. XVII).

58.7b–26a After the period of preparation, Allogenes receives a vision of the divine hierarchy in ascending order: Autogenes, the Thrice-male Youth, Protophanes, Kalyptos, Barbelo, and the Triply-powered Invisible Spirit.

The Thrice-male Youth is called the "savior" and he is located hierarchically between Autogenes and Protophanes.

As in 49.6–7, the triad of Autogenes, Protophanes, and Kalyptos is associated with goodness and blessedness.

The Triply-powered Invisible Spirit, while having no origin itself, is the primal origin of everything and is itself the whole (the Entirety) of everything transcendent.

¹⁰ ріос ᾱτε †ϩελπιс ᾱϣα ене[ϩ]
¹¹ есмеϩ евол ϩ̄ν оүм̄ᾱтхс
    ¹²аїнаү епіагаθос ᾱаүтоге
¹³ ннс ᾱνоүте м̄ᾱ пісωт[нр]
¹⁴ ете паї пе піϣм̄ᾱтϩо[оү]т
¹⁵ ᾱтеліос ᾱναλοу· м̄ᾱ †м̄ᾱт
¹⁶ агаθос ᾱте паї· піпрωто
¹⁷ фаннс ᾱϩармндωн ᾱтелі
¹⁸ ос ᾱνоүс м̄ᾱ †м̄ᾱтмака
¹⁹ ріос ᾱте пікалуптос· м̄ᾱ †
²⁰ ϣорп̄ ᾱархн ᾱте †м̄ᾱтма
²¹ каріос· піеωн ᾱβᾱрвнлω
²² ечмеϩ евол ϩ̄ν оүм̄ᾱтноу
²³ те м̄ᾱ †ϣорп̄ ᾱархн ᾱте
²⁴ піатархн· піϣм̄ᾱт6ом ᾱа
²⁵ ϩоратон м̄п̄ν̄а̄· пітнрч̄ ет
²⁶ хосе етеліос·
                    етаүторп̄ ⟨т̄⟩
²⁷ евол ϩ̄ітоотч̄ м̄піоүоеін
²⁸ ᾱϣα енеϩ· евол ϩ̄ітоотч̄
²⁹ м̄піендума еттое ϩ̄іω
³⁰ ωт. аүω аүхіт еϩраї ех̄ν

58.26 Manuscript reads: етаүторп̄ч̄.

The ascent begins

58.26b–38a See pp. 9–12.

This section is a turning point in the text: the ascent itself is now described.
Allogenes is "seized" out of his "garment" (body) by the "eternal light," a
reference to divine power and perhaps also to the mystical, illuminating nature
of the experience itself.

In Gnostic texts, the term ендума ("garment"), or a similar term (such as
χιτών or ἱμάτιον), is often a metaphor for the body. As Rist has shown,
however, such terms can also be used as metaphors for any accretions of the
soul (passions, and so forth; see Rist, *Plotinus*, chapter 14).

The description of the "place" to which Allogenes is taken is so general that
we can say only that it is completely transcendent. There he sees those things
or beings (ерооу can be understood impersonally or personally) about which
he has previously only heard. This seems a little odd in that he has just had a
vision of the divine hierarchy, including the Triply-powered. The sentence may

¹⁰ of eterna[l] hope,
¹¹ full with goodness.
     ¹²I saw the good, divine
¹³ Autogenes and the savi[or]
¹⁴ who is the perfect Thrice-ma[l]e
¹⁵ Youth; and (I saw) the goodness
¹⁶ of that one, the
¹⁷ perfect, noetic Protophanes Harmedon;
¹⁸ and (I saw) the blessedness
¹⁹ of Kalyptos; and (I saw) the
²⁰ primal origin of blessedness,
²¹ the aeon of Barbelo,
²² full of divinity;
²³ and (I saw) the primal origin of
²⁴ he who has no origin, the Triply-powered
²⁵ Invisible Spirit, the Entirety that
²⁶ surpasses perfection.
     After ⟨I⟩ had been seized
²⁷ by an eternal light
²⁸ from (out of)
²⁹ the garment that clothed
³⁰ me and I had been taken up to

58.12 "Autogenes" means "self-generated one."
58.17 "Protophanes" means "first-appearing one."
58.19 "Kalyptos" means "hidden one."
58.24–25 "Triple-powered Invisible Spirit" or: "invisible, spiritual Triply-powered."

be understood as a subsequent explanation of the vision described in 58.12–26a.

Valantasis argues unconvincingly that this passage does not refer to an ascent, but rather to an ascetic withdrawal (see *Spiritual Guides*, 127). In his view, Allogenes' being seized from his garment refers "to his being stripped of the power of distinction in which he was clothed by the Father of All" at 51.24–33 (p. 140). Such an understanding of the passage grossly misunderstands the nature of the hierarchical structure of power described in the text. In fact Allogenes is able to achieve his spiritual progression only through empowerment from above. To "receive power" indicates spiritual progression; to be stripped of that power would indicate the opposite. The motif of an extrabodily ascent is also well attested in apocalyptic literature and in philosophical mysticism (see Plotinus, *Ennead* I.6.7,5–7).

³¹ ογτοπος εϥογααβ· πη ε
³² τε ⲙⲙⲛϭⲟⲙ ⲛⲧⲉⲉⲓⲛⲉ ⲛ
³³ ⲧⲁϥ ⲟⲩⲱⲛⲅ̄ ⲉⲃⲟⲗ ⲅ̄ⲙ ⲡⲕⲟⲥ
³⁴ ⲙⲟⲥ· ⲧⲟⲧⲉ ⲉⲃⲟⲗ ⲅ̄ⲓ̄ⲧ̄ⲛ̄ ⲟⲩ
³⁵ ⲛⲟϭ ⲙ̄ⲙ̄ⲛ̄ⲧ̄ⲙⲁⲕⲁⲣⲓⲟⲥ ⲁⲓ̈
³⁶ ⲛⲁⲩ ⲉⲛⲏ ⲧⲏⲣⲟⲩ ⲉⲧⲁⲉⲓ
³⁷ ⲥⲱ̄ⲧ̄ⲙ̄ ⲉⲣⲟⲟⲩ ⲁⲩⲱ ⲁⲉⲓ
³⁸ ⲥⲙⲟⲩ ⲉⲣⲟⲟⲩ ⲧⲏⲣⲟⲩ
ⲁⲓ̈

59   ¹ [ⲁⲅⲉⲣ]ⲁⲧ ⲅ̄ⲓ̄ⲭ̄ⲛ̄ ⲧⲁⲅⲛⲱⲥⲓⲥ· ⲁ[ⲓ̈]
² [ⲕⲱⲧ]ⲉ ⲉⲅⲟⲩⲛ ⲉϯⲅⲛⲱⲥⲓⲥ [ⲛ̄]
³ [ⲧⲉ] ⲛⲓⲡⲧⲏⲣ̄ϥ̄· ⲡⲓⲉⲱⲛ ⲛ̄ⲃⲁⲣⲃ[ⲏ]
⁴ [ⲗⲱ·]

Allogenes' final reaction is praise. The content of the praise may be recorded in the hymn on page 54. At any rate, the text follows the order that is to be expected in mystical progression: 1) study of books or auditory instruction, 2) vision, and 3) finally praise. (Compare NHC VI.6 *Discourse on the Eighth and Ninth*; *Corpus Hermeticum* 13.17; *StSeth* 127.11–21; see *TLZ* 98 [1978], 502.)

58.38b–59.4a Allogenes now prepares for the vision and revelation which will come.

The sentence ⲁⲓ̈ⲁⲅⲉⲣⲁⲧ ⲅ̄ⲓ̄ⲭ̄ⲛ̄ ⲧⲁⲅⲛⲱⲥⲓⲥ ("I stood upon my knowledge of myself"; 58.38b–59.1a) reflects the ideal of stability expressed repeatedly in *Allogenes*. This theme has been studied at length by Williams (see *The Immovable Race* and "Stability"), who concludes:

This description in *Allogenes* (59.9–61.22) of the decisive revelatory experience as the attainment to stability, the participation in that which is truly stable, is not unique in Gnostic literature as far as the concept is concerned, and even the technical expression which is so visible here, 'to stand at rest,' is now well-attested in several other Gnostic texts as a technical term for the stability to which the Gnostic returns through the reception of gnosis.   ("Stability," 821)

Williams adduces two pertinent examples from non-Gnostic texts to demonstrate how widespread this theme is in Platonic thought: Plotinus, *Enneads* V.5.8.5–15; VI.9.11.4–16 and Philo, *Post.* 22–28. His summaries are worth quoting at length:

³¹ a place that is holy—that (place) of which it is true that
³² it is not possible for an image of
³³ it to appear in the world—
³⁴ then, through a
³⁵ great blessedness, I
³⁶ saw all those things about which I
³⁷ had heard. And I
³⁸ praised them all.
    I

59   ¹ [took a st]and upon my knowledge of myself; [I]
       ² [tur]ned toward knowledge
       ³ [concerning] the entireties, the aeon of Barb[elo].

> **58.34–35** "Through a great blessedness" can be understood either as 1) "By means of great blessedness" or 2) "being in a state of great blessedness."
> **58.36–37** Or: "those beings about whom I had heard."

The mystical ascent according to Plotinus involves the retreat of the self from the unstable realm of sense perception, the realm of opinion, in which the self falls prey to deceptive fantasies that give rise to turbulent passions. The self withdraws alone unto itself in contemplation, waiting in tranquility for the vision of the One.   ("Stability," 822)

Together with the examples from Plotinus and *Allogenes*, the evidence from Philo points to the existence of an underlying model for the retreat of the wise man to a condition of participation in the stability of the Transcendent—a condition in which knowledge of the Transcendent is received.   ("Stability," 826)

Plotinus' description of the role of stability in the ascent is similar conceptually to the description of the ascent in *Allogenes*: Allogenes achieves a stability through knowledge of himself. He has overcome his own agitation of soul and come to perfection and divinity (52.6–13). On this basis he now "turns" toward the Entirety. (Plotinus, too, uses the metaphor of "turning" with reference to the mystical ascent; see, for example, *Ennead* VI.9.9.) Stability leads to new knowledge through vision and auditory revelation.

Williams notes, too, that the ideal of stability does not originate with Philo, but that he, Plotinus, and the Gnostics are all drawing upon a theme that goes back at least to Plato (see *Phaedo* 79C–D; *Parmenides* 138B–C; 145E–146A; *Sophist* 255B ff.; "Stability," 826–828).

ⲁⲩⲱ ⲁⲉⲓⲛⲁⲩ ⲉϩⲉⲛϬⲟⲙ ⲉ[ⲩ]
5 [ⲁⲁ]ⲃ ⲉⲃⲟⲗ ϩⲓⲧⲟⲟⲧⲟⲩ ⲛ̄ⲛⲓⲫⲱ[ⲥ]
6 [ⲧⲏ]ⲣ ⲛ̄ⲧⲉ ϯⲃⲁⲣⲃ[ⲏⲗ]ⲱ ⲛ̄ϩⲟⲟⲩ[ⲧ]
7 ⲙ̄ⲡⲁⲣⲑⲉⲛⲟⲥ ⲉⲩ[ϫⲱ] ⲙ̄ⲙⲟ[ⲥ ⲛⲁⲓ̈]
8 [ϫ]ⲉ *ϯⲛⲁϬⲙϬⲟⲙ ⲡⲓⲣⲁⲛ ⲉⲧⲁϥ
9 ϣⲱⲡⲉ ϩⲙ̄ ⲡⲕⲟⲥⲙⲟⲥ·

ⲡⲁⲗⲗⲟ
10 [ⲅ]ⲉⲛⲏⲥ ⲉⲛⲁⲩ ⲉϯⲙ̄ⲛ̄ⲧⲙⲁⲕⲁⲣⲓ
11 ⲟⲥ ⲉⲧⲛ̄ⲧⲁⲕ ⲛ̄ⲑⲉ ⲉⲧϣⲟⲟⲡ
12 ϩⲛ̄ ⲟⲩⲥⲓⲅⲏ· ⲧⲏ ⲉⲧⲉⲕⲉⲓⲙⲉ ⲉ
13 ⲣⲟⲕ ⲛ̄ϩⲏⲧⲥ̄ ⲕⲁⲧⲁⲣⲟⲕ· ⲁⲩⲱ ⲁⲣⲓ

59.7 The supralinear stroke above the first ⲙ is restored.
59.8–9 The restoration ⲡⲓⲣⲁⲛ ⲉⲧⲁϥ . . . ⲡⲁⲗⲗⲟ was suggested by Wolf-Peter Funk, who notes that what Turner understood to be a circumflex above the ⲟ in *Allogenes* is a trace of the stem of ϥ in ⲉⲧⲁϥ. See Funk, *Concordance des Textes Séthiens*, 657. Moreover, the Coptic translator has mistakenly translated indirect speech in Greek into direct speech in Coptic. Turner notes no corruption here. For further discussion, see the exegetical note to 59.4b–9a.

In 59.1b–4, the Aeon of Barbelo is directly identified with *gnosis,* "the knowledge of the Entirety" (see pp. 6–8). Note the close association of self-knowledge with knowledge of the Entirety, mediated through Barbelo. (Compare Plotinus, *Ennead* VI.9.8–9.)

The revelation to Allogenes by the Powers concerning the ascent
The ascent occurs as the Powers have foretold

59.4b–9a Concerning the Luminaries of the Aeon of Barbelo, see above, note to 56.14b–37; pp. 6 and 45. The "holy powers" also are located in the realm of Barbelo and function as mediators of revelation (compare *Zost* 46.15–30).

The text at 59.8–9 is clearly corrupt. One would expect a direct quotation following ϫⲉ. It may be that the Coptic translator has mistakenly translated indirect speech in Greek into direct speech in Coptic. (Coptic has no form for indirect speech.) In this case, the direct quotation proper would first begin only at 59.9 with "Allogenes."

Moreover, the grammatical structure of the indirect quotation is extremely difficult, leaving the nominal phrase hanging without a clear reference. It may be that the whole statement ϯⲛⲁϬⲙϬⲟⲙ ⲡⲓⲣⲁⲛ ⲉⲧⲁϥϣⲱⲡⲉ ϩⲙ̄ ⲡⲕⲟⲥⲙⲟⲥ ("I will find power, the name that came into being in the world") is either a secondary gloss or was misplaced. W.-P. Funk has suggested that ϯⲛⲁϬⲙϬⲟⲙ might be a miscopying of an original ϯ ⲛⲁϬⲛ̄Ϭⲟⲙ.

Discerning the sense of the phrase is also difficult. In the only other place

⁴And I saw [hol]y Powers
⁵ by means of the Lumi[nar]ies
⁶ of the ma[le],
⁷ virginal Bar[bel]o; they [said to me]
⁸ (that) I will find power, the name that
⁹ came into being in the world.
¹⁰ "Allo[g]enes, look silently upon the blessedness
¹¹ which is yours as it (truly) is,
¹² that in which you know
¹³ yourself as you (truly) are. And,

> **59.4–9** Here the Coptic text is corrupt, probably due to indirect speech in Greek being mistakenly translated into direct speech in Coptic (Coptic has no form of indirect speech). The English translation adds (that) in parentheses to indicate this error.

the term κόσμος ("world") occurs (58.33–34), it is used as a contrast to the transcendent nature of the holy place to which Allogenes has gone. Here the "name" has come into being in the world. Grammatically, "name" best refers to "Allogenes," implying perhaps that his name refers to the nature of his true transcendent self that he is to seek within. As was stated above, "Allogenes" can be translated as the "foreigner" or "he of another race." This name points to the fact that he does not truly belong to the world below, yet his true self (that is, his name) has come into being in the world. Knowing this will make him strong; it will help him find power for the journey he must make. Alternatively, it is possible that "the name that came into being in the world" will be a source of strength for Allogenes, but specifically what that name is remains obscure. At any rate, the speech of the Holy Powers only begins properly at 59.9b with the injunction to Allogenes to look silently upon his own blessedness.

59.9b–61.22a This long section can be divided into two parallel sections: 59.9b–60.12a and 60.12b–61.22a. In the first section, the Powers give Allogenes advice and tell him what is going to occur in the ascent. The second section records the actual ascent and mystical apprehension. 60.12b–14a provides the transition between the two sections.

Parallel portions of the two sections will be considered together below.

59.9b–13a; 60.14b–18 Allogenes begins in silence and self-knowledge of his blessedness. The metaphor of 60.14–18 indicates that, on the one hand, he exists in a stillness of silence; on the other hand, he hears his blessedness. The implication is that one cannot "hear" one's true nature, except in silence. Silence emphasizes the transcendent basis of true self-knowledge.

The theme of silence as a description both of the stability of the transcendent and of the moment of cultic revelation is well-attested in antiquity.

¹⁴ ⲁⲛⲁⲭⲱⲣⲓ ⲉ̄ⲝ̄ⲛ̄ ϯⲙ̄ⲛ̄ⲧⲱⲛⳁ̄
¹⁵ ⲉⲕⲕⲱⲧⲉ ⲛ̄ⲥⲱⲕ· ⲧⲏ ⲉⲧⲉⲕⲛⲁ
¹⁶ ⲛⲁⲩ ⲉⲣⲟⲥ ⲉⲥⲕⲓⲙ· ⲁⲩⲱ ⲉⲙ̄ⲛ̄
¹⁷ ϭⲁⲙ ⲛ̄ⲅⲁⳁⲉⲣⲁⲧ̄ⲕ̄· ⲙ̄ⲡ̄ⲣ̄ⳁⲟⲧⲉ
¹⁸ ⲗⲁⲁⲩ. ⲁⲗⲗⲁ ⲉⲩⲱⲡⲉ ⲉⲕⲩⲁⲛ
¹⁹ ⲟⲩⲱⲩ ⲉⲁⳁⲉⲣⲁⲧ̄ⲕ̄· ⲁⲣⲓⲁⲛⲁⲭⲱ
²⁰ ⲣⲓ ⲉ̄ⲝ̄ⲛ̄ ϯⳁⲩⲡⲁⲣⳅⲓⲥ· ⲁⲩⲱ ⲉⲕⲉ
²¹ ⳁⲉ ⲉⲣⲟⲥ ⲉⲥⲁⳁⲉⲣⲁⲧ̄ⲥ̄ ⲁⲩⲱ ⲉⲥ
²² ⳁⲟⲣ̄ⲕ̄ ⲙ̄ⲙⲟⲥ ⲕⲁⲧⲁ ⲡⲓⲛⲉ ⲙ̄ⲡⲏ
²³ ⲉⲧⳁⲟⲣ̄ⲕ̄ ⲙ̄ⲙⲟϥ ⲟⲛⲧⲱⲥ·
²⁴ ⲁⲩⲱ ⲉϥⲁⲙⲁⳁⲧⲉ ⲛ̄ⲛⲁ̈ⲓ ⲧⲏⲣⲟⲩ
²⁵ ⳁ̄ⲛ̄ ⲟⲩⲕⲁⲣⲱϥ ⲙ̄ⲛ̄ ⲟⲩⲙ̄ⲛ̄ⲧⲁ
²⁶ ⲧⲉⲛⲉⲣⲅⲓⲁ·

(Compare, for example, *The Mithras Liturgy* which places the theme of silence in the context of theurgic ascent and mystic vision [555–630, 725; Meyers, 8–12, 20]. See also Motley, "The Theme of Silence," 197–202.) A particularly appropriate example is from the ritual of ascent described in *Three Steles of Seth*:

> For they all bless these individually and at one place, and afterwards these shall be silent. And as they are ordained; they ascend and after the silence, they descend. From the third they bless the second; after these (they bless) the first. The way of ascent is the way of descent.
>
> (127.11–21)

The ritual begins with praise, but the ascent itself requires silence in the face of the transcendent. Since the transcendent is ineffable, the proper attitude is silence. As discussed on p. 16, *Three Steles of Seth* and *Allogenes* seem to share knowledge of a Sethian ritual of ascent.

The phrase ⲛ̄ⲑⲉ ⲉⲧⲩⲟⲟⲡ ⳁ̄ⲛ̄ ⲟⲩⲥⲓⲅⲏ ("according to the manner which exists in silence"; 59.11–12) can be understood as an adverb modifying either ⲉⲛⲁⲩ ("see") or modifying ⲉϯⲙ̄ⲛ̄ⲧⲙⲁⲕⲁⲣⲓⲟⲥ ⲉⲧⲛ̄ⲧⲁⲕ ("the blessedness which is yours").

59.13b–18a; 60.19–24a The goal of the ascent is self-knowledge. The Powers tell Allogenes to look in silence upon himself and to ascend "seeking yourself" (59.15).

60.19–20 states, however, that Allogenes withdrew up to Vitality, seeking *it*, not *himself* as he was told in 59.14–16. The next sentence explains, however, that he "entered it (Vitality) together with it." The phrase may indicate that there is little difference between seeking oneself and seeking the higher realities (see 57.7–17). This principle is confirmed directly concerning "Subsistence" at 60.30–37.

¹⁵ªseeking yourself,
¹⁴ withdraw up to the Vitality
¹⁵ᵇthat you will
¹⁶ see in motion. And when you are
¹⁷ not able to stand, do not fear
¹⁸ at all. But whenever you
¹⁹ desire to stand, withdraw
²⁰ up to the subsistence and you will
²¹ find it standing and
²² at rest according to the image of that
²³ which is truly at rest.
²⁴ªAnd it is
²⁵ in silence and inactivity
²⁴ᵇthat it embraces all these things.

The first stage of the ascent is toward Vitality. As was discussed above pp. 22–28, Vitality belongs to the triad: Vitality, Intellection, and Existence. Here the figure is hypostasized and presented as the first and lowest level of Allogenes' ascent.

Williams has argued that Intellection, not Vitality, is the lowest level of the ascent, and that Allogenes had already achieved this level through revelation and self-knowledge at 58.30–37 ("Stability," 821–822). Turner agrees (see "Allogenes," 260). It is more probable, however, that Intellection is portrayed at the highest level of the ascent, that is, that the realm of Intellection as a part of the transcendent Triply-powered is best characterized by the unknowing knowledge Allogenes receives through a vision, not his initial act of self-knowledge (see below, note to 59.26b–60.12a; 60.37b–61.28a; and 67.20b–24a, 32–35a).

Vitality, by its nature as Life, is in motion and hence Allogenes is not able to stand firmly, but he does achieve a kind of "quiet" stability, an allusion perhaps to his state of silence. The Powers warn him that he must not be afraid because of Vitality's instability (his fear would only increase it; 59.17–18).

The type of motion which belongs to Vitality is described at greater length in 60.24–28. It is eternal, noetic, and undivided. This description seems to accord well with Plato's notion of the movement of reason or Soul (see *Timaeus* 34A, 36E–37; *Laws* 898A) except for the additional statement that this motion is "formless, not bounded by any boundary" (60.27–28). With this qualification, it now comes much closer to Plotinus' description of the One. At *Ennead* V.1.7, he describes how that which has Intellect, Existence, and Life proceeds from the One, which is undivided and not confined by any form. The description of Vitality here exposes the same problematic discussed

ⲁⲩⲱ ⲉⲕϣⲁⲛϫⲓ ⲛ̄

27 ⲟⲩⲱⲛ̄ϩ ⲉⲃⲟⲗ ⲛ̄ⲧⲉ ⲡⲁⲓ̈· ⲉⲃⲟⲗ

28 ϩⲓⲧⲟⲟⲧ̄ϥ ⲛ̄ⲟⲩϣⲟⲣⲡ̄ ⲛ̄ⲟⲩ

29 ⲱⲛ̄ϩ ⲉⲃⲟⲗ ⲛ̄ⲧⲉ ⲡⲓⲁⲧⲥⲟⲩⲱ

30 ⲛ̄ϥ· ⲡⲏ ⲉⲧⲉ ⲉϣⲱⲡⲉ ⲉⲕ

31 ϣⲁⲛⲉⲓⲙⲉ ⲉⲣⲟϥ. ⲁⲣⲓⲁⲧⲉⲓ

32 ⲙⲉ ⲉⲣⲟϥ· ⲁⲩⲱ ⲉⲕϣⲁⲛⲣ̄

33 ϩⲟⲧⲉ ⲙ̄ⲡⲓⲙⲁ ⲉⲧⲙ̄ⲙⲁⲩ ⲁⲣⲓ

34 ⲁⲛⲁⲭⲱⲣⲓ ⲉⲡⲁϩⲟⲩ ⲉⲧⲃⲉ ⲛⲓ

35 ⲉⲛⲉⲣⲅⲓⲁ· ⲁⲩⲱ ⲉⲕϣⲁⲛⲣ̄

36 ⲧⲉⲗⲓⲟⲥ ⲙ̄ⲡⲓⲧⲟⲡⲟⲥ ⲉⲧⲙ̄

37 ⲙⲁⲩ ϩⲣⲟⲕ ⲙ̄ⲙⲟⲕ· ⲁⲩⲱ

38 ⲕⲁⲧⲁ ⲡⲓⲧⲩⲡⲟⲥ ⲉⲧϣⲟⲟⲡ

39 ⲛ̄ϩⲏⲧⲕ̄· ⲉⲓⲙⲉ ⲟⲛ ⲛ̄ϯϩⲉ

60 1 [ⲭ]ⲉ ⲉϥϣⲟⲟⲡ ⲛ̄ϯϩⲉ ϩⲛ̄ ⲛ[ⲁⲓ̈ ⲧⲏ]

2 [ⲣⲟ]ⲩ ⲕⲁⲧⲁ ⲡⲉⲓ̈ⲥⲙⲟⲧ. ⲁⲩ[ⲱ]

3 [ⲙⲡ̄]ⲣ̄ϫⲱⲱⲣⲉ ⲉⲃⲟⲗ ⲛ̄ϩⲟⲩⲟ [ϩⲓⲛⲁ]

4 [ⲭ]ⲉ ⲉⲕⲉⲃⲙⲃⲟⲙ ⲛ̄ⲁϩⲉⲣⲁⲧ̄[ⲕ̄]

5 [ⲟ]ⲩⲧⲉ ⲙ̄ⲡⲣⲟⲩⲱϣ ⲉⲣⲉⲛ[ⲉⲣⲅⲓ]

6 [ϩⲓ]ⲛⲁ ϫⲉ ⲛⲉⲕϩⲉ ⲉⲃⲟⲗ ⲡⲁⲛⲧ[ⲱⲥ]

7 [ϩⲓ] ⲡⲓⲁⲧⲉⲛⲉⲣ[ⲣ]ⲓ[ⲁ] ⲉⲧϩⲣⲁⲓ̈ ⲛ̄ϩ[ⲏ]

8 [ⲧⲕ̄] ⲛ̄ⲧⲉ ⲡⲓ[ⲁⲧⲥ]ⲟⲩⲱⲛ̄ϥ ⲙ̄ⲡⲣⲉ[ⲓ]

9 [ⲙ]ⲉ ⲉⲣⲟϥ[·] ⲡⲁⲓ̈ ⲅⲁⲣ ⲟⲩⲙⲛ̄ⲧⲁⲧ

60.8 Supralinear stroke above the first ⲛ is restored.

above pp. 22–28: How can Life (movement and multiplicity) be ascribed to or derived from the transcendent One? Vitality in *Allogenes* is an hypostasization of the *potential* to produce living beings; the *potential* of the Unknowable (or Invisible Spirit) is hypostasized as the Triply-powered (whose triplicity is described as Vitality, Intellection, and Existence).

59.18b–26a; 60.28b–37a Here is described the second level of the ascent, Subsistence. The term ὕπαρξις ("subsistence") is used in the Chaldaean Oracles as a designation for the first term of the Intelligible Triad and by Porphyry as a designation for the One. (See the discussion of Rist, "Mysticism," 223.) Plotinus, however, uses the term only as a designation for lower hypostases. The use of the term here as practically a synonym for ⲡⲉⲧϣⲟⲟⲡ ("That-which-exists") in the triad Vitality, Intellection, and Existence shows a closer similarity to Plotinus than to the Chaldaean Oracles.

²⁶And when you receive
²⁷ a revelation about this
²⁸ through a first
²⁹ revelation of the Unknowable—
³⁰ that one who, when you
³¹ know it, you must be ignorant
³² of it—and when you become
³³ frightened in that place,
³⁴ withdraw back on account of the
³⁵ activities. And when you have become
³⁶ perfect in that place,
³⁷ be at rest. And
³⁸ according to the pattern that exists
³⁹ in you, know also in this manner

60   ¹ᵃth[at] it is
² in this way
¹ᵇthat it exists thus in [al]l th[ese]. An[d]
³ [do not] be greatly dispersed, [so that]
⁴ you will have power to stan[d].
⁵ [Ne]ither desire to be ac[tive]
⁶ [le]st you should fall away completely
⁷ from that state of inacti[v]it[y] that is
⁸ i[n you] which belongs to the [Un]knowable. Do not [kn]ow
⁹ it—for that is impossible.

Subsistence is "standing" and "at rest" (see above, note to 58.38b–59.4a). Subsistence is stable, not in and of itself, but as an "image of that which is undivided and truly at rest" (59.22–23; 60.33–37), that is, the Unknowable or Invisible Spirit. Only it can be said to be undivided (compare Plotinus, *Ennead* V.1.7) and perfectly at rest, since only it completely transcends movement and change of any kind. Subsistence, even as the potential of those things which exist, is stable only by its connection with the Unknowable (as an image of it), not by its connection with the existents (as the potential for Existence). The relation of Subsistence to the existents is expressed metaphorically: it embraces all these things (the existents) in silence and inactivity (59.24–26a). "Silence" and "inactivity" again stress the lack of movement and change.

The self-seeking nature of the ascent is again expressed at 60.33–35: in ascending to Subsistence, Allogenes finds in it the pattern of his own stability

¹⁰ бом те· алла евол ϩⲓⲧⲛ ⲟⲩ
¹¹ ⲉⲛⲛⲟⲓⲁ ⲉⲥⲉ ⲛ̄ⲟⲩⲟⲉⲓⲛ ⲉⲕⲓⲙ[ⲉ]
¹² ⲉⲣⲟϥ· ⲁⲣⲓⲁⲧⲉⲓⲙⲉ ⲉⲣⲟϥ·
                                  ⲛⲁⲓ̈
¹³ ⲇⲉ ⲛⲉⲓ̈ⲥⲱⲧⲙ̄ ⲉⲣⲟⲟⲩ ⲉⲩϫⲱ ⲙ̄
¹⁴ ⲙⲟⲟⲩ ⲛ̄ϭⲓ ⲛⲏ ⲉⲧⲙ̄ⲙⲁⲩ· ⲛⲉϥ
¹⁵ ϣⲟⲟⲡ ⲛ̄ϭⲓ ⲟⲩϩⲣⲟⲕ ϩⲣⲁⲓ̈ ⲛ̄ϩⲏⲧ
¹⁶ ⲛ̄ⲧⲉ ⲟⲩⲥⲓⲅⲏ· ⲁⲉⲓⲥⲱⲧⲙ̄ ⲉϯ
¹⁷ ⲙ̄ⲛ̄ⲧⲙⲁⲕⲁⲣⲓⲟⲥ ⲧⲏ ⲉⲧⲁⲓ̈ⲉⲓⲙⲉ
¹⁸ ⲉⲣⲟⲓ̈ ⲉⲃⲟⲗ ϩⲓⲧⲟⲟⲧⲥ̄ ⲕⲁⲧⲁⲣⲟ⟨ⲓ̈⟩
       ¹⁹ⲁⲩⲱ ⲁⲉⲓⲡ̄ⲁⲛⲁⲭⲱⲣⲓ ⲉⲝ̄ⲛ ϯⲙⲛ̄ⲧ
²⁰ ⲱⲛ̄ϩ ⲉⲓ̈ⲕⲱⲧⲉ ⲛ̄ⲥⲱⲥ· ⲁⲩⲱ
²¹ ⲁⲉⲓⲣ̄ϣⲃⲏⲣ ⲛ̄ⲃⲱⲕ ⲉϩⲟⲩⲛ ⲉⲣⲟⲥ
²² ⲛ̄ⲙⲙⲁⲥ· ⲁⲩⲱ ⲁⲉⲓⲁϩⲉⲣⲁⲧ ⲛ̄
²³ ϩⲣⲁⲓ̈ ϩⲛ̄ ⲟⲩⲧⲁϫⲣⲟ ⲁⲛ· ⲁⲗⲗⲁ ϩⲛ̄
²⁴ ⲟⲩϩⲣⲟⲕ· ⲁⲩⲱ ⲁⲓ̈ⲛⲁⲩ ⲉⲩⲕⲓⲙ
²⁵ ⲛ̄ϣⲁ ⲉⲛⲉϩ ⲛ̄ⲛⲟⲉⲣⲟⲛ ⲛ̄ⲁⲧ
²⁶ ⲡⲱⲣϫ̄· ⲉⲡⲁⲛⲓϭⲟⲙ ⲧⲏⲣⲟⲩ ⲡⲉ
²⁷ ⲛ̄ⲛⲁⲧⲉⲓⲇⲟⲥ ⲛ̄ⲛⲁⲧϯ ⲧⲟϣ
²⁸ ⲉⲣⲟϥ ϩⲛ̄ ⲟⲩϯ ⲧⲟϣ· ⲁⲩⲱ ⲉ
²⁹ ⲧⲁⲉⲓⲟⲩⲱϣ ⲉⲁϩⲉⲣⲁⲧ ϩⲛ̄ ⲟⲩ
³⁰ ⲧⲁϫⲣⲟ· ⲁⲉⲓⲡ̄ⲁⲛⲁⲭⲱⲣⲓ ⲉⲝ̄ⲛ

60.12 Turner does not note that dots above final ⲓ are restored.
60.18 Manuscript reads: ⲕⲁⲧⲁⲣⲟⲥ.
60.20 Turner emends: ⲉⲓ̈ⲕⲱⲧⲉ ⲛ̄ⲥⲱ⟨ⲓ̈⟩·.

(ⲛ̄ⲧⲉ ⲡⲏ ⲉⲧⲧⲟⲉ ϩⲓⲱⲱⲧ). One wonders here if the use of the phrase "image and likeness" is in any way related to Genesis 1.26 (LXX). The fact that Allogenes is "clothed" with such an image and likeness would then indicate even more clearly Allogenes' divinity, his likeness to God.

59.26b–60.12a; 60.37b–61.28a (and 67.20b–24a, 32b–35a) Having reached the level of Subsistence, Allogenes becomes filled with a "primary revelation of the Unknowable" (59.26–30; 60.37–61.1; 61.8–11; 61.28–32). The understanding that results from this revelation is described as an unknowing or ignorant knowledge (59.30–32; 60.10–12; 61.1–2; 61.17–19). This "knowledge" is the limit of what Allogenes can achieve. To seek after more threatens his stability; again and again he is cautioned not to go further lest he endanger his stability and the inactivity (or rest) which he has achieved

¹⁰ Rather, when, through a
¹¹ luminous insight, you know
¹² it: be ignorant of it."
    ¹³And I heard those ones speaking
¹⁴ these things.
¹⁵ A stillness of silence existed in me.
¹⁶ I heard that
¹⁷ blessedness by which I knew
¹⁸ myself as ⟨I⟩ am.
    ¹⁹And I withdrew up to the Vitality,
²⁰ seeking it. And
²¹ I entered it together
²² with it. And I stood
²³ not firmly, but
²⁴ quietly. And I saw an
²⁵ eternal, noetic,
²⁶ undivided motion to which all the powers pertain,
²⁷ formless, not bounded
²⁸ by a(ny) boundary. And when
²⁹ I desired to stand
³⁰ firmly, I withdrew up to

(59.32–35; 60.2–10; 61.25–28; 67.20–24, 32–35; see also above, note to 58.38b–59.4a).

The prefix ⲘⲚⲦ governs the entire complex ϣⲟⲣⲡ̄ ⲛ̄ⲟⲩⲱⲛϩ ⲉⲃⲟⲗ (60.39–61.1).

The distinction between revelation and primary revelation concerns the difference between auditory and direct (visual) apprehension. Plotinus makes a similar distinction between written or oral instruction and vision:

> "Not to be told; not to be written": in our writing and telling we are but urging towards it (unity with the One): out of discussion we call to vision; to those desiring to see, we point the path; our teaching is of the road and the travelling; the seeing must be the very act of one that has made this choice.   (*Ennead* VI.9.4)

From none is that Principle absent and yet from all: present, it remains absent save to those fit to receive, disciplined into some accordance, able to touch it closely by their likeness and by that kindred power within

31 †ⲌⲨⲠⲀⲢⲌⲒⲤ ⲦⲎ ⲈⲦⲀⲈⲒⲞⲚⲦⲤ

32 ⲈⲤⲀⲌⲈⲢⲀⲦⲤ· ⲀⲨⲰ ⲈⲤⲌⲞⲢⲔ

33 ⲘⲘⲞⲤ ⲔⲀⲦⲀ ⲞⲨⲌⲒⲔⲰⲚ ⲘⲚ

34 ⲞⲨⲈⲒⲚⲈ ⲚⲦⲈ ⲠⲎ ⲈⲦⲦⲞⲈ ⲌⲒⲰ

35 ⲰⲦ. ⲈⲂⲞⲖ ⲌⲒⲦⲚ ⲞⲨⲰⲚⲌ ⲈⲂⲞⲖ

36 ⲚⲦⲈ ⲠⲒⲀⲦⲠⲰⲱ ⲘⲚ ⲠⲎ ⲈⲦ

37 ⲌⲞⲢⲔ ⲘⲘⲞϤ·

ⲀⲈⲒⲘⲞⲨⲌ ⲈⲂⲞⲖ

38 ⲌⲚ ⲞⲨⲰⲚⲌ ⲈⲂⲞⲖ· ⲈⲂⲞⲖ ⲌⲒ

39 ⲦⲚ ⲞⲨⲘⲚⲦⲱⲞⲢⲠ ⲚⲞⲨⲰⲚⲌ

61 1 ⲈⲂⲞⲖ ⲘⲠⲒⲀⲦⲤⲞⲨⲰⲚϤ· Ⲍ[ⲰⲤ]

2 ⲈⲒⲈ ⲚⲚⲀⲦⲈⲒⲘⲈ ⲈⲢⲞϤ· ⲀⲒⲈⲒ[ⲘⲈ]

3 ⲈⲢⲞϤ ⲀⲨⲰ ⲀⲈⲒⲬⲒ ϬⲞⲘ ⲌⲢⲀⲒ Ⲛ

4 [Ⲍ]ⲎⲦϤ· ⲈⲀⲈⲒⲬⲒ ⲚⲞⲨⲬⲢⲞ Ⲛ2ⲎⲦ

5 [Ⲛ]ⲱⲀ ⲈⲚⲈⲌ· ⲀⲈⲒⲤⲞⲨⲰⲚ ⲠⲎ Ⲉ[Ⲧ]

6 [ⲱ]ⲞⲞⲠ Ⲛ2ⲎⲦ ⲘⲚ ⲠⲒⲱⲘⲦϬⲞ[Ⲙ]

7 ⲘⲚ ⲠⲒⲞⲨⲰⲚⲌ Ⲉ[ⲂⲞ]Ⲗ ⲚⲦⲈ Ⲡ[Ⲓ]

61.3 The supralinear stroke above ⲛ is restored.
61.7 The supralinear stroke above ⲙⲛ is restored.

themselves through which, remaining as it was when it came to them from the Supreme, they are enabled to see in so far as God may at all be seen.   (*Ennead* VI.9.4)

The role of teaching is to prepare the soul that is fit through discipline for the road it must travel. The vision, on the other hand, is a goal itself (although the highest goal for Plotinus is not vision, but unity with the One). Similarly in *Allogenes*, the revealed teachings serve as preparation for the goal of "primary revelation," the direct apprehension of the Unknowable, as far as is possible.

Allogenes' revelation is described as an unknowing or ignorant knowledge. This type of knowledge is direct, intuitive apprehension, not the type of knowledge that is the result of discursive thought. Plotinus writes that awareness of the One is beyond Intellect and any kind of knowing since the act of knowing implies a distinction between knower and known that is antithetical to the goal of unity with the One (*Ennead* VI.9.4). One can also see a close similarity of *Allogenes* to the language used by the author of the anonymous *Parmenides* commentary regarding contemplation of the One:

31 the subsistence, which I found
32 standing and at rest
33 according to an image and
34 a likeness of that with which I am clothed
35 through a revelation
36 of That which is undivided and That which is
37 at rest.
    I became full
38 with a revelation through
39 a primary revelation

61   1 of the Unknowable. So [far as]
        2 I was ignorant of it, I came to kn[ow]
        3 it and I was empowered
        4 [b]y it. After I had received an eternal strength,
        5 I came to understand wha[t]
        6 [e]xists in me, and the Triply-power[ed],
        7 and the revela[t]ion of wh[at]

Καὶ οὕτως οὔτε ἐκπίπτειν εἰς κένωμα ἐνέσται οὔτε τολμᾶν τι ἐκείνῳ
προσάπτειν, μένειν δ' ἐν ἀκαταλήπτῳ καταλήψει καὶ μηδὲν ἐννοούσῃ νοήσει
ἀφ' ἧς μελέτης συμβήσεταί σοί ποτε καὶ ἀποστάντι τῶν δι' αὐτὸν
ὑπο⟨στάν⟩των τῆς νοήσεως στῆναι ἐπὶ τὴν αὐτοῦ ἄρρητον προέννοιαν τὴν
ἐνεικονιζομένην αὐτὸν διὰ σιγῆς οὐδὲ ὅτι σιγᾷ γιγνώσκουσαν οὐδὲ ὅτι
ἐνεικονίζεται αὐτὸν παρακολουθοῦσαν οὐδέ τι καθάπαξ εἰδυῖαν, ἀλλ' οὖσαν
μόνον εἰκόνα ἀρρήτου τὸ ἄρρητον ἀρρήτως οὖσαν, ἀλλ' οὐχ ὡς γιγνώσκουσαν, εἴ μοι ὡς χωρῶ λέγειν δύναιο κἂν φανταστικῶς παρα-
κολουθῆσαι.

(Hadot, *Porphyre et Victorinus*, vol. II, 68, 70)

And thus it is possible neither to fall into emptiness nor to dare to
attribute something to That one, but to remain in an incomprehensible
comprehension and an intellection which conceives nothing. From this
exercise, it is possible for you at some time, turned away from the
intellection of the things which have been hypostasized through him, to
stand still at the ineffable preconception of him, which gives an image of
him by means of silence, not knowing that it is silent, nor understanding
that it is imaging him, nor knowing anything at all, but being only an
image of the ineffable, since it is ineffably the Ineffable, but not as though

⁸ ⲁⲧϣⲱⲡ ⲉⲣⲟϥ ⲉ[ⲧⲛ̄]ⲧⲁϥ· ⲁⲩ[ⲱ]
⁹ ⲉⲃⲟⲗ ϩ̣ⲓⲧⲛ̄ ⲟⲩⲙ̄ⲛ̄ⲧϣⲟⲣ̄ⲡ̄ ⲛ̄[ⲟⲩ]
¹⁰ ⲱⲛ̄ϩ̄ ⲉⲃⲟⲗ ⲛ̄ⲧⲉ ⲡⲓϣⲟⲣ̄ⲡ̄ ⲛ̄ⲁⲧ
¹¹ [ⲥ]ⲟⲩⲱⲛϥ̄ ⲛⲁⲩ ⲧⲏⲣⲟⲩ. ⲡⲛⲟⲩ
¹² ⲧⲉ ⲉⲧⲭⲟⲥⲉ ⲉⲧⲉⲗⲓⲟⲥ ⲁⲓ̈ⲛⲁⲩ
¹³ ⲉⲣⲟϥ ⲙ̄ⲛ̄ ⲡⲓϣⲙ̄ⲧ6ⲟⲙ ⲉⲧϣⲟ
¹⁴ ⲟⲡ ⲛ̄ϩⲏⲧⲟⲩ ⲧⲏⲣⲟⲩ· ⲛⲉⲓ̈ⲕⲱ
¹⁵ ⲧⲉ ⲛ̄ⲥⲁ ⲡⲛⲟⲩⲧⲉ ⲛ̄ⲛⲁⲧϣⲁⲭⲉ
¹⁶ ⲙ̄ⲙⲟϥ ⲙ̄ⲛ̄ ⲡⲓⲁⲧⲥⲟⲩⲱⲛϥ̄·
¹⁷ ⲡⲁⲓ̈ ⲉⲧⲉ ⲉϣⲱⲡⲉ ⲉⲣϣⲁⲛⲟⲩⲁ
¹⁸ ⲉⲓⲙⲉ ⲉⲣⲟϥ ⲡⲁⲛⲧⲱⲥ ϣⲁϥⲣ̄ⲁⲧ
¹⁹ ⲉⲓⲙⲉ ⲉⲣⲟϥ· ⲡⲓⲙⲉⲥⲓⲧⲏⲥ ⲛ̄ⲧⲉ
²⁰ ⲡⲓϣⲙ̄ⲛ̄ⲧ6ⲟⲙ ⲡⲏ ⲉⲧⲕⲏ ϩ̄ⲛ̄ ⲟⲩ
²¹ ϩⲣⲟⲕ ⲙ̄ⲛ̄ ⲟⲩⲕⲁⲣⲱϥ· ⲁⲩⲱ ⲉϥⲉ
²² ⲛ̄ⲁⲧⲥⲟⲩⲱⲛϥ̄·

ⲛⲁⲓ̈ ⲇⲉ ⲉⲓ̈ⲧⲁ
²³ ⲭⲣⲏⲩ ⲛ̄ϩⲏⲧⲟⲩ· ⲡⲉⲭⲁⲩ ⲛⲁⲓ̈ ⲛ̄
²⁴ 6ⲓ ⲛⲓ6ⲟⲙ ⲛ̄ⲧⲉ ⲛⲓⲫⲱⲥⲧⲏⲣ ⲭⲉ

61.8 Turner reads: ⲁ[ⲩⲱ].

it were knowing the Ineffable—if you are able, though only in imagination, to follow me, to the extent that I am able to describe this.

(trans. Williams, *The Immovable Race*, 79)

The similarities between this passage and *Allogenes* occur primarily in certain
shared terms or metaphors; a closer study than is offered here would need to be
done to show precisely whether or not these terms convey a shared conceptualization. The terms appear to belong, however, to the same circle of
thought: the One is ineffable and unknowable; knowledge of the One can be
described as an "unknowing knowledge" or "incomprehensible comprehension," a kind of ignorance or "intellection which conceives nothing"; the use
of terms related to the ideal of stability, such as "remain" and "stand" in the
context of mystical ascent or contemplation (see Williams, *The Immovable
Race*, 74–82); the silence of the one who "stands."

The ⲉⲛⲉⲣⲅⲓⲁ of 59.35, against which Allogenes must beware, are perhaps
his own fears (59.32–33) or his own impossible longings to know more than
can be attained (60.8–12).

The two phrases, ⲡⲓⲧⲩⲡⲟⲥ ⲉⲧϣⲟⲟⲡ ⲛ̄ϩⲏⲧⲕ̄ ("the pattern that exists in
you"; 59.38–39) and ⲡⲓⲁⲧⲉⲛⲉⲣⲅⲓⲁ ⲉⲧϩⲣⲁⲓ̈ ⲛ̄ϩⲏⲧⲕ̄ ⲛ̄ⲧⲉ ⲡⲓⲁⲧⲥⲟⲩⲱⲛϥ̄ ("that
state of inactivity that is in you which belongs to the Unknowable"; 60.7–8),
both emphasize the point made in 60.33–37 that Allogenes' stability has its

⁸ is illimitable o[f it]. An[d]
⁹ through a primary
¹⁰ [re]velation of the First
¹¹ (which is) un[k]nown to all,
¹² I saw the God that surpasses perfection
¹³ and the Triply-powered that
¹⁴ exists in them all. And I was seeking
¹⁵ the ineffable
¹⁶ and Unknowable God—
¹⁷ that which is such that if one
¹⁸ knows it at all, one is
¹⁹ ignorant of it—the mediator of
²⁰ the Triply-powered, that which is situated in
²¹ stillness and silence, and is
²² unknowable.

    When I was
²³ᵃstrengthened by these things,
²⁴ the Powers of the Luminaries
²³ᵇsaid to me:

basis in the stability of the Unknowable. And this is true not only for Allogenes, but for anything which partakes of stability (see 59.37–60.2).

The phrases "to become perfect" and "be still" or "silent" occur often in antiquity in a cultic setting, especially in the Mysteries (see above, note to 59.9b–13a). But here, though the terms certainly may carry over from the cultic setting of the ascent, they also imply again the theme of stability. In 59.35–37, the context is an admonition not to become active or "dispersed," but to become perfect and still. Like stability, stillness and silence are imitations of the state belonging to the Unknowable (see 61.20–22).

Concerning ϫⲓ ϭⲟⲙ ("giving power"; 61.3), see above, note to 45.22b–30. Here the power is described as "eternal strength" (ⲟⲩϫⲣⲟ ⲛ̄ϩⲏⲧ ⲛ̄ϣⲁ ⲉⲛⲉϩ; 61.4–5). Compare also 61.22–23.

ⲡⲓⲙⲉⲥⲓⲧⲏⲥ (61.19) is in grammatical apposition to ⲡⲛⲟⲩⲧⲉ in line 15. The difficulty here is that it is the Triply-powered who is presented throughout the rest of the text as the mediator between the Invisible Spirit (or Unknowable God) and the existents (or the Aeon of Barbelo). The idea that the Unknowable is a mediator is clearly mistaken. It may be an example of the translator's difficulty in understanding technical Greek. One would expect a description of the Unknowable such as: "that of which the Triply-powered is a mediator."

25 ϩⲱ ϭⲉ ⲉⲕϫⲱⲱⲣⲉ ⲉⲃⲟⲗ ⲙⲡⲓⲁ

26 ⲧⲉⲛⲉⲣⲅⲓⲁ ⲉⲧϣⲟⲟⲡ ⲛ̄ϩⲏⲧⲕ̄

27 ⲉⲃⲟⲗ ϩ̄ⲓⲧⲟⲟⲧϥ̄ ⲙ̄ⲡⲓⲕⲱⲧⲉ ⲛ̄

28 ⲧⲉ ⲛⲓⲁⲧⲧⲁϩⲟⲟⲩ· ⲁⲗⲗⲁ ⲥⲱⲧ̄ⲙ̄

29 ⲉⲧⲃⲏⲏⲧϥ̄ ⲕⲁⲧⲁ ⲑⲉ ⲉⲧⲉ ⲟⲩⲛ̄

30 ϭⲟⲙ ⲉⲃⲟⲗ ϩ̄ⲓⲧⲛ̄ ⲟⲩⲙⲛ̄ⲧϣⲟ

31 ⲣ̄ⲡ ⲛ̄ⲟⲩⲱⲛ̄ϩ ⲉⲃⲟⲗ ⲙⲛ̄ ⲟⲩⲱ

32 ⲛ̄ϩ ⲉⲃⲟⲗ·

The revelation to Allogenes by the Powers concerning the Unknowable

61.22b–67.38 This section contains the last revelation of the text. It is given by the Powers of the Luminaries of the aeon of Barbelo to Allogenes at the height of his ascent. He has ascended as far as was possible and received a primary (visual) revelation of the Unknowable. Now the Powers stop him from disturbing the stability he has gained by seeking the impossible, and instead give him an oral revelation containing a description of the Unknowable "as is possible" (61.28–32). (For further discussion of the Unknowable God, see also pp. 16–19.)

The content of the revelation concerning the Unknowable is given in the following six formulations:

I. It is *neither* this *nor* that *but* something better.

This formulation is expressed by any of the following combinations:

a. ⲟⲩⲧⲉ…ⲟⲩⲧⲉ…ⲁⲗⲗⲁ
b. negative . . . ⲁⲗⲗⲁ
c. ⲉⲡⲓⲇⲏ…ⲁⲗⲗⲁ
d. ⲟⲩⲧⲉ…ⲟⲩⲧⲉ . . . plus circumstantial

For example:

a. "Neither is it divinity nor blessedness nor perfection, rather it itself is something incomprehensible." (62.27–32)

b. "As it is boundless and powerless and non-existent, it cannot give existence, but rather it accepts them all being at rest, taking its stand." (66.25–30)

c. "For it is not among those things which exist, but rather it is something else more exquisite." (63.17–19)

d. "Because of this, neither does it have any need of intellect nor life nor anything else at all since it is more exquisite than all of them in its privation and incomprehensibility." (62.17–22)

²⁵ "You have hindered enough the
²⁶ inactivity that exists in you
²⁷ by seeking
²⁸ incomprehensible things. Rather, hear
²⁹ about it (the Unknowable) as is
³⁰ possible—through a primary
³¹ revelation and a revelation.
   ³²But (may one properly say of it that) it exists as

II. It is (or is not) something *lest* it not be transcendent in some respect.

This statement is formulated either positively (with ⲉⲡⲓⲆⲏ) or negatively (with ⲟⲩⲧⲉ):

a. ⲉⲡⲓⲆⲏ...ϫ︦ⲓⲛⲁ
b. ⲟⲩⲧⲉ...ϫ︦ⲓⲛⲁ

For example:

a. "For it possesses silence and stillness lest it should be limited by those who are not limited." (62.24–27)

b. "Neither is it even with regard to itself that it is active in order that it should remain still. Nor is it a subsistence lest it should be in want." (65.26–30)

III. It is *not* this; it is *not* that.
Is it this? Is it that? No, it is *neither* this *nor* that.

This formulation always expresses that *neither* element in a pair of opposites can be predicated of it.

The formulation may be either a) two positive statements or b) questions are posed that are given negative answers; the questions are posed with ⲏ︦; the answer is given using ⲟⲩⲧⲉ...ⲟⲩⲧⲉ... or ⲉⲙ︦ⲛ︦ⲧ︦ⲁϥ.

For example:

a. "It is not corporeal; it is not incorporeal. It is not great; it is not small. It is not a number; it is not a creature." (63.5–8)

b. "But (may one properly say of it that) it exists as something appropriate to the manner in which it exists or that it exists and will come into being? or does it act? or does it know? (or) is it living?—since it has no intellect nor life nor subsistence . . ." (61.32–38; see also 64.10–30)

qϣOOΠ ⲁⲉ ⲚⲚOⲨ
33 ⲗⲁⲁⲨ ⲚⲐⲈ ⲈⲦⲈϥϣOOΠ· Ⲏ ⲬⲈ
34 ⟨ⲉ⟩qϣOOΠ ⲀⲨⲱ ⲈϥⲚⲀϣⲱΠⲈ
35 Ⲏ ⲈϥⲢⲈⲚⲈⲢⲄⲒ Ⲏ ⲈϥⲈⲒⲘⲈ ⲈϥO
36 Ⲛⲍ ⲈⲘⲚⲦⲀϥ ⲚⲚOⲨⲚOⲨⲤ·
37 OⲨⲦⲈ OⲨⲱⲚⲍ· OⲨⲦⲈ OⲨⲌⲨ
38 ΠⲀⲢⲬⲒⲤ· OⲨⲦⲈ ⟨...⟩ ΠⲒⲀⲦⲌⲨΠⲀⲢ
39 ⲌⲒⲤ ⲌⲚ OⲨⲘⲚⲦⲀⲦⲦⲀⲌOⲤ·

61.34 Turner does not note corruption.
61.38 Turner does not note corruption. Following OⲨⲦⲈ, a noun with the indefinite article is expected.

IV. It is this; it is that.

This formulation always expresses that *both* elements in a pair of opposites can be predicated of the Unknowable God.

For example:

"On the one hand, it is corporeal existing in a place; on the other hand, it is incorporeal as is fitting for it, since it has subsistence that is not subject to becoming." (65.30–33)

V. It is of such a kind.

This formulation is simply a positive statement. These occur often with a negative adjective so that even though the formulation is positive, the content is negative.

For example:

"For it is incomprehensible, being a breathless place of boundlessness." (66.23–25)

"For that one is of such a kind that it is unknowable to them all in every respect." (64.6–8)

VI. It is more this or that than anything else.

Positive statements are also often framed as comparisons intended to express its surpassing excellence.

For example:

"For in beauty it surpasses all those who are fair." (64.4–6)

One also may find combinations of the above. For example, V and VI:

³³ something appropriate to the manner in which it exists or
   that
³⁴ it exists and will come into being?
³⁵ or does it act? or does it know? (or) is it
³⁶ living?—Since it has no intellect
³⁷ nor life nor
³⁸ subsistence nor ⟨. . .⟩   that which is subsistenceless
³⁹ incomprehensibly—

"For it is a comprehension of itself, since it is something unknowable of
this sort, and since it is in its unknowability more exquisite than those
who are good since it possesses blessedness and perfection and silence."
(63.28–35)

Though the formulation of each type listed above differs, every statement
describes the transcendence of the Unknowable, either by expressing its superiority or priority to everything or its transcendence of opposites. The point in
every case is to stress its transcendence. As such, the entire passage represents
an important and early example of so-called "negative" or "apophatic" theology.

61.22b–28a Seeking after incomprehensible things is an inappropriate
desire which causes one to be agitated and hence hinders the stability necessary
for the vision. (See also the discussion of Williams, "Stability," 821–22.)

Turner suggests that the distinction between "revelation" and "primary
revelation" refers to a distinction between positive theology ("revelation")
and negative theology ("primary revelation"). In my view, the primary revelation refers to the vision, revelation refers to both positive and negative
discourse. (See note to 59.26b–60.12a.)

The text reads ⲛ̄ⲧⲉ after ⲕⲱⲧⲉ (61.27–28) when one would expect ⲕⲱⲧⲉ
ⲛ̄ⲥⲁ.

61.32b–62.24a The construction of this section is extremely well-bal-
anced stylistically. It consists of two parallel sections of rhetorical questions
introduced by (ⲉ)ϥϣⲟⲟⲡ ⲛ̄ⲛⲟⲩⲗⲁⲁⲩ (61.32; 62.1). These questions are by
rhetorical implication to be answered with negatives: the questions are followed by circumstantial and I Present constructions with ⲟⲩⲧⲉ...ⲟⲩⲧⲉ...
that make their negative import clear (see above, formulation III.b). Each
section concludes with a parenthetical remark: ⟨...⟩ⲡⲓⲁⲧϩⲩⲡⲁⲣϫⲓⲥ ϩ̄ⲛ
ⲟⲩⲙ̄ⲛ̄ⲧⲁⲧⲧⲁϩⲟⲥ ("that which is subsistenceless incomprehensibly"; 61.38–
39) and ⲉⲧⲉ ⲧⲁⲓ̈ ⲧⲉ ϯϩⲩⲡⲁⲣϫⲓⲥ ⲛ̄ⲛⲁⲧϣ̄ϣⲱⲡⲉ ("that is, the subsistence that is
not subject to becoming"; 62.22–24).

This construction can be summarized schematically as follows:

62 ¹ [ⲁ]ⲩⲱ ⲉϥϣⲟⲟⲡ ⲛ̄ⲛⲟⲩⲗⲁⲁⲩ ⲙ̄ⲛ
    ² [ⲛ]ⲏ ⲉⲧϣⲟⲟⲡ ⲉⲧⲛ̄ⲧⲁϥ· ⲟⲩⲧⲉ
    ³ [ⲉ]ⲛⲥⲉϣⲱⲭⲡ̄ ⲙ̄ⲙⲟϥ ⲁⲛ ⲕⲁⲧⲁ
    ⁴ [ⲗ]ⲁⲁⲩ ⲛ̄ⲥⲙⲟⲧ· ϩⲱⲥ ⲉϥϯ ⲛ̄ⲟ[ⲩ]
    ⁵ [ⲗ]ⲁⲁⲩ ⲉϥⲭⲟⲛⲧ̄· ⲏ̄ ⲉϥⲧ̄ⲃⲃⲟ [ⲏ̄]
    ⁶ [ⲉ]ϥϫⲓ ⲏ̄ ⲉϥϯ· ⲟⲩⲧⲉ ⲉⲙⲉⲩ
    ⁷ [ϣⲁ]ⲭⲍ̄ϥ ⲕⲁ[ⲧⲁ] ⲗⲁⲁⲩ ⲛ̄ⲥⲙⲟⲧ
    ⁸ [ⲏ̄ ⲉ]ⲃⲟⲗ ϩ̄ⲓ[ⲧⲛ̄] ⲡⲉϥⲟⲩⲱϣⲉ ⲟⲩ[ⲁ]
    ⁹ [ⲁ]ϥ ⲏ̄ ⲉϥϯ· ⲏ̄ ⲉϥⲭⲓ ⲉⲃⲟⲗ ϩ̄ⲓⲧⲟ
   ¹⁰ ⲟⲧ̄ϥ ⲛ̄ⲕⲉⲟⲩⲁ· ⲟⲩⲧⲉ ⲙ̄ⲙ̄ⲛⲧⲁ[ϥ]
   ¹¹ ⲗⲁⲁⲩ ⲛ̄ⲟⲩⲱϣⲉ ⲉⲃⲟⲗ ⲙ̄ⲙⲟ[ϥ]
   ¹² ⲟⲩⲁⲁϥ· ⲟⲩⲧⲉ ⲉⲃⲟⲗ ϩ̄ⲓⲧⲛ̄ ⲕⲉ

62.2 Turner restores: [ⲡ]ⲏ.
62.5 The supralinear stroke above ⲧⲃ is restored; letters are clear.

Can existence be predicated of it? How can it be conceived?
    Does it exist only with reference to itself or does it exist by some
    other cause?
        Is it active being?
        Is it noetic being?
        Is it living being?

No (by rhetorical implication), since:
    It has no mind.
    It has no life.
    It has no subsistence.
(It is subsistenceless incomprehensibly.)

Can one then predicate existence of it insofar as it is productive, that is,
with reference to its products?
No, since it is true that:
    Nothing can be derived from it that would imply that:
    1. There are remains left over after they are produced, when
       production is conceived of as:
           assaying,
           purifying,
           giving,
           receiving.
    2. It is limited:
           by its own desire,
           by giving anything to anything else,
           by receiving from anything else.

62 ^{1a}and is it with
   ² those existents which belong to it
   ^{1b}that it exists as something?—(Since) neither
   ³ does it remain left over in
   ⁴ any way as though it gives anything
   ⁵ that is assayed or (as though) it purifies (anything) or
   ⁶ (as though) it receives or gives; nor is it
   ⁷ limited in any way
   ⁸ either through its own desire
   ⁹ or (by) giving or receiving from
   ¹⁰ anything else; neither does it possess
   ¹¹ any desire from itself
   ¹² alone nor is it through anyone

> **62.7, 16, 26, 27** For the translation "limited," see Schenke, "Bemerkungen," 419–420.

>   3. It is subject to desire:
>   from itself,
>   from anything else.

Conclusion: It has no need of intellect, nor life, nor anything else, since it is more exquisite than any predication or conception could imply. Its privation consists in the inability to predicate anything of it. It is incomprehensible. (It is non-existing subsistence.)

These questions, introduced by the disjunctive ⲏ̄, set out the central problematic of the whole section (61.32–62.24): what can be predicated of the Unknowable?

The first section, 61.32–36, raises the question of whether the triad Existence, Life, and Intellect can be predicated of it. This proposition is given a final negative conclusion in 61.36–38 (and again at 62.17–22). (For further discussion of the triad Existence, Life, and Intellect, see pp. 22–28.)

The text following ⲟⲩⲧⲉ at 61.38 is corrupt. To read "it possesses neither intellect, nor life, nor subsistence, nor that which is subsistenceless incomprehensibly" makes no sense. We expect a noun with an indefinite article followed by something like ⲁⲗⲗⲁ ⲉϥϣⲟⲟⲡ ⲛ̄ⲡⲓⲁⲧϩⲩⲡⲁⲣϫⲓⲥ ϩ̄ⲛ ⲟⲩⲙ̄ⲛ̄ⲧⲁⲧⲧⲁϩⲟⲥ "but rather it exists incomprehensibly as that which is without subsistence." (Compare the types of constructions analyzed by Tardieu, *Écrits Gnostiques*, 250.) As it stands, the phrase is an incomplete parenthetical construction.

The topic of how the Unknowable exists continues at 62.1–24a. The first set of questions asked if it can be said to exist in and of itself. Now the question

¹³ ογα· ⲛⲛⲉϣⲁϥⲉⲓ ⲁⲛ ⲉⲍⲣⲁⲓ ⲉ
¹⁴ ⲣⲟϥ· ⲁⲗⲗⲁ ⲟⲩⲧⲉ ⲛⲧⲟϥ ⲛϥϯ
¹⁵ ⲛⲛⲟⲩⲗⲁⲁⲩ ⲁⲛ ⲉⲃⲟⲗ ⲍⲓⲧⲟⲟⲧϥ
¹⁶ ⲍⲓⲛⲁ ϫⲉ ⲛⲉϥϣⲱⲡⲉ ⲉⲩϣⲱⲭⲍ
¹⁷ ⲙⲙⲟϥ ⲕⲁⲧⲁ ⲕⲉⲥⲙⲟⲧ· ⲉⲧⲃⲉ
¹⁸ ⲡⲁⲓ ⲟⲩⲧⲉ ⲙⲁϥⲣ̄ⲭⲣⲓⲁ ⲛⲛⲟⲩ
¹⁹ ⲛⲟⲩⲥ ⲟⲩⲧⲉ ⲟⲩⲱⲛ̄ⲍ· ⲟⲩⲧⲉ ⲗⲁ
²⁰ ⲁⲩ ⲣⲱ ⲉⲡⲧⲏⲣϥ· ⲉϥⲥⲟⲧ̄ⲡ ⲉⲛⲓ
²¹ ⲡⲧⲏⲣϥ ⲍ̄ⲛ ϯⲙⲛⲧⲣ̄ⲍⲁⲉ ⲉⲧⲛⲧⲁϥ
²² ⲙⲛ ϯⲙ̄ⲛⲧⲁⲧⲥⲟⲩⲱⲛ̄ⲥ· ⲉⲧⲉ
²³ ⲧⲁⲓ ⲧⲉ ϯⲍⲩⲡⲁⲣϫⲓⲥ ⲛⲛⲁⲧϣⲱ
²⁴ ⲡⲉ·

ⲉⲡⲓⲇⲏ ⲟⲩⲛ̄ⲧⲁϥ ⲙⲙⲁⲩ ⲛ̄
²⁵ ⲟⲩⲥⲓⲅⲏ ⲙ̄ⲛ ⲟⲩⲍⲣⲟⲕ· ⲍⲓⲛⲁ ϫⲉ
²⁶ ⲛⲉⲩϣⲁⲍ̄ⲭϥ ⲉⲃⲟⲗ ⲍⲓⲧⲟⲟⲧⲟⲩ
²⁷ ⲛ̄ⲛⲏ ⲉⲧⲉ ⲙⲉⲩϣⲁⲍϫⲟⲩ·

ⲟⲩ
²⁸ ⲧⲉ ⲛ̄ⲛⲟⲩⲙ̄ⲛ̄ⲧⲛⲟⲩⲧⲉ ⲁⲛ ⲡⲉ

is whether existence can be predicated of it with regard to the existents derived from it ("and is it with those existents which belong to it that it exists as something?" 62.1–2). As above, the answer is no. To say otherwise compromises its essential unity, immutability, and transcendence. As Plato puts it, the object of reason is "the self-identical Form, ungenerated and indestructible, neither receiving anything other into itself from any direction nor itself passing in any direction into another, invisible and in all ways imperceptible by sense" (*Timaeus* 52A). To say that the Unknowable gives or desires might imply that it is itself limited or limitable. It is therefore completely without need of anything—even of Intellect or Life. Its Existence is in no way subject to becoming. This position is in contrast with that taken by the *Apocryphon of John*, which states that certain things can be predicated of the Invisible Spirit (the One), not because he possesses them in and of himself, but because he is their source (II,*1*, 4.1–10). A similar point is made in *Allogenes* about the Triply-powered (see 47.26–33; 48.14–35).

Concerning the phrase, ⲟⲩⲧⲉ ⲙⲁϥⲣ̄ⲭⲣⲓⲁ ⲛ̄ ("neither does he have need of"; 62.18), see Tardieu, *Écrits Gnostiques*, 251.

62.24b–27a To say that the Unknowable possesses silence and stillness, things which are themselves privative (the absence of sound and movement), is merely another way of saying that nothing positive can be predicated of it that might indicate it could be limited in any way. (Compare Plotinus, *Ennead* V.1.4.)

¹³ else that any desire comes upon
¹⁴ it, but neither does it give
¹⁵ anything from itself
¹⁶ lest it should become limited
¹⁷ in another way. Because of
¹⁸ this, neither does it have any need of
¹⁹ intellect nor life nor anything
²⁰ else at all since it is more exquisite than
²¹ all of them in its privation
²² and incomprehensibility;
²³ that is, the subsistence that is not subject to becoming.
    ²⁴For it possesses
²⁵ silence and stillness lest
²⁶ it should be limited by
²⁷ those that are not limited.
    ²⁸Neither is it divinity

62.21 "all of them" or: "the entireties."

62.27b–63.28a This section closely resembles the *Apocryphon of John* (BG 24.6–25.10; II, 3.17–36; III, 5.2–6.3; IV, 4.28–5.23). Both works make similar statements concerning the highest figure of the divine hierarchy:

> It is not divinity nor blessedness nor perfection,
> but it is superior to these.
>
> It is not corporeal; it is not incorporeal.
>
> It is not great; it is not small.
>
> It is not anything which exists such that one can know it,
> but is superior to everything which exists.
>
> It does not participate in an aeon (eternity) or in time.
>
> It does not receive anything from another.

The purpose of these statements is to indicate the transcendence of the highest figure of the divine hierarchy, termed the One or Invisible Spirit in both *Allogenes* and the *Apocryphon of John*. Tardieu's summary concerning the *Apocryphon of John* can stand for *Allogenes* as well:

> The articulation of the apophatic argument rests not only on rejecting these contraries from the One, but upon the transcendence of the First by rapport with the sum total of the opposed terms:

29 ογτε ογⲙⲛ̄ⲧⲙⲁⲕⲁⲣⲓⲟⲥ
30 ογτε ογⲙⲛ̄ⲧⲧⲉⲗⲓⲟⲥ· ⲁⲗⲗⲁ
31 ογⲗⲁⲁγ ⲛ̄ⲧⲁϥ ⲡⲉ ⲛ̄ⲛⲁⲧⲥⲟγ
32 ⲱⲛ̄ϥ ⲙ̄ⲡⲏ ⲁⲛ ⲉⲧⲛ̄ⲧⲁϥ· ⲁⲗ
33 ⲗⲁ ⲉⲕⲉⲟγⲁ ⲛ̄ⲧⲟϥ ⲡⲉ ⲉϥⲥⲟ
34 ⲧ̄ⲡ ⲉϯⲙⲛ̄ⲧⲙⲁⲕⲁⲣⲓⲟⲥ ⲙⲛ̄
35 ϯⲙⲛ̄ⲧⲛⲟγⲧⲉ ⲙⲛ̄ ογⲙⲛ̄ⲧ
36 ⲧⲉⲗⲓⲟⲥ· ογⲧⲉ ⲅⲁⲣ ⲛ̄ⲛⲟγ
37 ⲧⲉⲗⲓⲟⲥ ⲁⲛ ⲡⲉ· ⲁⲗⲗⲁ ⲉⲕⲉⲛ̄

63

1 ⲕⲁ ⲡⲉ ⲉϥⲥⲟⲧⲡ̄· ογⲧⲉ ⲛ̄[ⲛογ]
2 ⲁⲧⲛ̄ⲁⲣⲏⲭ̄ϥ ⲁⲛ ⲡⲉ· ογⲧⲉ ⲛ̄[ⲥⲉ]
3 ϯ ⲧⲟⲱ ⲉⲣⲟϥ ⲁⲛ ⲉⲃⲟⲗ ϩⲓ̄ⲧⲟⲟ[ⲧ̄ϥ]
4 [ⲛ̄ⲕ]ⲉⲟγⲁ· ⲁⲗⲗⲁ ⲉγⲛ̄ⲕⲁ ⲉϥⲥⲟ
5 ⲧ̄ⲡ ⲡⲉ· ⲛ̄ⲛογⲥⲱⲙⲁ ⲁⲛ ⲡⲉ [ⲛ̄]
6 ⲛογⲁⲧⲥⲱⲙⲁ ⲁ[ⲛ] ⲡⲉ· ⲛ̄[ⲛογ]
7 ⲛⲟϭ ⲁⲛ ⲡⲉ ⲛ̄ⲛογ[ⲕⲟ]γⲉⲓ [ⲁⲛ ⲡⲉ]
8 ⲛ̄ⲛογⲏⲡⲉ ⲁⲛ ⲡⲉ ⲛ̄ⲛογⲧⲁ[ⲙⲓⲟ]
9 [ⲁ]ⲛ ⲡⲉ· ογⲧⲉ ⲛ̄ⲛογⲗⲁⲁγ ⲁⲛ

63.5 The supralinear stroke above ⲧⲡ is restored.
63.8 The supralinear stroke above the third ⲛ is restored; letter is clear.

limited—unlimited
corporeal—incorporeal
great—small
quantity—quality
time—eternity   (*Écrits Gnostiques*, 251)

Not only are the content and language of the two texts similar, but also the order in which the statements are given. These similarities may indicate a literary dependency. Antoinette Clark Wire considers this section to be borrowed from previous tradition ("Introduction," 177). Tardieu has pointed out, however, that the two passages may not be literarily dependent, but that both could reflect knowledge of Plato's *Parmenides* 137C–142.A, where the problem of knowing the One is considered (see *Écrits Gnostiques*, 249–251). In his view, each author drew independently upon this source, using it as the basis for a scholastic exercise, either embellishing or compressing their own presentations (see *Écrits Gnostiques*, 250). Both passages definitely seem acquainted with the well-known *Parmenides* passage and may have fashioned their views accordingly.

[29] nor blessedness
[30] nor perfection, rather
[31] it itself is something incomprehensible.
[32] (It is) not that which it possesses, but
[33] rather is something else more exquisite
[34] than blessedness and
[35] divinity and
[36] perfection. For neither is it
[37] perfect, but it is another

63 [1] thing that is more exquisite. Neither is it
[2] bound[le]ss nor is it
[3] bounded by
[4] [any o]ther thing, but rather it is something which is
[5] more exquisite. It is not corporeal;
[6] it is no[t] incorporeal. It
[7] is not great; [it is not sm]all.
[8] It is not a number; it is [n]ot a crea[ture].
[9] Neither is it anything

Plato posits that the One by definition cannot be many. From this premise he goes on to propose that the One cannot have parts or be whole; it can have no beginning, middle, or end and is therefore unlimited and without form; it cannot be in a place nor be in anything or in itself; it is not at rest nor in motion, and therefore cannot be the same as or other than itself or another; it can be neither equal nor unequal to itself or another, and therefore cannot be greater or less than itself or another; it has nothing to do with time and does not exist in time. All this means that the One does not partake of being at all; it is not even one. The final deduction is that, since it has no share in being at all, nothing pertains or belongs to it; it has no name; nor is any description or knowledge or perception or opinion of it possible.

Allogenes makes several statements concerning the Unknowable which are similar to Plato's portrait of the One, for example, that it is not possible to predicate place, substance, quantity, quality, or time of the Unknowable.

Allogenes' statement that the Unknowable is neither boundless nor bounded (63.1–5) reflects Plato's point that the One cannot be said to be in any place. (Compare Plotinus, *Ennead* VI.7.17.)

Since the One does not partake of the same or the other, it cannot be said to be corporeal or incorporeal, great or small (63.5–7). Neither is it number or

¹⁰ [ⲡ]ⲉ ⲉϥϣⲟⲟⲡ· ⲡⲁⲓ̈ ⲉⲧⲉ ⲟⲩⲛ̄ϭⲟⲙ
¹¹ [ⲛ̄]ⲧⲉⲟⲩⲁ ⲉⲓⲙⲉ ⲉⲣⲟϥ· ⲁⲗⲗⲁ ⲉⲕⲉ
¹² [ⲗⲁ]ⲁⲩ ⲛ̄ⲧⲁϥ ⲡⲉ ⲉϥⲥⲟⲧⲡ̄· ⲡⲏ ⲉ
¹³ [ⲧ]ⲉ ⲙ̄ⲙⲛ̄ϭⲟⲙ ⲛ̄ⲧⲉⲟⲩⲁ ⲉⲓⲙⲉ
¹⁴ [ⲉ]ⲣⲟϥ· ⲉⲩϣⲟⲣⲡ̄ ⲛ̄ⲟⲩⲱⲛ̄ϩ̄ ⲉ
¹⁵ ⲃⲟⲗ ⲡⲉ ⲙ̄ⲛ̄ ⲟⲩⲅⲛⲱⲥⲓⲥ ⲛ̄ⲧⲁϥ
¹⁶ ⲉⲛⲧⲟϥ ⲟⲩⲁⲁϥ ⲉⲧⲉⲓⲙⲉ ⲉⲣⲟϥ·
¹⁷ ⲉⲡⲓⲁⲏ ⲛ̄ⲗⲁⲁⲩ ⲁ[ⲛ] ⲡⲉ ⲛ̄ⲧⲉ ⲛⲏ
¹⁸ ⲉⲧϣⲟⲟⲡ· ⲁⲗⲗⲁ ⲉⲕⲉⲛ̄ⲕⲁ ⲡⲉ
¹⁹ ⲉϥⲥⲟⲧⲡ̄ ⲛ̄ⲧⲉ ⲛⲏ ⲉⲧⲥⲟⲧⲡ̄·
²⁰ ⲁⲗⲗⲁ ⲛ̄ⲑⲉ ⲙ̄ⲡⲏ ⲉⲧⲛ̄ⲧⲁϥ· ⲁⲩⲱ
²¹ ⲙ̄ⲡⲏ ⲁⲛ ⲉⲧⲛ̄ⲧⲁϥ· ⲟⲩⲧⲉ ⲉϥϫⲓ
²² ⲁⲛ ⲉⲃⲟⲗ ϩ̄ⲛ̄ ⲟⲩⲉⲱⲛ· ⲟⲩⲧⲉ
²³ ⲉϥϫⲓ ⲁⲛ ⲉⲃⲟⲗ ϩ̄ⲛ̄ ⲟⲩⲭⲣⲟⲛⲟⲥ·
²⁴ ⲟⲩⲧⲉ ⲉⲙⲉϥϫⲓ ⲗⲁⲁⲩ ⲉⲃⲟⲗ ϩ̄ⲓ
²⁵ ⲧⲛ̄ ⲕⲉⲟⲩⲁ· ⲟⲩⲧⲉ ⲉⲛⲥⲉϣⲱ
²⁶ ⲭ̄ϩ̄ ⲙ̄ⲙⲟϥ ⲁⲛ· ⲟⲩⲧⲉ ⲉϥϣⲱⲭ̄ϩ̄
²⁷ ⲛ̄ⲗⲁⲁⲩ ⲁⲛ· ⲟⲩⲧⲉ ⲛ̄ⲛⲟⲩⲁⲧϣⲁ
²⁸ ⲭ̄ϥ̄ ⲁⲛ ⲡⲉ·

63.10 The dots above ι are restored.

creature (63.8–9). Tardieu argues that ⲏⲡⲉ ("number") is an interpretation of quantity, ποσόν (*Écrits Gnostiques*, 251). The *Apocryphon of John* reads ⲟⲩⲏⲣ (BG 24.18). Tardieu has also argued that ⲧⲁⲙⲓⲟ ("creature") is a corruption of the Greek ποιόν ("quality") to ποιητόν ("creature"; *Écrits Gnostiques*, 251). If this is the case, then the "original" text would have intended these phrases to deny that quantity or quality can be predicated of the Unknowable. Compare Albinus *Didask.* X (ed. Hermann, *Plato*, VI, 165 line 9). The passage then provides yet another example of the distortion that may have taken place in the translation from Greek to Coptic.

The Unknowable does not exist in an aeon (eternity) nor does it have anything to do with time (63.21–23). (See Tardieu, *Écrits Gnostiques*, 250–251.)

It has no quantity such that it can give or receive, be added to or limited (63.24–28).

The point of clearest congruity between *Parmenides* and *Allogenes*, however, lies in the proposition that the One is unknowable and nothing can properly be predicated of it, not even Existence (see 63.9–16). But unlike *Parmenides*, *Allogenes* stresses that transcendence indicates superiority—even

¹⁰ that exists such that it is possible
¹¹ [fo]r one to know it, but rather it is some[th]ing
¹² else that is more exquisite, such tha[t]
¹³ it is not possible for anyone to know
¹⁴ [i]t, though it is a first revelation
¹⁵ and a knowledge of itself since it is that
¹⁶ alone which knows itself.
¹⁷ For it is no[t] among those things
¹⁸ that exist, but rather it is something else
¹⁹ more exquisite; (it is not) even among those that are exquisite,
²⁰ but rather (it exists) like that which pertains to it and
²¹ not (like) that which pertains to it; neither does it participate in
²² an aeon nor
²³ does it participate in time,
²⁴ nor does it receive anything from
²⁵ any other thing; neither is it limitable,
²⁶ nor does it limit
²⁷ anything nor is it unlimitable.
²⁸For it is a comprehension

63.25–28 For the translation "limitable," "limit," and "unlimitable," see Schenke, "Bemerkungen," 419–420.

to those qualities most applicable to the highest being—for example, the statement of *Allogenes* that the Unknowable is not divinity nor blessedness nor perfection but is more exquisite than these (62.27–63.1). The same point is implied at 63.17–21 where it is clearly stated that the Unknowable cannot be included among the existents; it is beyond or superior to them. The synthesis of opposites which follows presses this point home: the Unknowable is like that which pertains to it and *not* like that which pertains to it.

This insistence that nothing can be predicated of the One leads to two problems. The first is reminiscent of the Stranger's interjection in Plato's *Sophist*. He objects:

But tell me, in heaven's name, are we really to be so easily convinced that change, life, soul, and understanding have no place in that which is perfectly real—that it has neither life nor thought, but stands immutable in solemn aloofness, devoid of intelligence?   (*Sophist* 249A)

ⲡⲁⲓ ⲇⲉ ⲟⲩⲧⲉ2ⲟ
²⁹ ⲛ̄ⲧⲁ4 ⲟⲩⲁⲁ4 ⲡⲉ· 2ⲱⲥ ⲉⲩⲗⲁ
³⁰ ⲁⲩ ⲛ̄†2ⲉ ⲡⲉ ⲛ̄ⲛⲁⲧⲥⲟⲩⲱⲛ4·
³¹ 2ⲱⲥ ⲉ4ⲥⲟⲧⲡ̄ ⲉⲛⲏ ⲉⲧⲛⲁⲛⲟⲩ
³² ⲟⲩ 2̄ⲛ †ⲙⲛ̄ⲧⲁⲧⲥⲟⲩⲱⲛⲥ̄·
³³ ⲉⲩⲛ̄ⲧⲁ4 ⲛ̄ⲛⲟⲩⲙⲛ̄ⲧⲙⲁⲕⲁ
³⁴ ⲣⲓⲟⲥ ⲙⲛ̄ ⲟⲩⲙⲛ̄ⲧⲧⲉⲗⲓⲟⲥ
³⁵ ⲙⲛ̄ ⲟⲩⲕⲁⲣⲱ4 ⟨ … ⟩ ⲙ̄ⲡⲓⲙⲁⲕⲁⲣⲓ
³⁶ ⲟⲥ ⲁⲛ· ⲟⲩⲧⲉ ⲛ̄†ⲙⲛ̄ⲧⲧⲉ
³⁷ ⲗⲓⲟⲥ ⲁⲛ· ⲙⲛ̄ ⲟⲩ2ⲣⲟⲕ· ⲁⲗⲗⲁ
³⁸ ⲟⲩⲗⲁⲁⲩ ⲛ̄ⲧⲁ4 ⲡⲉ ⲉ4ϣⲟⲟⲡ·
³⁹ ⲡⲏ ⲉⲧⲉ ⲙⲙⲛ̄6ⲟⲙ ⲛ̄ⲧⲉⲟⲩⲁ

64   ¹ [ⲉⲓ]ⲙⲉ ⲉⲣⲟ4 ⲁⲩⲱ ⲉ42ⲟⲣⲕ̄ ⲙ̄
² [ⲙ]ⲟ4· ⲁⲗⲗⲁ ⲉ2ⲉⲛⲗⲁⲁⲩ ⲛⲉ ⲛ̄
³ [ⲧⲁ]4 ⲛ̄ⲛⲁⲧⲥⲟⲩⲱⲛⲟⲩ ⲛⲁⲩ
⁴ ⲧⲏⲣⲟⲩ· ⲉ4ϫⲟⲥⲉ ⲇⲉ 2̄ⲛ †ⲙ̄[ⲛ̄ⲧ]
⁵ ⲥⲁⲉⲓⲉ ⲛ̄2ⲟⲩⲟ ⲉⲛⲁⲓ ⲧⲏⲣⲟⲩ

63.35–36 Turner emends: ⟨ⲛ̄†ⲙⲛ̄ⲧ⟩ⲙⲁⲕⲁⲣⲓⲟⲥ.
64.5 Dots above second ı are restored; letter is clear.

It seems that the Sethian must make the same objection: "But can we really say that the Unknowable does not possess divinity and blessedness and perfection!" The problem is addressed in *Allogenes* by a synthesis of opposites: the Unknowable both does and does not possess what rightly pertains to it.

The fact that the One cannot be known, however, raises a second problem: Can the Unknowable possess any self-consciousness, that is, if it is completely unknowable can it know itself? The problem was put forth first most clearly by Plato in the *Sophist* 248D–E. The problem is simply that knowing implies a certain duality between the one who knows and what is known, a duality between acting on something and that which is acted upon. The problem was a serious one for Plotinus. On the one hand, he did not wish to exclude Intellection from the One; on the other hand, he would in no way brook compromise with the essential Unity of the One. (See Rist's clear presentation of this issue in *Plotinus*, 38–52.)

Allogenes, like Plotinus, follows Aristotle in insisting that God thinks Itself (63.9–16; see also Aristotle *Metaphysics* 1074B.15–1075A.12). For Plotinus, this self-contemplation is itself transcendent so that the duality that applies to thinking with regard to finite things is not applicable to the One's self-knowl-

²⁹ of itself, since it is something
³⁰ unknowable of this sort,
³¹ᵃ(and) since it is
³² in its unknowability
³¹ᵇmore exquisite than those which are good,
³³ since it possesses blessedness
³⁴ and perfection
³⁵ and silence. ⟨. . .⟩ neither that blessedness
³⁶ nor the perfection
³⁷ with stillness, but rather
³⁸ it itself is something existing—
³⁹ something which no one is able

64   ¹ to kn[ow]—and being at res[t].
² ⟨. . .⟩ but they are things
³ be[long]ing to it that are unknowable for them
⁴ all. For in b[e]auty it
⁵ surpasses all those

edge. Though the question has no sure answer, it is possible to ask if this problem is not precisely what *Allogenes* attempts to overcome by insisting that the Unknowable is "a first revelation and knowledge of itself, since it alone knows itself" (63.14–16). (Compare 63.28–31; Plotinus, *Enneads* II.9.9; V.3.5; VI.7.41.)

Concerning the construction of the Greek ἀλλά with the Coptic circumstantial ⲁⲗⲗⲁ ⲉⲕⲉ (62.32–33), see Shisha-Halevy, "The Circumstantial Present as an Antecedentless Relative," 134–37, especially 135–136.

63.28b–64.10a The statements in this section are directed toward emphasizing that knowledge of the Unknowable is impossible.

Concerning the self-comprehension of the Unknowable (63.28b–30), see above, note to 62.27b–63.28a.

ⲍⲉⲛⲗⲁⲁⲩ ⲛⲉ ⲛ̄ⲧⲁϥ ("the things which belong to it," 64.2–3) refers to all those things which are predicated of it (such as perfection and blessedness). Thus the statement in 63.33–35 that it possesses blessedness, perfection, and silence is explained in 64.2–4: It possesses these things in such a manner that they are unknowable. The implication is simply that whatever pertains to the Unknowable belongs to it in a way that lower beings cannot comprehend. This point is simply repeated by the (rather confused) lines at 63.35–64.2. As soon as the text states that the Unknowable possesses blessedness, perfection, and silence, the text qualifies itself by saying that it did not mean what it said. The

⁶ [ετν]ανο[γ]ογ· παϊ λε ν†ϩε
⁷ [ογα]τϲο[γ]ωνϥ πε νаγ τη
⁸ ρ[ο]γ κατα ϲμοτ νιμ· аγω
⁹ εβολ ϩιτο[ο]τογ τηρογ εϥ
¹⁰ ϩραϊ ν̄ϩητογ τηρογ
                                ν̄†ʳνω
¹¹ ϲιϲ ογααϲ αν ν̄νατϲογων̄[ϲ̄]
¹² τη ετϣοοπ καταροϥ· аγ[ω]
¹³ εϥϩοτπ̄ εβολ ϩιτοοτϲ̄ ν̄†м[ν̄τ]
¹⁴ ατϲογων̄ϲ̄ ετναγ εροϥ· н̄
¹⁵ ϫε ν̄аϣ ν̄ϩε ϥε ν̄νατϲογω
¹⁶ ν̄ϥ· н̄ εϣϫε [о]γν̄ ογα εϥναγ
¹⁷ εροϥ κατα θε ετεϥϣοοπ м̄
¹⁸ моϲ κατα ϲμοτ νιμ· н̄ εϣ
¹⁹ ϫε ογν̄ ογα ναϫοοϲ εροϥ ϫε
²⁰ εϥϣοοπ ν̄ογλααγ ν̄θε ν̄ογ
²¹ γνωϲιϲ· аϥρϲεβηϲ εроϥ
²² εγν̄ταϥ ν̄ογϩαπ ϫε м̄πεϥ
²³ ϲογων πνογτε· ν̄νεϥνα
²⁴ ϫι ν̄ογϩαπ αν εβολ ϩιτοοτϥ̄
²⁵ м̄πη ετм̄μαγ· πη ετεϲρ̄

64.11 Supralinear stroke above fourth n is restored.

64.14 Turner restores [εϣ] and emends the text by suggesting that an entire line has been left out: н̄ [εϣ]⟨ϫε ογ̄νоγа εϥναγ εроϥ⟩ ("[Whe]⟨ther one sees⟩"). This is unnecessary to yield a good sense. εϣ is not necessary before ϫε and can appear only where there is no other direct relative element. ϫε in line 15 introduces a direct question. In addition, the restoration of εϣ at the end of line 14 makes the line inordinately long.

purpose seems to be to push the hearer's imagination beyond any limitations implied in the definitions. The Unknowable exists, but in a manner such that it is impossible to know it (63.37–64.1) and that does not imply any compromise to its stability (64.1–2).

In lines 64.4–8, another example is given. Beauty is commonly ascribed to the highest Being by Plato (*Symposium* 210a–212a) through Plotinus (*Ennead* I.6.7). *Allogenes* states simply that the beauty of the Unknowable is superior to the beauty of anything else. The following statement (64.6–8), however, elaborates again the point that even in this respect, It is unknowable.

64.10b–37 The formulation in this section is again a series of rhetorical questions, this time about whether the Unknowable can be known—the

⁶ [who] are [f]ai[r]. For that one is of such a kind
⁷ (that) it is [u]nkno[w]able to them all
⁸ in every respect. And it is
⁹ through them all, it is
¹⁰ in them all.
      Is it
¹¹ not this unknowabl[e] knowledge alone
¹² that expresses what it is? An[d]
¹³ it is with incomprehensi[bil]ity
¹⁴ which sees it that it is joined. Or
¹⁵ how is it unknowable?
¹⁶ Or does anyone exist who sees
¹⁷ it as it exists
¹⁸ in every respect? Or
¹⁹ would one say about it that
²⁰ it exists as something like
²¹ knowledge? (Such a person) would be impious towards it
²² (and) would receive judgement on the charge of not
²³ knowing god. It is not from That one that (such a person) will
²⁴ receive judgement, (since)
²⁵ That one which does not

---

answer is clearly no. The condemnation in 64.21–33 of persons who have inappropriate conceptions of the Unknowable stresses quite sharply that any other answer to such questions is simply wrong.

The unknowability of the Unknowable raises the issue, not only of *if* but also of *how* it then can be known. Two answers are given corresponding to "revelation and primary revelation" (compare 61.25–32). With regard to oral revelation, only "unknowable knowledge" expresses what it is as it is in itself (64.10–12). Thus negative theology is the only adequate way of verbally expressing what the Unknowable is with any correctness. With regard to the "primary revelation," one can only be joined with it through an incomprehensible vision (64.12–14). Such a joining, however, does not express the kind of unity usually enjoyed by the mystic, as is indicated by the fact that Allogenes wants something more, but the knowledge he is seeking is not possible (compare 61.8–28). One cannot even really know how the Unknowable is unknowable (64.14–16).

²⁶ ⲙⲉⲗⲓ ⲛⲁϥ ⲁⲛ ϩⲁⲗⲁⲁⲩ· ⲟⲩⲧⲉ
²⁷ ⲙⲙ̅ⲛ̅ⲧϥ̅ ⲗⲁⲁⲩ ⲛ̅ⲟⲩⲱϣⲉ ⲙ̅
²⁸ ⲙⲁⲩ· ⲁⲗⲗⲁ ⲛ̅ⲧⲟϥ ⲉⲃⲟⲗ ⲙ̅ⲙⲟϥ
²⁹ ⲟⲩⲁⲁϥ ϫⲉ ⲙ̅ⲡⲉϥϭⲓⲛⲉ ⲛ̅ϯⲁⲣ
³⁰ ⲭⲏ ⲉⲧϣⲟⲟⲡ ⲟⲛⲧⲱⲥ· ⲁϥⲣ̅ ⲃ̅ⲗ̅
³¹ ⲗⲉ ⲛ̅ⲥⲁⲛⲃⲟⲗ ⲙ̅ⲡⲓⲃⲁⲗ ⲉⲧϩⲟ
³² ⲣ̅ⲕ ⲙ̅ⲙⲟϥ ⲛ̅ⲧⲉ ⲡⲓⲟⲩⲱⲛϩ̅
³³ ⲉⲃⲟⲗ· ⲡⲏ ⲉⲧⲉⲩⲣ̅ⲉⲛⲉⲣⲅⲓ
³⁴ ⲉⲣⲟϥ ⲡⲓⲉⲃⲟⲗ ϩ̅ⲙ ⲡⲓϣⲙ̅ⲛⲧ
³⁵ ϭⲟⲙ ⲛ̅ⲧⲉ ϯϣⲟⲣⲡ̅ ⲛ̅ⲉⲛⲛⲟⲓ
³⁶ ⲁ ⲛ̅ⲧⲉ ⲡⲓⲁϩⲟⲣⲁⲧⲟⲛ ⲙ̅ⲡ̅ⲛ̅ⲁ̅
³⁷ ⲡⲁⲓ̈ ⲛ̅ϯϩⲉ ⲉϥϣⲟⲟⲡ ⲉⲃⲟⲗ

64.28 Turner emends: ⲁⲗⲗⲁ ⲛ̅ⲧⲟϥ ⟨ϥ⟩ⲉⲃⲟⲗ ⲙ̅ⲙⲟϥ. Emendation is not necessary, however. Compare 65.24.

The next two questions (64.16–21) receive the strongest negative rebuke. It is impossible that anyone could see it as it exists in every respect. Nor does it exist in any way that can be comprehended by knowledge. These two sentences qualify the previous statement (64.10–14) that might have appeared to indicate that it was knowable (through apophatic theology and vision). But these sentences deny that the vision will allow one to see it as it truly is in every respect or that any kind of knowledge of it is possible. To think otherwise is impious (64.21).

The unreserved manner in which the text convicts the ignorant person of impiety shows how emphatic the author is on this point. It is a strong statement condemning "outsiders," persons who hold opposing views; these persons are "blind"; they are "outside of the quiescent eye of the revelation."

Judgement is one of the paradigmatic elements of ancient apocalyptic. *Allogenes* stresses, however, that judgement is not a characteristic of the Unknowable; rather the punishment is given solely by the impious person himself or herself (64.23–30). The individual is punished not by the gods, but by his or her own behavior; such persons are blind; their punishment consists primarily in not finding their way to that other region which is free from evil, described by *Allogenes* as "the origin which truly exists" (64.29–30). (Compare Plato, *Theaetetus* 176E–177A.)

The condemned person is described as blind and ⲛ̅ⲥⲁⲛⲃⲟⲗ ⲙ̅ⲡⲓⲃⲁⲗ ⲉⲧϩⲟⲣ̅ⲕ ⲙ̅ⲙⲟϥ ⲛ̅ⲧⲉ ⲡⲓⲟⲩⲱⲛϩ̅ ⲉⲃⲟⲗ ("outside of the quiescent eye of the revelation"; 64.31–33). Metaphors of seeing and blindness are commonly used in ancient literature to refer to the capacity or incapacity for comprehension. The term "eye" might simply refer to the capacity to see, that is, to possess knowledge. The image of a *"quiescent* eye of the *revelation"* alludes to

²⁶ show concern for anything nor

²⁷ have any desire,

²⁸ but rather (such a person) (will receive judgement) from himself/herself

²⁹ alone for that one did not find the origin

³⁰ that truly exists. That person became blind,

³¹ (being) outside of the quiescent eye

³² of the revelation—

³³ the (eye) that has active existence (and)

³⁴ that derives from the Triply-

³⁵ powered of the First Thought

³⁶ of the Invisible Spirit.

³⁷ It is from . . . that that one thus exists. . .

two other themes in *Allogenes*: the ideal of stability and knowledge achieved though visionary revelation.

But the term "eye" is used in other Sethian texts with a more specific meaning. It can refer to the archetypal Human, Adam, from whom Seth and his seed derive. *Zostrianos* reads:

> Since Adam, the perfect man, is an eye of Autogenes, it is his knowledge which comprehends that the divine Autogenes is a word of [the] perfect mind of truth. The son of Adam, Seth, comes to each of the souls as knowledge sufficient for them. Therefore [the] living [seed] came into existence from him.
>
> (30.4–14; trans. Sieber, *Nag Hammadi Codex VIII*, 85)

Or the *Gospel of the Egyptians*:

> For this one, Ad[amas], is [a light] which radiated [from the light; he is] the eye of the [light].   (IV.61.8–10; trans. Böhlig and Wisse,
> *Nag Hammadi Codices III,2 and IV,2*, 93)

(See also *TriProt* 38.5; 46.28–29; and *Zost* 13.6; compare *SJC* III.105.12–15=*BG* 108.10–11.)

These cases lead one to wonder if the term "eye" in *Allogenes* might be an oblique reference to the Divine Adam. Perhaps to say that the ignorant person is "outside the quiescent eye of the revelation" is another way to talk about those who do not share in the light of primal revelation through Adam, that is, those who do not belong to the Sethians. One cannot claim, however, without further research that such a metaphor refers to a distinct social group. The designation might simply be a kind of spiritual code, a type of "insider" language.

65 ¹⁻¹⁴ [   ]

¹⁵ [.....].[   ]

¹⁶ [...]ⲗⲁⲁⲩ ⲁ[   ]

¹⁷[...]ⲡ̣ⲏⲟⲩ ⲉⲛ[........ⲟ]ⲩ

¹⁸ [ⲙ̄]ⲛ̄ⲧⲥⲁⲉⲓⲉ ⲙ̄ⲛ ⲟ[ⲩⲱ̄ⲣ]ⲡ̄ ⲛ̄ⲱϣⲉ

¹⁹ ⲛ̄ⲧⲉ ⲟⲩⲅ̄ⲣⲟⲕ· ⲙ̄ⲛ [ⲟⲩ]ⲕⲁⲣⲱϥ

²⁰ ⲙ̄ⲛ ⲟⲩⲙ̄ⲛ̄ⲧ̄ⲅ̄ⲣⲟⲕ ⲙ̄ⲛ ⲟⲩⲙ̄ⲛ̄

²¹ [ⲧ]ⲛⲟϭ ⲛ̄ⲛⲁⲧ̄ⲛ̄ⲡⲁⲧ̄ⲥ ⲉⲁϥⲟⲩⲱ

²² ⲛ̄ⲅ̄ ⲉⲃⲟⲗ·

         ⲛ̄ⲛⲉϥⲣ̄ ⲭⲣⲓⲁ ⲁⲛ ⲛ̄ⲟⲩ

²³ ⲭⲣⲟⲛⲟⲥ ⲟⲩⲧⲉ ⟨ⲛ̄ⲛⲉϥϣⲱⲡ⟩ ⲉⲃⲟⲗ ⲅ̄ⲛ ⲟⲩⲉ

²⁴ ⲱⲛ⟨ⲁⲛ⟩· ⲁⲗⲗⲁ ⲛ̄ⲧⲟϥ ⲉⲃⲟⲗ ⲙ̄ⲙⲟϥ

²⁵ ⲟⲩⲁⲁϥ ⲉⲩⲁⲧ̄ⲛ̄ⲡⲁⲧ̄ϥ ⲡⲉ ⲅ̄ⲛ ⲟⲩⲙ̄ⲛ̄ⲧ̄

²⁶ ⲁⲧ̄ⲛ̄ⲡⲁⲧ̄ⲥ· ⲉϥⲉⲛⲉⲣⲅⲓ ⲁⲛ ⲟⲩ

²⁷ ⲧⲉ ⲉⲣⲟϥ ⲅ̄ⲓⲛⲁ ϫⲉ ⲉϥⲉϣⲱⲡⲉ

²⁸ ⲉϥⲅ̄ⲟⲣ̄ⲕ̄ ⲙ̄ⲙⲟϥ· ⲟⲩⲧⲉ ⲛ̄ⲛⲟⲩ

²⁹ ⲅ̄ⲩⲡⲁⲣⲝⲓⲥ ⲁⲛ ⲡⲉ ⲅ̄ⲓⲛⲁ ϫⲉ ⲛⲉϥ

³⁰ ⲣ̄ⲅ̄ⲁⲉ·

65.17 Turner restores: [ⲧⲁϫ]ⲣⲏⲟⲩ.
65.20 Supralinear stroke above second ⲙⲛ is restored; letters are clear.
65.23-24 This sentence, though elliptical, is clear in sense as it stands but is grammatically deficient. It is possible that this error is due to the elliptical character of the underlying Greek text. Turner emends: ⟨ⲛ̄ⲛⲉϥϫⲓ ⲁⲛ⟩. Douglas Parrott suggests: ⟨ⲛ̄ⲗⲁⲁⲩ⟩.

The term ⲣ̄ⲉⲛⲉⲣⲅⲓ (64.33) is a technical term describing that mode of being which is not potential but actual.

†ϣⲟⲣⲡ̄ ⲛ̄ⲉⲛⲛⲟⲓⲁ ("First Thought"; 64.35-36) may be a Coptic rendering of Protennoia.

65.16-22a These lines, disrupted though they are by the lacuna of 65.1-14, appear to describe the primary revelation of the Unknowable. The last phrase, "it appeared" (65.21-22) can also be translated, "it was revealed." The preceding terms ("beauty" and "stillness and silence and quiescence and untraceable greatness") describe the experience of that appearance or revelation. All are privatives, reminding the readers that even greatness emanates from the Unknowable without leaving a trace of it. It is only in this sense that the Unknowable can "appear."

The restored expression ⲱ̄ⲣⲡ̄ ⲛ̄ϣⲉ (65.18) is a *Prae-verbal* (see Funk, "Zur Syntax des Koptischen Qualitativus II.," 94-114). The verbal expression is substantivized by ⲟⲩ.

65 [1-15] [   ]

[16] [   ] something [   ]

[17][   ] . . . . . . [a]

[18] beauty and an [ema]nation

[19] of stillness and silence

[20] and quiescence and

[21] untraceable great[n]ess when it appeared.

[22]It is not of time that it has need,

[23] nor ⟨does it derive⟩ from an

[24] aeon, but rather out of itself

[25] alone because it is untraceable untraceably.

[27] In order that it should

[28a]remain still,

[26] it is not active even with regard to itself.

[28b]Nor is it a

[29] subsistence lest it should

[30] be in want.

65.22b–66.30a The point of 65.22–26 is comparable to that made already at 63.21–23: The Unknowable has no need of time or eternity. That is to say, it is not subject to time. Compare Plato's *Parmenides* 140E–141E. The Coptic is corrupt (see note to text), but the meaning in context is clear.

The term ⲁⲉⲟⲛ (65.23–24) carries connotations of both time (eternity) and place. Hence the term expresses a transition from the first point (time does not pertain to the Unknowable; 65.22–23) to the second point (place does not pertain to it; 65.25–26). The Unknowable does not derive from a place of eternity, but out of itself alone. One cannot say that place pertains to it in any way that would limit it. Compare *Parmenides* 138A–B. Rather its "place" or "existence" is untraceable (65.25–26). Compare Plotinus, *Ennead* VI.7.17, where Intellect is described as a "trace" of the One, while denying that this imputes any multiplicity to the One itself.

One cannot impute activity to the Unknowable even with regard to itself lest again that would seem to imply multiplicity (65.26–28). Since activity presumes one thing acting upon another, to say it was active with regard to itself would imply a certain duality within the One. Rather it is more proper to say (metaphorically speaking) that the Unknowable is still.

To say that the Unknowable is in want implies that it lacks something, that it is incomplete—and this notion is, of course, false (65.28–30). As the *Parmenides* points out, however, existence itself implies a lack of unity and

OYCⲰMA MEN ⲠE Eϥ

31 ⲌⲚ OYTOⲠOC· OYATCⲰMA

32 ⲗE ⲠE EϥⲌⲚ OYHEI· EYⲚTⲁϥ

33 ⲚNOYⲌYⲠAPϪIC ⲚATϢⲰⲠE

34 EϥϢOOⲠ NⲁY THPOY* EPOϥ

35 EⲘⲚTⲁϥ ⲗⲁⲁY ⲚOYⲰϢ Ⲙ

36 Mⲁy·

ⲁⲗⲗⲁ OYⲌOYE ϪICE

37 ⲠE ⲚTE OYⲘⲚTNOϬ· ⲁYⲰ

38 EϥϪOCE EⲠEϥⲌPOK· ⲌINⲁ

66 1-14 [   ]

15 [   ].NH[   ]

16 [... ⲠI ⲠⲚⲀ ⲚNAT]NⲁY EPO[ϥ]

17 ⲁϥϯ[NⲁY ⲚNⲁï THP]OY ENC[Ⲣ̄]

18 MEⲗI Nⲁ[Y AN] Ⲙ[N]H ETⲘMⲁY [Ⲛ̄]

19 ⲗⲁⲁY· OYTE EϢⲰⲠE EϢⲁOYⲀ

20 ϪI EBOⲗ ⲘMOϥ· MEϥϪI ϬOM· OY

65.34 Turner does not note corruption, but the text as it stands cannot be translated. The ЄPOϥ is left hanging.

66.16–17 Turner restores: ⲁϥ]NⲁY EPO[OY] ⲁϥϯ[ϬOM EPOOY THP]OY ("[He sa]w th[em] and em[powered them a]ll.").

66.17 Turner restores: [EⲢ̄].

66.18 Supralinear stroke above second M is restored; letter is clear.

hence an incompleteness. Therefore the Unknowable cannot be said to be subsistence. (Compare 63.17–21.)

The shocking statement that the Unknowable is corporeal (65.30–31) is clarified by the circumstantial clause "possessing a non-existing subsistence" (65.32–33). It is corporeal "being in a place," that is, as the underlying potential of all things. (Compare 66.23–25: "For it is incomprehensible, being a breathless place of boundlessness.") The problem is also somewhat mitigated by the formal synthesis of opposites (corporeal and incorporeal, 65.30–32) in non-existing subsistence (64.32–33; compare also 63.5–6.)

The Coptic ⲌⲚ OYHEI ("in a house") is an infelicitous translation of the Greek dative ἐν τῷ οἰκείῳ ("belonging to, conformable to, fitting"). Thus the meaning of the underlying Greek is "it is incorporeal as is fitting for it." (Compare the use of this phrase in Plato, *Timaeus* 42E.5–6 and Plotinus, *Ennead* V.4.2.22, 35.) Accepted by Turner (see King, "Neoplatonism").

The text appears to be corrupt at 65.34–36, although the sense of the

On the one hand, it is corporeal, existing
³¹ in a place; on the other hand, it is incorporeal
³² as is fitting for it, since it has
³³ a subsistence that is not subject to becoming.
   ³⁴It is for them all that it exists* for itself,
³⁵ not having any desire.
   ³⁶But it is a high exaltation
³⁷ of greatness and
³⁸ it is more exalted than its own stillness in order that. . .

66 ^{1–14} [   ]
   ¹⁵ [   ] those [   ]
   ¹⁶ [. . . the In]visible [Spirit]
   ¹⁷ gave [all these to them] though they did not [show]
   ¹⁸ concern for [them at]
   ¹⁹ all. Nor if one
   ²⁰ receives from him, does one receive power.
   ²¹ Nor does anyone act upon him, in

> **65.31–32** Although an accurate translation of the Coptic here means "it is incorporeal being in a house," the meaning is nonsense. Here the Coptic has misunderstood a Greek prepositional phrase. The meaning in Greek is more like "it is incorporeal as is fitting for it." See exegetical note below.

sentence is clear. To exist for itself and to be the ground of all existents are the same thing. To think otherwise would be to presume that the Unknowable desires something, and that would be wrong since it again implies division and incompleteness within the One. (Compare 62.6–17; Plotinus, *Ennead* III.9.9; see also Armstrong on Plotinus, *Cambridge History*, 240.)

Although the conclusion of 65.36–38 disappears in a lacuna, the point seems to be simply to express the Unknowable's exalted superiority in greatness and stillness. This language is again more poetry and praise than philosophy.

The fragmentary character of the first lines of page 66 makes it difficult to determine what the precise sense of lines 15–19 is.

One does not receive even power (=existence) from the Unknowable (66.19–20). Compare 62.1–17 where it is clearly stated that giving anything might seem to imply that something remains left over or that the Unknowable is itself limited. The Unknowable is the potential of all things, but not in any manner that would imply it gives power.

²¹ ⲧⲉ ⲙⲉⲣⲉⲗⲁⲁⲩ ⲉⲛⲉⲣⲅⲓ ⲉⲣⲟϥ ⲕⲁ
²² ⲧⲁ ϯⲙⲛ̄ⲧⲟⲩⲱⲧ ⲉⲧ2ⲟⲣⲕ̄ ⲙ̄ⲙⲟ[ⲥ]
²³ ⲟⲩⲁⲧⲥⲟⲩⲱⲛ̄ϥ ⲅⲁⲣ ⲡⲉˑ ⲉⲩⲧⲟ
²⁴ ⲡⲟⲥ ⲅⲁⲣ ⲡⲉ ⲛ̄ⲛⲁⲧⲛⲓϭⲉ ⲛ̄ⲧⲉ
²⁵ ϯⲙⲛ̄ⲧⲁⲧⲛ̄ⲁⲣⲏⲭ̄ⲥ̄ˑ 2ⲱⲥ ⲉⲩⲁ
²⁶ ⲧⲛ̄ⲁⲣⲏⲭ̄ϥ ⲡⲉ ⲙ̄ⲛ ⲟⲩⲁⲧϭⲁⲙˑ
²⁷ ⲁⲩⲱ ⲟⲩⲁⲧϣⲱⲡⲉˑ ⲛ̄ⲛⲉϥϯ
²⁸ ⲙ̄ⲡϣⲱⲡⲉ ⲁⲛˑ ⲁⲗⲗⲁ ⲉϥϣⲱⲡ
²⁹ ⲛ̄ⲛⲁⲓ̈ ⲧⲏⲣⲟⲩ ⲉⲣⲟϥ ⲉϥ2ⲟⲣⲕ̄
³⁰ ⲙ̄ⲙⲟϥ ⲉϥⲁ2ⲉⲣⲁⲧ̄ϥ
                         ⲉⲃⲟⲗ 2ⲙ̄
³¹ ⲡⲏ ⲉⲧⲁ2ⲉⲣⲁⲧ̄ϥ ⲛ̄ⲟⲩⲟⲉⲓϣ
³² ⲛⲓⲙˑ ⲉⲁϥⲟⲩⲱⲛ2 ⲉⲃⲟⲗ ⲛ̄ϭⲓ
³³ ⲟⲩⲱⲛ2 ⲛ̄ϣⲁ ⲉⲛⲉ2ˑ ⲡⲓⲡ̄ⲛ̄ⲁ̄
³⁴ ⲛ̄ⲁⲧⲛⲁⲩ ⲉⲣⲟϥ ⲁⲩⲱ ⲛ̄ϣⲙ̄ⲛ̄ⲧ
³⁵ ϭⲟⲙˑ ⲡⲓⲟⲩⲁ ⲉⲧ2̄ⲛ̄ ⲛⲁⲓ̈ ⲧⲏⲣⲟⲩ
³⁶ ⲉⲧϣⲟⲟⲡˑ ⲁⲩⲱ ⲉϥⲙ̄ⲡⲉⲩ
³⁷ ⲕⲱⲧⲉ ⲧⲏⲣⲟⲩ ⲉϥϫⲟⲥⲉ ⲉ
³⁸ ⲣⲟⲟⲩ ⲧⲏⲣⲟⲩˑ
                         ⲟⲩ2ⲁⲓ̈ⲃⲉⲥ

The phrase "the oneness which is at rest" (66.22) clarifies why nothing can act upon the Unknowable. According to Plato's *Parmenides*, movement of any kind cannot be attributed to the One, since parts (that is, multiplicity) are needed in order for one thing to act upon another. Since the One has no parts, it cannot be acted upon nor act upon anything else. The One is at rest.

Similarly, actuality applies to the class of existents, but the Unknowable is non-existing. (Compare Plotinus, *Ennead* II.5.1.)

One can say that place pertains to the Unknowable only if "place" is redefined to include what is appropriate for the Unknowable: boundlessness (66.23–25). The place of the Unknowable is Boundlessness. This "place" is "breathless," without life or movement or activity. It is incomprehensible. (Compare 49.9; 63.1–5.)

Existence is defined by limit, power, and being. Since the Unknowable does not possess any of these, it cannot give existence (66.25–30). On the other hand, it is in some sense the ground of all things. *Allogenes* expresses its connection with the existents by saying that the Unknowable contains them all in such a manner as is appropriate for its rest and stability.

66.30b–38 This passage is extremely important since here, for the first

²² accord with the oneness that is at rest.
²³ For he is incomprehensible, being a
²⁴ breathless place of
²⁵ boundlessness. As he is
²⁶ boundless and powerless
²⁷ and not subject to becoming, he does not give
²⁸ existence, but rather he accepts
²⁹ them all, being at rest,
³⁰ taking his stand.
　　It is from
³¹ that one who stands at every time
³³ that eternal life
³² appeared, that is, (from) the
³⁴ Invisible and Triply-
³⁵ powered Spirit, the One who is in all those
³⁶ that exist and who encompasses
³⁷ them all, since he surpasses
³⁸ them all.
　　A shadow. . .

time in the revelation from the Powers, the Unknowable seems to be identified with the Triply-powered Invisible Spirit. Interestingly enough, the connection is made in a context where the topic has switched from an affirmation of the transcendence of the Unknowable to the topic of generation. Above (66.28–30), *Allogenes* states that "it" contains the existents. The identity of this figure is now made clear: it is the Triply-powered Invisible Spirit who stands at every time; he is "the One who is in all those who exist and who encompasses them all since he surpasses them all." (See pp. 19–20.)

Eternal life came forth from the Triply-powered Invisible Spirit (66.32–35). The reader is surely meant to connect ⲱⲛϩ ("life") with ⲘⲚⲦⲱⲛϩ ("Vitality"; compare 49.26–36 and 60.19–20), one member of the triad Vitality-Existence-Intellection associated with the Triply-powered and the first level achieved by Allogenes in his ascent.

Turner and Layton both understand ⲉϥⲁϩⲉⲣⲁⲧϥ (66.30) as a circumstantial, rather than a second tense. The sense remains the same, although it is not clear from their translations that "the Triply-powered Invisible Spirit" is in apposition with "the one who stands continually."

In Gnostic myths, the term ϩⲁⲓⲃⲉⲥ ("shadow"; 66.38) is often used as a metaphorical term concerning that which derives from light or that which

67 ¹⁻¹⁴ [   ]
¹⁵ [. .] . [   ]
¹⁶ [. .]ϵⲧⲁϥ·ⲣ[. . . . . . ⲁⲩ]
¹⁷ [ⲙⲁ]ⲍ̄ϥ ⲉⲃⲟ[ⲗ ⳍⲓⲧⲛ̄ ⲟⲩϬⲟⲙ· ⲁⲩⲱ]
¹⁸ [ⲁϥ]ⲁⲍⲉⲣⲁⲧ̄ϥ ⳍ[ⲁ]ⲑⲏ [ⲛ̄]ⲛⲁ[ⲓ̈] ⲉϥ†
¹⁹ Ϭⲟⲙ ⲛ̄ⲛⲁⲓ̈ ⲧⲏⲣⲟⲩ. ⲁϥⲙⲟⲩⳍ
²⁰ ⲛ̄ⲛⲁⲓ̈ ⲧⲏⲣⲟⲩ ⲉⲃⲟⲗ·

ⲁⲩⲱ ⲉ
²¹ [ⲧ]ⲃⲉ ⲛⲁⲓ̈ ⲙⲉⲛ ⲧⲏⲣⲟⲩ ⲁⲕⲥⲱ
²² ⲧ̄ⲙ ⳍⲛ̄ ⲟⲩⲧⲁⳃⲣⲟ· ⲁⲩⲱ ⲙ̄ⲡ̄ⲣ
²³ ⲕⲱⲧⲉ ⲛ̄ⲥⲁ ⲗⲁⲁⲩ ⲛ̄ⳍⲟⲩⲟ̄·
²⁴ ⲁⲗⲗⲁ ⲙⲟϣⲉ ⲛⲁⲕ·

/   ⲟⲩⲧⲉ ⲛ̄
²⁵ ⲧ̄ⲛⲥⲟⲟⲩⲛ ⲁⲛ ⳁⲉ ⲟⲩⲛ̄ⲧⲉ
²⁶ ⲡⲓⲁⲧⲥⲟⲩⲱⲛ̄ϥ ⲟⲩⲛ̄ⲧⲁϥ
²⁷ ⲛ̄ⳍⲉⲛⲁⲅⲅⲉⲗⲟⲥ· ⲟⲩⲧⲉ ⳍⲉⲛ
²⁸ ⲛⲟⲩⲧⲉ· ⲟⲩⲧⲉ ⲡⲏ ⲉⲧⳍⲟⲣⲕ̄
²⁹ ⲙ̄ⲙⲟϥ· ⳁⲉ ⲛⲉⲟⲩⲛ̄ⲧⲁϥ ⲛ̄ⲟⲩ
³⁰ ⲗⲁⲁⲩ ⳍⲣⲁⲓ̈ ⲛ̄ⳍⲏⲧ̄ϥ ⲛ̄ⲥⲁⲃⲏⲗ ⲉ
³¹ ⲡⲓⳍⲣⲟⲕ ⲉⲧⲉ ⲡⲁⲓ̈ ⲡⲉ ⳁⲉ ⲛ̄ⲧⲟϥ ⟨ . . . ⟩

67.17 Turner restores: [ⲙⲟ]ⲍ̄ϥ, but the variant ⲁ for ⲟ is normative for this text and well within the range of possible variations within Sahidic (see Introduction p. 69).
67.31 Turner does not note corruption, but sense requires more than is given in the manuscript.

lacks light. Sometimes it has a positive valence ("the shadow of light," *ApJohn* BG 54.6); sometimes a negative valence ("the shadow of death," *ApJohn* BG 55.2). In *Three Steles of Seth*, it is used to describe Barbelo. She is called "the first shadow of the Father" (122.1–3). It is not possible even to speculate how the term is to be understood here due to the lacuna.

67.16–20a This statement ends the discussion of the generation of existents and their relationship to the Unknowable begun at 66.25.

Though the antecedent of the subject pronoun is lost in the lacuna, comparison with 45.36–38 suggests that the subject here is Barbelo (m.). It is he who was filled by power and was prior to the individual existents in stability. Out of his own power, he filled all the individual existents, that is, he gave them substantial existence. Compare Plotinus' description of the generation of all things through the filling of Intellect:

67 ¹⁻¹⁵ [   ]
   ¹⁶ [   ] which was [. . . He]
   ¹⁷ was [fil]led [by power and]
   ¹⁸ [he] stood ea[rli]er [than] the[y]; giving
   ¹⁹ power to them all, he filled
   ²⁰ them all.

And
   ²¹ on the one hand, you have heard a[b]out all these things
   ²² with surety. And do not
   ²³ seek anything more;
   ²⁴ rather go.

Neither do
   ²⁵ we understand whether
   ²⁶ the Incomprehensible possesses
   ²⁷ angels or
   ²⁸ gods; nor (do we know regarding) that one who is at rest
   ²⁹ whether it had
   ³⁰ anything in it except
   ³¹ this very stillness. For it ⟨. . .⟩

At first it was not Intellect looking upon the Good; it was a looking void of Intellection. We must think of it not as looking but as living; dependent upon That, it kept itself turned Thither; all the tendance taking place There and upon That must be a movement teeming with life and must so fill the looking Principle; there is no longer bare Act, there is a filling to saturation. Forthwith it becomes all things . . .

                                               (*Ennead* VI.7.16)

Barbelo fills the role in *Allogenes* that is played by Intellect in Plotinus's thought. (Compare 49.7-21; 53.8-17.)

67.20b-38 The trustworthiness of the revelation is now affirmed (67.20b-22a). (Compare 47.5-7.)

The theme of the limitation of what can be known begun at 59.26-60.12 and 61.25-28 is taken up again at 67.22b-24a, 32b-35a. The revelation is nearing its end. The Powers warn Allogenes not to seek more. The phrase ⲙⲟⲩⳋⲉ ⲛⲁⲕ infers that he should "let go of it, leave off seeking." It is not proper (to his achieved stability) to continue seeking again and again (67.32b-35a).

Lines 67.24b-32a seem to interrupt the Powers' warning with a short

³² ϩⲓⲛⲁ ϫⲉ ⲛ̄ⲛⲉⲩϣⲁϩ𝑥̄ϥ·

ⲟⲩ

³³ ⲧⲉ ⲙ̄ⲡⲉⲧⲉϣϣⲉ ⲁⲛ ⲡⲉ ⲉ

³⁴ ϫⲱⲱⲣⲉ ⲉⲃⲟⲗ ⲛ̄ϩⲟⲩⲟ ⲛ̄ⲟⲩ

³⁵ ⲏⲡⲉ ⲛ̄ⲥⲟⲡ ⲉⲕⲕⲱⲧⲉ· ⲛⲉⲥ

³⁶ ⲙ̄ⲡϣⲁ ⲛ̄ⲧⲉⲧⲛ̄ⲉⲓⲙⲉ ⟨ⲉⲣⲟϥ⟩ ⲟⲩ

³⁷ ⲁⲉⲧϥ̄· ⲁⲩⲱ ⟨ … ⟩ ⲛ̄ⲥⲉϣⲁϫⲉ

³⁸ ⲙ̄ⲛ̄ ⲕⲉⲟⲩⲁ· ⲁⲗⲗⲁ ⲉⲕⲁϫⲓⲧⲟⲩ

68 ¹⁻¹⁴ [   ]

¹⁵ [   ]··[   ]

¹⁶ [··ⲁⲩⲱ ⲡ]ⲉϫ[ⲁϥ ⲛⲁ]ⲓ̈ ϫⲉ ⲥϩⲁ[ⲓ̈ ⲛ̄]

¹⁷ [ⲛ]ⲏ ⲉⲧ̄ⲛⲁϫ[ⲟⲟ]ⲩ ⲛⲁⲕ· ⲁⲩ[ⲱ]

¹⁸ ⲉⲧ̄ⲛⲁⲧ̄ ⲙⲉⲉⲩⲉ ⲛⲁⲕ ⲉⲧⲃⲏ

¹⁹ ⲏⲧⲟⲩ ⲛ̄ⲛⲁⲓ̈ ⲉⲧⲛⲁⲣ̄ⲙ̄ⲡϣⲁ ⲙ̄

²⁰ ⲙ̄ⲛ̄ⲛ̄ⲥⲱⲕ· ⲁⲩⲱ ⲉⲕⲉⲕⲱ ⲙ̄

²¹ ⲡⲉⲓ̈ϫⲱⲱⲙⲉ ϩⲓϫⲛ̄ ⲟⲩⲧⲟⲟⲩ

²² ⲛ̄ⲅ̄ⲙⲟⲩⲧⲉ ⲉϩⲣⲁⲓ̈ ⲟⲩⲃⲉ ⲡⲓⲣⲉ[ϥ]

²³ ⲁⲣⲉϩ ⲉⲙⲟⲩ ⲫⲣⲓⲕⲧⲟⲥ·

67.36 Or: ⟨ⲉⲣⲟⲟⲩ⟩. Turner emends ⲛ̄ⲧⲉⲧⲛ̄ⲉⲓⲙⲉ ⲟⲩ ⲁⲉⲧ ⟨ⲧⲏⲛⲉ⟩·.
68.16 Dots above ι are restored.
68.19 Supralinear stroke above second ⲙ is restored; letter is clear.

excursus on whether or not the Incomprehensible possesses angels or gods or whether it has anything in it except stillness. Not only is the placement of these sentences odd, their meaning is surely not in line with the rest of the revelation where the Unknowable is presented as a completely unitary and transcendent being. They are probably a secondary addition.

According to Merlan, the location of gods and daimons (including angels) was a topic of considerable interest to later Platonists (see "Greek Philosophy," 32–37). The presence of theurgic materials in *Allogenes* itself leads one to speculate upon the belief in such gods and angels by Sethians and the role this belief may have played in their cult (see pp. 14–16). The skepticism it expresses about the place of gods and daimons and their existence is interesting. It surely seems as though such belief, based as it is upon a Stoic view of the harmony of the universe, may not be consistent with Sethian myth. It is definitely not consistent with the exalted description of the Unknowable contained in the immediately preceding pages.

³² in order that it will not be limited.
    ³³Nor is it fitting to
³⁴ hinder yourself more
³⁵ seeking again and again. It would be
³⁶ worthy for you to know ⟨it⟩
³⁷ alone and ⟨. . .⟩ for them to speak
³⁸ with another one. But you will receive them . . .”

68 ¹⁻¹⁵ [   ]
¹⁶ [. . And he s]aid [to me]: “Writ[e] down
¹⁷ [the]se things, which I will t[el]l to you an[d]
¹⁸ which I will recall to your mind
¹⁹ for those who will become worthy
²⁰ after you. And you shall place
²¹ this book upon a mountain
²² and you shall adjure the
²³ guardian: ‘Come, Horrible One!’”

> **67.32** For the translation “limited,” see Schenke, “Bemerkungen,” 419–420.
> **67.36** Or: “⟨them⟩.”

The last lines of the page are incomplete and corrupt (67.35b–38). The sense is difficult to establish.

The revelation of the Powers ends somewhere in the lacuna.

The final command to Allogenes

68.16–23a The identity of the revealer here is unclear. It is, however, a single masculine figure (see 68.24), so it can be neither Iouel, who is female, nor the Powers collectively. Various suggestions have been made. Turner suggests that it may be one of the Luminaries or powers (“Allogenes,” 266). Valantasis suggests that the speaker might be Barbelo (*Spiritual Guides*, 143; but see also p. 144 where he assumes wrongly that it is Iouel). Schenke suggests that this revealer could be identified also with the revealer who gave Allogenes his first revelation at the opening of the text. In that case, the speech of this revealer frames *Allogenes*. This figure moreover might be identified with the helper who was given to him (45.9–12) and the power that clothed Allogenes when he was sent below (50.24–32). Schenke suggests that comparison with other Sethian texts could lead to the conclusion that this figure is the heavenly Adam, the father of Seth (“Bemerkungen,” 421–422). The

ⲛⲁ̈ⲓ

²⁴ ⲁⲉ ⲛ̄ⲧⲉⲣⲉϥϫ̄ⲟⲟⲩ ⲁϥⲡⲱⲣⲝ̄

²⁵ ⲉⲃⲟⲗ ⲙ̄ⲙⲟ̈ⲓ· ⲁⲛⲟⲕ ⲁⲉ ⲁ̈ⲓⲙⲟⲩ\2

²⁶ ⲉⲃⲟⲗ ⲅ̄ⲛ ⲟⲩⲣⲁ\ϣⲉ· ⲁ̈ⲓⲥⲅⲁ̈ⲓ ⲁⲉ

²⁷ ⲙ̄ⲡⲉ̈ⲓϫⲱⲱⲙⲉ ⲉⲧⲁⲩⲧⲱ\ϣ

²⁸ ⲛⲁ̈ⲓ ⲡⲁⲩⲏⲣⲉ ⲙⲉⲥⲥⲟⲥ· ϫⲉ

²⁹ ⲉ̈ⲓⲉ6ⲱⲗⲡ̄ ⲛⲁⲕ ⲉⲃⲟⲗ ⲛ̄ⲛⲏ ⲉ

³⁰ ⲧⲁⲩⲧⲁⲩⲉ ⲟⲉⲓⲩ ⲙ̄ⲙⲟⲟⲩ ⲛⲁ

³¹ \2ⲣⲁ̈ⲓ ⲛ̄\2ⲏⲧ ⲡⲩⲟⲣⲡ̄ ⲁⲉ ⲁ̈ⲓϫⲓ

³² ⲧⲟⲩ ⲅ̄ⲛ ⲟⲩⲛⲟ6 ⲛ̄ⲥⲓⲅⲏ[.] ⲁⲩⲱ

³³ ⲁⲉⲓⲁ\2ⲉⲣⲁⲧ ⲕⲁⲧⲁⲣⲟ̈ⲓ ⲉ̈ⲓⲥⲟⲃ

³⁴ ⲧⲉ ⲙ̄ⲙ[ⲟ]ⲉⲓ· ⲛⲁ̈ⲓ ⲛⲉ ⲛⲏ ⲉⲧⲁⲩ

³⁵ 6ⲟⲗⲡⲟ[ⲩ] ⲛⲁ̈ⲓ ⲉⲃⲟⲗ ⲱ̄ ⲡⲁⲩⲏ

69   ¹ [ⲣⲉ ⲙⲉⲥⲥⲟⲥ   ]

   ²⁻¹³ [   ]

   ¹⁴ [

lacuna at the beginning of the text and in the first half of page 68 makes any solution uncertain.

The revealer delivers a simple message. He tells Allogenes to write down what he is told and the things which he will recall to Allogenes' mind. The book is for "those who will become worthy after you," probably fellow Sethians (see pp. 35–43). He is to place the book upon a mountain and adjure the Guardian to watch over it by calling his name, "Phriktos" ("Horrible One").

These elements are standard among apocalypses. Good examples for comparison are the Hermetic *Discourse on the Eighth and Ninth* 61.18–63.32; *GosEgypt* 68.1-end; *ApJohn* II,*1*,31.28–34. In these cases the book is also to be placed upon a mountain. It is possible that Phriktos is the guardian spirit of the mountain.

The notion of secret books and esoteric teaching is common in Gnosticism, but is not unique to it. Even Plotinus would agree that holy matters are not for general distribution (see *Ennead* IX.9.11). The fact that Messos receives this information and is told below to "proclaim it" is not inconsistent with the essentially esoteric content of the writing. It is meant only for a select number of "worthy persons," of whom Messos is clearly one (contrary to Valantasis, [*Spiritual Guides*, 135–36] who understands Iouel's teaching as philosophical instruction and that of the Powers as ascetical experience). He further con-

²⁴Then after he said these things, he parted

²⁵ from me. But I was filled

²⁶ with joy. Then I wrote

²⁷ this book which was ordained

²⁸ for me, O my son Messos, so that

²⁹ I might disclose to you those things

³⁰ that were proclaimed

³¹ in my presence inside me. For first I received

³² them in a great silence. And

³³ I stood as was appropriate for me, preparing

³⁴ my[s]elf. These are those things that were

³⁵ disclosed to me, O my so[n]

69   ¹ [Messos. . .   ]
      ²⁻¹³ [   ]
       ¹⁴ [   ]

cludes that: "This implies that philosophical formation best emerges from a relationship with a singular guide and ascetical formation best occurs in a community" [133], a thesis that has no foundation in the text.)

Allogenes' final response

68.23b–69.1 After the revealer departs, Allogenes experiences joy.

Allogenes wrote this book, as he was intended to do, disclosing all the things which were proclaimed to him. The spiritual nature of the contents is emphasized by noting that the experience itself was internal (68.30–31).

The book is addressed to "his son, Messos," and may indicate that the book is framed as an epistle. (See note to 45.1–5 above.)

At the end of all his experiences, Allogenes has achieved the ideal state of silence and stability. It is unclear what he is now preparing for, perhaps another revelation or ascent, or perhaps the final return to "that which is his" (see 50.33–34).

Williams has suggested that the language of "standing" refers here, not only to the ideal of stability, but to the actual posture of the visionary. He writes:

> . . . the author of *Allog(enes)* may be depicting a physical pose for the seer which is appropriate to the condition of noetic stability that is achieved in the vision.   (*The Immovable Race*, 86)

ⲧⲁϣⲉ]
15 ⲟⲉⲓϣ ⲙ̄[ⲙⲟⲟⲩ ⲱ̄ ⲡⲁ]
16 ϣⲏⲣⲉ ⲙⲉ[ⲥⲥ]ⲟⲥ [· ⲧⲧⲉ ⲛ̄]
17 ⲥⲫⲣⲁⲅⲓⲥ [ⲛ̄]ⲧⲉ [ⲛⲓⲭⲱ]
18 ⲱⲙⲉ ⲧⲏⲣⲟⲩ ⲛ̄[ⲧⲉ]
19 ⲡⲁⲗⲗⲟ[ⲅⲉ]ⲛⲏⲥ
20 ⲡⲁⲗ[ⲗ]ⲟⲅⲉⲛⲏⲥ

69.15 Supralinear stroke above ⲙ is restored; letter is clear.
69.16 Restoration by H.-M Schenke, "The Phenomenon and Significance of Gnostic Sethianism," 603. Turner restores: [ⲛ̄ⲧ].
69.18 Supralinear stroke above ⲛ is restored.

The command to Messos

69.14–19 The final lines contain the last admonition of Allogenes to his son Messos and the name of the treatise. These lines are set apart and emphasized in the manuscript by decoration.

Concerning the restoration of the "five seals" (69.16–17), see pp. 13–14 above.

Regarding the "books," see pp. 40–41.

¹⁵[Pro]claim t[hem, O my]
¹⁶ son Me[ss]os, [these five]
¹⁷ seals [o]f all [the]
¹⁸ [bo]oks o[f]
¹⁹ Allo[ge]nes!
²⁰Al[l]ogenes

Title of the Tractate

69.20 It is the usual orthographic practice in Coptic epigraphy to place the title of the tractate at the end of the text. The title is emphasized by decoration.

NHC XI,55 and 56. Two sides of the most heavily damaged leaf in *Allogenes*: the top third of the leaf is missing altogether, and less than half of the bottom two-thirds survives. The two pages contain part of the revelation from Iouel to Allogenes about the nature of the divine world. *Photographs courtesy of the Institute for Antiquity and Christianity, Claremont, California. Used by permission.*

Works Consulted

Aland, Barbara, ed. *Gnosis. Festscrift für Hans Jonas* (Göttingen: Vandenhoeck and Ruprecht, 1978).

Armstrong, Arthur Hilary. "Eternity, Life and Movement in Plotinus' Accounts of NOYC" in *Le Néoplatonisme* (ed. Schull, P. M. and Hadot, P.; Paris: Centre national de la recherche scientifique, 1971), 67–74. Reprint in *Plotinian and Christian Studies* (London: Variorum Reprints, 1979), 67–74.

———. "Gnosis and Greek Philosophy" in *Gnosis* (ed. Barbara Aland), 87–124.

———. "Plotinus," in *The Cambridge History of Later Greek and Early Medieval Philosophy* (Cambridge: Cambridge University Press, 1967), 195–268.

———. *Plotinus* (5 vols.; Loeb Classical Library; Cambridge, MA: Harvard University Press, 1966–1984).

———, ed. *The Cambridge History of Later Greek and Early Medieval Philosophy* (Cambridge: Cambridge University Press, 1967).

Barbara, S. "Allogenes, Supreme" in *The Zondervan Pictoral Encyclopedia of the Bible* (ed. M. C. Penney, et al.; Grand Rapids: Zondervan, 1975), vol. 1, 107.

Berlin Arbeitskreis für koptische-gnostische Schriften. "Die Bedeutung der Texte von Nag Hammadi für die moderne Gnosisforschung" in *Gnosis und Neues Testament* (ed. Karl-Wolfgang Tröger; Berlin: Gütersloher Verlaghaus, 1973), 13–76.

Berchman, Robert M. "Arcana Mundi between Balaam and Hecate: Prophecy, Divination, and Magic in Later Platonism," in *SBLSP* (ed. David J. Lull; Atlanta, GA: Scholars Press, 1989), 107–185.

———. *From Philo to Origen. Middle Platonism in Transition* (Brown Judaic Studies 69; Chico, CA: Scholars Press, 1984).

———. "Magic and Philosophy in Late Antiquity: Toward a Theory of Magic in Neoplatonism" (manuscript).

Bianchi, Ugo, ed. *Le Origini dello Gnosticismo: Colloquio di Messina 13–18 Aprile 1966* (Leiden: E. J. Brill, 1967).

Böhlig, Alexander. "Triade und Trinität in den Schriften von Nag Hammadi" in *The Rediscovery of Gnosticism* (ed. Bentley Layton), vol. II, 617–634.

Böhlig, Alexander and Frederik Wisse (ed. and trans.) *Nag Hammadi Codices III,2 and IV,2. The Gospel of the Egyptians* (NHS 4. Leiden: E. J. Brill, 1975).

Bréhier, Émile. *The Philosophy of Plotinus* (trans. Joseph Thomas; Chicago: University of Chicago Press, 1958).

Burkert, Walter. *Lore and Science in Ancient Pythagoreanism* (trans. Edwin L. Minar, Jr.; Cambridge, MA: Harvard University Press, 1972).

Bury, R. G. *Plato. Timaeus, Critias, Cleitophon, Menexenus, Epistles* (Loeb Classical Library; Cambridge, MA: Harvard University Press, 1929).

Cerny, Jaroslav. *Coptic Etymological Dictionary* (Cambridge: Cambridge University Press, 1976).

Collins, John J. "Introduction: Towards a Morphology of a Genre" in *Apocalypse* (ed. John J. Collins), 1–20.

187

———, ed. *Apocalypse. The Morphology of a Genre* (*Semeia* 14, 1979).

Colpe, Carsten. "Die gnostische Gestalt des Erlösten Erlösers" in *Der Islam* 32 (1956/57), 195–214.

———. "Heidnische, Jüdische, und Christliche Überlieferung in den Schriften aus Nag Hammadi" in *Jahrbuch für Antike und Christentum* 15 (1972), 5–18; 16 (1973), 106–126; 17 (1974), 109–125; 18 (1975), 144–165; 19 (1976), 120–138; 20 (1977), 149–170; 21 (1978), 125–146; 22 (1979) 98–122; 23 (1980), 108–127; 25 (1982), 65–101.

———. "Die 'Himmelreise der seele' ausserhalb und innerhalb der Gnosis" in *Le Origini Dello Gnosticismo* (ed. U. Bianchi), 429–447.

———. *Die religionsgeschichtliche Schule: Darstellung und Kritik ihres Bildes vom gnostischen Erlösermythus* (Göttingen: Vandenhoeck and Ruprecht, 1961).

———. "Vorschläge des Messina-Kongresses von 1966 zur Gnosisforschung," in *Christentum und Gnosis* (ed. Walther Eltester; Beiheft zur ZNW 37; Berlin: Alfred Töpelmann, 1969), 129–132.

Crum, Walter. *Coptic Dictionary* (Oxford: Clarendon Press, 1939).

Des Places, É. *Oracles chaldaïques* (Paris: Budé, 1971).

———. *Numénius. Fragments* (Paris: Budé, 1973).

Dillon, John. "The Descent of the Soul in Middle Platonic and Gnostic Theory" in *The Rediscovery of Gnosticism* (ed. B. Layton), I, 357–364.

———. *The Middle Platonists. A Study of Platonism 80 B.C. to A.D. 220* (London: Duckworth, 1977).

Dodds, E. R. *The Greeks and the Irrational* (Berkeley and Los Angeles: University of California Press, 1951).

———. "Numenius and Ammonius" in *Les Sources de Plotin* (Entretiens sur l'antiquité classique, V; Vandoeuvres-Genève: Fondation Hardt, 1960), 3–32.

———. "The *Parmenides* of Plato and the Origin of the Neoplatonic 'One'" in *Classical Quarterly* 22 (1928), 129–142.

———. *Proclus. The Elements of Theology* (Oxford: Clarendon Press, 1933).

Dörrie, H. "Die Frage nach dem Transzendenten im Mittelplatonismus" in *Les Sources de Plotin* (Entretiens sur l'antiquité classique V; Vandoeuvres-Genève: Fondation Hardt, 1960), 193–223.

———. *Platonica Minora* (München: Wilhelm Fink Verlag, 1976).

Doresse, Jean. "Les reliures des manuscrits gnostiques coptes découverts à Khènoboskion" in *Revue d'Egyptologie* 13 (1961), 27–49.

———. *The Secret Books of the Egyptian Gnostics* (trans. P. Mairet; New York: Viking Press/London: Hollis and Carter, 1960).

——— and Togo Mina. "Nouveaux textes gnostiques coptes découverts en Haute-Egypte: La bibliothèque de Chénoboskion" in *VC* 3 (1949), 129–141.

Dornseiff, F. *Das Alphabet in Mystik und Magie* (2nd ed.; Leipzig: B. G. Teubner, 1925).

Elsas, Christoph. *Neoplatonische und gnostische Weltablehnung in der Schule Plotins* (Berlin: Walter de Gruyter, 1975).

Emmel, Stephen. "Proclitic Forms of the Verb † in Coptic" in *Studies Presented to H. J. Polotsky* (ed. D. W. Young; E. Glouchester, MA: 1981), 131–146.

———. "Unique Photographic Evidence for Nag Hammadi Texts: CG IX-XIII.*1*" *BASP* 16 (1979), 263–75.

Enslin, M. S. "Allogenes, Supreme" in *Interpreter's Dictionary of the Bible* (ed. G. H. Buttrick; New York and Nashville: Abingdon Press, 1962), vol. 1, 84–85.

——. "Messos, Apocalypse of" in *Interpreter's Dictionary of the Bible* (ed G. A. Buttrick; New York and Nashville: Abingdon Press, 1962), vol. 3, 365–366.

The Facsimile Edition of the Nag Hammadi Codices (Leiden: E. J. Brill, 1972–1978).

Fallon, Francis F. "The Gnostic Apocalypses" in *Apocalypse* (ed. John J. Collins), 123–158.

Festugière, R. P. *La révélation d'Hermès Trismégiste. IV. Le dieu inconnu et la gnose* (Paris: Librairie Lecoffre, 1954).

Foerster, Werner. *Gnosis. A Selection of Gnostic Texts* (trans. R. McL. Wilson; 2 vols.; Oxford: Clarendon Press, 1972, 1974).

Fowler, Harold North. *Plato: Cratylus, Parmenides, Greater Hippias, Lesser Hippias* (Loeb Classical Library; Cambridge, MA: Harvard University Press, 1926).

——. *Plato: Euthyphro, Apology, Crito, Phaedo, Phaedrus* (Loeb Classical Library; Cambridge, MA: Harvard University Press, 1928).

Funk, Wolf-Peter. "Beiträge des mittelägyptischen Dialekts zum koptischen Konjugationssystem" in *Studies Presented to H. J. Polotsky* (ed. D. W. Young; East Glouchester, MA: Pirtle and Polson, 1981), 177–210.

——. "'Blind' oder 'unsichtbar'? Zur Bedeutungsstruktur deverbaler negativer Adjektive im Koptischen" in *Studien zum Menschenbild in Gnosis und Manichäismus* (ed. Peter Nagel; Halle: Wissenschaftliche Beiträge der Martin-Luther-Universität Halle-Wittenberg, 1979/39), 55–65.

——. *Concordance des texte Séthiens platonisants. Trois Stéles de Seth. Zostrien. Allogène.* Québec: Université Laval, 1994.

——. "Eine frühkoptische Ausgleichsorthographie für Unter- und Mittelägypten" in *Bulletin de la Société d'Egyptologie, Genève* 4 (1980), 33–38.

——. "How Closely Related are the Subakhmimic Dialects?" in *ZÄS* 112 (1985), 124–139.

——. "Koptische Isoglossen im oberägyptischen Raum: 1. ⲉⲱϫⲉ 'wenn'" in *ZÄS* 112 (1985), 19–24.

——. "Koptische Isoglossen im oberägyptischen Raum: 2. Die Satellitenparadigmen de Präsenssystems" in *ZÄS* 113 (1986), 103–114.

——. "Koptische Isoglossen im oberägyptischen Raum: 3. Die Konjugationsformen des Konditional, 4. Die Pluralform des absoluten Possessivpronomens" in *ZÄS* 114 (1987), 45–54.

——. "Die Morphologie der Perfektkonjugation im NH-subachmimischen Dialekt" *ZÄS* 111 (1984), 110–30.

——. "Toward a Synchronic Morphology of Coptic" in *The Future of Coptic Studies* (ed. R. McL. Wilson), 104–124.

——. "Zur Negation des Präsens in den oberägyptischen Dialekten" in *ZÄS* 114 (1987), 101–102.

——. "Zur Syntax des koptischen Qualitativs," Part I in *ZÄS* 104 (1977), 25–39; Part II, "Die koptischen Präverbale und ihr Gebrauch beim Qualitativ" in ZÄS 105 (1978), 94–114.

——. *Die Zweite Apokalypse des Jakobus aus Nag Hammadi Codex V: Neu herausgegeben, übersetzt und erklärt* (Berlin: Akademie Verlag, 1976).

Hadot, I. "The Spiritual Guide" in *Classical Mediterranean Spirituality. Egyptian, Greek, Roman* (ed. A. H. Armstrong; New York: Crossroad, 1986), 436–459.

Hadot, Pierre. "Etre, vie, pensée chez Plotin et avant Plotin" in *Les sources de Plotin* (Entretiens sur l'antiquité classique, V; Vandoeuvres-Genève: Fondation Hardt, 1960), 107–157.

——. *Porphyre et Victorinus* (2 vols.; Paris: Études Augustiniennes, 1968).

Hamilton, Edith and Huntington Cairns, ed. *Plato. The Collected Dialogues including the Letters* (Bollingen Series LXXI; Princeton: Princeton University Press, 1961).

Hancock, Curtis L. "Negative Theology in Gnosticism and Neoplatonism" in *Neoplatonism and Gnosticism* (ed. Richard T. Wallis and Jay Bregman; Studies in Neoplatonism: Ancient and Modern 6; Albany: State University of New York Press, 1992), 167–186.

Hedrick, Charles W. "The Apocalypse of Adam: A Literary and Source Analysis" in *SBLSP* (1972), 581–590.

——. "Gnostic Proclivities in the Greek *Life of Pachomius* and the *Sitz im Leben* of the Nag Hammadi Library" in *NovTest* 22 (1980), 78–94.

Hellholm, David. "The Problem of Apocalyptic Genre and the Apocalypse of John" in *Semeia* 36 (1986), 13–64.

Henry, Paul and Hans-Rudolf Schwyzer. *Plotini Opera* (Oxford: Oxford University Press, 1982).

Hermann, C. F., ed. *Plato* (Leipzig: B. G. Teubneri, 1921–1936).

Horner, G. *The Coptic Version of the New Testament in the Southern Dialect* (7 vols.; Oxford: Clarendon Press, 1911–1924).

Jaeger, Werner. *Early Christianity and Greek Paideia* (Oxford: Oxford University Press, 1977).

Jonas, Hans. "Delimitation of the Gnostic Phenomenon—Typological and Historical" in *Le Origini dello Gnosticismo* (Supplement to *Numen*, 12; Leiden: E. J. Brill, 1967), 90–108.

——. *The Gnostic Religion. The Message of the Alien God and the Beginnings of Christianity* (Boston: Beacon Press, 1958).

——. "The Soul in Gnosticism and Plotinus" in *Philosophical Essays. From Ancient Creed to Technological Man* (Englewood Cliffs, NJ: Prentice-Hall, 1974), 324–334.

Jufresa, Montserrat. "Basilides. A Path to Plotinus" in *VC* 35 (1981), 1–15.

Kahle, Paul. *Bala'izah: Coptic Texts from Deir El-Bala'izah in Upper Egypt* (2 vols.; London: Oxford University Press, 1954).

Kasser, Rodolphe. *Compléments au dictionnaire copte de Crum* (Le Caire: Imprimerie de l'Institut français d'Archéologie Orientale, 1964).

——. *Compléments morphologiques au dictionnaire de Crum* (Paris: Bulletin de l'Institut français d'Archéologie orientale 64, 1966).

——. "Les Dialectes coptes" in *Bulletin de l'Institut français d'archéologie orientale* 73 (1973), 71–101.

——. "Dialects" in *The Coptic Encyclopedia* (ed. Aziz S. Atiya; New York: Macmillan Publishing Company, 1991), VIII, 87–97.

——. "Orthographe et phonologie de la variété subdialectale lycopolitaine des textes gnostiques coptes de Nag Hammadi" *Muséon* 97 (1984), 261–312.

————. "Prolégomènes à un essai de classification systématique des dialectes et subdialectes coptes selon les critères de la phonétique" Part I, "Principes et terminologie" in *Muséon* 93 (1980a), 53–112; Part II, "Alphabets et systèmes phonètiques" in *Muséon* 93 (1980b), 237–97; Part III, "Systèmes orthographiques et catégories dialectales" in *Le Muséon* 94 (1981), 91–152.

————. "Relations de généalogie dialectale dans le domaine lycopolitain" *Bulletin de la Société d'égyptologie, Genève* 2 (1979), 31–36.

Katz, Joseph. *The Philosophy of Plotinus* (New York: Appleton-Century-Crofts, 1950).

King, Karen L. "Neoplatonism and Gnosticism in NHC XI.*3 Allogenes*" Society of Biblical Literature Annual Meeting, November, 1988.

————. "Ridicule and Rape, Rule and Rebellion" in *Gnosticism and the Early Christian World. Vol. II of Essays on Antiquity and Christianity in Honor of James M. Robinson* (ed. James E. Goehring, Charles W. Hedrick, Jack T. Sanders with Hans Dieter Betz; Sonoma, CA: Polebridge Press, 1990), 1–22.

————, ed. *Images of the Feminine in Gnosticism* (Studies in Antiquity and Christianity; Philadelphia: Fortress Press, 1988).

Klijn, A. F. T. *Seth in Jewish, Christian and Gnostic Literature* (Supplements to *NovTest* 46; Leiden: E. J. Brill, 1977).

Kraemer, H.-J. *Der Ursprung der Geistmetaphysik: Untersuchungen zur Geschichte des Platonismus zwischen Platon und Plotin* (Amsterdam: P. Schippers, 1964).

Krause, Martin. "Die koptische Handschriftenfund bei Nag Hammadi: Umfang und Inhalt" in *Mitteilungen des deutschen archäologischen Instituts, Abteilung Kairo* 18 (1962), 121–132.

————. "Zum koptischen Handschriftenfund bei Nag Hammadi" in *Mitteilungen des deutschen archäologischen Instituts. Abteilung Kairo* 19 (1963), 106–113.

————, ed. *Essays on the Nag Hammadi Texts in Honor of Pahor Labib* (NHS 6; Leiden: E. J. Brill, 1975).

————, ed. *Gnosis and Gnosticism* (NHS 8; Leiden: E. J. Brill, 1977).

Lamb, W. R. M. *Platon. Lysis, Symposium, Gorgias* (Loeb Classical Library; Cambridge, MA: Harvard University Press, 1925).

Layton, Bentley. *Coptic Grammar* (unpublished manuscript).

————. *The Gnostic Scriptures. A New Translation with Annotations and Introductions* (Garden City, NY: Doubleday and Company, 1987), esp. 141–148.

————. *The Rediscovery of Gnosticism: Proceedings of the International Conference on Gnosticism at Yale, New Haven, Connecticut, March 28-31, 1978* (2 vols.; Studies in the History of Religons 41; Leiden: E. J. Brill, 1981).

————, ed. *Nag Hammadi Codex II, 2-7* (2 vols.; NHS 20 and 21; Leiden: E. J. Brill, 1989).

Leemans, E.-A. *Studie Over den Wijsgeer Numenius van Apamea mit Uitgave der Fragmenten* (Bruxelles: Palais des Académies, 1937).

Leisegang, H. *Die Gnosis* (1st ed.; Leipzig: A. Kroner, 1924).

Lewy, Hans. *Chaldaean Oracles and Theurgy. Mysticism, Magic and Platonism in the Later Roman Empire* (ed. Michel Tardieu; Paris: Études Augustiniennes, 1978).

Liddel, H. G. and Robert Scott. *A Greek-English Lexicon* (8th ed.; New York: American Book Company, 1897).

Lubac, Henri de. *Origen: On First Principles* (Glouchester, MA: Peter Smith, 1973).

MacKenna, Stephen. *Plotinus. The Enneads* (4th ed. revised by B. S. Page; London: Faber and Faber Limited, 1956).

MacRae, George. "Seth in Gnostic Texts," *SBLSP* (1977), 17–24.

Majercik, Ruth Dorothy. *Chaldean Oracles. Text, Translation, Commentary* (Ph.D. diss., University of California Santa Barbara, 1982).

Manchester, Peter. "The Noetic Triad in Plotinus, Marius Victorinus, and Augustine" in *Neoplatonism and Gnosticism* (ed. Richard T. Wallis and Jay Bregman; Studies in Neoplatonism: Ancient and Modern 6; Albany: State University of New York Press, 1992), 207–222.

McKeon, Richard, ed. *The Basic Works of Aristotle* (New York: Random House, 1941).

Menard, J.-É., ed. *Les Textes de Nag Hammadi. Colloque du Centre d'Histoire des Religions (Strasbourg, 23–25 octobre 1974)* (NHS 7; Leiden: E. J. Brill, 1975).

Merlin, P. "Greek Philosophy from Plato to Plotinus," in *The Cambridge History of Later Greek and Early Medieval Philosophy* (ed. A. H. Armstrong; Cambridge: Cambridge University Press, 1967), 14–132.

Meyer, Marvin (ed. and trans.) *The "Mithras Liturgy"* (Text and Translations 10, Graeco-Roman Religon Series 2; Missoula, MT: Scholars Press, 1976).

Motley, R. "The Theme of Silence in Clement of Alexandria," *JTS* 24 (1973), 197–202.

Nagel, Peter. "Akhmimic" in *The Coptic Encyclopedia* (ed. Aziz S. Atiya; New York: Macmillan Publishing Company, 1991), VIII, 19–27.

———. "Grammatische Untersuchungen zu Nag Hammadi Codex II," in *Die Araber in der Alten Welt* (ed. F. Altheim and R. Steihl; Berlin: De Gruyter, 1969), 393–469.

———. "Lycopolitan (or Lydo-Diospolitan or Subakhmimic)" in *The Coptic Encyclopedia* (ed. Aziz S. Atiya; New York: Macmillan Publishing Company, 1991), VIII, 151–159.

———. *Studia Coptica* (Berlin: Akademie Verlag, 1974).

———, ed. *Probleme der koptischen Literatur* (Halle: Wissenschaftliche Beiträge der Martin-Luther-Universität Halle-Wittenburg, 1968).

O'Daly, Gerard P. *Plotinus' Philosophy of the Self* (New York: Harper and Row, 1973).

O'Meara, Dominic J. "Gnosticism and the Making of the World in Plotinus" in *The Rediscovery of Gnosticism* (ed. Bentley Layton), vol. I, 365–378.

Pagels, Elaine. *The Gnostic Gospels* (New York: Random House, 1979).

Pearson, Birger A. "Egyptian Seth and Gnostic Seth" in *SBLSP* (1977), 25–43.

———. "The Figure of Seth in Gnostic Literature" in *The Rediscovery of Gnosticism* (ed. Bentley Layton), vol. II, 472–514.

———. "The Figure of Seth in Manichaean Literature" in *Manichaean Studies: Proceedings of the First International Conference on Manichaeism* (ed. Peter Bryder; Lund Studies in African and Asian Religions, 1; Lund: Plus Ultra, 1988), 147–155.

————. "Theurgic Tendencies in Gnosticism and Iamblichus's Conception of Theurgy" in *Neoplatonism and Gnosticism* (ed. Richard T. Wallis and Jay Bregman; Studies in Neoplatonism: Ancient and Modern 6; Albany: State University of New York Press, 1992), 253–276.

————. "The Tractate Marsane (NHC X) and the Platonic Tradition" in *Gnosis* (ed. Barbara Aland), 373–384.

————, ed. *Nag Hammadi Codices IX and X* (NHS 15; Leiden: E. J. Brill, 1981).

Pépin, Jean. "Theories of Procession in Plotinus and the Gnostics" in *Neoplatonism and Gnosticism* (ed. Richard T. Wallis and Jay Bregman; Studies in Neoplatonism: Ancient and Modern 6; Albany: State University of New York Press, 1992), 297–336.

Perkins, Pheme. "Beauty, Number, and Loss of Order in the Gnostic Cosmos" in *Neoplatonism and Gnosticism* (ed. Richard T. Wallis and Jay Bregman; Studies in Neoplatonism: Ancient and Modern 6; Albany: State University of New York Press, 1992), 277–296.

————. "Deceiving the Deity: Self-Transcendence and the Numinous in Gnosticism" in *Proceedings of the Tenth Annual Institute for Philosophy and Religion, Boston University, 1979* (Notre Dame: Notre Dame, 1981).

————. *The Gnostic Dialogue. The Early Church and the Crisis of Gnosticism* (New York: Paulist Press, 1980).

Peters, F. E. *Greek Philosophical Terms. A Historical Lexicon* (New York: New York University Press, 1967).

Polotsky, H. J. *Collected Papers* (Jerusalem: Magnes Press, 1971), 99–316; 341–440; 645–714.

————. "The Coptic Conjugation System" *Orientalia* 29 (1960), 392–422.

Pope, M. H. "Number" in *The Interpretor's Dictionary of the Bible* (Nashville: Abingdon Press, 1962), vol. III, 564–565.

Puech, Henri-Charles. "Découverte d'une bibliothèque gnostique en Haute-Égypte" in *Encyclopédie Française* 19 (Paris: Société Nouvelle de l'Encyclopédie Française, 1957), 19.42.4–19.42.13.

————. "Fragments retrouvés de l''Apocalypse d'Allogène'" in *Mélanges Franz Cumont* (Brusselle: Annuaire de l'Institute de Philologie et d'Histoire Orientales et Slaves de l'Université Libre de Bruxelles 4, 1936), 935–62.

————. "Les nouveaux écrits gnostique découverte en Haute-Égypte (premier inventaire et essai d'identification)" in *Coptic Studies in Honor of Walter Ewing Crum* (Boston: The Byzantine Institute, 1950), 91–154.

Rackham, H. *Aristotle: Politics* (Loeb Classical Library; Cambridge, MA: Harvard University Press, 1932).

Rist, John. "Mysticism and Transcendence in Later Neoplatonism" in *Hermes* 92 (1964), 213–25.

————. *Plotinus. The Road to Reality* (Cambridge: Cambridge University Press, 1967).

Robbins, Frank Egleston. "The Tradition of Greek Arithmology" in *Classical Philology* 16 (1921), 97–123.

Robinson, James M. "The Coptic Gnostic Library" in *NovTest* (1970), 81–85.

————. "The Coptic Gnostic Library Today" in *NTS* 14 (1968), 356–401.

————. "The Discovery and Marketing of Coptic Manuscripts. The Nag Hammadi Codices and the Bodmer Papyri," in *Sundries in Honour of Torgny Säve-Söderbergh* (ed. R. Holthoer and T. Linders; Uppsala: University of Uppsala Press, 1984), 97–114.

————. "The Discovery of the Nag Hammadi Codices" in *Biblical Archaeologist* 42 (1979), 206–224.

————. "The Future of Papyrus Codicology" in *The Future of Coptic Studies* (ed. R. McL. Wilson), 23–70.

————. "The Jung Codex: The Rise and Fall of a Monopoly" in *RSR* 3 (1977), 17–30.

————. "On the Codicology of the Nag Hammadi Codices," in *Les Textes de Nag Hammadi* (ed. J.-É. Menard), 15–31.

————. "On the Construction of the Nag Hammadi Codices," in *Essays on the Nag Hammadi Texts in Honour of Pahor Labib* (ed. Martin Krause), 170–190.

————. "Preface," *The Facsimile Edition of the Nag Hammadi Codices. Codices XI, XII, and XIII* (Leiden: E. J. Brill, 1973), vii-xvii.

————. "The Three Steles of Seth and the Gnostics of Plotinus" in *Proceedings of the International Colloquium on Gnosticism* (ed. Geo Widengren; Kungl. Vitterhets Historie och Antikvitets Akademiens Handlingar, Filologisk-filosofiska serien 17; Stockholm: Almquist & Wiksell International; Leiden: E. J. Brill, 1977), 132–142.

————, ed. *The Nag Hammadi Library in English* (1st ed.; San Francisco: Harper and Row, 1977).

Rudolph, Kurt. *Gnosis. The Nature and History of Gnosticism* (trans. R. McL. Wilson; San Francisco: Harper and Row, 1983).

————. "Die 'sethianische' Gnosis—Eine häresiologische Fiktion?" in *The Rediscovery of Gnosticism* (ed. Bentley Layton), vol. II, 577–578.

Satzinger, H. "On the Origin of the Sahidic Dialect" in *Acts of the Second International Congress of Coptic Studies, Rome, 22–26 September 1980* (ed. Tito Orlandi and Frederik Wisse; Rome, 1985), 307–312.

Säve-Söderbergh, Torgny. "Holy Scriptures or Apologetic Documentations? The *Sitz im Leben* of the Nag Hammadi Library" in *Les Textes des Nag Hammadi* (ed. J.-É. Ménard), 3–14.

Schenke, Gesine. *Die Dreigestaltige Protennoia* (Nag-Hammadi-Codex XIII) *herausgegeben, übersetzt und kommentiert* (TU 132; Berlin: Akademie-Verlag, 1984).

Schenke, Hans-Martin. "Bemerkungen zur Apokalypse des Allogenes (NHC XI,3)" in *Coptic Studies: Acts of the Third International Congress of Coptic Studies, Warsaw, 20–25 August, 1984.* (ed. Wlodzimierz Godlewski. Varsovie: PWN-Éditions scientifiques de Pologne, 1990), 417–24.

————. "Hauptprobleme der Gnosis. Gesichtspunkte zu einer neuen Darstellung des Gesamtphänomens" in *Kairos* 7 (1965), 114–123.

————. *Das Matthäus-Evangelium im mittelägyptischen Dialekt des Koptischen (Codex scheide)* (TU 127; Berlin: Akademie-Verlag, 1981).

————. "Notes on the Edition of the Scheide Codex" in *Acts of the Second International Congress of Coptic Studies (Roma, 22–26 September 1980)* (ed. Tito Orlandi and Frederik Wisse; Roma: C.I.M., 1985), 313–321.

———. "On the Middle Egyptian Dialect of the Coptic Language" in *Enchoria* VIII Sonderband (1978), 43* (89)–(104) 58*.

———. "The Phenomenon and Significance of Gnostic Sethianism" in *The Rediscovery of Gnosticism* (ed. Bentley Layton), vol. II, 588–616.

———. "The Problem of Gnosis" in *Second Century* 2.3 (1983), 73–87.

———. Review: "Elsas, Christoph: *Neuplatonische und gnostische Weltablehnung in der Schule Plotins*" in *TLZ* 102 (1977), 644–646.

——— "Das sethianische System nach Nag-Hammadi-Handschriften" in *Studia Coptica* (ed. Peter Nagel), 165–174.

———. *Das Thomasbuch* (Nag-Hammadi-*Codex II,7*) (TU; Berlin: Akademie-Verlag, 1989).

Schmidt, Carl. *Plotins Stellung zum Gnostizismus und kirchlichen Christentum* (TU nf. 5/4; Leipzig, 1901).

Schmidt, Carl and Violet MacDermot. *The Books of Jeu and the Untitled Text in the Bruce Codex* (NHS XIII; Leiden: E. J. Brill, 1978).

Scholem, Gerschom. *Jewish Gnosticism, Merkabah Mysticism, and Talmudic Tradition* (New York: Jewish Theological Seminary of America, 1960).

———. "Merkabah Mysticism and Jewish Gnosticism" in *Major Trends in Jewish Mysticism* (Jerusalem: Schocken Publishing House, 1946), 40–79.

Scholer, David. *Nag Hammadi Bibliography 1948–1969* (NHS 1; Leiden: E. J. Brill, 1971) with annual supplements in *NovTest* (1972–1994).

Scopello, Maddalena. "Contes apocalyptiques et apocalypses philosophiques dans la biblothèque de Nag Hammadi" in *Apocalypses et voyages dans l'au-dela* (ed. C. Kappler; Paris: Les Éditions du Cerf, 1987), 321–330.

———. "Youel et Barbélo dans le traité de l'*Allogène*" in *Colloque international sur les textes de Nag Hammadi tenu à Québec du 22 au 25 août 1978* (ed. Bernard Barc; Québec: Les Presses de l'Université Laval/Louvain: Éditions Peeters, 1981), 374–382.

Schottroff, Luise. "Animae naturaliter salvandae. Zum Problem der himmlischen Herkunft des Gnostikers" in *Christentum und Gnosis* (ed. Walther Eltester; BZNT 37; Berlin: Alfred Töpelmann, 1969), 65–97.

Sevrin, Jean-Marie. *Le dossier baptismal séthien. Études sur la sacramentaire gnostique* (Bibliothèque copte de Nag Hammadi, Section Études, 2; Québec: Les presses de l'Université Laval, 1986).

Shisha-Halevy, Ariel. "Apodotic ⲉϥⲥⲱⲧⲙ: A Hitherto Unnoticed Late Coptic Tripartite Pattern Conjugation-form and its Diachronic Perspective" in *Le Muséon* 86 (1973), 455–466.

———. "The Circumstantial Present as an Antecedentless (i.e., Substantival) Relative in Coptic" in *JEA* 62 (1976), 134–137.

———. "The Coptic Circumstantial Present with an Empty (Impersonal) Actor-suffix and Adverb Function" in *JEA* 61 (1975), 156–157.

———. "'Koptische Isoglossen im oberägyptischen Raum' and Adverb Function" in *JEA* 61 (1975), 256–257.

———. "Protatic ⲉϥⲥⲱⲧⲙ. A Hitherto Unnoticed Coptic Tripartite Conjugation-form and its Diachronic Connection" in *Orientalia* 43 (1974), 369–381.

———. "Protatic ⲉϥⲥⲱⲧⲙ. Some Additional Material" in *Orientalia* 46 (1977), 127–128.

———. "Sahidic" in *The Coptic Encyclopedia* (ed. Aziz S. Atiya; New York: Macmillan Publishing Company, 1991), VIII, 194–202.

Shorey, Paul. *Plato. Republic* (2 vols.; Loeb Classical Library; Cambridge, MA: Harvard University Press, 1930–1935).

Sieber, John. "The Barbelo Aeon as Sophia in *Zostrianos* and Related Tractates" in *The Rediscovery of Gnosticism* (ed. Bentley Layton), vol. II, 788–795.

———. "An Introduction to the Tractate Zostrianos from Nag Hammadi" in *NovTest* 15 (1973), 233–237.

———, ed. *Nag Hammadi Codex VIII* (NHS 31; Leiden: E. J. Brill, 1991).

Smith, Richard (managing editor) and James M. Robinson (general editor). *The Nag Hammadi Library in English* (3rd ed.; San Francisco: Harper and Row, 1988).

Stowers, Stanley K. *Letter Writing in Greco-Roman Antiquity* (Philadelphia: The Westminster Press, 1986).

Stroumsa, Gedaliahu A. G. *Another Seed: Studies in Gnostic Mythology* (NHS 24; Leiden: E. J. Brill, 1984).

Tardieu, Michel. *Écrits Gnostiques. Codex de Berlin* (Paris: Les éditions du Cerf, 1984).

———. "La gnose valentinienne et les Oracles chaldaïques" in *The Rediscovery of Gnosticism* (ed. Bentley Layton), vol. I, 194–237.

———. "Les livres mis sous le nom de Seth et les séthiens de l'hérésiologie" in *Gnosis and Gnosticism* (ed. Martin Krause), 204–210.

———. "Les trois stèles de Seth. Un Écrit gnostique retrouvé à Nag Hammadi" in *Revue des sciences philosophiques et théologique* 57 (1973), 545–575.

Tredennick, Hugh. *Aristotle: Metaphysics* (Loeb Classical Library; Cambridge, MA: Harvard University Press, 1935).

———. *Aristotle: The Organon* (Loeb Classical Library; Cambridge, MA: Harvard University Press, 1938).

Tröger, Karl-Wolfgang. *Mysterienglaube und Gnosis in Corpus Hermeticum XIII* (Berlin: Akademie-Verlag, 1971).

Turner, John. "The Gnostic Threefold Path to Enlightenment. The Ascent of Mind and the Descent of Wisdom" in *NovTest* 22 (1980), 324–351.

———. "Gnosticism and Platonism: The Platonizing Sethian Texts from Nag Hammadi in their Relation to Later Platonic Literature" in *Neoplatonism and Gnosticism* (ed. Richard T. Wallis and Jay Bregman; Studies in Neoplatonism: Ancient and Modern 6; Albany: State University of New York Press, 1992), 425–460.

———. "Sethian Gnosticism. A Literary History" in *Nag Hammadi, Gnosticism, and Early Christianity* (ed. Charles W. Hedrick and Robert Hodgson, Jr.; Peabody, MA: Hendrickson Publishers, 1986), 55–86.

——— with Orval S. Wintermute. "Allogenes. Transcription and Translation" and (Turner only) "Allogenes. Notes" in *Nag Hammadi Codices XI, XII and XIII* (ed. Charles W. Hedrick; NHS 28; Leiden: E. J. Brill, 1990), 192–267.

Usener, Hermann. "Dreiheit" in *Rheinisches Museum für Philologie* 58 (1903), 1–47, 161–208, 321–362.

Valantasis, Richard. *Spiritual Guides of the Third Century. A Semiotic Study of the Guide-Disciple Relationship in Christianity, Neoplatonism, Hermetism, and Gnosticism* (Harvard Dissertations in Religion 27; Minneapolis, MN: Fortress Press, 1991), 105–145.

Vogel, C. J. de. *Greek Philosophy. A Collection of Texts with notes and explanations. Vol. III The Hellenistic-Roman Period* (3rd ed.; Leiden: E. J. Brill, 1973).

———. "III. On the Neoplatonic Character of Platonism and the Platonic Character of Neoplatonism" in *Mind* 62 (1953), 43–64.

Wallis, Richard T. "The Spiritual Importance of Not Knowing," in *Classical Mediterranean Spirituality. Egyptian, Greek, Roman* (ed. A. H. Armstrong; New York: Crossroad, 1986), 460–480.

——— and Jay Bregman, ed. *Neoplatonism and Gnosticism* (Studies in Neoplatonism: Ancient and Modern 6; Albany, NY: State University of New York Press, 1992).

Wekel, Konrad. "Die drei Stelen des Seth" in *TLZ* 100 (1975), 571–180.

———. *Die Drei Stelen des Seth (NHC VII,5). Text–Übersetzung–Kommentar* (Dr. Theologiae diss., Humboldt-Universität, Berlin, 1977).

Westendorf, Wolfhart. *Koptisches Handwörterbuch* (Heidelberg: Carl Winter Universitäts-Verlag, 1977).

Whittaker, John. "ΕΠΕΚΕΙΝΑ ΝΟΥ ΚΑΙ ΟΥΣΙΑΣ" in *VC* 23 (1969), 91–104.

———. "Neopythagoreanism and Negative Theology" in *Symbolae Osloenses* 44 (1969), 109–125.

———. "Neopythagoreanism and the Transcendent Absolute" in *Symbolae Osloenses* 48 (1973), 77–86.

———. "Self-Generating Principles in Second-Century Gnostic Systems" in *The Rediscovery of Gnosticism* (ed. Bentley Layton), vol. I, 176–193.

Williams, Michael A. *The Immovable Race. A Gnostic Designation and the Theme of Stability in Late Antiquity* (NHS 29; Leiden: E. J. Brill, 1985).

———. "Stability as a Soteriological Theme in Gnosticism" in *The Rediscovery of Gnosticism* (ed. Bentley Layton), vol. II, 819–829.

Wilson, Robert McL., ed. *The Future of Coptic Studies* (Leiden: E. J. Brill, 1978).

Wire, Antoinette Clark. "Allogenes. Introduction" in *Nag Hammadi Codices XI, XII, and XIII* (ed. Charles W. Hedrick; NHS 28; Leiden: E. J. Brill, 1992), 173–191.

Wisse, Frederik. "Flee Femininity. Antifemininity in Gnostic Texts and the Question of Social Milieu" in *Images of the Feminine in Gnosticism* (ed. Karen L. King), 297–307.

———. "Gnosticism and Early Monasticism in Egypt" in *Gnosis* (ed. Barbara Aland), 431–440.

———. "The Nag Hammadi Library and the Heresiologists" in *VC* 25 (1971), 205–223.

———. "The Sethians and the Nag Hammadi Library" in *SBLSP* (1972), 601–607.

———. "Stalking Those Elusive Sethians" in *The Rediscovery of Gnosticism* (ed. Bentley Layton), vol. II, 563–576.

——— and Alexander Böhlig, ed. *Nag Hammadi Codices III,2 and IV,2. The Gospel of the Egyptians* (NHS 4; Leiden: E. J. Brill, 1975).

Witt, R. E. *Albinus and the History of Middle Platonism* (Cambridge: Cambridge University Press, 1971).

Wolfson, H. A. "Albinus and Plotinus on Divine Attributes" in *HTR* 45 (1952), 115–130.

————. "The Knowability and Describability of God in Plato and Aristotle" in *Harvard Studies in Classical Philology* 56–57 (1947), 233–249.

————. "Negative Attributes in the Church Fathers and the Gnostic Basilides" in *HTR* 50 (1957), 145–156.

Zandee, J. *The Terminology of Plotinus and of Some Gnostic Writings, Mainly the Fourth Treatise of the Jung Codex* (Uitgaven van het Nederlands Historisch-Archaeologisch Institut te Istanbul XI; Istanbul: Nederlands Historische-Archaeologisch Institut in het Nabije Oosten, 1961).

Index

Conjugation System

Bipartite Pattern

I. Present

† 50.15
ϥ 47.[9]; 54.22; 55.[21]; 61.32; 64.15
c 66.17
ⲧⲛ̄ 67.25
ⲥⲉ 55.22, 23; 57.21, 23; 62.3; 63.[2], 25

Circumstantial of Present
ⲉⲓ̈ 57.33; 60.20; 61.2, 22; 68.33
ⲉⲕ 59.15; 60.11; 61.25; 67.35
ⲉϥ 45.26; 47.[10], [17], 20, 23, 32; 48.16,
    20, [29]; 49.16, 30; 51.19, 21, 27, 28,
    30, 30; 53.17, 19; 56.16; 58.22, 31;
    61.21, ⟨34⟩, 35, 35, 35; 62.1, 4, 5, 5,
    [6], 6, 9, 9, 20, 33; 63.1, 4, 10, 12, 19,
    21, 23, 26, 31, 38; 64.1, 9, 16; 65.26,
    28, 30, 32; 66.28, 29, 30, 36, 37;
    67.[18]
ⲉⲥ 45.29, 36, 38; 46.[7], 8; 53.34, 35;
    54.27; 58.11; 59.16, 21, 21; 60.11, 32,
    32
ⲉⲩ 45.6, 7, [8]; 46.6, [6], [14]; 49.37; 53.22;
    57.20; 59.[4], 7; 60.13; 62.16

With Relative Converter

ⲉⲧⲉⲕ 59.12
ⲉⲧⲉϥ 61.33; 64.17
ⲉⲧϥ̄ 46.[15]
ⲉⲧⲉⲥ 64.25
ⲉⲧⲥ̄ 45.32
ⲉⲧⲉⲩ 64.33
ⲉⲧⲟⲩ 57.10, 14, 15

With Relative Pronoun
ⲉⲧ 45.10, 14, 21; 46.(9), 19, 21, [28], [29];
    48.11, 11, [15], 37; 49.[10], [13], 17,
    20, 27, 35; 50.[6], 12, 13, 13, 29, 31,
    34; 51.12, 16; 52.[11], 12, 17, 23, 28,
    30, 33; 53.11, 18; 54.[9], 14, 21, 25,
    31, 32, 34; 55.[15], [16], [23], 24, [25];
    56.10, 12, [17], 19, 20; 57.[13], 13;
    58.25, 29; 59.[8], 11, 11, 23, 38; 60.7,

I. Future
-ⲛⲁ 64.19
†ⲛⲁ 59.8

Circumstantial of Future

ⲉϥⲛⲁ 61.34

With Relative Converter Future
ⲉ†ⲛⲁ 68.17, 18
ⲉⲧⲉⲕⲛⲁ 52.19; 59.15

With Relative Pronoun Future
ⲉⲧⲛⲁ 68.19

34, 36; 61.[5], [8], 12, 13, 20, 26; 62.2,
2, 21, 32; 63.16, 18, 19, 20, 21; 64.12,
14, 30, 31; 66.22, 31, 35, 36; 67.28; see
also ⲙⲙⲁⲩ

Preterit of I. Present
ⲛⲉⲣⲉ- 49.[14–15]
ⲛⲉⲓ̈ 57.30, 32; 60.13; 61.14
ⲛⲉϥ 60.14
ⲛⲉⲥ 67.35
ⲛⲉⲩ 47.[29]

II. Present   *II. Future*
ⲉⲕ 55.20; 56.[36]
ⲉϥ 48.15; 49.[14]; 51.[13]; 52.36; 59.24;   ⲉϥⲛⲁ 64.23
    60.1; 64.4, 13, 20, 37; 65.22, ⟨23⟩, 34,
    38; 66.27
ⲉⲥ 51.[9]; 52.34
ⲉⲩ 47.[13]; 55.26; 56.[12]

Tripartite Pattern

I. Perfect Affirmative   *I. Perfect Negative*
ⲁ- 50.16; 52.16
  ⲁ- (prenominal) occurs only in
  extraposition of the conjugation base.
ⲁⲉⲓ 50.[1], [2], 9, [10]; 52.[8], [8], [9], [10],   ⲙ̄ⲡⲓ 57.27
    12; 55.12, [31]; 57.29; 58.37; 59.4;
    60.16, 19, 21, 22, 30, 37; 61.3, 5;
    68.33
ⲁⲓ̈ 58.12, 35, 38; 59.[1]; 60.24; 61.2, 12;
    68.25, 26, 31
ⲁⲕ 47.[5]; 52.18; 67.21
ⲁϥ 45.24, 25, 28; 46.31; 50.13; 53.10, 15,   ⲙ̄ⲡⲉϥ 64.22, 29
    16; 58.[9]; 64.21, 30; 66.17; 67.[18],
    19; 68.24
ⲁⲥ 45.[30], 31; 49.18; 50.16, 20; 52.6, 13,
    15, 16; 53.32, 38; 54.26; 57.26, 26
ⲁⲩ 45.[23]; 50.24; 58.30; 67.[16]   ⲙ̄ⲡⲟⲩ 57.18

Circumstantial of Perfect Affirmative   *Circumstantial of Perfect Negative*
                                           ⲉⲙⲡⲉ- 49.21
ⲉⲁⲉⲓ 61.4
ⲉⲁϥ 46.14; 65.21
ⲉⲁⲥ 53.35

With Relative Converter ⲛ̄ⲧ-
ⲛ̄ⲧⲁⲉⲓ 45.[9]
ⲛ̄ⲧⲁϥ 45.[10]
ⲛ̄ⲧⲁⲥ 45.11, [17]
ⲛ̄ⲧⲁⲩ 47.[27]

With Relative Converter ⲉⲧ-
ⲉⲧⲁⲉⲓ 57.35, 37; 58,36; 60.31
ⲉⲧⲁⲓ̈ 57.28; 60.17
ⲉⲧⲁϥ 50.25–26, 34–35; 59.[8]; 67.16
ⲉⲧⲁⲥ 53.26
ⲉⲧⲁⲩ 54.36; 68.27, 29–30, 34

Subordinate Clause Conjugations:
Conjunctive
ⲛ̄ⲧⲉ- 57.39; 58.32; 63.[11], 13, 39
ⲛ̄ⲧ 50.33; 56.[28]; 59.17; 68.22
ⲛ̄ⲧⲉⲧⲛ̄ 67.36
ⲛ̄ⲥⲉ 67.37

Temporalis
ⲛ̄ⲧⲁⲣⲓ 49.38–39; 55.[12]
ⲛ̄ⲧⲉⲣⲉⲥ 53.37
ⲛ̄ⲧⲁⲣⲉⲥ 46.13
ⲛ̄ⲧⲉⲣⲉϥ 68.24

Conditional
ⲉⲣϣⲁⲛ- 46.36; 47.[22]; 61.17
ⲉϣⲁ- 66.19
ⲉⲕϣⲁⲛ 56.[15], [31]; 59.18, 26, 30–31, 32, 35
ⲉϥϣⲁⲛ 46.[22], [26–27], 32; 48.18; 57.16
ⲉⲥϣⲁⲛ 46.[16]; 57.[7]
ⲉⲩϣⲁⲛ 48.[8], 33; 49.[7]

Coptic Words and Forms

ⲁⲗⲟⲩ (nn. m.) youth 45.[18]; 51.37; 58.15
ⲁⲙⲁϩⲧⲉ (tr.) grasp, embrace, apprehend 57.[7], [8]; 59.24
ⲁⲛ (negating particle):
   (negating nominal sentence) 48.[6]
   (negating present circumstantial) 63.22, 23, 27; 65.26
   (negating relative present) 64.26
   (negating word) 48.14; 53.20; 60.23
   (negating unknown element) 53.7
ⲛ̄...ⲁⲛ (negating nominal sentence) 63.17
   (negating I. present) 55.22, 23–[24]; 57.21–22; 62.3, 14–15; 63.2–3, [17], 25–26; 64.10–11; 66.17–[18]; 67.24–25
   (negating word) 63.36–37
ⲙ̄...ⲁⲛ (negating nominal sentence) 52.25–26; 67.33
   (negating word) 62.32; 63.21, 35–56
ⲛ̄ⲛ...ⲁⲛ (negating nominal sentence) 62.28, 36–37; 63.[1]–2, 5, [5–6], [6]–7, [7], 8, 8–9, 9, 27–28; 65.28–29
   (negating II. present) 65.22, ⟨23⟩–⟨24⟩; 66.27–28
   (negating II. habitual) 62.13
   (negating II. future) 64.23–24
ⲁⲛⲟⲕ (independent personal pronoun 1 sg.):
   (in extraposition) 49.38; 50.8; 55.11–[12]; 57.27, 32; 68.25

ⲁⲣⲏⲭ- (nn.) limit, end:
   ⲛ̄ⲁⲣⲏⲭ- bring limit:
   ⲁⲧⲛ̄ⲁⲣⲏⲭ- limitless, boundless:
   ⲁⲧⲛ̄ⲁⲣⲏⲭϥ̄ 53.13; 63.[2]; 66.25–26
   ⲙ̄ⲛ̄ⲧⲁⲧⲛ̄ⲁⲣⲏⲭⲥ̄ boundlessness 49.[9]; 66.25
ⲁⲧ- (privative adjective prefix) See ⲁⲣⲏⲭ-, ⲉⲓⲙⲉ, ⲕⲓⲙ, ⲙⲓⲥⲉ, ⲛⲁⲩ, ⲛⲓϥⲉ, ⲡⲱⲣⲝ, ⲡⲱϣ, ⲣⲁⲛ, ⲣⲁⲧ-, ⲥⲃⲱ, ⲥⲟⲟⲩⲛ, ⲧⲁϩⲟ, ⲧⲟϣ, ⲱⲡ, ϣⲓ, ϣⲱⲡ, ϣⲱⲡⲉ, ϣⲁⲭⲉ, ϣⲱⲭϩ̄, ϭⲟⲙ, ϫⲡⲟ; ἀρχή, εἶδος, ἐνέργεια, μορφή, σῶμα, οὐσία, ὕλη
ⲁⲧⲟ (nn. m.) multitude 50.2, 32
ⲁⲩⲱ (conjunction) and 45.[7], [10], 23, [25], 28, [31]; 46.8, 13, 16; 47.14, [15], 17, [31], 33; 48.21, 29; 49. 13, 14, 31, 36; 50.1, [11], 17, 21, 30, 33; 51.29, 38; 52.7, [9], 13; 53.[9], 15, 35, 38; 55.[14], [29], [31], [33]; 56.27, 35, 36, 57.11, 13, 14, 21, 23, 30, 36; 58.30, 37; 59.4, 13, 16, 20, 21, 24, 26, 32, 35, 37; 60.[2], 19, 20, 22, 24, 28, 32; 61.3, [8], 21, 34; 62.[1]; 63.20; 64.1, 8, [12]; 65.37; 66.27, 34, 36; 67.[17], 20, 22, 37; 68.[16], [17], 20, 32
ⲁϣ (interrogative pronoun) what 49.14; 64.15
ⲃⲱⲕ (intr.) go, depart:
   with ⲉϩⲟⲩⲛ ⲉⲣⲟ- go in, enter 53.15; 60.21

є2н (nn.) forepart: see 2н
єⲝ̄ⲛ- (prep.) upon, over 59.14, 20; 60.19,
    30
    є2ⲣⲁï єⲝ̄ⲛ- up 58.30
ηєι (nn.m.) house 65.32
єι (intr.) come, go 48.8; 50.28; 57.16;
    62.13
    єⲙⲟⲩ (imp.) 68.23
єιⲙє (intr.) know, understand 45.26, 29,
    30; 46.[11]; 49.12; 50.6, 32; 51.27;
    52.18; 53.22; 54.21; 55.20; 56.17,
    [18], [28]; 57.13, 15; 59,12, 31, 39;
    60.[8–9], 17; 61.[2], 18, 35; 63.11, 13,
    16; 64.[1]; 67.36
    ιⲙє 54.22; 60.[11]
    ⲁⲧєιⲙє without knowledge, ignorant
        55.[20]; 61.2
    ⲣ̄ ⲁⲧєιⲙє be or become unknowing,
        ignorant 61.18–19
    ⲁⲣιⲁⲧєιⲙє (imp.) 59.31–32; 60.12
    єιⲙє (subst.) knowledge, understanding
        55.19–[20]
    ⲙ̄ⲛ̄ⲧєιⲙє (nn.) intellection 49.27, 33–34;
        53.15, 24–25; 54.15; 55.[11]
єιⲛє (tr.) bring, bear 58.[9]
    ⲛ̄- See ⲁⲣηⲭ⸗, ⲣⲁⲧ⸗
    єιⲛє єⲃⲟⲗ bring forth, produce:
    ⲛ̄ єⲃⲟⲗ 49.[21]
єιⲛє (nn. m.) likeness 58.32; 60.34
    ιⲛє 53.30; 59.22
єιⲣє (tr.) act, become, etc. 50.16
    ⲣ̄- See ⲃ̄ⲗⲗє, єιⲙє, ⲙ̄ⲡⲱⲁ, ⲛⲟⲩⲧє,
        ⲟⲩⲟєιⲛ, ⲱⲃηⲣ, ⲱⲟⲣ̄ⲡ, 2ⲁє, 2̄ⲙⲙє,
        2ⲟⲧє, 6ⲃⲃє; ἀναχωρεῖν, ἀσεβής,
        ἐνεργεῖν, μέλει, νοεῖν, τέλειος, χρεία.
    ⲣ̄ єⲃⲟⲗ 52.[8]
    є⁺ 45.6; 48.[29]; 49.37; 50.31, 34;
        52.33; 53.17; 61.2, 21; 64.15; see also
        ⲟⲩⲟєιⲛ, ⲱⲟⲣ̄ⲡ
    ⲟ⁺ 45.38; 46.7; 47.10
    ⲁⲣι (imp.) See єιⲙє; ἀναχωρεῖν
єιⲱⲧ (nn. m.) father:
    ιⲱⲧ 50.26
ⲕє- (adjectival prefix) other, different 53.14;
    62.17, 37; 63.11, 18; see also ⲟⲩⲁ
ⲕⲟⲩєι (nn.) small person or thing 63.[7]
    ⲙ̄ⲛ̄ⲧⲕⲟⲩєι (nn.) smallness 57.23–24
ⲕⲱ (tr.) place, set, quit, abandon, leave, etc.
    68.20; see also ⲣⲟ
    ⲕⲁ-: See ⲣⲟ
    ⲕⲁⲁ⸗:
    ⲕⲁⲁⲧ 57.26–27
ⲕη⁺ be, lie, exist, be situated 45.7;
    48.[11]; 49.[10]; 51.[9]; 61.20
    ⲕη⁺ є2ⲣⲁï be put down, be laid down
        48.20
ⲕιⲙ (intr.) move, be moved 53.10; 59.16

ⲕιⲙ (subst.) motion, movement 60.24
    ⲁⲧⲕιⲙ immovable, unmoved;
    ⲙ̄ⲛ̄ⲧⲁⲧⲕιⲙ (nn.) immovability 53.[10]
ⲕⲱⲧє (tr.) turn 49.11; 59.[2]
    ⲕⲟⲧ⸗:
    ⲕⲟⲧⲧ 50.[2]; 52.9
    ⲕⲱⲧє (intr.) seek 67.35
    ⲕⲱⲧє with (є)-/єⲣⲟ⸗ (intr.) surround
        52.[11]
    ⲕⲱⲧє with ⲛ̄ⲥⲁ-/ⲛ̄ⲥⲱ⸗ seek 59.15;
        60.20; 61.14–15; 67.23
    ⲕⲱⲧє (subst.) turning, surrounding
        61.27; 66.37
ⲗⲁⲁⲩ (indef. pron.):
    (under the domain of negation or doubt;
        non-affirmed context):
    (in absolute usage): (not) anyone,
        anything 47.23; 49.21; 62.19–20;
        63.17, 24, 27; 64.26; 66.21; 67.23
    (in attributive usage) (not) any 57.19, 21;
        62.[4], 7, 11; 64.27; 65.35
    (in adverbial usage) (not) at all 59.18
    ⲛ̄ⲗⲁⲁⲩ 66.[18]–19
    (following indef. art. or equivalent)
        something:
    (in non-affirmed context) 62.[5], 15; 63.9;
        67.30
    (in affirmed context) 50.17; 55.[37];
        57.[8]; 61.33; 62.1, 31; 63.[12], 29–30,
        38; 64.2, 20
    (context indeterminate) 65.16
ⲗⲁєιⲃє (nn.f.) cause, excuse 48.[20]; 49.17
    ⲗⲟєιⲃє 52.33
ⲙⲁ (nn.m.) place 45.8; 46.7, 22, 30; 48.8,
    11; 50.28; 55.15, [24]; 59.33
ⲙⲕⲁ2 (intr.) suffer:
    ⲙⲟⲕ2⁺ be hard, difficult 50.29
ⲙⲙⲁⲩ (adv.) there:
    (with ⲟⲩⲛⲧⲁ⸗) 46.10; 52.29; 62.24
    (with ⲙ̄ⲙ̄ⲛ̄ⲧ̄ϥ-/ⲙ̄ⲛ̄ⲧⲁϥ) 64.27–28; 65.35–36
    єⲧⲙⲙⲁⲩ that 45.[30]; 53.11; 57.9; 59.33,
        36–37; 60.14; 64.25; 66.18
ⲙ̄ⲙ̄ⲛ̄ (predicates non-existence) there is/are
    not:
    ⲙ̄ⲛ̄- 47.35; see also 6ⲟⲙ
    (ⲙ̄ⲙ̄ⲛ̄ⲧє)-/ⲙ̄ⲙ̄ⲛ̄ⲧⲁ⸗ (negative of predicate
        of possession) have not:
    ⲙ̄ⲙ̄ⲛ̄ⲧⲁϥ 62.10
    ⲙ̄ⲙ̄ⲛ̄ⲧϥ 64.27
    ⲙ̄ⲛ̄ⲧⲁϥ 61.36; 65.35
ⲙ̄ⲛ̄- (prep.) with, together with, and 45.15;
    47.35, 38; 48.15, 21, [22], [23], 24, 25,
    [25], [26], [27], [28], [31], 34; 49.6, 26,
    27, 30, 33, 35; 50.14, 35; 51.[7], 15,
    35; 52.11, 17, 21, 32; 53.[8], 9, 25, 29,
    30, 31, 32; 54.[9], 15; 55.15, [23], 24,
    27, [28], 29; 56.11, 25, [25]; 57.9, 34;

ⲛ̄- (introducing object) 45.31; 46.7; 47.12;
    48.7, [17]; 49.[5], 29, 32; 50.13, 16;
    51.[6], 14, 31; 53.36; 54.36; 56.32;
    57.[7], 20; 59.24, 26; 62.4, 24; 63.27;
    64.22, 24, 27, 29; 65.22; 66.29; 67.20,
    27, 29; 68.[16], 29
ⲙ̄- 46.10, 23; 48.15; 49.35; 51.18, 25, 32;
    61.25; 66.28; 68.20, 27
ⲛ̄ⲛ- (reduplication before a vowel) 47.25;
    58.9; 61.36; 62.15, 18; 63.33; 65.33
ⲙ̄ⲙⲟ⸗:
ⲙ̄ⲙⲟⲓ̈ 57.29, 32
ⲙ̄ⲙⲟⲉⲓ 68.[34]
ⲙ̄ⲙⲟⲕ 56.[33]
ⲙ̄ⲙⲟϥ 47.[22–23]; 48.19; 49.8; 57.10, 14;
    62.3, 17; 63.26; see also ϣⲁϫⲉ
ⲙ̄ⲙⲟⲥ 49.⟨11⟩; 54.27; 57.[8]; 59.[7]
ⲙ̄ⲙⲟⲟⲩ 45.33; 47.7; 56.[37]; 60.13–14;
    68.30; 69.[15]
ⲛ̄- (prep.) in, through, etc. 47.16; 49.14, 22;
    50.25; 54.25; 61.4; 64.15; 66.31; see
    also ϩⲉ
ⲙ̄- 59.33, 36; 64.31; 66.36
ⲙ̄ⲙⲟ⸗:
ⲙ̄ⲙⲟⲉⲓ 57.30–31
ⲙ̄ⲙⲟⲕ 59.37
ⲙ̄ⲙⲟϥ 51.9–10; 59.23; 60.37; 64.1–[2],
    32; 65.28; 66.30; 67.29
ⲙ̄ⲙⲟⲥ 46.[16]; 53.34; 59.22; 60.33;
    64.17–18; 66.[22]
ⲙ̄ⲙⲟⲟⲩ 52.24
ⲉⲃⲟⲗ ⲛ̄-:
ⲉⲃⲟⲗ ⲙ̄ⲙⲟⲓ̈ 57.26; 68.25
ⲉⲃⲟⲗ ⲙ̄ⲙⲟϥ 62.11; 64.28; 65.24; 66.20
ⲉⲃⲟⲗ ⲙ̄ⲙⲟⲥ 54.10; 54.⟨16⟩
ⲛ̄- (forming adv.): See ⲗⲁⲁⲩ, ϣⲟⲣⲡ̄,
    ϩⲟⲩⲟ
ⲛ̄- (dative prep.) to, for 45.37; 49.15, 17;
    52.22; 67.19
ⲙ̄- 50.13; 66.18
ⲛⲁ⸗:
ⲛⲁⲓ̈ 52.15; 55.17, 33; 58.9; 59.[7]; 61.23;
    68.[16], 28, 35
ⲛⲁⲕ 51.[6]; 54.36; 56.[22]; 67.24; 68.17,
    18, 29
ⲛⲁϥ 64.26
ⲛⲁⲩ 47.11; 61.11; 64.3, 7; 65.34;
    66.[17], [18]
ⲛⲉ (preterit): See preterit of I. present
    ⲛⲉ with ⲟⲩⲛ̄ⲧⲁ⸗ 67.29
ⲛⲉⲁ⸗ (adj. verb) be great:
    ⲛⲉⲁϥ 47.[15]; 50.[8]; 57.12
    ⲛⲉⲁⲩ 57.22
ⲛⲟⲃⲉ (nn. m.) sin 51.31
ⲛ̄ⲕⲁ (nn. m.) thing 62.37–63.1; 63.4, 18
ⲛⲓⲙ (adj.) every 47.17, [30], 32, 33; 48.17;
    53.17; 54.26; 57.20, 22, 24; 64.8, 18;

66.32; see also ⲟⲩⲟⲛ
ⲛⲁⲛⲟⲩ⸗ (adj. verb) be good, fair:
    ⲛⲁⲛⲟⲩϥ 54.23
    ⲛⲁⲛⲟⲩⲟⲩ 63.31–32; 64.[6]
ⲛ̄ⲥⲁ- (prep) behind, after, for 47.33; 61.15;
    67.23
ⲛ̄ⲥⲱ⸗:
ⲛ̄ⲥⲱⲕ 59.15
ⲛ̄ⲥⲱϥ 48.17]
ⲛ̄ⲥⲱⲥ 60.20
ⲛ̄ⲥⲁⲃⲏⲗ with ⲉ- (prep.) except for 67.30
ⲛ̄ⲥⲁ(ⲛ)ⲃⲟⲗ with ⲛ̄-/ⲙ̄ⲙⲟ⸗ (prep.) outside
    of, beyond 49.[22]; 51.[9]; 64.31
ⲛ̄ⲧⲉ- (prep.) from, with, circumscription of
    genitive, possessive 45.[14]; 46.[8], 21,
    [26], 33, [35]; 47.[24], 37; 48.[7], 9–10,
    [16], [30], [31], 36, 37; 49.9; 50.27;
    51.15, 16, 18, 28; 53.6, 14, 24; 54.24,
    33; 56.[11], [23], [25], [26], [32]; 58.6,
    [8], 10, 16, 19, 20, 23; 59.[2–3], 6, 27,
    29; 60.8, 16, 34, 36; 61.7, 10, 19, 24,
    27–28; 63.17, 19; 64.32, 35, 36; 65.19,
    37; 66.24; 69.[17], [18]
ⲛ̄ⲧⲁ⸗:
ⲛ̄ⲧⲁⲕ 54.[9], 14; 59.11
ⲛ̄ⲧⲁϥ 58.32–33; 61.[8]; 62.2, 21, 32;
    63.15, 20, 21, 29; 64.2–[3]
ⲛ̄ⲧⲁⲩ 48.[6]
ⲛ̄ⲧⲉⲩ 51.34
ⲛⲟⲩⲧⲉ (nn. m.) god 46.11, 19, 20; 47.35,
    36; 51.26, 33–34; 56.20, [35]–36;
    58.[6–7], 13; 61.11–12, 15; 64.23;
    67.28
    ⲣ̄ ⲛⲟⲩⲧⲉ become divine 52.12–13
    ⲙ̄ⲛ̄ⲧⲛⲟⲩⲧⲉ (nn.) divinity 47.[30]; 48.31,
    32; 54.11; 55.[27]; 58.22–23; 62.28,
    35
ⲛ̄ⲧⲕ̄- (subject pron. of nominal sentence 2
    sg.) "you are" 54.6, 11, 12, 21, 22, 22–
    23
ⲛ̄ⲧⲟⲕ (independent personal pron. 2 sg.)
    54.24, 32, 35
ⲛ̄ⲧⲛ̄- (prep.) in, by, with, etc.:
    ⲛ̄ⲧⲟⲟⲧ⸗:
    ⲉⲃⲟⲗ ⲛ̄ⲧⲟⲟⲧⲕ̄ 50.10–11
ⲛ̄ⲧⲟϥ (independent personal pron. 3 sg. m.)
    67.31 (?)
    ⲛ̄ⲧⲟϥ (in nominal sentence) 47.[26];
    49.28
    ⲛ̄ⲧⲟϥ (in circumstantial of nominal
    sentence) 46.[17]; 63.16
    ⲛ̄ⲧⲟϥ (in reduced cleft sentence) 48.18;
    49.20
    ⲛ̄ⲧⲟϥ (as particle with ⲁⲗⲗⲁ) but 62.14,
    33; 64.28; 65.24
    ⲛ̄ⲧⲁϥ 62.31; 63.12, 38
ⲛ̄ⲧⲟⲟⲩ (indep. personal pron. 3 pl.) 49.[25]

ⲁⲧⲡⲱϣⲉ 51.[10]–11
ⲡⲁϩⲟⲩ (nn. m.) back:
  ⲉⲡⲁϩⲟⲩ (adv.) backwards 59.34
ⲡⲉⲭⲉ- say:
  ⲡⲉⲭⲁ⸗:
  ⲡⲉⲭⲁϥ 68.[16]
  ⲡⲉⲭⲁⲥ 50.18, 21; 52.15; 55.17, [33]
  ⲡⲉⲭⲁⲩ 61.23
ⲣⲟ (nn. m.) mouth:
  ⲣⲱ⸗:
  ⲕⲱ ⲛ̄ⲣⲱ⸗ be silent:
  ⲕⲱ ⲛ̄ⲣⲱⲥ 53.35
  ⲕⲁⲣⲱϥ (nn.) silence 53.24; 59.25; 61.21;
    63.35; 65.19
  ⲣⲱ (adv.) indeed, same, again, etc. 48.[14];
    62.20
ⲣⲟⲙⲡⲉ (nn. f.) year 56.22; 57.31; 58.[8]
ⲣⲁⲛ (nn. m.) name: 59.[8]
  † ⲣⲁⲛ give name, call:
  ⲁⲧϯⲣⲁⲛ ⲉⲣⲟ⸗ unnamed, unnameable:
  ⲁⲧϯⲣⲁⲛ ⲉⲣⲟϥ 47.19; 54.37–55.[1]
ⲣⲁⲧ⸗ (nn. m.) foot: see ⲱϩⲉ
  ⲛ̄ ⲣⲁⲧ⸗ follow foot, trace:
  ⲁⲧⲛ̄ⲣⲁⲧ⸗ untraceable:
  ⲁⲧⲛ̄ⲣⲁⲧϥ 65.25
  ⲁⲧⲛ̄ⲣⲁⲧⲥ̄ 65.21
  ⲙⲛ̄ⲧⲁⲧⲛ̄ⲣⲁⲧⲥ̄ (nn.) untraceability 65.25–
    26
ⲣⲉϥ (prefix forming actor nouns): see
  ⲥⲁϩⲛⲉ, ϩⲁⲣⲉϩ, ϫⲓⲟⲟⲣ
ⲣⲁϣⲉ (nn. m.) gladness, joy 68.26
ⲥⲁ (nn. m.) side, part: see ⲛ̄ⲥⲁ, ⲛ̄ⲥⲁ(ⲛ)ⲃⲟⲗ
ⲥⲁⲉⲓⲉ (nn. m.) beautiful person:
  ⲙⲛ̄ⲧⲥⲁⲉⲓⲉ (nn.) beauty 64.[4]–5; 65.[18]
  ⲙⲛ̄ⲧⲥⲁⲉⲓ 47.38
ⲥⲃⲱ (nn. f.) doctrine, teaching 50.11, 16;
    52.16
  ⲁⲧⲥⲃⲱ ignorant, unlearned 52.27
ⲥⲟⲃⲧⲉ (tr.) prepare, set in order 57.29;
    68.33–34
ⲥⲙⲟⲩ (intr.) bless, praise 54.26; 58.38
ⲥⲙⲟⲧ (nn. m.) form 60.2; 62.4, 7, 17; 64.8,
    18
ⲥⲛⲁⲩ (m.) two:
  ⲙⲉϩⲥ̄ⲛⲧⲉ (f.) second 53.25; 54.14–15
  ⲙⲁϩⲥ̄ⲛⲧⲉ 48.38
ⲥⲟⲡ (nn. m.) occasion, time, turn: see ⲏⲡⲉ,
    ⲙⲏⲏϣⲉ
ⲥⲱⲧⲙ̄ (tr.) hear 47.[5]; 49.39; 50.10, 22;
    52.25; 53.37; 55.[12]; 57.28, 37–38;
    58.37; 60.13, 16; 67.21–22
  ⲥⲱⲧⲙ̄ (imp.) 47.9; 52.18; 61.28
ⲥⲱⲧⲡ̄ (tr.) choose:
  ⲥⲟⲧⲡ̄⁺ be chosen, exquisite 62.20, 33–
    34; 63.1, 4–5, 12, 19, 19, 31
ⲥⲟⲟⲩⲛ (tr.) know 45.[33]; 49.20; 67.25
  ⲥⲟⲩⲱⲛ- 61.5; 64.23

ⲥⲟⲩⲱⲛ⸗:
  ⲁⲧⲥⲟⲩⲱⲛ⸗ unknowable:
  ⲁⲧⲥⲟⲩⲱⲛϥ̄ 59.29–30; 60.8; 61.1, 10–
    [11], 16, 22; 62.31–32; 63.30; 64.[7],
    15–16; 66.23; 67.26
  ⲁⲧⲥⲟⲩⲱⲛⲥ̄ 64.[11]
  ⲁⲧⲥⲟⲩⲱⲛⲟⲩ 50.[14]–15, 31; 64.3
  ⲙⲛ̄ⲧⲁⲧⲥⲟⲩⲱⲛⲥ̄ (nn.) unknowability,
    incomprehensibility 62.22; 63.32;
    64.[13]–14
ⲥϩⲁⲓ̈ (tr.) write 68.26
  ⲥϩⲁⲓ̈ (imp.) 68.[16]
ⲥⲁϩⲛⲉ (intr.) provide, supply 47.33;
    48.[16]–17
  ⲥⲁϩⲛⲉ (subst.) provision, supply 48.[30–
    31]
  ⲣⲉϥⲥⲁϩⲛⲉ (nn. m.) provider 48.30
ⲧ- (def. art. f. sg.) 46.20; 47.26, [29], 36;
    48.16, 32, 34, 36; 49.9, 26, 27, 30, 32,
    33, 33; 55.18; see also ϩⲉ, ϩⲏ (as a
    constituent part of the monogrammatic
    spelling ⲑ of ⲧϩ)
ⲧⲉ⸗ (poss. art. f. sg.):
  ⲧⲁ- 50.16; 52.[7]; 59.1
  ⲧⲉⲕ- 52.16
  ⲧⲉϥ- 47.37; 49.19, 29; 57.16
ⲧⲁ (poss. prefix) 50.19; 52.14; 55.[34];
    57.25
ⲧⲱ⸗ (poss. pron.):
  ⲧⲱⲥ 46.12
ⲧⲁⲓ̈ (dem. pron. f. sg.) this 62.23
ⲧⲉⲓ̈- (dem art. f. sg.) 51.38; 57.20
ⲧⲏ (dem. pron.f. sg.) that 50.25; 54.10, 15;
    59.12, 15; 60.17, 31
ⲧⲏ (in cleft sentence) 64.12
† (dem.art. f. sg.) 45.10, 16; 46.19, 25, [29];
    47. [5], 38; 49.34; 50.11; 51.16, 32;
    53.6, 15, 19, 24, 25, 27, 31, 32, 38;
    54.8, 9, 11, 13, 14, 15, 16; 56.11; 57.6,
    31; 58.8, 10, 15, 18, 19, 20, 23; 59.2, 6,
    10, 14, 20; 60.16, 19, 31; 62.21, 22,
    23, 34, 35; 63.32, 36; 64.4, 10, 13, 29,
    35; 66.22, 25; 69.[16]; see also ϩⲉ
ⲧⲉ (dem. pron. f. sg. in nominal sentence)
    45.38; 46.12, [20]; 48.[6], 9, ⟨36⟩;
    54.10, 16; 60.10; 62.23
ⲧⲉ (dem. pron. f. sg. in cleft sentence) 45.11
† (tr.) give 48.15; 53.35; 62.4, 6, 9, 14;
    66.17, 27
  †- See ⲙⲉⲉⲩⲉ, ⲟⲥⲉ, ⲣⲁⲛ, ⲧⲟϣ, ϣⲓ, ⲃⲟⲙ
  ⲧⲁⲁ⸗:
  ⲧⲁⲁϥ 45.9
† ϩⲓⲱⲱ⸗ clothe, lay upon:
  † ϩⲓⲱⲱⲕ 50.24–25
  ⲧⲁⲁⲥ ϩⲓⲱⲱⲕ 50.26
  ⲧⲟⲉ⁺ ϩⲓⲱⲱⲧ 58.29–30; 60.34–35
  ⲧⲟ⁺ ϩⲓⲱⲱⲧ 50.9–[10]

ⲕⲁⲧⲁ ⲟⲩⲁ (adverbial usage) individually
45.38; 46.[6], [15]; 51.30
ⲟⲩⲁⲁ⸗/ⲟⲩⲁⲉⲧ⸗ self, alone:
ⲟⲩⲁⲁⲧ 52.[10]
ⲟⲩⲁⲁⲕ 54.35
ⲟⲩⲁⲁϥ 53.16; 62.8–9, 12; 63.16, 29;
64.29; 65.25
ⲟⲩⲁⲉⲧϥ 67.36–37
ⲟⲩⲁⲁⲥ 64.11
ⲟⲩⲁⲁⲩ 50.[23]; 57.39
ⲟⲩⲃⲉ (prep.) toward, against:
ⲉϩⲣⲁⲓ ⲟⲩⲃⲉ 68.22
ⲟⲩⲁⲁⲃ⁺ be pure, holy 58.31
( )ⲁⲁⲃ (a sort of haplography: ⲉⲩⲁⲁⲃ
appears in the text instead of ⲉⲩⲟⲩⲁⲁⲃ)
59.[5]
ⲟⲩⲟⲉⲓⲛ (nn. m.) light 45.[16]; 52.10–11;
57.34; 58.27
ⲣ̄ ⲟⲩⲟⲉⲓⲛ shine, make light:
ⲉ⁺ ⲛ̄ⲟⲩⲟⲉⲓⲛ be light 60.11
ⲟⲩⲟⲛ (indef. pron.) someone, something:
ⲟⲩⲟⲛ ⲛⲓⲙ everyone, everything 49.[16];
50.22; 52.22–23
ⲟⲩⲛ̄ (predicates existence) there is/are
64.[16], 19 [as auxiliary construction
for I. present (verb only)/ I. future
(with indef. nominal subject)]; see also
ϭⲟⲙ
( )ⲩⲛ (elision of ⲟⲩ following ⲉ-) 50.9
ⲟⲩⲛ̄ⲧⲉ-/ⲟⲩⲛ̄ⲧⲁ⸗ (predicates possession)
have:
ⲟⲩⲛ̄ⲧⲉ (in extraposition) 49.31–32;
67.25
ⲟⲩⲛ̄ⲧⲁⲕ 52.29
ⲟⲩⲛ̄ⲧⲁϥ 47.11–12; 49.[5], 29; 51.32;
62.24; 67.26, 29
( )ⲩⲛ̄ⲧⲁϥ (elision of ⲟⲩ following ⲉ-)
51.14, 17, 25; 63.33; 64.22; 65.32
ⲟⲩⲛ̄ⲧⲁⲥ 46.[10]
ⲟⲩⲛ̄ⲧⲉⲥ 49.32
( )ⲩⲛ̄ⲧⲁⲥ (elision of ⲟⲩ following ⲉ-)
49.34–35
ⲟⲩⲛ̄ⲧⲁⲩ 47.[25]
( )ⲩⲛ̄ⲧⲁⲩ (elision of ⲟⲩ following ⲉ-)
57.19
ⲟⲩⲱⲛ̄ϩ (tr. in intran./passive usage) be
revealed, appear:
ⲟⲩⲱⲛ̄ϩ ⲉⲃⲟⲗ 45.[17]; 53.16–17, 26–27,
32–33; 58.33; 65.21–22; 66.32
ⲟⲩⲱⲛ̄ϩ (nn.) revelation, appearance
48.[7]; 50.7–8; 51.[7]; 55.[32]; 59.27,
28–29; 60.35, 38; 61.[7], 31–32;
63.14–15; 64.32–33
ϣⲟⲣⲡ̄ ⲛ̄ⲟⲩⲱⲛ̄ϩ ⲉⲃⲟⲗ (nn.) first
revelation:
ⲙ̄ⲛ̄ⲧϣⲟⲣⲡ̄ ⲛ̄ⲟⲩⲱⲛ̄ϩ ⲉⲃⲟⲗ (nn.) primary
revelation 60.39–61.1; 61.9–10, 30–31

ⲟⲩⲱⲧ (adj.) single, alone, any 45.20
ⲙ̄ⲛ̄ⲧⲟⲩⲱⲧ (nn.) singleness 66.22
ⲟⲩⲱⲧⲃ̄ (subst.) passing over 47.37
ⲟⲩⲱϣ (tr.) desire 59.19; 60.5, 29
ⲟⲩⲉϣ- 47.23
ⲟⲩⲱϣⲉ (subst.) desire 62.8, 11; 64.27
ⲟⲩⲱϣ 65.35
ⲟⲩⲟⲉⲓϣ (nn. m.) time, occasion 47.16–17;
54.25–26; 66.31
ⲟⲩⲱϩ (tr.) put, set:
ⲟⲩⲏϩ⁺ be placed, dwell 51.30
ⲟⲩϫⲁⲓ (subst.) health, salvation 49.15;
51.34
ⲱⲙⲉⲥ (tr. in intr./pass. usage) sink 53.12
ⲱⲛ̄ϩ (intr.) live 46.[37]
ⲟⲛϩ⁺ be alive 61.35–36
ⲱⲛ̄ϩ (subst.) life 49.31, 35; 61.37; 62.19;
66.33
ⲙ̄ⲛ̄ⲧⲱⲛ̄ϩ (nn.) vitality 48.34; 49.26, 30,
32; 54.8; 59.14; 60.19–20
ⲱⲡ (tr.) count, esteem
ⲏⲡⲉ (nn. f.) number 48.[22]; 63.8
ⲟⲩⲏⲡⲉ ⲛ̄ⲥⲟⲡ (in adverbial usage) a
number of times 67.34–35
ⲁⲧⲏⲡⲉ numberless 48.23
ⲱϣ (subst.) cry, announcement 53.30
ⲱϩⲉ (intr.) stand, etc.:
ⲁϩⲉⲣⲁⲧ⸗ have a stand (BP); take a stand
(TP):
ⲁϩⲉⲣⲁⲧ 59.[1]; 60.22, 29; 68.33
ⲁϩⲉⲣⲁⲧⲕ̄ 59.17, 19; 60.[4]
ⲁϩⲉⲣⲁⲧϥ̄ 66.30, 31; 67.[18]
ⲁϩⲉⲣⲁⲧⲥ̄ 46.[13]; 59.21; 60.32
ϣ- (prefixed verb) be able, permitted 50.22
ϣⲁ- (prep.) until: See ⲉⲛⲉϩ
ϣⲉ (intr.) go 65.18
ϣⲉ (numeral) hundred 56.[21]; 57.31; 58.8
ϣⲓ (tr.) measure:
ϣⲓ (subst.) measure, weight 50.14
† ϣⲓ set measure, restrict:
ⲁⲧ†ϣⲓ ⲉⲣⲟ⸗:
ⲁⲧ†ϣⲓ ⲉⲣⲟϥ unmeasured, unrestricted
45.15
ϣⲃⲏⲣ (nn.) friend, comrade:
ⲣ̄ ϣⲃⲏⲣ with ⲉ- befriend, be partner 57.18;
60.21
ϣⲟⲙⲛ̄ⲧ (numeral) three:
ϣⲟⲙⲧ̄ 49.36, 37; 51.8, 33; 52.30; 55.[21]
ϣⲙ̄ⲛ̄ⲧ-/ϣⲙ̄ⲧ- See ϩⲟⲟⲩⲧ, ϭⲟⲙ
ⲙⲉϩϣⲟⲙⲧ̄ third 53.23–24
ϣⲓⲛⲉ (tr.) seek 56.[15]
ϣⲓⲛⲉ (subst.) inquiry 56.16; 57.[5]
ϣⲱⲡ (tr.) receive, contain, take 65.⟨23⟩,
⟨24⟩
ϣⲱⲡ with (ⲉ)-/ⲉⲣⲟ⸗ (tr.) take to self,
contain 66.28
ⲁⲧϣⲱⲡ ⲉⲣⲟ⸗ uncontainable:

ⲛ̄ϩⲏⲧⲟⲩ 47.17–[18]; 50.12; 57.29–30;
　61.14, 23
ⲉⲃⲟⲗ ϩⲛ̄- out of, from 45.19; 48.33–34;
　51.31–32, 36; 58.11, 22; 60.37–38;
　63.22, 23; 65.23; 68.26
ⲉⲃⲟⲗ ϩⲙ̄- 45.[13]; 56.[33]; 64.34; 66.30
ⲉⲃⲟⲗ ⲛ̄ϩⲏⲧⲟⲩ 45.[25–26]
(ⲛ̄)ϩⲣⲁⲓ̈ ϩⲛ̄- 53.8; 60.22–23
ϩⲣⲁⲓ̈ ϩⲙ̄- 53.11
ϩⲣⲁⲓ̈ ⲛ̄ϩⲏⲧ 60.15
ϩⲣⲁⲓ̈ ⲛ̄ϩⲏⲧⲕ̄ 60.[7–8]
(ⲛ̄)ϩⲣⲁⲓ̈ ⲛ̄ϩⲏⲧϥ̄ 47.[12]; 49.[10]–11, 13;
　52.34; 61.3–[4]; 67.30
ϩⲣⲁⲓ̈ ⲛ̄ϩⲏⲧⲟⲩ 64.10
ϩⲉⲛ- (indef. art. pl.) 49.25; 59.4; 64.2;
　67.27, 27
　ϩⲛ̄- 48.[30]
ϩⲟⲩⲛ (nn. m.) inward part:
ⲉϩⲟⲩⲛ (adv.) to inside, inward: see ⲉ-
　/ⲉⲣⲟ⸗, ϩⲱⲛ.
ϩⲱⲛ (intr.) be nigh, approach:
　ϩⲛⲁⲛ:
　ϩⲛⲁⲛ ⲉϩⲟⲩⲛ 58.[7]
ϩⲁⲡ (nn. m.) judgement 64.22, 24
ϩⲱⲡ (tr.) hide:
　ϩⲏⲡ⁺ be hidden 48.16
ϩⲣⲁⲓ̈ (nn.) upper side; (nn.) lower side: see
　ϩⲛ̄-.
ⲉϩⲣⲁⲓ̈ (adv.) See ⲉ-, ⲉϫⲛ̄-, ⲕⲱ, ⲟⲩⲃⲉ-.
ϩⲣⲟⲕ (intr.) with (prep.) ⲙ̄ⲙⲟ⸗ (reflexive) be
　quiet, become quiet:
　ϩⲣⲟⲕ (imp.) with ⲙ̄ⲙⲟ⸗ 59.37
　ϩⲣⲟⲕ⁺ with ⲙ̄ⲙⲟ⸗ 53.34; 59.22, 23;
　　60.32, 37; 64.1, 31–32; 65.28; 66.22,
　　29; 67.28
　ϩⲣⲟⲕ (subst.) quietness 60.15, 24; 61.21;
　　62.25; 63.37; 65.19, 38; 67.31
　ⲙⲛ̄ⲧϩⲣⲟⲕ (nn.) state of quietness,
　　quietude 65.20
ϩⲱⲣⲕ (tr.) make quiet:
　ϩⲟⲣⲕ⸗:
　ϩⲟⲣⲕϥ̄ 45.[22–23]
ϩⲣⲟⲟⲩ (nn. m.) voice, sound 53.36
ϩⲁⲣⲉϩ (intr.) keep, guard 52.[20]
　ⲣⲉϥⲁⲣⲉϩ (nn.) guardian 45.8; 68.[22]–23
ϩⲏⲧ (nn.) heart: see ϭⲃⲃⲉ
ϩⲟⲧⲉ (nn. f.) fear:
　ⲣ̄ ϩⲟⲧⲉ be afraid 50.[1], 15; 59.17, 32–33
ϩⲓⲧⲛ̄- (prep.) through, by:
　ⲉⲃⲟⲗ ϩⲓⲧⲛ̄- 50.7; 53.33; 58.34; 60.10, 35,
　　38–39; 61.9, 30; 62.[8], 12; 63.24–25;
　　67.[17]
　ⲉⲃⲟⲗ ϩⲓⲧⲙ̄- 49.18; 57.[8–9]
　ⲉⲃⲟⲗ ϩⲓⲧⲟⲟⲧ⸗:
　ⲉⲃⲟⲗ ϩⲓⲧⲟⲟⲧ 53.20
　ⲉⲃⲟⲗ ϩⲓⲧⲟⲟⲧϥ̄ 56.[23]–24; 57.9–10;
　　58.27, 28; 59.27–28; 61.27; 62.9–10,

15; 63.[3]; 64.24
　ⲉⲃⲟⲗ ϩⲓⲧⲟⲟⲧⲥ̄ 48.12–13; 53.13–14;
　　60.18; 64.13
　ⲉⲃⲟⲗ ϩⲓⲧⲟⲟⲧⲟⲩ 47.20–[21]; 59.5; 62.26;
　　64.9
ϩⲱⲧⲣ̄ (tr.) join:
　ϩⲟⲧⲡ⁺ be joined 45.8; 64.13
ϩⲟⲩⲟ (nn. m.) greater part, greatness:
　ϩⲟⲩⲉ- 47.37; 65.36
　ⲛ̄ϩⲟⲩⲟ (adv.) more, greater 50.[8]; 57.12,
　　13; 60.3; 64.5; 67.23, 34
ϩⲟⲟⲩⲧ (nn. m.) male 45.18, 37–[38];
　46.[24]; 51.20, 33; 59.[6]
　ϣⲙⲛ̄ⲧϩⲟⲟⲩⲧ thrice-male 46.[18]; 55.[36];
　　56.[14]; 58.[14]
ϩⲓϫⲛ̄- (prep.) upon, over 46.[13]; 59.1;
　68.21
ϩⲓϫⲱ⸗:
　ϩⲓϫⲱϥ 47.36
ϫⲉ (conj.):
　ϫⲉ (before direct statement or question)
　　50.18, 21; 52.15; 53.36; 54.28;
　　55.[19], [35]; 59.[8]; 61.24; 64.15, 19;
　　68.16
　ϫⲉ (explicative) that, namely 45.[36]
　　(following ⲉⲓⲙⲉ) 49.12, 13; 55.20; 60.[1]
　　(following ⲛⲁⲩ) 46.37
　　(following ⲥⲟⲟⲩⲛ) 49.20; 67.25, 29
　ϫⲉ (causal) for, because, since 45.22, [30];
　　46.[7]; 48.17; 49.7, 20; 52.22; 57.35;
　　61.33; 64.22, 29; 67.31
　ϫⲉ (before final clause) 55.31; 56.29;
　　68.28
　ϫⲉ (with ἵνα) 49.12; 50.30, 32; 53.12;
　　60.[4], 6; 62.16, 25; 65.27, 29; 67.32
ϫⲓ (tr.) take, get, bring, accept, receive 48.7,
　12, 33, 33; 56.[31], [36]; 59.26; 61.4;
　62.6, 9; 63.21, 23, 24; 64.24; 66.20
ϫⲓ-: See ϭⲟⲙ.
ϫⲓⲧ⸗:
　ϫⲓⲧ 58.30
　ϫⲓⲧⲟⲩ 67.38; 68.31–32
ϫⲱ (tr.) say, speak, tell 54.27; 59.[7]; 60.13
　ϫⲟⲟ⸗:
　ϫⲟⲟⲥ 64.19
　ϫⲟⲟⲩ 52.22, 26; 57.24; 68.[17], 24
ϫⲱⲕ (tr.) complete, finish 56.33
　ϫⲏⲕ⁺ ⲉⲃⲟⲗ be ended, complete 56.[16]
　ϫⲱⲕ ⲉⲃⲟⲗ (subst.) completion, end
　　56.[34]; 58.[8]
ϫⲱⲱⲙⲉ (nn. m.) sheet, roll of papyrus,
　book 68.21, 27; 69.[17]–18
ϫⲱⲛⲧ̄ (tr.) try, test:
　ϫⲟⲛⲧ̄⁺ be tried, tested 62.5
ϫⲡⲟ (tr.) beget, bring forth 54.36
　ϫⲡⲟ (subst.) birth, begetting 46.35
　ⲁⲧϫⲡⲟ unbegotten 54.34, 34

Greek Words

63.28; 64.4, 6; 65.32; 68.24, 25, 26, 31
εἶδος (nn.) form 48.[23]; 51.7, 15
ⲁⲧⲉⲓⲁⲟⲥ 48.[23]–24; 60.27
εἰκών (nn. f.) likeness, image:
ϩⲓⲕⲱⲛ 51.16, 21, 27; 60.33
εἴτε (conjunctive particle) either . . . or . . .
51.22, 23, 24
ἐλπίς (nn. f.) hope:
ϩⲉⲗⲡⲓⲥ 58.10
ἔνδυμα (nn. f.) garment 58.29
ἐνεργεῖα (nn. f.) action, actuality, existence
in action:
ⲉⲛⲉⲣⲅⲓⲁ 48.[28], 35; 49.1; 53.14, 25–26,
33–34; 54.9–[10], [13]–14; 59.35
ⲁⲧⲉⲛⲉⲣⲅⲓⲁ inactive 48.[29]; 60.7; 61.25–
26
ⲙⲛⲧⲁⲧⲉⲛⲉⲣⲅⲓⲁ (nn.) state of inactivity
59.25–26
ἐνεργεῖν (intr.) be in action, operate:
ⲉⲛⲉⲣⲅⲓ 65.26; 66.21
ⲣ̄ ⲉⲛⲉⲣⲅⲓ 45.32; 51.21; 60.[5]; 61.35;
64.33
ⲣ̄ ⲉⲛⲉⲣⲅⲉⲓ 51.29
ἔννοια (nn. f.) thought, conception 46.20;
48.[13]; 53.27–28; 56.[32]; 60.11;
64.35–36
ἐπειδή (causal conjunction) since, seeing
that:
ⲉⲡⲓⲁⲏ 48.9; 52.15–16; 53.21; 62.24;
63.17
ἐπιστήμη (nn. f.) knowledge, scientific
knowledge 51.23–[24]; 53.[9]
ἤ (conjunction) or:
ⲏ 61.33, 35, 35; 62.5, [5], 6, [8], 9, 9;
64.14, 16, 18
ἵνα (conjunction) that, in order that:
ϩⲓⲛⲁ 49.[12]; 50.28–29; 53.12; 60.[3],
[6]; 62.16, 25; 65.27, 29, 38; 67.32
καλυπτός covered, hidden 45.[31]; 46.[31],
[33]; 51.17; 58.19
κατά (prep.) according to, etc. 49.37; 51.20,
26–27, 29; 54.[8], 13; 55.[37]; 59.22,
38; 60.2, 33; 62.3, [7], 17; 64.8, 18;
66.21–22; see also ⲟⲩⲁ, ϩⲉ.
ⲕⲁⲧⲁⲣⲟ⸗:
ⲕⲁⲧⲁⲣⲟⲓ̈ 60.⟨18⟩; 68.33
ⲕⲁⲧⲁⲣⲟⲕ 59.13
ⲕⲁⲧⲁⲣⲟϥ 64.12
κόσμος (nn. m.) order, cosmos, world
58.33–34; 59.9
μακάριος blessed 47.15–16; 57.34–35;
63.35–36
ⲙⲛⲧⲙⲁⲕⲁⲣⲓⲟⲥ (nn.) blessedness 47.[32];
49.[6]; 52.31; 54.16–17; 55.27–[28];
58.[9]–10, 18–19, 20–21, 35; 59.10–
11; 60.17; 62.29, 34; 63.33–34

μέλει (impersonal) is concerned:
(ⲥ)ⲣ̄ ⲙⲉⲗⲓ 64.25–26; 66.[17]–18
μέν (conjunctive particle) indeed, truly
57.35; 67.21
(with δέ) on the one hand 46.[6]; 53.19;
55.35; 56.37 (?); 65.30
μερικόν particular 51.25
μέρος (nn. m.) part 51.29
μεσίτης (nn. m.) mediator 61.19
μήπως (conjunction) lest 50.[15]–16
μορφή (nn. f.) form, shape 48.[24]
ⲁⲧⲙⲟⲣⲫⲏ formless, shapeless 48.[24–25]
μυστήριον (nn.) mystery 52.[21]–22
νοεῖν (tr.) perceive, think, suppose:
ⲣ̄ ⲛⲟⲉⲓ 47.[22]; 48.19; 49.8
νοερόν intellectual, noetic 51.18; 60.25
νόησις (nn. f.) mental perception, intelligence,
mentality:
ⲛⲟⲏⲧⲏⲥ 49.30–31, 34
νοῦς (intellect) 45.[9], 35; 46.[25]; 51.20;
58.18; 61.36; 62.19
ὄντως (adv.) really, actually 59.23
ⲟⲛⲧⲱⲥ with ϣⲟⲟⲡ truly exist 45.[14–
15], [22]; 46.9, [9] (note: ϣⲟⲟⲡ is
added by emendation; ⲟⲛⲧⲱⲥ appears
twice due to a scribal error), [28]; 48.38;
49.17; 51.15; 55.25; 56.[12], 21; 64.30
οὐσία (nn. f.) substance 47.34; 48.[26];
55.37
ⲁⲧⲟⲩⲥⲓⲁ substanceless 48.[26–27];
53.31–32
ⲙⲛⲧⲁⲧⲟⲩⲥⲓⲁ (nn.) substancelessness
47.34; 49.33; 55.[29], [38]
οὐτέ (adv. joining negative clauses) 49.[22],
23, 23–[24], 24; 52.25; 60.[5]; 61.37,
37, 38; 62.2, 6, 10, 12, 14, 18, 19, 19,
27–28, 29, 30, 36; 63.1, 2, 9, 21, 22,
24, 25, 26, 27, 36; 64.26; 65.23, 26–
27, 28; 66.19, 20–21; 67.24, 27, 28,
32–33
πάλιν (adv.) again 55.[17]
παντέλειος all-perfect:
ⲡⲁⲛⲧⲉⲗⲓⲟⲥ 55.14, [16]
πάντως (adv.) altogether, at all 60.[6]; 61.18
παρά (prep.) beyond 50.17
παρθένος (nn.) virgin 45.18; 59.7
πειράζειν (tr.) test
ⲡⲓⲣⲁⲍⲉ 59.8
περιούσια (nn. f.) surplus, abundance 47.[6]
πηγή (nn. f.) fount, source, origin 47.[26];
48.21
πνεῦμα (nn. n.) spirit:
ⲡⲛ̅ⲁ̅ (nn. m.) 51.9; 66.[16], 33
ⲁϩⲟⲣⲁⲧⲟⲛ ⲙ̄ⲡⲛ̅ⲁ̅ Invisible Spirit 45.[27];
47.[8]– 9; 49.9–[10]; 51.35; 58.24–25;
64.36

Proper Names

Magical Utterance